The Gun Digest® Book of

GUNS For Personal Defense

Arms & Accessories for Self-Defense

Edited by

Kevin Michalowski

© 2004
by KP Books

Published by

kp books
An imprint of F+W Publications, Inc.

700 East State Street • Iola, WI 54990-0001
715-445-2214 • 888-457-2873

Our toll-free number to place an order or obtain a free catalog is 800-258-0929.

Manuscripts, contributions and inquiries, including first class return postage, should be sent to the Guns for PERSONAL DEFENSE Editorial Offices, Krause Publications, 700 E. State Street, Iola, WI 54990-0001. All materials received will receive reasonable care, but we will not be responsible for their safe return. Material accepted is subject to our requirements for editing and revisions. Author payment covers all rights and title to the accepted material, including photos, drawings and other illustrations. Payment is at our current rates.

CAUTION: Technical data presented here, particularly technical data on the handloading and on firearms adjustment and alteration, inevitably reflects individual experience with particular equipment and components under specific circumstances the reader cannot duplicate exactly. Such data presentations therefore should be used for guidance only and with caution. Krause Publications, Inc., accepts no responsibility for results obtained using this data.

Library of Congress Catalog Number: 2004105219

ISBN: 0-87349-931-X

Designed by Patsy Howell and Tom Nelsen
Edited by Kevin Michalowski

Printed in the United States of America

Contents

Features

Repetition Builds Skill *by Kevin Michalowski* 5
Laser Sights: Real Benefit With A Warning *by Kevin Michalowski* .. 8
Dry Practice: Build Confidence and Skills Off the Range
  by Dan Donarski 11
GPS of Personal Defense: Grip, Presentation
  and Stance *by Dan Donarski* 16
The Alpha and Omega: Complete Training *by Dan Donarski* 21
Buying Used Firearms Without Guilt, and With Low Risk
  by Patrick Sweeney 26
Bring Out the Big Guns *by M.D. Johnson* 30
The Trend Toward Autoloaders *by M.D. Johnson* 36

Catalog

Modern Gun Values 44
Current Handguns
  Autoloaders, Service & Sport 84
  Double Action Revolvers, Service & Sport 108
  Miscellaneous 115
Current Shotguns
  Military & Police 117
Grips 118
Metallic Sights 124
Laser Sights 128

Reference

Compendium of State Laws Governing Firearms 131
Guide to Right-to-Carry Reciprocity and Recognition 134
Product & Service Directory 152

Introduction

Choosing a firearm for use as a defensive tool is a big decision. It is a statement about your willingness to accept the responsibility for your safety and the safety of those you love. A gun brings the power of life and death to your hands. Once you make the choice to wield such power you can only move ahead with the utmost diligence and care.

Understand that in a violent encounter all that you have learned, all that you believe and all the skills you have worked to acquire will be put to the test in a few terrifying seconds. Your survival and that of your loved ones will bear upon all of your decisions up to that point. Conversely, following such an encounter your skills, training and perhaps even your beliefs and attitudes may be subject to extreme scrutiny by the legal system. The choices you make must be correct. To be correct they must be based on facts collected through solid research and evidence presented by reliable sources.

So, now you have decided to keep a firearm for self-defense. Which gun is right for you? Unfortunately the criteria are quite subjective. The parameters are intensely personal. Will you be defending yourself in your home or on the street? Will you carry the gun concealed on your person or in a fanny pack, purse or attaché case? Do you have the physical strength and dexterity to handle firearm of a certain style or size? Which caliber will work best? That question alone can open the door to hours of debate that will not result in a clear answer.

Those who prefer to be glib might say, "The best gun to have in a gunfight is the gun you have with you when the gunfight starts." That's a non-answer. How do you get from having no gun to making a knowledgeable decision about choosing an appropriate firearm for self-defense? You do research. This book is one portion of that research. It should by no means be your only point of reference. You will need this book and others. You will also need plenty of practical experience and advice from people you trust. This book will show you what's available and give you a good look at some of the options you have when it comes to choosing a gun for self-defense. Further research will help you narrow the field. Practical experience will show what works for you and what doesn't. Effective professional training will make you proficient.

You may never need to use your firearm for self-defense, but when you do, nothing else will really do. And nothing but action backed up by confidence in your decisions will get you through such a trial.

You've made the choice. Now you begin gaining the confidence.

Kevin Michalowski
Editor

Once you've made the choice to use a handgun for self-defense, you need to get competent instruction to be able to use the gun effectively.

Repetition Builds Skill

By Kevin Michalowski

Whether you are swinging a golf club, dribbling a basketball or firing a round at the center of a target, the key to success is repetition. I read somewhere that a person must complete something like 7,000 repetitions to truly master a skill. Doing so teaches the muscles how the activity should feel. Once the muscles know what it feels like to complete an action, you begin to move almost instinctively. Once that happens you begin to see true consistency in your shooting and can work on increasing the speed of the sequence.

This, of course, works on the presupposition that your practice is based on proper techniques.

Therefore, the first step to effective practice is proper training. This is especially true when handling firearms for self-defense. A knowledgeable expert must teach you, and you must work diligently to emulate that training in your practice sessions. I will not pretend that an article of this length can cover all the salient points and subtle nuances of defensive firearms training. That training must be done on a range, under the watchful eyes of an expert. Find a school. Spend the money and while you are involved in the training, immerse yourself in the teachings of your instructor.

Then come home and practice… regularly.

Here are some tips to improve the quality of your practice sessions:

Focus on the fundamentals: High hand, crush-grip, front sight, roll the trigger. During the StressFire course Mas Ayoob made a clear point of telling every shooter that consistently accurate shooting cannot be expected with inconsistent firearms manipulation. In layman's terms: Hold the gun the same way every time. And to that end Mas wanted us to squeeze the gripframe hard for every shot. After that, focus on the front sight and control that trigger. Think about fundamentals and practice using them until they are ingrained. You high school coach was right when he said "you play like you practice." The skills you need come only from muscle memory. While training at Front Sight in Nevada, I was constantly reminded that in a real fight I would perform at only about half the level at which I performed in training. By focusing on the fundamentals I was able to raise my training scores to the point where I was confident that 50 percent would be good enough.

Practice from real positions: In a gunfight you will be shooting from cover or concealment. You will be shooting while moving to cover. You might even be shooting from odd or unstable positions. Within the bounds of safe shooting and range rules, shoot from non-standard positions. Use a post to simulate a barricade. Go prone. If it is safe to do so move to within 7 yards of the target and shoot while backing up. Just

It takes 7,000 repetitions to build the muscle memory needed to master a skill. That means you have to practice the skill correctly 7,000 times before your body knows what it should be doing.

remember all the while to focus on the fundamentals.

Start slowly: Speed kills. Going to town with serious rapid-fire training can cause you to forget the fundamentals. First, get good going slowly. Then get great going slowly. Then speed up.

Quit when you get tired: No matter how tough and strong you are, fatigue will compromise your shooting skills. If your performance starts to fade, stop the practice session. To build your endurance, don't practice longer, that could encourage you to adopt sloppy habits. Instead practice more often.

Get a range bag: Keeping an organized range bag is one of the best ways to insure productive practice. If you have everything you need in one place — ammo, hearing protection, targets, staple gun, etc. — all you need to do is grab your pistol and the bag and head to the range. When the practice session is over, simply put everything back in the bag and you're ready for the next outing.

Don't draw to the shot: While it might seem like a good idea to practice drawing the pistol from your holster and shooting at the target, resist that urge. Remember, practice builds muscle memory and teaches us to reflexively complete the action. Most of the time when you pull a gun you will be holding someone at gunpoint and the situation may be defused without firing. If you have trained yourself to draw and reflexively fire, you may end up facing an angry district attorney who believes you could have solved the problem without firing a shot. A better means of practice is to draw (keep your finger off the trigger), and then command your "adversary" to stop and put down the weapon before you decide to fire. That's more likely the sequence you'll go through in a real self-defense scenario.

What about ammo?

All of this means you'll have to make an investment in ammunition. For several years I opted to reload ammo for my pistols and revolvers. Not having the latest and greatest reloading gear I soon found that I couldn't keep up. Figuring my time was worth something, I started looking at the real cost of reloading and determined that for my needs I was better off buying my ammunition in bulk.

At this writing I can, from any mail-order house, get 1,000 rounds of Wolf brand .40 S&W for $125 plus shipping. At most gun shows I can save the cost of shipping. I use Wolf as an example because when I started shooting it a few people I know looked down their noses at this "imported surplus" ammo. They did so until I completed the 400-round StressFire handgun course without so much as a hiccup and qualified with a score of 299 out of 300. Wolf ammo may be imported, but it certainly is not surplus. I've never had reason to complain about its performance or accuracy and especially not the price. If there was one drawback to Wolf Ammo, it was

Competent instruction insures that the foundation of skills you need will be laid correctly. No one can expect to simply pick up a handgun and use it efficiently.

Well-organized gear makes practice easier and more efficient. It also takes away any excuse not to head to the range. Find a good source of inexpensive ammo and hone the skills you've been taught.

that the cases were lacquer-coated. Some people with really fast trigger fingers and lots of high-capacity magazines might, and I repeat "might" have experienced a jam if the chamber got hot enough to melt the lacquer. I never had it happen and never saw it happen even while watching thousands of rounds go downrange. But it gave some people a reason so complain. That reason is now gone. For 2004 the folks at Wolf replaced the lacquer with an advanced-technology polymer coating to several of their most popular center-fire calibers. I thought the stuff worked great before. They say it works better now.

There are lots of other ammunition suppliers out there and the shelves are full of books that can teach you all you need to know about reloading. Choose one supplier, or build your own reloading bench and get some ammo for you firearm. The bottom line is this. You need to practice and dry practice, while very important, can only take you so far. Shoot real ammo and shoot as much as you can afford. Building skill takes time and practice, but the benefits far outweigh the costs. ✪

Start slowly. Establish good form make sure you practice that form. Speed will come only after the basics are mastered.

LASER SIGHTS: Real Benefit With A Warning

By Kevin Michalowski

Almost since the invention of the laser people have been trying, with varying degrees of success, to use the instrument as a sighting device for firearms. As technology improved and dependable lasers became small enough to easily handle and mounting hardware began to provide repeatable accuracy, the dream of a laser sight became a reality.

Today you can, quite easily, equip a firearm with a laser, focus the dot on a target and fire for effect. And they work. Modern laser sights are small, light and durable. Modern batteries provide adequate power and the adjustments can be held in place under all but the most violent recoil. So, with all the hype and hoopla, should you or should you not equip your defensive firearm with a laser sight?

This is where the subjective nature of the debate takes over.

Yes, laser sights work. Some work quite well. But you need to review your personal needs and desires before you choose something on which you will stake your life.

Some of the benefits laser sights offer include:

Instinctive Activation — Most lasers are pressure-activated. Just grip your gun naturally and the laser comes on. No on/off switch to find. No extra button to push. No fumbling when seconds count.

Rapid Target Acquisition — The laser beam can be quickly directed to your target. In a life-threatening situation your eyes often lock on to the threat. With the beam projected on the target you can find it quickly and position it precisely.

Enhanced Accuracy From Various Positions — Without the need to acquire a traditional sight picture you can bring accurate fire to bear from a wide variety of positions, even those in which you are at a tactical disadvantage.

A Measure Of Deterrence — The jury is still out on the reaction of a thug when faced with the flash of a laser sight. Some will cease hostilities. Some will only pause. Others may never even notice the presence of the laser. Remember, violent encounters happen

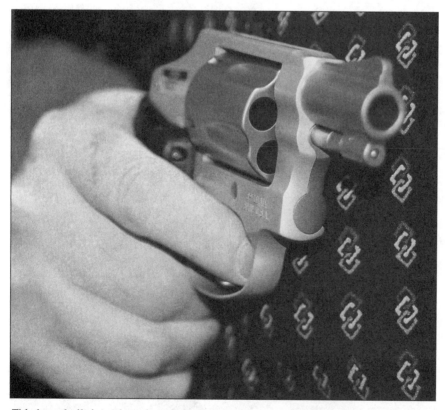

This laser built into the grip panel of a J frame revolver is both unobtrusive and effective. Adding the sight requires no changes in the type of holster required or additional bolt-on gear outside the gun.

quickly and the attacker may not be paying attention to a tiny red dot on his chest.

The Other Side Of The Coin

Just as it is true that for every action there is an equal and opposite reaction, any discussion of laser sight must include a review of their drawbacks. Laser sights are not perfect.

One major concern associated with laser sights is that all mechanical devices will eventually fail. Traditional iron sights are very tough, very simple and rarely fail. While the failure rate of laser sights may be very low, there is still the possibility that the shooter will engage the switch and have

nothing happen. And if that possibility becomes a reality, the owner of a laser-sighted pistol has to shift focus immediately. This shift in focus is both literal and figurative. With the laser sight in operation, all your attention can be focused on the attacker. That's a natural instinct and that's where the red dot from the laser is projected. Should that red dot fail, the shooter is required to develop an effective sight picture immediately and while under extreme stress. The stress is not only that of a violent encounter, but also the understanding that your aiming system has failed. To achieve a proper sight picture with your iron sights you must shift focus from the target to the front sight. The front sight must

be aligned with the rear sight and the combination placed on the target. To aim effectively, the sight must remain in focus and the target will appear out of focus. If you have come to rely on your laser sight and suppressed or completely forgotten the sequence of establishing a proper sight picture, this shift under stress can be very tough and will likely result in errant shots.

The ability to focus on the front sight during a high-stress and violent encounter is something that must be learned through repetitive practice. The common knock against laser sights is that they reinforce poor shooting habits. Used regularly, the laser sight can teach shooters to look over or around the gun and focus on the target, thus

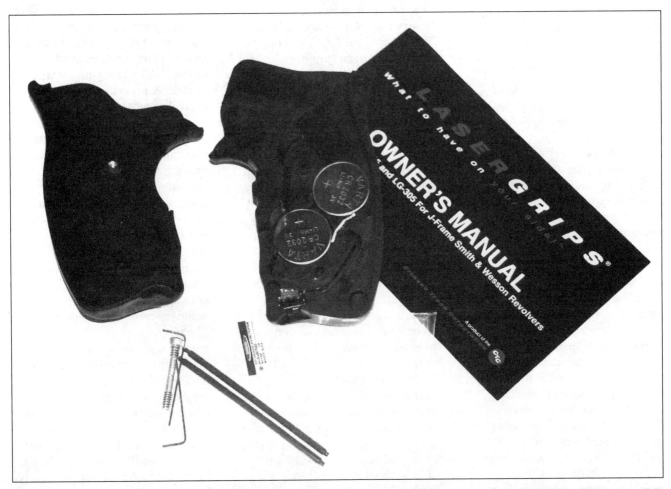

Inside the grip a laser sight is very simple, but there are things that can go wrong. Batteries can go dead and connections can fail. Still, the durability of many modern laser sights rivals that of adjustable iron sights.

when the front sight is really needed the shooter will, under stress, forget that basic element of accurate shooting. Solve that problem by not using the laser sight regularly. Sight-in the laser at an adequate self-defense distance and leave it alone. Practice only with the iron sights. Run every type of drill you can think of using only the iron sights. Switch on the laser sight's master control only when you are not in a practice situation, but well before you find yourself in a self-defense situation. There's no need to be fumbling for a master switch under the stress of an attack.

Crimson Trace, makers of the Laser Grip laser sight, also embraces this philosophy. Here's a passage directly from their Internet site:

At Crimson Trace, we believe you should always be able to sight and shoot a handgun without a laser. This new technology was never meant to replace your fixed sights, but to supplement them in difficult situations, like firing on the move or from awkward positions, defending yourself in close quarters, aiming in low light where iron sights are difficult to see, and any time that you're under stress. Under these kinds of conditions, our natural and automatic reaction is to focus on the threat, not the gun sights.

That's a powerful statement from the maker of a tested and battle-proven product. While the comment points out the importance of acquiring and continuing to practice good marksmanship skills; it stops short of reminding those who carry firearms for self-defense that one of the toughest things to do under stress is shift focus from the threat to the sights of a handgun. To do so effectively requires continued practice in the fundamentals of good

marksmanship. Anything short of such practice will leave the shooter ill-prepared for the encounter. In that case, a laser sight should not be considered a quick fix. No competent firearms instructor would suggest anything but that a shooter first acquire proficiency with iron sights before moving to a laser.

With all that said, there are indeed some instances where laser sights provide a definite advantage. Indeed, in some situations a laser will work when almost nothing else will. In a close-quarters fight that quickly devolves in a struggle for your weapon a laser sight will help you get an aimed shot off even if you can't see the sights. This is where the laser sight really (excuse the pun) shines. In such a struggle one of the key elements of using a firearm at such close range is to insure you don't shoot yourself. The laser sight lets you know precisely where round will impact, regardless of your shooting position. Police officers can use a laser to sight around a tactical shield. This is not something the average armed citizen will be faced with, but it shows the ability to fire from an awkward position.

One often overlooked element of the laser sight is its benefit as a training tool. During dry practice the beam of the laser shows a shooter exactly what happens when a trigger is jerked. It can also prove to the shooter that double-action can be nearly as accurate as single-action, as long as the basic elements of marksmanship are adhered to.

The most talked about benefit of the laser sight has to be its performance in low light. Most attacks occur in low light and a laser will indeed help you get off an aimed shot. But it is still a shot in the dark. The best option for low-light fighting is to carry a light. Positive target

identification is of paramount importance. Not only will such identification prevent the tragedy of shooting an innocent person, it will also bolster your claim of self-defense during the inevitable investigation following the use of lethal force. With a light you know exactly who your target is and can clearly judge his intent. Streamlight offers a weapon-mounted light/laser combination or a Laser Grip accompanied by a hand-held light will accomplish the same things. Either way, the first rule of shooting is to know your target.

The other downside of a using a laser in a dark environment is that, like tracers, lasers work both ways. If your laser sight is casting beam directly from you to your target, it is also casting a beam from your target to you. The realistic odds of this having a huge bearing on the outcome of the shootout may be pretty slim, but it is a factor. Another factor could be the accidental activation of the laser when you are trying to hide. A pressure switch activates most lasers when the firearm is held in the firing grasp. In a high-stress situation, you can count on grasping your firearm tightly enough to activate the switch. Will that give away your position? Again, the odds are slim that you'll be in such a situation, but it is something to consider.

In the end, the decision to use a laser sight is intensely personal. In a real-world self-defense scenario, a laser will likely help you. But nothing is perfect and you should not stake your entire defensive plan on the benefits of a laser. Such a sight may indeed help in times of intense stress and in situations that require rapid response. Combine a solid base of effective shooting skills with a well-built laser sight and you will certainly have a combination capable of saving your life. ✪

Dry Practice:
Building Confidence and Skills Off the Range

By Dan Donarski

At the range with live bullets, shooting at standard silhouettes or, better yet, inside simulated scenario theaters, is far and away the finest way you can practice your weaponry skills. Or is it?

Firing on a range will definitely verify that our handgun actually fires bullets. Range firing will show us that our sights are aligned properly and our sight picture is correct. But, when push comes to shove, that is really all range firing does.

Now, if you live so close to a range that you go every day and you have an unlimited supply of ammunition, then, by all means, use the range for practice. Most of us don't live next door to a range, however. Getting to the range becomes a problem of time whether we like it nor not. Nor is our ammunition supply unlimited.

So, how are we going to practice on a regular basis to get the skills necessary in a life-and-death situation? How are we going to maintain and improve upon the skills we have been taught?

Dry Practice: What is it? Why is it Essential?

That's where something called "dry practice" comes in. You may have heard of this before being referred to as "cold practice." No matter what you call it, dry practice is the method of building your skill and confidence level without the range and without bullets.

And, take care not to call this "dry fire" as it is impossible to fire an unloaded weapon without bullets. This distinction becomes

Dry practice is the single most important training you will do. It trains everything from the grip to the presentation at the ready; to the surprise break to the quick and final check when the action is completed. Range firing validates your dry practice drills. It does not build them.

absolutely vital on a range. There can be no confusion on this. It is called dry practice. Period.

No bullets, no punching holes in paper– how can that help? Actually it can, and does help more than you'd think. In fact, dry practice training is absolutely necessary to improving and ingraining your skills.

Think about it for a moment. The firing pin or hammer dropping on the primer, the bullet leaving the chamber and barrel of the gun, traveling to a target, is all the result of one single action. The trigger break is all that's needed. It is something as simple as curling your index finger.

In order to get to that simple step you need to master a number of other vital steps that occur before, as well as after, that simple finger curl. That's what makes dry practice so crucial. It allows you to practice the entire sequence of events from start to finish, from bringing the pistol to the ready position to re-holstering after the action.

There's another reason dry practice is essential. There are a lot of ranges that will not allow you to practice your skills with a handgun from a holstered or concealed position. We're not talking about target practice per se in this book, we're talking about personal defense. How many times will you be in a real personal defense situation when your handgun is already out of its holster and aimed at the target?

You need to practice realistically in order to practice perfectly in order to achieve perfect performance. Your handgun doesn't need practice in order to have the bullet leave the barrel. That process is simple mechanics. You need the practice, however, so your movements before and after the hammer fall become just as mechanical.

Target acquisition, putting the front sight on the target's center mass, is certainly a critical skill to dry practice. It should become intuitive – where you point the bullet will travel– so you don't have to hunt for the front sight. Then it's time to take the slack out and get that surprise break, the terminal end of target acquisition.

There is no way to mimic, or practice, one thing that will happen when faced with a potentially deadly situation. That one thing is the body's biologic response to the stress involved.

In a life-threatening engagement, your body will be under stress, a huge amount of stress. That stress will release a load of adrenaline. Adrenaline will have a huge negative impact on your body's ability to function coherently. Your mind will become a bit scrambled, your fine motor coordination will be significantly impacted in a negative way. Under these conditions you can only expect your body to be half as effective as it is under a non-stressful situation.

Dry practice, perfect dry practice done consistently, will help alleviate a good percentage of that degradation. When the movements and the skills become ingrained through practice drills, your body's ability to perform those skills under times of stress will not be as significantly impacted. You'll be better. Much better.

The Front Sight Firearms Training Institute puts it this way, "When faced with the stress of a life-threatening engagement, we don't rise to the occasion, we descend to our level of training."

The Mind Set and Practice Location

It starts and ends between your ears. Safety is completely up to you and your ability to engage that computer located above your neck and set it to safe. Mechanical devices, devices like handguns, are not the safety issue. You are.

Dry practice is serious business, it is not play. You are practicing with a tool that, when coupled with the conscious act of trigger squeeze and ammunition, can take a life. The only thing missing in dry practice is the bullet. That is all. And that's everything.

As you become familiar with your handgun there is a better than good possibility that you will reach a point of familiarization where you "know" everything there is to know about it. At that point is when you become complacent. You and your familiarity have just become lethal.

Negligent discharges can be and often are the result of this complacency. In reality there is

Before you go up on the range to validate a new skill, instructors run you through dry practice drills to ensure you know the movements. Think of dry practice as an extension of these drills and work them regularly to instill the muscle memory needed for the skills to become second nature.

no excuse for a negligent discharge. None. During dry practice you must be absolutely focused on the task at hand. There can be no distractions. It must be structured. It must be serious. When it is there won't be any need for excuses. You'll never have to say, "I didn't mean to shoot."

Choosing a practice environment is crucial to the success of your dry practice sessions. The number one rule in choosing a practice location is that you must have absolute control over it. There can be no distractions.

The TV needs to be turned off. Same with the stereo. If there are family members in the house or apartment send them outside, the fresh air will do them good. Close the drapes. Take the phone off the hook. The point here is the dry practice room needs to be its own isolated environment. There can be no distractions. You must make this room as safe as physically and mentally possible.

Physical safety comes in the form of where you choose to do your dry practice. In the best of worlds you will have a room in the house that has a wall capable of stopping bullet. True, this practice is without ammunition, but...

Cinder block walls are ideal for this, so maybe the basement will be your best bet. The point is this, you want to use the absolute safest room possible, and then you make it even safer by taking out the distractions.

Target Choice and Ammunition Separation

It is all too easy to find a "convenient" target. Dry practice is not convenient, and neither should targets be those of convenience.

Targets should be specific. A simple piece of paper with a silhouette drawn on it is perfect. You can, and you should, dry practice at different distances,

using larger and smaller silhouette drawings to the feeling of depth. Tape these targets to a wall that could stop a bullet.

Never use a light switch or the corner of a room. Never a picture and never a television screen. In order to maintain the proper mindset, in order to maintain the controlled, distraction-free environment, your target(s) must be specific. They also must be used only during dry practice situations.

You can probably see why televisions, paintings and the like shouldn't be used. They are always around you and you may, at one point or another, be tempted to "practice" when you are not entirely focused. That is a very dangerous situation.

It is also very dangerous to have any ammunition anywhere near you during dry practice training. You need to separate yourself entirely from all ammunition.

The first step is to unload the weapon. Place the ammunition in

Dry practice includes all the skills you have learned on the range and in the classroom, without bullets, including skills like tactical reloading.

and safe. We have made targets specific for the purpose of dry practice. And finally we have ensured that there is no ammunition in the room in which we are practicing. It's time to actually dry practice.

What to Practice

In one word, everything. Every skill you know, every skill you have been taught needs to be practiced. Now is not the time to try out something new, however. Only practice those skills and techniques you are familiar with. Practicing beyond your scope of knowledge is downright dangerous and leads to ingraining bad habits in your memory.

Practicing the movements associated with loading and unloading must be covered. Remember, movements only. Gaining muscle memory is the reason for this. By repetition we learn.

Target acquisition, too. This includes a proper stance, a proper grip and bringing the

a container of some sort. Empty your pockets, ensuring there are no bullets. Take off any devices used to store ammunition such as magazine holders, speed loaders and all magazines. Empty the ammunition from all of these into the container you used when you emptied the weapon.

When all devices are empty and the ammunition is in one storage container, take that container and place it in another, entirely separate room. Return to

the dry practice room and double-check all of the carrying devices to ensure that they are free of all ammunition.

You will need the carrying devices to do your dry practice drills so return them now to their normal position on your belt or harness when you are armed.

So, where are we?

We have gained the proper mindset and are entirely focused. We have found a proper location to practice, free of all distractions

Another skill that needs to be trained regularly to retain muscle and mental memory is what to do in the case of a malfunction. There are three basic types and all need to be practiced.

handgun up so that the front sight is centered on the target. From there, practice aligning the front and back sights, concentrating on the front sight to gain an absolute focus.

And, it includes the potentially deadly action of the trigger squeeze. This includes taking up the slack and getting the surprise click of the hammer falling on an empty chamber. The front sight must not move during the hammer fall. If the front sight does move then it wasn't a surprise at all. At the range, or in a life-and-death situation, any movement of that front sight during the hammer fall will send the bullet off target.

Then there are malfunction problems to practice, practicing to replace empty magazines or use speed loaders, checking your surroundings after the hammer fall for any other potential threats– all must be practiced.

These skills mentioned above are just the basics. They apply to everyone in any situation imaginable.

There are different ways we carry our handguns however, different places we position them so they are available if the time comes. These contingencies must also be practiced in dry practice sessions.

For instance, say you have a handgun in your nightstand. If you do not practice the entire movement from opening the nightstand and establishing a proper grip and sight alignment then really how effective is that handgun in the nightstand? If you carry a handgun in a holster under a light jacket how effective can you be at a moment's notice if you haven't practiced gripping and clearing that pistol and bringing it to a firing position? What about inside a purse or a fanny pack? The point is this– you need to practice as close to real situations as you can.

Speed will be a concern to you at first. Everyone wants to be fast. But, at least initially, you should not consider speed at all. You need to practice absolutely correct techniques. After a period of time when you have used dry practice sessions in an absolutely correct manner you will find your speed improving. This is over time, not overnight.

A Final Thought

Back at the beginning of this chapter we talked about the range and live fire not being the best training for personal defense. Most ranges don't allow shooting from a holster, much less a concealed carry position. Ranges don't have nightstands or desk drawers. You can't get to them on a regular basis in most cases. Bullets cost a fair amount of money. Yet, all of these things must become second nature, they must become ingrained into your muscle and nervous system memory for you to be consistently effective.

Have regularly scheduled dry practice sessions, say twice weekly. Use the range to verify your dry practice sessions. The dry practice sessions are where you will build upon your skills. ✪

The Front Sight Firearms Training Institute, located in Aptos, California, with its primary training center located just outside of Las Vegas, Nevada, has put together a comprehensive checklist to follow when engaged in dry practice. The institute's president, Dr. Ignatius Piazza, has graciously allowed its reproduction in this chapter.

Front Sight Training Institute Dry Practice Checklist

- Set a realistic dry practice goal before you start. A long practice session is not necessarily better because quality— not quantity— is the goal.
- Establish the proper mind-set for dry practice.
- Establish and maintain control of your dry practice environment to eliminate all possible distractions.
- UNLOAD THE WEAPON AND YOURSELF and place the ammunition in another room.

Chamber check the weapon to verify that it is unloaded and say, "The weapon is unloaded and I am ready for dry practice."

- Select an appropriately sized target and place it on a solid surface capable of stopping a bullet.
- Chamber check the weapon again and then begin dry practice.
- Terminate the dry practice session before significant physical and mental fatigue set in.
- Remove the dry practice target immediately upon finishing the dry practice session.
- Return the weapon to fighting mode— loaded and placed in its usual location such as a holster, fanny pack, briefcase, or nightstand.
- Say aloud, "The weapon is loaded and dry practice is over."

Copyright 2004 Front Sight Firearms Training Institute. Used by permission.

GPS of Personal Defense:

Grip, Presentation and Stance

By Dan Donarski

The absolute beginning and end of personal protection, of self-defense, is your ability to fight through the adrenaline and yes, the fear factor, involved in a life-threatening situation. No matter how good you may be on the range, it is under conditions of intense stress that your abilities to protect yourself and your family or friends will be tested.

On the range there is no threat. You have plenty of time to load or reload, to align the sights on the paper or steel target, and easily take the slack out of the trigger and get that surprise trigger break sending the bullet downrange.

On a darkened street with an armed assailant or suddenly awaken from a sound sleep with a home invader those seconds disappear. Now is not the time to monkey around ensuring you have a proper grip. Your grip must be perfect. Now is not the time to wave the handgun around squinting at the sights trying to align them. Your sight alignment must be perfect.

In another chapter of this book you'll find a complete discussion of a style of training called "dry practice." In that chapter you'll find just how important this style of training is to your ability to function properly when the time comes. But, there are a few things you should consider before you start to dry practice in order to get the most out of it. Some of these won't change no matter how you choose to carry your handgun,

Grip, stance and presentation are the ingredients for consistent accuracy. Range firing validates the practice that goes in to ensure all three are perfect.

or even where you place it so it is ready at a moment's notice. Some will however.

The Basic Grip and Presentation

The one, single, most important skill to perfect is the basic grip. Calling it basic is almost a disservice as this basic grip is the end point in consistent shooting both on the range and in a life and death situation. There are not any variables in this. It must be done the same way each time your handgun is pointed downrange.

For the sake of clarification the grip is something you do, not something that is on the weapon. You grip the weapon by the tang.

No matter how the weapon is carried or stored you must grip

the weapon with the firing hand high on the tang. If your weapon is an autoloader the soft flesh found between your thumb and index finger is just underneath the slide. If your weapon is a revolver it is just underneath the hammer. That index finger of yours should be along the frame, just above the trigger and completely out from the inside of the trigger guard.

Once the weapon is cleared from its carrying position or stored position the weapon is brought up. Here you will be dropping and rotating your firing arm shoulder just a bit. The end result is that your firing arm elbow will end up being tucked into the area just below your firing side ribs. Your firing arm forearm will be parallel with the ground and the weapon will be pointed in the direction of the threat. The trigger finger throughout all of this remains alongside the frame and away from the trigger.

Now, in one smooth and sharp move you use your firing arm to push the weapon forward while the supporting hand comes up to meet the firing hand. The thumb of the supporting hand covers the thumb of the firing hand while the fingers of the supporting hand cover the middle, ring and little finger of the firing hand. During this movement the safety on your weapon, if it has one, is disengaged.

The movement of the supporting hand to the firing hand is not a lazy, curvy move. It is done sharply. Think of it this

Notice the position of the handguns of the two right shooters, both in the close contact position. On the far right, the shooter's handgun is pointed into the ground in front of him, not at the potential threat to his front. On his left, the shooter's handgun is pointed in the direction of the threat, ready to be used. This shooter is executing the close contact position correctly.

way: The firing hand and arm, when thrust forward, is like a boxer throwing a jab. There is no curve to it, no bowling-like move. When the supporting hand comes up to meet the firing hand at the beginning of the move they should meet with authority and a slight clap heard when they do meet. Throughout this move the trigger finger remains alongside the frame away from the trigger.

Your firing arm elbow should have a slight bend to it. It should be a bit relaxed. The elbow should be pointed down with just a slight outward angle. If you lock out the elbow with a straight arm on the firing side you, will not be able to get a solid, unwavering sight picture. Your barrel will quiver in the least, which will throw any bullets off your desired target. The elbow of the supporting arm will have a pronounced bend with the elbow pointing straight down. Neither of the elbows is pushed out from the body. Rather, both are relatively tight to the body.

Your eyes are focused on the front sight, placing the sight center mass on the target. To put it simply, you are dead serious at this point.

A firm grip. Arms thrust out; firing arm straight but not locked; elbows close in to the body; trigger finger along the frame and the handgun brought up to the eyes and the eyes locked on the front sight, not brought down to the gun and sight; all these make up getting the ready position right. Follow these rules and the shot, if the need arises, will be on target.

Let's review where we are. We've established a grip high on the tang of the weapon. The weapon was brought up to a position close in to the body with the barrel pointed towards the target and the firing elbow tucked into the body and the firing shoulder dropped just a bit. From there the weapon was thrust forward towards the target while at the same time the supporting hand comes up and meets the firing hand with the supporting hand fingers overlapping. You are focused on the front sight and on the target and you mean business.

The next step in the grip is the meat of the matter. You can mess up any of the initial steps and while you will be compromised in one way or another, you can still be effective if this next step is done with precision. You must take that quiver out of the barrel. This is the accuracy step. Everything else is the presentation leading up to the accuracy.

Now you must match the tension that your supporting hand and your firing hand are applying to the tang of the weapon. The tension on your

firing hand will be that of a push. On the supporting hand the tension is a pull.

Your firing hand will be applying the push tension, pushing the weapon away from you, with the base of the palm where it meets the backside of the tang. Your supporting hand will be applying the pull tension, pulling the weapon back into your body, with the fingers wrapped over the firing hand fingers on the front of the tang. These must be equal because if they are not your bullets will not find there desired place on the target. They will go low if the push is greater, or go high if the pull is greater.

This is an exercise in isometrics. The force is applied on both sides equally, thereby creating a stable object, in this case, a stable handgun. It is this stability that leads to your bullet leaving the gun and reaching its desired target.

At this stage your trigger finger remains alongside the frame when in the ready to fire position or mode. It is a simple thing to drop the finger to the trigger and take up the slack, when in the point-and-shoot mode.

No matter if you are firing from a sitting position, like from behind a desk or sitting up in bed, or from a standing position, this basic grip will be a deadly asset to master. The grip, when done properly, is stable. When coupled with the precise presentation just covered, it is a lethal combination.

When you learn this basic grip and presentation to the point that the mechanics become second nature from regular practice there will be only one conscious thought left. That one conscious thought and decision is whether or not to terminally complete the trigger break and send that bullet off to meet its target. That is the only thought or concern you want to have running around inside your head when the time comes. It's the only one you can afford to have.

Nightstands, Desks and the Like

You know the grip, you know the presentation. Now, just where in that desk or in that nightstand are you going to place your weapon? The care you take with that answer, and the care

Use another person to check your isometric, push-pull pressure of your grip. This will help you determine the proper amounts of pressure, and the placement of that pressure, when you grip the handgun.

A good grip looks and feels strong. An instructor can tell if you're doing things correctly by allowing you to apply your grip to her forearm.

you take to make your decision a lasting one is vital.

First off there are not two or three good choices. There is only one. What works for me isn't necessarily the best for you. Before you decide on the where part of the equation you need to take extra care to ensure that the where, except for the handgun, is sterile.

Here are a few things to consider. Your handgun will be loaded, or the magazine holding the bullets will be filled and next to the gun. You will need to ensure that when the time comes the gun, and the ammunition-filled magazine if the gun is not loaded, is easy to reach with nothing in the way.

This means that nothing else should be in that desk or night stand drawer. Nothing– no papers or pens, no loose change, no loose ammunition. Nothing but the gun. It must be in a ready-to-fire state and you must be able to get to it without fumbling through a bunch of junk.

If you are just now going out to purchase a desk or night stand you are in luck because you can ensure that the "gun drawer" is at the front of the decision making process. If you already own one, then you are going to have to empty the drawer chosen as the gun drawer and put the junk in other places. Assuming a right-handed shooter, the desk drawer should be on the right as well.

How you place the gun in the drawer is also vitally important to your quick access to it when the need arises. It must be placed in the exact same place each time. Front or back is up to you, but keep in mind that when you open the drawer there is going to be a chance for that gun to move.

In a desk drawer, by keeping the gun in the far right, front corner you have two sides of the drawer to stabilize the gun in position. The grip should be closest to you with the barrel pointing directly to the right. The magazine well, or butt of the handgun's tang should be snugged up along the front edge of the drawer. Placing it here affords a more natural angle to gain access to the gun. There are no hard corners to bend your arms or wrists around, just a smooth outstretch of the firing arm and the gun will be in a secure grip in your hand ready to be used.

In a nightstand the placement of the gun remains to the far right, front corner of the drawer. The magazine well or butt still remains closest to you but this time the barrel is snugged up against the front edge of the drawer. Why the difference?

When pulling out a desk drawer it is natural to pull with the firing hand, the hand on the same side as the drawer. In a nightstand, particularly after you've been become suddenly startled, it is a natural tendency to roll over and open the drawer with your left hand. As you'll be somewhere between lying down in bed and sitting up in bed, placing the gun in this way provides a more natural access.

Keep in my mind here that nothing works for everyone in gun placement. What matters most is to keep your gun stored and ready so YOU can get access quickly and naturally. Try a number of placements until you find the one that works for you. When you do make sure each time you put the gun into its drawer it is in the exact place every time.

Purses and Handbags

With purses and handbags the discussion about the clutter inside becomes possibly more vital than the discussion about the clutter in drawers. There are going to be other items in the purse or handbag than the gun. You must deal with that fact from the start.

True, there are special holsters that are made to clip inside these things but that still doesn't overcome the ease of access problem. Even a holster securely clipped to the inside of a purse doesn't make access easy if assorted stuff is in the way on your way to secure the handgun. You can't afford the time involved in rearranging that stuff when faced with an ugly situation. You need free and easy access now.

No matter the style of purse, the most logical place to store the gun is at the front. The barrel should pointed down with the barrel snugged into the front edge and the tang extending back along the top. With a purse holster this is a relatively easy thing to do. If you don't own a holster then take the purse to a shoemaker or seamstress and have them sew in an extra triangle-shaped pocket that coincides with your gun's dimensions. Make sure the pocket sits right up to the top edge of the purse as you don't want anything to get jostled around and find its way on top of the tang thereby blocking your grip.

It should go without saying but nothing else goes into that special pocket but the gun. Ever. Like with the discussion about drawers, you'll have to find the best way to draw the gun out of the purse. You also must decide what style is best for you.

Are you going to use the supporting hand to grip the bag while the firing hand unzips or unbuckles the purse and then grip the gun? Is a zipper or buckle the best purse style or is one of those clam-shell types, the ones with a simple toggle at the top that, when undone, causes the purse to open on its own. The choice here is obviously yours, but keep in mind that the choice to complete the trigger break is yours, too. Like most every thing when it comes to personal defense, the more exact you are, the more exact and precise your practice makes you, the better off you are. Seconds, or even their mere fractions, often count.

What About Those Feet?

We're talking about stance here, how you are going to place your feet and your body when you need to.

One of the best, and easiest stances to master is the modified

The position of your feet should be at a 30-degree angle from parallel to the target/threat. This will feel a bit uncomfortable at first so practice is key. This position gives the shooter a more stable platform to shoot from than other varieties.

Weaver stance. Basically this stance is one just shy of parallel to the threat or target. Your supporting side foot becomes the front foot. Your firing side foot becomes the trail foot.

Imagine a 30-degree angle cut back from the parallel firing line on a range, or back from parallel from an attacker. Your feet should be aligned along that 30-degree angle, as should your lower body up to the waist. From your waist you slightly turn your firing side shoulder into the target. The jab-like movement you make when you bring the gun up from alongside your body and he clapping of your supporting to complete the grip in the ready position will make this turn naturally for you.

While it is true that this stance does give any attacker a larger profile than a perpendicular stance would, a perpendicular stance is not at all stable. Much more than 30 degrees off parallel and your firing arm will become fully extended making it unstable. Much less, and the unstable body part becomes the supporting arm and sometimes even the firing arm.

Thirty degrees is a magic number here. Initially it will feel more than a little uncomfortable. After a few hours of practice it will become second nature.

In fact, everything we've discussed in this chapter will become second nature with enough practice. It needs to be second nature if you want to be pro-active in your own personal defense. As the name implies, it is personal, as in YOUR defense. How you prepare for it can mean the difference between successful defense and, if you live through it, an episode you rather not remember. If you haven't read the chapter on dry practice now would be a good time. ✪

The Alpha and Omega: *Complete Training*

By Dan Donarski

Yes, except for those convicted of felonies, or those with a history of mental illness and a few other qualifiers, everyone else in the United States of America has the right to own a firearm. With some states there are a few more hoops to jump through, particularly with handguns, but thanks in large part to a vigorous defense of the 2nd Amendment the rest of have the right to keep and bear arms.

Without getting into a debate over something in which I have a deep and abiding belief, The Bill of Rights in all its glory, let me say this: Just because you have the right doesn't free you from the responsibility that goes along with exercising that right. I can think of no other freedom we have, that of owning firearms, that bears such a weighty responsibility. That beautifully simple freedom gives us the tool to take a life.

Nay-sayers to this belief would have us believe that guns kill people. Most of us would say that people kill people. Recently, while at the Front Sight Firearms Training Institute near Las Vegas I came to realize that both are rather trite. At Front Sight they have a saying that goes something like this: You are the weapon, the gun is the tool. It may be an exaggeration to say that seeing it put this way was an epiphany, but it was damn close. So close that it still sits at the forefront of my personal defensive posture. I am, you are, the weapon.

The Importance of Complete Training

Just as you wouldn't want a 16-year-old kid to climb into a motor vehicle and take off down the highway without first going through structured training that includes a test of some sort, you

Training will only be as good as the instructors who conduct it. Look for a small instructor-to-shooter ratio, nothing higher than one instructor to five students. This gives you the assurance of personal attention.

probably also do not want any Tom, Dick, or Harry to go out, buy a gun and start carrying that gun concealed or blasting away without some sort of instruction. Preferably structured instruction rather than a single lesson from Uncle Joe or even the relatively simplistic training that is required by most states in order to get a carry permit.

And, no, definitely not, this is not to step on the 2nd Amendment. It is most certainly the realization that there are deadly serious responsibilities that go along with that right.

These responsibilities don't have an ending point. If you ever have to launch a bullet at an attacker and the attacker falls, well, your responsibilities and their consequences have just begun. They do have a beginning, however. It is the responsibility of making the decision to use lethal force, or not to use lethal force, if and when the time comes. From that first thoughtful decision to the bullet being launched and beyond, is complete training.

The mechanics involved in taking up the trigger slack, experiencing the surprise break in the trigger releasing the hammer or firing pin onto the primer and launching the bullet is basic. The thought process leading up to that point is most likely the most advanced mental gymnastics you'll ever deal with. Complete training takes all of this, the mental and the physical, into consideration. It trains both the mind and the body to work in concert with one another to create an effective tool. It also asks the most important question you'll ever ask yourself right at the beginning.

Complete training trains the mind along with the body to function as one. Two-day courses, four-day courses and even longer should include both the mind and the body. You should, in choosing a course of instruction, make sure that both are covered. If one aspect is missing, and generally it is the mental part that will be missing, you are not training completely.

In writing his book, *Men Against Fire*, S.L.A. Marshall studied and personally researched all sorts of things that happen to men on the battlefield. One of the things he was able to document had to do with soldiers firing their weapons. It seems that barely 15 percent of those under fire would actually return fire at enemy personnel or positions. Even in the best-trained units that percentage was not more than 25 percent — one in four. That's right, the rest didn't fire back. At all.

Keep in mind that the men involved were under fire. Their buddies were getting killed. Their lives were in severe danger. They had the legal sanction of war to fire back without threat of civil or criminal repercussion. And the vast majority didn't shoot back. Certainly fear was a factor but there was another factor, too. This leads us to the question.

The Ultimate Question, The Ultimate Consequence

Are you prepared, willing and able to use deadly force to stop a robbery or an assault in your home or where you work? How

Defensive handgun training is right for everyone. If you are going to carry, or place a handgun in the home for protection, then a complete training course should be taken.

about a rape? What about an attacker preying on you, a family member, or someone you don't even know in the park?

If you own a gun then you certainly have the ability. If you have been well trained to use that gun then you are prepared. That leaves us with "willing." So, let's ask again, "Are you willing to use deadly force in situations like this?"

There is no single correct answer. The willing part of the question is a question on morals and ethics. How you answer these questions is purely personal, based on your moral and ethical beliefs. Morals are generally a personal reflection on right and wrong. Ethics are based collectively on the area you live in and coincide with generally accepted conduct.

In a course of complete instruction where should this question be raised? The answer is quite simple — right at the beginning. A course that doesn't ask this question in a serious manner is simply a course in handling firearms, not a personal defense course. Without a solid answer to the different scenarios you will not be properly prepared to defend yourself or your loved ones when the time comes.

At the Front Sight Firearms Training Institute the instructors ran us through a variety of scenarios in the classroom. They ranged from an attacker who wouldn't stop, to a roadside accident where one of the drivers became an aggressor. In each we were asked when or if we would present the handgun and when we would shoot. In more than one case the aggressor became the victor thanks to hesitation on the defender's part, hesitation in answering that question.

That's why your answer to the ultimate question is so important and why it must be asked early on during your personal defense training. Knowing the answer to the question when posed in different ways gives you the prior knowledge that you will act in a specific way. There will be no hesitation. You already know the answer.

Your training course also needs to go over the ramifications of what will happen to you if you are forced to use lethal force to stop an assailant. There are a myriad of civil and criminal liabilities to consider. You quite possibly will be cuffed and arrested. Legal costs in defending yourself against a criminal complaint filed by the District Attorney and/or a civil liability case where the attacker's family sues you are a definite possibility. So is being pilloried in the press for acting in what they will call a "rash" manner. These are just a few of the consequences of your actions in a justified shooting.

When you know that you are willing to take the ultimate action in defending yourself or your loved ones your training absolutely needs to take the next step. The "when to shoot" question must be asked and answered.

Justification Training

Going hand-in-hand with the willing part of the equation, any personal defense course you participate in must include a good discussion of when the use of deadly force is justified. We use deadly here for a very specific reason. While you are training with your gun to stop an attacker, not to kill him or her, there is a real probability that when your bullet hits center mass on the assailant that you will, indeed, kill him.

Here's something to keep in mind throughout the discussion. No matter how justified you may feel, no matter how justified you actually are, whether or not it was reasonable or necessary may often rely on what the investigating officers and a jury of 12 may think. In other words the best gunfights, as that is what they are, are the ones you can avoid. Unfortunately there may come a time when avoidance is out of the question.

There are no hard and fast rules any personal defense course can give you to determine with absolute certainty when a shooting will be ruled justified. There is, however, a definite thought process involved that

will make the shoot/don't shoot question easier to answer. This thought process must be in your course for you to be prepared.

Questions that you must be able to answer after the course and when faced with an attacker would include these:

- Was the force used necessary rather than excessive?
- Was the use of force unavoidable?
- Was there an immediate threat rather than an imminent threat?
- Was it a threat to life or serious injury to the body?
- Are you free from any fault, from any instigation or escalation?

Did your attacker have the ability, intent and opportunity to kill you or cause serious injury?

These are just a few of the questions that you need to be trained to quickly think about. In a study by Mike Waidelich in the early 1980s, he found that the average armed assailant can travel just over 20 feet in one and a half seconds and cause a fatal wound. Waidelich also found that it takes that same amount of time for an average person to draw his weapon from his holster and fire one bullet into the center mass of a target. Basically that

means you have precious little time, and you are in immediate danger, when an armed attacker is within a distance of 10 yards. If these considerations aren't in the course you are thinking about signing up for you need to find another.

You should also look for a section of the course to include a thorough discussion on ways to persuade an attacker that his course of action is not all that bright. No, you are not going to become a psychologist here, but you will attempt to quickly persuade the attacker to quit his actions. Your vocal cords come into play here with simple things like yelling, "Don't come any closer," or "Stop! I will shoot," while you are presenting the weapon into the ready-to-shoot position.

At the end of this section of your personal defense course you must be able to positively determine if your shooting in specific situations is justified. If you have to wrestle through the answer you most likely shouldn't be shooting. Nothing is more serious than a gunfight. There are no winners– one side just loses a hell of a lot more. The so-called winner now gets to face the possible wrath of the police and the courts, the press, and

You walk before you run. You also practice from close range before going for distance. It is at close range that most gunfights will begin and end. Center mass is the target, two-shot groups the goal.

the inner questions and turmoil that will mark the rest of his or her life.

If you don't understand that the best gunfight is the one you avoid then you need to go back and take another course that thoroughly goes through the justification and ramifications of the use of deadly force.

A well-respected lawyer, and someone I hold in high personal regard, Doug Chester, offers these final thoughts on the subject of consequence and justification.

"It's interesting that you hit right on the big question. It is one thing to pull the trigger in a sanctioned situation, i.e., military. Your conscience is given a "free pass," and you have society's sanction (more or less) to terminate another human being," said Chester. "Not that this gets you totally out from under, as you still have to live with yourself, and you still have to wonder if you were right.

"In a non-sanctioned situation, like a burglar breaking into your home, or a street fight, the question is a lot tougher, and you will likely be subject to unsympathetic review. I find it infuriating when people second-guess cops for a split-second decision made in a dark hallway when they were telling some

eggplant to freeze and show his hands, and the eggplant does neither, and points a cell phone at the cops, and gets shot. Boards of inquiry and Courts will spend weeks re-hashing a second by second account of a shooting. This is totally unfair to the cop. It is also what you should expect as a civilian involved in a shooting, only you'll get worse. The problem is that the bad guy is not subject to these limitations. He acts on instinct without consideration of consequences. This gives him a major advantage."

Up until now the course of complete instruction has only touched on the mental process involved in the use of firearms or weapons in self-defense. And that's how the course should be laid out. Mental exercises, the mental debate, are by far the hardest to come to grips with. They are the defining quotient on the use of weapons for personal defense. On the range, with a weapon in hand, the rest of a complete training course becomes simple mechanics.

Weapons Training

That's not to downplay the importance of the correct way to use a weapon. The weapon is only as good as the person using

it. You need to know your weapon inside and out.

A complete weapons course will start from the beginning, showing how the weapon works and how it is taken care of. It should include a wide range of weapons in various actions as well as barrel lengths and grip sizes and styles. Just because you are a revolver fan doesn't mean it is the best choice for you. Just because that .44 Magnum with the 8-inch barrel is in your gun safe doesn't mean that it the right choice for carrying in a holster or placing in a purse or desk drawer. Only by using different styles will you be able to make a good decision on which one is right for you.

A basic defensive weapons course should start with you and your choice of weapon at short range, say 5 yards. First the instructors should go through the mechanics involved in the grip, stance and presentation of the handgun to the target gaining a good focus on both the front sight and the target. When this is mastered you begin firing two shot groups so that the hits are center mass on a human silhouette. After you reach a high degree of consistency the distance should be increased to seven, then 10 and on out to 25 yards.

Your course should teach you basic malfunction drills. You need to know how to clear a dud from your gun, clear a shell that has mis-fed into the chamber and execute tactical reloading all with the handgun in the point position. These should become reflexive actions, the only intellectual action is whether to actually shoot.

Actions after the shot is taken, checking the surrounding environment for any other threats, needs to be covered. You'll have a single focus after the shot, and that single focus must be broken to ensure the area is clear from danger. Front

Initially speed will not be an issue. As the complete training course builds on your skills, speed training, with revolving targets will prove critical, and should be stressed.

Training should also include tactical scenarios or simulator training. Here we see an instructor putting a student through a shoot/don't shoot situation where every decision made and shot taken will be evaluated thoroughly. Even seasoned shooters get a bit nervous doing these, but such simulations build mental and physical confidence, the key to complete training.

Sight uses the quick-check and final check method. It is one that is highly recommended.

After the shot(s) are taken you execute a simple head movement, looking both left and right with the weapon in the ready position. You then execute the final check by taking a step, left or right, and then rotating your head and torso as one, like a tank turret, while keeping the gun in the ready position. This is done after every shooting sequence. You must become reflexive in breaking through that tunnel vision.

A basic two-day course will build upon each technique. It should only go as fast as you can be taught. A rushed course serves no one but the instructor's wallet. What you want to accomplish in a basic course is the fundamentals involved. You want to be able to reflexively get into a firing stance. Reflexively go through the presentation of the weapon from a holster to the point position. Taking the slack out of the trigger, getting the surprise break and the reset of the

trigger without putting the slack back. You need to be able to hit center mass on the target.

Actual speed of presentation and firing, and the speed involved in clearing a malfunction will only become "fast" after a great deal of practice. Another chapter of this book goes through something called "Dry Practice," an excellent method of building speed through regular practice even when you are not on a range. You'll also find a chapter on grip, stance and weapon presentation and placement. Each stresses the reflexive nature of everything except the intellectual decision on whether to shoot or not. Everything except taking the shot must be reflexive and a good course will help get you to that point.

The basic course should also include at least one scenario where you will be shooting at photo targets, or choosing not to shoot in some cases, while inside a mock-up of a house or alley. One instructor should be tied to you for safety one way or another, and another acts as the voice of

the bad guy in the background, screaming and making noise, putting your shoot/don't shoot reasoning to the test.

A more advanced four-day course would start with all of the above but get into even more tactical situations. It should cover shooting from a variety of positions as well as shooting under limited light. Clearing areas such as doorways, around corners, and engaging multiple targets should also be trained. And there should be a wide variety of tactical scenarios that you go through.

In all cases a defensive weapons course, be it handgun, rifle, shotgun or edged weapon, must be a skill-building course. You didn't run before you could first walk, and you won't be good with a weapon until you first learn how it works and how it is to be used effectively in a step-by-step manner.

You say you don't need training? That you have all the bases covered? There is really no such thing as "complete training" as you must continue to train, to practice, to keep your skills sharp and your mind focused. Having the skills leads to confidence and confidence will lead to performance. Skills not practiced and refreshed are soon lost. Complete training means regular and proper training. It just doesn't end. ✪

(Author's note: The mental processes involved in the training for personal defense, along with the need for continued practice on a regular basis, was brought home after attending the Front Sight Firearms Training Institute's two-day Defensive Handgun Training course. Even after a career as an infantry officer where I was trained on all sorts of weapons, qualifying expert in each I might add, I have never been to a more professional course. It, or its four-day counterpart course, is a course I would highly recommend to anyone considering having a defensive weapon in the home or applying for a carry permit.)

Buying Used Firearms Without Guilt, and With Low Risk

By Patrick Sweeney

Let's face it, new guns can be expensive. And even though people can make the argument, "What price is your life worth?" when you are buying a gun for personal defense, sooner or later, we all give in to the temptation of a used firearm. You might spot one that you've always wanted. Or one just like the one you learned to shoot with, and foolishly sold because someone offered you "a lot of money" for it. Or, someone has a solid firearm at a rock-bottom price, but there is no time because he is leaving town tomorrow or getting divorced next week.

Yes, it could be a great deal. Or, it could be a series of headaches, each more expensive than the last. How do you avoid the hassles? Firearms transactions occur in one of two settings; A retail establishment or on the open market. (In states where all transactions must go through a dealer, the open market is the black market. You were warned. Do not write me from jail, bemoaning your fate.)

Dealing with a retail establishment has its own etiquette. The main thing you need to remember is to follow the advice your father gave you when he was trying to get you educated on appliances, vehicles and life insurance: Buy from an established firm that has been around a long time. Yes, you'll pay their markup. But what that markup gets you is their experience and a willingness to stand behind their product. You may be seeing your second-ever (fill in the model name or number) but an active gun shop will have been at it for years, and likely seen dozens of them.

Ask the store staff what the return policy is. Don't assume there is one, and don't assume it is printed on the back of the receipt. It would be prudent for the store to print it, but a lot don't. You can usually expect to be able to return a firearm if it isn't as promised. If all the particulars check out as presented (correct headspace, straight barrel, clean bore, correct caliber) but the 80-year-old revolver you just bought shoots poorly, that was part of the risk you assumed when you paid $79 for it.

A firearm should perform within the parameters of its type. If it doesn't, then you should be able to return it. If you buy a Winchester or Marlin saddle carbine, and it shoots two to three inch groups at one hundred yards, you have no cause for complaint. That is the expected average for such rifles. If the group is two feet to the right or left, then you have cause for return.

You can protect yourself in many cases by asking for a test period. In the two weeks following your purchase you should have a gunsmith inspect your new firearm, and test-fire it. If anything is wrong, you can return it within the time limit. (Be sure to get this in writing.) Car dealers do it, dog breeders do it, and many gun dealers also do it.

You have lots of choices on the used gun market. Be careful and choose wisely. Clockwise from lower left – Smith & Wesson, Glock, S & W Lady Smith, Taurus PT111.

How your used gun shoots might have something to do with the ammunition. Try several kinds to see what works best. A used gun in good shape should function with nearly all factory-loaded ammunition.

When you test, test honestly. Don't assume your new Tactical rifle will shoot sub-MOA groups with the grungy surplus ammo you keep behind the seat of your truck. Give it a fair test and feed it new factory match-grade ammo. If it won't perform, have someone else shoot it. I know we're all good shots, but let a better shot try it if you aren't having any luck. In fact, test any new purchase with factory ammo. Yes, We are all competent and accomplished reloaders, but now is not the time to be using them. Test with factory ammo, ideally with factory ammo that has a track record you are sure of. If you buy a used P-38 because you've always wanted one, and it won't shoot your 9mm reloads at all, where's the blame? You don't know. But if it won't shoot groups with Remington Match 9mm ammo that are smaller than a Volvo, you know the gun is at fault.

On the open market such as at a gun show, you have to keep in mind the Latin phrase Caveat Emptor. "Let the buyer beware."

You probably won't be offered a chance to return it, nor will you have a chance to test it and have it inspected. How can you protect yourself when buying a firearm on the open market? Get a written receipt, with a description of the firearm and accessories or features. Get the owner's name and address. If you agree to a return policy, write it on the back of the receipt. Both of you sign it. A receipt so-described is a contract, and with it you can later go to small claims court if you can't get the owner to take it back and return your money.

You can minimize your chances of getting shafted, and stuck with a bad deal, if you give the prospective new purchase a thorough inspection. You can't do a test-fire at the store or gun show (that would put us all in a very bad light) but you can look for the things that alert you to a bad deal.

First, look it over. Does the blueing/Parkerizing/hard chrome have the correct color? A reblued gun will look different than a factory blue job. The best bluers

cannot match what the factory did. It may look better, but a reblue isn't original. If the seller is telling you it is factory-new, but the color is off, you might ask why. Or just put it down and walk on. While you're checking the color, look at the edges and markings. A reblue job entails polishing, and a heavy-handed polisher will leaves traces on the markings. You can see them "pulled" or "faded." A pulled marking has the buffing wheels marks dragged from the lettering. A faded marking has the letters partially obliterated. (You can do a lot of the visual inspection without even picking it up.) Do all the parts match in wear? Or is one part obviously newer? Is the blueing evenly worn, or is it worn in spots? Many lever guns have the blueing worn off on the bottom at the balance point, not a cause for concern. Is the stock equally worn? Or does the rifle have new wood and old blueing? Any mismatch is cause for concern and questioning. On rifles and shotguns, look over the stock. More than dents and dings (which can be treated later) you're interested in cracks and repairs. Look at the wrist of the stock, behind the tang. Is it cracked? If it is it won't shoot accurately, and probably will crack further when you shoot it. Look at the forend. Does the forend of a shotgun come off easily, too easily? Does it need to be wrestled off? Too easy and wrestling are bad signs. On rifles look at the barrel channel. Some shooters cannot help themselves, they must experiment. If someone has "free-floated" the barrel by way of a wood rasp and router, you've got to wonder what else they did. On handguns, look for dents and dings on the edges and muzzle. Dropped handguns often leave distinct marks from their fall and impact. Dropped guns can be subtly damaged, and not ever be accurate again. Once your potential new gun passes the visual inspection, check the function. Does the bolt, lever, or operating rod move smoothly and freely? Does the safety click on and off? Does the safety actually prevent the mechanism from firing when it is on? What, the owner won't let you cycle the action or dry-fire it? Put it down and walk away. Yes, I know that many owners and dealers at gun shows want to keep their firearms from being excessively handled. Yes, I know that constant handling can wear blue and put dings in the stock. But if I'm in the market to buy something and the current owner won't let me perform safety and function tests, I walk on. I don't need the financial risk, and I've wasted too much time in the past trying to change small minds.

Having said that, would I make exceptions? Perhaps. But only if I was dealing with someone with a known reputation, and I had the return policy in writing.

Open the action and look down the bore. Rifle, shotgun, handgun, they all have to have a clean and unpitted bore to shoot well. If the bore is shiny but slick, get a rod and patch to wipe it out. A pitted bore can be disguised by putting a heavy application of oil in it, and then carefully wiping the bore until the pits are hidden but the rifling (if any) shows. Don't put too much faith in bore scopes. Unless the barrel you are looking at is a top-grade match tube, with few rounds through it, the bore will look bad when magnified 10 or 25 times. A rifle with a slightly pitted bore may still shoot well (I have several that do) but you won't know until you test it. If you can't test and return, pass on the deal.

If it can be disassembled without using tools, then strip it. Look the parts over and see if they are matching in color, texture and wear. If you're contemplating buying a recently shipped M1 Garand that came from the CMP, you probably won't find a lot of matching parts. But, you can ask to see the CMP papers.

If you're buying a new or used AR-15, then you'll definitely want to open it up and see if there are any M-16 parts that have slipped in. (Some shooters don't know the difference, and install whatever works or is cheapest.) Inspect the internals for tool marks and ground-on parts. Many shooters who have tried to assemble an AR ended up doing a lot of grinding and filing. If the receivers or barrel are altered, pass on it. Look at the front sight casting to see if you can spot any hammer marks. If someone took the sight off, they were probably up to no good. If the internal parts are ground-on, whittle the price down by their replacement costs.

Manufacturers who ship assembled AR's make sure the upper and lower match in color. If the AR you're looking at is two different colors, it is probably a parts gun. Be extra careful.

On self-loading pistols in general, check to make sure the magazine goes in smoothly and without binding. Then see that it falls out under its own weight when you push the mag release button. Some won't, like Glocks with early magazines or S&W's or Browning Hi Powers with magazine disconnectors. Does the magazine lock the slide open? Rack the slide and find out. Does the safety work? If it is a hammer-drop model, does the hammer drop? Drop a pencil down the bore, eraser end first, point it up and safety-drop the hammer again. While the pencil jiggles from the vibration, it shouldn't be launched. If it does, the safety isn't blocking the firing pin. Don't worry too much about slide to frame fit. On most guns a bit of play is no big deal.

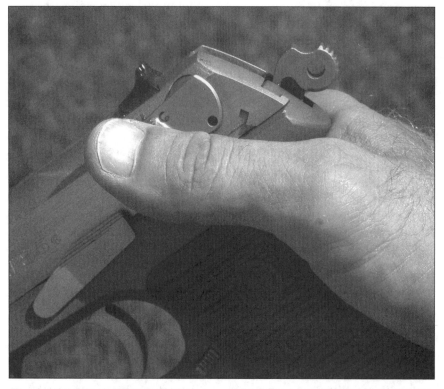

Check the safety or decocking lever on every pistol you are considering for purchase. An inexpensive pistol with a bad safety is no bargain.

However, if the gun in question is offered as a high-end custom gun "with a few mags through it" and the slide wobbles on the frame, don't buy it. The choices are all bad: it may not be custom, it may have a lot more ammo through it, or it may be someone's first "custom" work.

What to look for on 1911's could take a whole book. Make sure the safeties work and that the bore isn't pitted. Remove the barrel and look at the lugs. They should sharp and clean, with square edges and not be peened. If they are peened, the pistol probably needs a new slide and barrel, an expensive repair. If you're contemplating buying a used 1911 that has been a competition gun, check the grip safety. Many old competition guns have the grip safety pinned or deactivated.

On revolvers, check to see that the cylinder turns smoothly. Slowly cock the hammer for each chamber, watching the cylinder. On each chamber, the cylinder should come fully into position when the hammer is cocked. Failure to "carry up" is a sign of hard use, and will need to be repaired. It can mean simply a new hand, or some minor extractor star work, or it could mean a new hand and extractor. If it won't carry up, open and look a the extractor. If it has been filed or ground on, pass on it. Grab the cylinder with your off hand and try to move it fore and aft. If it moves more than a few thousandths, it has endshake. Endshake is another bad sign, and will have to be dealt with by a gunsmith by stretching the crane or installing bushing washers. Look at the forcing cone. Is it clean and sharp, or dark and eroded? A heavily eroded forcing cone can be corrected by setting the barrel back, but it takes a skilled gunsmith or a bit of practice to do it right.

So how do you gain all this knowledge so you can assess a firearm? Read. Talk to experienced shooters and collectors. Ask questions. Cruise the gun shows and look at hundreds of guns. Strike up a relationship with a local gun shop, and drop in once a week or so to see what's new. If you want to get into a particular area of collecting or competition, then read up on it. Yes, it can be expensive to buy a couple of hundred dollars worth of books to read, but you could lose that and more on one bad acquisition. Talk to the experienced shooters and long-time collectors at your gun club. And as with any other gambling, don't play with money you can't afford to lose. Keep at it long enough and you'll make a mistake or two, but even a bad used gun is knowledge gained.   ✪

The etiquette of buying a used gun in a gun shop is different than buying on the open market. In the shop you can ask about the warranty and sometimes be allowed to test fire the gun.

Bring Out the Big Guns

By M.D. Johnson

Let's face it – There are few things available to the average U.S. citizen that can prove as intimidating in a threatening or hostile situation as can a shotgun. There's just something about staring down that black, bottomless, manhole-sized abyss that is a 12-gauge muzzle – I've looked while cleaning, not while on the receiving end, mind you – that quite completely defines the word *fear*. Combine that with the unmistakable *schlick-schlick* sound of a pump-gun action being worked in the darkness, and even the legendary strongman, Hercules, might think twice about stepping, uninvited, inside the doorway.

A Mossberg Model 500, with 18.5" barrel and synthetic, twin-bar forearm – a workhorse, and a proven piece for both home and field situations. Bad guys fear this.

And as if sight and sound weren't enough, there's the fact that while the man with the .32 ACP is shooting a single round with each pull of the trigger, he who carries a 12-bore filled with 2.75-inch shotshells containing OO buckshot can be secure in the knowledge that nine – NINE – of the same sized projectiles are headed downrange. Downsize to #4 buck in the same 2.75-inch shotshell, and he's increased that count to 27 .24-caliber pellets, each moving at roughly 1,300 feet-per-second (fps). That, my friend, is real power.

Despite these very obvious advantages, the shotgun as a self-defense firearm is not without is downsides. Let's take a look at the pros and cons.

Shotguns – The good

Let's discuss three factors why a shotgun might be considered for self-defense: Intimidation, Ease of Operation, and Margin of Error.

As mentioned before, there's just something intimidating about having a shotgun pointed at you, and often a 12-bore show of force has proved sufficient to end the threat before the situation has a chance to escalate. That's not to say that you should assume that the mere sight of a shotgun will be enough to strike fear into the heart of any burglar or would-be assailant. In such situations, you should never assume anything; however, instances where the

sight a home or shop owner armed with a 12-gauge has squelched an attack are numerous to the point of justifying the shotgun's role as Intimidator.

Ease of Operation means just that, that a shotgun can be an extremely simple machine to operate. And in a hostile situation simplicity can mean the difference between winning and losing. I say *can be* simple because a shotgun, like many other things, offers varying degrees of technological function – a point which will be discussed further in the section on Choosing an Action.

Finally, there is Margin of Error. With its multiple projectiles per round, the shotgun is may compensate for a number of variables, including fear, injury, target obstruction, target motion, and shooter movement. Any one of these could lead to inaccuracy and a delay or failure in subduing the threat. This element known as Margin of Error, when combined with the Intimidation Factor, can and often does contribute to a sense of confidence on the part of the defender or intended victim, and confidence is the first step to success and effectiveness. But simply having a margin of error does not mean to imply one does not have to aim a shotgun. Nor does it mean you should be firing rounds without positively identifying your target. A shotgun is a lethal weapon and all the same rules apply.

Shotguns – The not-so-good

On the downside, those who choose a shotgun for self-defense must deal with several factors limiting the gun's effectiveness. These include: Intimidation, Bulk and Recoil, and Ammunition Capacity.

In much the same way as a shotgun can be intimidating to a potential threat, the firearm can likewise be intimidating to the shooter. Shotguns are large, much larger than any pistol, and they kick hard. That can lead to a sense of reluctance; though, conversely, the shear size of most shotgun ammunition can also contribute to a sense of security. It's a double-edged sword there.

We've mentioned that shotguns are by nature much larger than handguns, and herein lies another consideration – bulk. In close quarters, shotguns, even short-barreled weapons, can prove cumbersome and unwieldy. This is particularly true for smaller-framed shooters. And unlike pistols that can, if necessary, be fired one-handed, shotguns are, save for extreme situations, a two-handed proposition. Ordinarily, this one-hand versus two-hands debate isn't a consideration where shotguns are concerned; however, there is that one time in a thousand – an injury, perhaps – where a single paw is all that's available. There is, also, the concealment factor. My personal home-defense shotgun, a Mossberg Model 500, measures, with 18-inch barrel, 38 inches overall, which is fine given the weapon spends most of its time perched in a corner. Compare this measurement, however, to the .45 caliber Glock Model G20's overall 7.5 inches, and it's easy to see – literally – what the shotgun lacks as a choice for concealed carry.

Along with the potential of being cumbersome, there's also a shotgun's recoil to be considered. True, this recoil is likely to be dismissed entirely in a life-threatening situation; however, it still does exist. And then there's the recoil associated with familiarizing oneself with the self-defense shotgun. Should recoil be an issue, there is the option of downsizing and/or customizing the shotgun so as to make it more user-friendly. These alterations might include choosing a .410-caliber or 20-gauge weapon as opposed to a 12-gauge, using reduced-recoil ammunition, or installing recoil-reducing elements such as pads or barrel ports.

A final thought – and I hesitate to include this in a section on Cons – involves shotguns and ammunition capacity. High-capacity semi-auto handguns, depending upon the caliber, can offer the shooter from 10 to in some cases, 17 rounds. Shotguns, on the other hand, will range from the single shot's solitary offering upwards of six to eight rounds in most traditional (non-custom) weapons; extended magazine tubes can increase this 8-round maximum by a round or two. Initially, the balance in terms of ammunition capacity

seems to swing in favor of the semi-automatic pistol; however, when one considers that each of a 12-gauge pump's six 2.75-inch shotshells are filled with nine .32-caliber #00 pellets – That's 54 individual .32-caliber projectiles – a slightly different picture begins to unfold. That explained, do the pump-gun's six rounds put the shotgunner at a disadvantage in a threatening situation? That may be open for debate.

Gauge or caliber

For many individuals, this is point at which the debate begins. A 12-gauge, some say, is too heavy and, therefore, too unwieldy. Others counter, there is the intimidation factor is huge. Throw in discussions on customized guns and aftermarket add-ons and the 12-gauge sometimes seems to have very few drawbacks.

On the other side of the coin, there are those who condemn the smaller gauges – the 20-gauge and the .410-caliber – as being less than perfect based on such variables as pellet count and, in the case of the .410, the availability of factory-loaded ammunition designed for self-defense. Still, these "small" guns do have their advocates – those

Big pellets, like this Environ-Metal "Hevi-Shot" 00 buckshot, stop fights quickly. This round and a good short-barreled shotgun make for an impressive combination.

who would say that gauge, which essentially translates into pellet count, plays a minor role in the case of a shotgun being used in self-defense given that such situations, particularly those encountered in the home, are occurring at extremely close distances – 10 feet or less, on average.

For those considering shotguns, the choices include –

The 12-gauge – Perhaps the most popular gauge in home or self-defense shotguns due in large part to the availability of both guns and specialty ammunition. The 12-gauge is available in all four actions – single, double, pump, and semi-auto – and in a wide variety of price ranges. Barrels, too, are widely available. An excellent choice.

The 16- and 28-gauges – I mention these simply so as not to exclude them; however, neither the 16- nor the 28-gauge get much call in terms of self-defense weaponry. The shotguns can prove rather expensive and somewhat difficult to procure. Likewise, the ammunition, which, when found, is typically better suited for the upland bird hunter than the individual protecting his or her home.

The 20-gauge – A good choice, particularly if the firearm is to be used in the home. The 20-gauge is light, widely available, and produces less recoil than the 12-gauge. Like the 12, specialty (factory-loaded) ammunition for the 20-gauge can be had, and it does lend itself well to handloading.

The .410 caliber – Some would say the .410 caliber is too small to serve well as a self-defense firearm, and that its 11/16-ounce maximum shot charge is far too light to allow for a sufficient number of the larger (#4 Buck and up) pellets. However, that same 11/16-ounce load **does** hold a more-than-adequate number of

#4 or #5 pellets, which will prove effective in a close-quarters situation. An accurately fired .410 round is potent. Maybe not as potent as a 12-gauge, but four pellets of 00 buck will make an impact on someone bent on doing evil. Though not nearly as common as either the 12-gauge or 20-gauge, .410 caliber shotguns are offered by several manufacturers, and in all five (including a lever action) action styles. Of the three most popular gauges/calibers, the .410 produces the least amount of recoil, and can be easily handled by most shooters. The bottom line? It's worth considering.

Action

Ease of operation, ammunition capacity, and personal preference help determine what type of shotgun action is *best* in the case of the home or self-defense shotgun. Regardless of the action chosen, however, familiarity with the firearm **before** a situation presents itself is paramount. That point cannot be over-emphasized.

Single-shot – Probably the least common type of shotgun action for home or self-defense is the single-shot. Recoil, particularly in the larger (12-gauge or 10-gauge) bores, can be considerable; however, it's the one-shot limitation that potential buyers find most undesirable. Add to this the need to cock the single-shot's hammer – a simple act on the range, but potentially troublesome in a darkened hallway when confronted adrenaline levels make fine motor skills difficult – and the single-shot becomes less and less an option. Specialty single-shots, however, are available. The Harrington & Richardson synthetic stocked *Tamer* single comes in a 20-inch barreled .410 version, while the H & R Topper series includes a 12- and 20-

The jury's still out on the .410 as a home or self-defense caliber. Is it, or isn't it?

gauge, as well as a .410, with a choice of 26 or 28-inch barrels. New England Firearms also offers a single-shot in their *Survivor Series*, available in 12- and 20-gauge and .410-bore configurations, with a lightweight synthetic stock and choice of 20 or 22-inch barrel. These options are easy on the budget, but if you can afford a different style of gun, you should look for one.

Side-by-Side or Over/Under – These days, save for those wielded by the sheriff in Old Western films, relatively few side-by-side (SxS) shotguns are seen in use or discussed as candidates for self-defense weapons, ousted, I believe, by the popularity, simplicity, and availability of the newer model pump-actions and semi-automatics. It's a shame, too, as the SxS makes for a fine choice for self-defense, despite its two-shot capacity which, the truth be known, isn't that much of a disadvantage as practice can smooth to rapidity the empty-break-load-empty routine. In most cases, the SxS offers a simple-to-operate piece, with an immediate choice in choke constrictions – typically, modified and full – a plus should an outdoors situation present longer distances. In addition, side-by-sides have been traditionally lightweight pieces, offering an ambidextrous top-mounted, and thus convenient, safety. Modern side-by-sides, such as the *Coach Gun* by Stoeger (12- and 20-gauge and .410, 20-inch barrel, double triggers) are without question a force to be reckoned with.

Years ago, I knew a gentleman who kept a pristine Ruger Red Label 12-gauge over/under (O/U), complete with 26-inch barrels, next to his headboard. It was, as he claimed, the best security blanket that money could buy. And while I certainly don't doubt his claim nor the Ruger's role as metal comforter, it's seldom if ever you find an O/U serving as a self-defense or home defense piece. True, there's very little difference between the SxS and the O/U, save for the barrel configuration, so I attribute this discrepancy to tradition.

Pump – The workhorse of the shotgun family, the pump-action or simply, pump, is perhaps the most popular action type for defensive use, and the one with which the general public – thanks, Hollywood – is most familiar. A pump, be it a modern Remington 870 Special Purpose or an older Winchester Model 1897 hammer gun, is a reliable piece, able to withstand the rigors of repeated fire and harsh treatment. Barrels ranging from 18 to 22 inches are available, and stock/fore-end combinations of woods and synthetics are offered. All gauges, 12 through 28, as well as .410-bore, are currently being manufactured, with the 12-gauge and 20-gauge being the most often encountered in the home or field.

An interesting safety note about the pump-action as a defense gun revolves around the fact that such weapons can be stored loaded – that is, the magazine filled to capacity – without a round in the chamber. A shotgun stored as such is much safer should it fall into young and/or untrained hands; however, the same piece can also be readied for action in a split-second simply by hitting the slide release and working the action and disengaging the safety

A plethora of pump-actions, either ready for home defense use or those easy-to-customize, are being made these days. These include models from Remington (M870 Express), Mossberg (M500), Winchester (The Camp Defender), and Ithaca Model 37.

Semi-Automatic – The advantage of the semi-automatic shotgun in a defense role rests in the weapon's rate of fire; that is, a round with every pull of the trigger just as quickly as the trigger can be pulled until the rounds, usually five to seven, are exhausted. The disadvantage, however, is the semi-auto's complicated innards – complicated, that is, in comparison to the less technically advanced pump-action and the downright simple side-by-side. There are simply fewer parts, and thus fewer malfunction potential, with the tried-and-true pump-action.

Also to be considered is the price factor, with semi-autos often costing two to two and one-half times that of a defense-specific pump-action. Pros and cons aside, the final word is that there are semi-autos available – the Remington 1100 and Winchester's Super X2 Practical MK II, for example – for those who might want them.

Barrel length and choke selection

In its simplest form, a shotgun barrel serves merely as a sighting plane. The longer the barrel, the longer the sighting plane. Take away, then, the need for this sighting plane, such as would be the case in a close-quarters defensive encounter, and this lengthy sighting plane becomes unnecessary. A constriction at the shotgun's muzzle, also known as a choke or choke tube, works to create or maintain pattern density. And pattern density is most vital in those instances where distances from the shooter to the intended target begin to increase; that is, a full choke, or a choke that places a minimum of 85 percent of a shotshell's available pellets within a 30-inch circle at 40 yards, is a moot point at 10 feet, yet becomes an important factor at, say, 100 feet.

Given these explanations and knowing that most self or home defense situations unfold at ranges between 3 and 15 feet from the shooter, it becomes understandable that the defensive shotgun would need neither a lengthy barrel *nor* any degree of barrel constriction/choke. In terms of barrels, a short barrel – a tube ranging from the 18-inch legal minimum up to 22 inches – is both lighter and more maneuverable in tight quarters. Chokes in such barrels are typically fixed; that is, there are no interchangeable choke tubes to deal with. These chokes are commonly referred to as *open*, *improved cylinder*, *spreader*, or simply, *none*. Such constrictions offer acceptable up-close patterns with a variety of shot sizes ranging from #00 Buck to #4 lead, and are the recommended chokes when using specialty or less-than-lethal ammunition.

Shotshells, shot size, and less-than-lethal ammunition

In the case of shotguns and personal defense, it is shot size more so than shotshell dimension that lends itself to debate. Members of the "One shot and out of commission" group have their valid argument with larger projectiles - #00 Buck, for example – while there are those who would say that

For shotgun defense work, 00 Buckshot is hard to beat.

smaller pellets such as #2 or #4 lead have energy and penetration sufficient to stop any threat while at the same time posing a less-than-great likelihood of collateral damage to innocents in adjoining rooms. This debate goes on and on and will not likely be ended here.

Both schools have their points; however, let's begin with shotshell dimension. Even in those shotguns chambered for either 3-inch or 3.5-inch rounds, there is really no need for anything larger than the traditional 2 3/4 -inch shotshell be used in a defense role. Such 2.75-inch rounds offer satisfactory pellet counts – 12-gauge = nine #00 Buck pellets, 27 #4 Buck, pellets or roughly 200 #4 lead – while keeping recoil to a minimum. These smaller rounds also allow for increased magazine capacity. An exception to this may be when considering 20-gauge firearms. Here, the choice of a 3-inch shotshell, one which closer approximates a 12-gauge in hull capacity, would be advised.

As for shot size, the scales, both from a private as well as a law enforcement standpoint, seem to swing toward the larger pellets – the #00 Buck and #4 Buck. The thinking here follows that should a shooting situation become unavoidable, you want the threat neutralized quickly and completely; that is, without an opportunity for return fire. In close-range encounters, the nine

and 27 pellets, respectively, of the aforementioned buckshot rounds provide an excellent chance for multiple hits on target, particularly in the case of the #4 Buck, along with more than adequate retained energy and penetration.

Furthermore, and even at close ranges, the nine #00 Buck pellets do disperse wider than do their smaller counterparts, thus adding to a margin of error on the side of the shooter.

The argument in favor of smaller pellets - #2 or #4 lead, for example – centers primarily on these pellets being less likely to cause collateral damage. With less mass, and therefore less energy and penetration, these smaller projectiles, it's thought by some, perform their task and stop the human threat without

problems of over-penetration. Whereas the larger buckshot pellets can potentially wreck havoc in adjoining rooms, the smaller pellets will more often than not fail to penetrate common interior barriers.

Pellet for pellet, the smaller projectiles simply cannot provide the one-shot stopping power of the larger; that is, a one-pellet hit with .32 caliber #00 Buck will draw considerably more attention than will the same hit with a single .12 caliber #4 lead projectile. At a range of 15 feet and with a pattern roughly the size of a turkey egg, a 1-1/2 ounce charge of #4 lead shot leaves little room for error, whereas the 9-pellet load of #00 Buck is a bit more forgiving… at least for the shooter.

Although primarily a focus of the nation's law enforcement agencies, less-than-lethal (LTL) shotgun ammunition offers an interesting and increasingly effective alternative to traditional shotshells. Currently,

Less-lethal ammunition exists, however many say it has no place in a home defense role. For police use, especially in a crowd-control situation, it can be very effective.

several different types of LTL ammunition are available, including rubber buckshot, large rubber balls (2 per 12-gauge round), .73 caliber rubber slugs, and flexible batons or beanbags. Some, such as Lightfield Ammunition Company's innovative *Super Star* and *Star Lite* "koosh ball" 12-gauge round or the 40-gram Flexible Baton (beanbag) round from MK Ballistics, are meant to be fired directly at a perpetrator. Others like the rubber shot pellets are skipped or bounced onto the target. General consensus among law enforcement officers and self/home defense trainers is that LTL rounds are best used as crowd control, and not in a self or home defense role.

Accessories

To me, accessorizing and customizing are two different things. Accessories are those things, slings for example, that work to make a firearm more user-friendly. Customizations, on the other hand, serve to make a weapon more functional and more field efficient. Such custom work might involve porting a barrel to reduce recoil, shortening or lengthening a stock, installing a non-traditional stock, mounting specialized optics or sighting devices, or extending a magazine tube thus increasing the weapon's ammunition capacity. These are the nitty-gritty; the accessories…well, they're often the gingerbread.

Still, both have their place in the realm of the self/home defense shotgun. Such accessories and customizations might include:

Stocks and grips – For a time, I had a black synthetic pistol grip on the Mossberg Model 500 that I maintain as a home defense firearm. And while it certainly did make the gun

lighter and much smaller, I didn't feel as though I had the same control over the piece as with the original walnut stock. Following some range time, I reversed my decision and reinstalled the original 13 1/4-inch stock. A recoil pad handles the recoil of the 2.75-inch #4 Buck rounds I've chosen, and the firearm, overall, provides me with something very substantial to hold on to.

The choice between a traditional (full-length) stock or a pistol-style grip on a self/home defense shotgun is one primarily based on fit, ability, and personal preference. Today's modern synthetic stocks are extraordinarily durable, not to mention being lightweight. Some, such as Mossberg's Model 590 synthetic, incorporate features such as the company's *Speedfeed Stock*, an altered piece capable of holding and quickly supplying four additional rounds. Traditional wood – often walnut – stocks are also an option, and often make for a less expensive, though just as reliable, piece.

Whereas a full stock offers a solid foundation and can contribute to improved accuracy, pistol-style grips also have their place. As mentioned, these short grips make for a somewhat easier-to-conceal weapon and cut down on the space necessary for storage – underneath a seat or mattress, for instance; however, the recoil of such short weapons can prove problematic or impossible to handle for smaller shooters. The bottom line in the stock versus grip debate rests then, elementally, with the individual. And finally, a hybrid. In the case of Mossberg's *HS (Home Security) .410*, a pistol grip is incorporated into the Model 500 pump-action's fore-end; a traditionally styled though synthetic full stock rounds out the piece. This hybridized fore-end allows for a

much surer, positive hold on that element of the weapon necessary to the firearm's repeated function, and is a definite plus when a shooter's hands are wet, either from rain or, understandably, perspiration.

Sights and sighting devices – Sights and self/home defense shotguns are, it seems, a relationship founded on personal preference and application. For the layperson who simply wants a dependable weapon for the purpose of protecting self, home, and property, a single front bead – the traditional shotgunner's sighting device – serves more than admirably. In most instances, the shotgun is pointed rather than aimed, and as such, a single sighting device like a lone front bead, is sufficient.

Military and law enforcement shotguns will often be seen with some type of after-market or customized sighting system; something other than a simple bead. Iron or buckhorn sights are one example, as is the large aperture *Ghost Ring* unit, a modern twist on the traditional peep sight, which allows for quick target acquisition. Laser or lighted sighting units are yet another option; however, and unless a quality unit is going to be purchased and professionally mounted, regularly maintained, and is made familiar through range time, it's advised that the fewer things to consider in the heat of a defense encounter, high-tech sights included, the better.

All in all, a shotgun is a wise choice for personal defense, especially in the home. While the gun can't really be concealed or easily carried, it works especially well if kept at the ready to defend against home invasions. In trained hands, all the elements that make a shotgun effective come to the fore and the gun serves as an outstanding fight-stopper. ✪

The Trend Toward Autoloaders

By M.D. Johnson

Autoloaders, like this Ruger P-89, are popular for many reasons. Chief among them is the speed of reloading.

The world of the handgunner is surprisingly large; but there are really just two types of defensive handguns – the revolver, and the semi-automatic pistol. Since the mid 1980s there has been a decided shift among law enforcement agencies to adopt autoloaders as their primary weapons. Before 1980 most cops carried revolvers. Many of those revolvers were chambered for the .38 Special. Some fired .357 Magnum rounds. There was a long-held philosophy that revolvers were more dependable, simpler and safer than autoloaders. We can argue the nuances of such thinking for the next 100 pages of text and never satisfy everyone. Things began to change as a result of

several high-profile shooting in which law enforcement officers were quite simply out-gunned. In a couple of those shootings officers died trying to reload their revolvers. Those events started a serious review of handgun policies and training. From the FBI down to local police agencies, the real-world needs of officers on the street were held up to the test of "what if." It became clear, rather quickly that the benefits of the magazine-fed pistol outweighed any perceived drawbacks. There was a wholesale change in the handgun philosophy of law enforcement officers.

People might not like to admit it, but the official adoption of a firearm by a government agency

can have a big impact on the buying public. The bigger the agency, the bigger the impact. Consider the Beretta Model 92 pistol. Once it was deemed good enough for the U.S. military, it suddenly became good enough for many police agencies and as a result, the general public fell in line. These days, while revolver sales are still holding their own, most people opt for a pistol when it comes time to think about self-defense. Here's why.

The semi-auto pistol defined

Semi-automatic as it refers to a handgun means precisely that. In other words, the weapon fires once for each pull of the trigger. At which time the shooter must fully release the trigger and pull it again. This can be done until such a time as the ammunition supply is exhausted. The internal workings of the weapon eject the spent cartridge, slide a fresh cartridge into the chamber under the firing pin, and close the action, thus making the weapon "live" once more. Often, such firearms are, however incorrectly, referred to as *automatics*. Unlike semi-autos, true or *full* automatics require but a single pull of the trigger in order to exhaust the supply of ammunition. The German MP-40, a.k.a. Schmeisser, is an example of such a fully automatic firearm. True, the MP-40 and the Ruger Model P89 are both recoil-operated *and* fire the same 9x19 round; however, beyond that, the similarities end, particularly when discussing semi-automatic versus true automatic fire.

Why semi-auto: Pros and Cons

Whether you're talking about a rolling pin or a Rolls Royce, everything short of perfection comes complete with a set of Pros and Cons. Such is the case with the semi-automatic pistol as a defensive firearm. And these variables, then, should be taken into consideration when you're deciding upon the category of firearm – revolver, semi-auto, or shotgun – which will be used in these defensive roles.

Pros

- Most modern semi-autos are relatively simplistic in design and operation
- Intermediate calibers – .380, 9mm, and .357 SIG – provide options for women or seniors
- Large capacity magazines offer seven to 17 rounds
- Reloading is faster and easier than with a revolver
- Modern autoloaders can be safely carried with a round in the chamber
- Several frame sizes are available to fit nearly every hand and every defensive option
- Autoloaders offer a choice of single-action, double-action, and double-action-only

Cons

- Some models may prove cumbersome, bulky, and/or heavy for some shooters
- Heavy recoil springs may cause trouble for some shooters
- Lacking pre-loaded magazines, reloading time

can increase dramatically over revolvers
- The operation of a semi-auto is more complicated than that of a revolver
- Improper ammunition choice or poor maintenance can lead to malfunctions

Large, medium, small, and compact

Before we delve into the details surrounding the various semi-automatic pistol frames and frame types, it makes sense that we first define this word – *frame* – as it applies to this particular firearm. The *frame* is *the main structure of the handgun to which the other components, e.g. grips, barrel, slide, trigger group, are attached.* In other words, the frame of the semi-automatic pistol can be compared to the foundation of your home. Construction begins with the foundation – the frame – and then everything is built on top of that.

In the past, the majority of semi-auto frames were constructed of either stamped or machined steel or aluminum. Today, however, an increasing number of these firearms, civilian, military and law enforcement styles, are being built on frames made of high-

tech synthetic polymer materials. Such frames are not only lighter than are their steel or aluminum counterparts, but they are also extremely low maintenance, impervious to changes in temperature, and virtually indestructible. On the *con* side, however, semi-autos sporting polymer frames, being lighter, will also exhibit increased felt recoil than will their heavier, steel-framed counterparts. That said, frame composition becomes a matter of fit, comfort, and recoil-handling ability.

Next is frame size. Modern semi-automatic pistols are offered in five different designations or classifications – large, medium, small, compact, and subcompact. Now, before you start thinking that a *large frame* means a large caliber and a *subcompact* denotes a smaller caliber, let me say that while it can be the case, it isn't necessarily the rule. For instance, 9mm semi-autos are available in large, medium, compact, and subcompact formats But you can also get a subcompact .45 ACP. It's a handful to shoot, but great to carry. Such choices, then, lend themselves to questions on the part of you, the shooter – What is your physical stature? How large are your hands? To what extent

There is an an auto-loading pistol for just about every need and every hand size. Shop around for one that fits both.

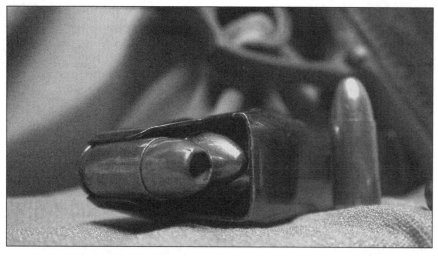

The magazine is the heart of the reloading operation. Good magazines are the key to effective function.

can you comfortably tolerate recoil? Will the firearm be carried concealed on your person? In a handbag or fanny pack? Or will the weapon be stored in a lockbox or bedside nightstand? The answers to these questions will help you decide which frame size, is best for you. Get to a gun shop or a gun show and handle several different sizes. If you can arrange it, go to the range and see if you can actually shoot some of the different models.

Choosing a caliber

The question of caliber as it relates to semi-automatic pistols used for self-defense can best be answered by asking several different questions. These include:

- Does this caliber deliver enough power so as to be capable of eliminating or disabling any threat immediately, where the key word here is **IMMEDIATELY**
- Is the caliber so large as to be uncomfortable or unwieldy to shoot, thus affecting accuracy
- Does the caliber offer a variety of bullet weights and designs
- Is the primary purpose of this caliber (firearm) to be

home defense, street defense, or will it serve double duty

In the long run, it's Question #1 which carries the most significance, for it's possible to possess a comfortable, accurate handgun lacking the stopping power necessary to eliminate the threat *before* that threat can do you bodily harm. Likewise, it is also possible to possess a firearm fully capable of performing well in a self-defense role which has been mismatched with improper ammunition, thus decreasing or negating the weapon's effectiveness.

With this in mind, let's take a look at a list of popular semi-automatic calibers and cartridges, with an emphasis on bullet weight and design.

The .22 Long Rifle (LR)

While it is undeniable that the venerable .22 rimfire is a joy to shoot, the caliber leaves quite a bit to be desired when it comes to self-defense. The problem? Even with high-velocity rounds leaving the muzzle at more than 1,300 feet per second (fps), the light 40-grain bullet – yes, even in a hollow point format – with their perhaps 150 foot-pounds of point-blank energy just don't have the immediate stopping power

necessary to classify them as a consistent, reliable self-defense bullet. Certainly, the perpetrator may eventually succumb to injuries received courtesy of a .22 LR, but the important term here is *eventually*.

Perhaps the .22 LR might best be used as a training tool on the range, with the intent being to upgrade to a larger caliber for applications either in the home or on the street.

The .25 ACP

There was a period during the early 1980s, I believe, when the tiny .25 ACP semi-auto pistols, particularly those manufactured by Raven Arms, became quite trendy. Why, I'm not certain, as it was my experience that Black Cat firecrackers made just as much noise *and* were, in most cases, as accurate as the .25 ACP.

True, the .25 semi-auto does offer a small variety of bullet weights and designs ranging from a 35-grain jacketed hollow point (JHP) to a 50-grain full metal jacketed (FMJ) round; however, with velocities approximately half of the High Velocity .22 LR and less than 50 percent the energy at the muzzle when compared with the same .22 rimfire, the .25 ACP, again, leaves much to be desired. And in terms of range practice, most would be better served with a mid- to high-end .22 rimfire semi-auto for accuracy, ammunition availability, and ammunition cost.

The .32 ACP

Some shooters consider the .32 ACP the bottom end of the self-defense ammunition curve. Others draw the line at .380. Regardless, the tale of the tape reveals the .32 ACP to have muzzle energy rating (120 to 135 ft/lbs) slightly less than a .22 High Velocity, and bullet weight options which include 60-, 65-, and 71-grain projectiles. Bullet designs include FMJ, JHP, and Federal's Hydra-Shok round in JHP.

Like the .22 rimfire, the .32 ACP is enjoyable and inexpensive to shoot, both considerations which should lead to individuals spending ample time on the range acquainting themselves intimately with the capabilities and limitations of this borderline self-defense caliber. Range time is vital, particularly with the .32 ACP, as familiarity with the firearm leads to elevated accuracy, which plays a major role in this cartridge's effectiveness or lack thereof.

The .380 ACP

Despite what was said earlier about the .32 ACP and the caliber's potential as a candidate for self-defense, it is with the .380 that many consider to be the least powerful cartridge for use in a self-defense pistol. Bullet weights for this popular caliber range from 85 to 102 grains, with a wide variety of bullet designs including Federal's Hi-Shok and Hydra-Shok JHP, FMJ, Remington's Brass JHP, and the Starfire Hollow Point, a quick-expansion offering from PMC. In comparison, muzzle energies for the .380 will be half again that of the .32 ACP, or from 180 to 200 ft/lbs. This brings the stopping power up to what some people might describe as "adequate" but is it still a long way from the "lightning bolt effect" you'd love to have when your life is on the line.

The .380 is head and shoulders above the .32 ACP in the realm of self-defense, but it's effective use still requires impeccable combat accuracy and perhaps working knowledge of human anatomy. If you know where to place the round and can put it in exactly the right spot, the .380 will work.

The 9mm

By far the world's most popular pistol cartridge, the 9mm, aka 9mm Parabellum or 9mm Luger, has earned itself a self-defense role with police departments, security forces, and private individuals around the globe. Dozens of makes and models of 9mm semi-auto pistols, both foreign and domestic and, of course, of varying quality and dependability, are available. Ammunition, too, is varied, abundant, and relatively inexpensive – a plus on the practice side of the equation. Shooters can choose a 9mm in any frame size and some guns like the Glock and Springfield Armory XD series provide identical controls and nearly identical ergonomics between the smallest and the largest models.

Muzzle energy ratings for the 9mm will run from 290 to 295 ft./lbs. into the high 400s and low 500s, with many manufacturers' offerings averaging from 325 to 370. On the low end, shooters can choose from a 95-grain Starfire HP from PMC up to several different 147-grain projectiles in configurations including FMJ and FMJ +P, JHP, and JHP +P. Here, the **+P** denotes a more powerful cartridge and indicates, on average, a 100 to 150 fps increase in muzzle velocity over traditional ammunition of an identical style (bullet weight and design). Bullets designed specifically for self-defense – the aforementioned +P, Federal's *Nyclad* (an encapsulated lead core with a patented nylon coating ensures reliable cycling in semi-autos), and the *MegaShock* (weight retention AND controlled expansion) by Lapua – are also available and might be considered. As previously mentioned, inexpensive FMJ ammunition is widely carried and can be used for familiarization and practice.

It's fine to use inexpensive ammo for practice at the range. In fact, you should use lots of it and practice often. But also make sure your pistol feeds and functions perfectly with the self-defense load you have chosen.

Recoil with the 9mm, even with some of the lighter smaller pistols, is still very manageable, even for those with smaller hands. And this decrease in recoil, or increase in controllability, does not necessarily translate into a corresponding decrease in the caliber's effectiveness as a self-defense choice.

The .357 SIG

This is the new kid on the block. Designed by the folks at SIG-Sauer, makers of some of the world's best semi-auto pistols, the .357 SIG was created to duplicate the power of the .357 Magnum in a round that would fit into and function perfectly in an autoloader. Since U.S. police agencies began the wholesale switch to auto-loading pistols in the mid-1980s there have been complaints that the 9mm is underpowered. Lots of law enforcement agencies were also concerned, knowledgeable shooters would say wrongly, that carrying a Model 1911 (with its bigger .45 ACP rounds) in the cocked and locked condition was "dangerous." The search for an alternative yielded the .40 S&W, which will be discussed below. And thus was spawned the .357 SIG, now just a few years old. Several law enforcement agencies have adopted the round and most report that is does indeed deliver the "lightning bolt effect" of the old .357 Magnum wheelgun.

Despite these capabilities, however, the 357 SIG may never enjoy the popularity of the 9mm. The 9mm and the .40 S&W already have the lion's share of the defensive pistol market, especially in the military and law enforcement areas.

Several bullet weights are available for the 357 SIG, with the 124-grain, 125-grain, and 147-grain being three of the more popular and most versatile options. You can expect sharper recoil as we continue to move up the power scale, but it is not oppressive. Where the .357 SIG really shines is accuracy. There are a couple handgun models on the market that allow the shooter to change from .357 SIG to .40 S&W by simply swapping barrels. The. .357 SIG will outshoot the .40 every time.

The .40 S&W

Introduced in 1990, the .40 S&W is quite honestly the product of litigation. To make a long story short, the FBI liked the 10mm, but some agents could not qualify with this monster cartridge and sued to be given a chance to shoot something smaller. When all was said and done, the FBI had to make serious change in policy and ammo companies and gunmakers came up with something to fill in the gap. Since 1990, the .40 S&W has taken the shooting world by storm, especially the area of law enforcement. This round takes up where to some the 9mm leaves off – and then some. Bullet choices for the .40 run the gamut from Federal's 135-grain Hydra-Shok JHP (1,190 fps and 420 ft/lbs at the muzzle) to a number of 180-grain loadings, including several +P rounds

Understandably, recoil will be more noticeable in the .40 S&W as compared to the 9mm; however, the lighter (135 and 150-grain) rounds, themselves proven better performers than the 180-grain offerings, are still quite manageable for all but the most recoil-conscious. You get only a little less power than the venerable .45 ACP and only a few less rounds than can be held by a high-capacity 9mm magazine.

The .45 ACP

Imagine, if you will, getting hit by a half-inch marble going 647 miles per hour. That's the .45 ACP, one of the most recognized and most popular handgun calibers in existence today. Popularity, performance, precision, power, reliability, availability, versatility – the .45 ACP has it all in terms of a self/home defense firearm; however, that's not to say that the tried-and-true .45 isn't without its downsides.

Yes, it is undeniably a powerful piece, yet that power comes with a price in the form of recoil and physical weight; still, and with an eye on firearm design and ammunition selection, both variables – recoil *and* weight – can be kept down to manageable levels for most shooters. Too, the .45 ACP's larger rounds translate into decreased magazine capacity in the smaller guns. – 10 rounds, commonly, for the 9mm and .40 S&W compared to the .45's eight. It is a concern for some, but perhaps not for the civilian masses. And the crafty gun designers are everyday working out ways to stuff the government-limited maximum 10 rounds into small and smaller .45 ACP pistols.

Versatility and variety are but two of the areas in which the .45 ACP excels. The cartridge offers a wide range of bullet weights – factory loads from 165 to 230 grains – and designs, along with an almost infinite number of makes and models from manufacturers worldwide.

Customizing your home/self-defense handgun

Webster defines the word, *customize*, in this way – To make according to individual specifications. My definition differs slightly, that being "to make so as to be more user-friendly, and in essence, a more effective or productive piece or whole." Those definitions stated, let's take a brief look here at the art of customizing the defensive pistol.

Before we get started, however, let's consider the case where no customization is needed. Rather, the firearm from an energy/power standpoint meets any and all defense criteria, fits comfortably, and functions properly and reliably. The piece points well, and the recoil is more than manageable given the factory-equipped grips. The out-of-the-box iron sights are large enough to allow for quick target acquisition, but not so big as to be visually obstructive – that, and they perform as well in daylight as they do in low light. Should this be your new semi-auto handgun, my suggestion is this – Don't mess with it. If you're already a shooter, practice. If you're not a skilled shooter, register for a firearms training and concealed carry workshop, pass it with flying colors... and then practice.

Granted, the scenario above is the ultimate. In many cases, an out-of-the-box handgun is like an off-the-rack suit – it's going to need a little alteration here and there. Below are some of the primary ways in which a handgun meant for self/home defense can be made more user-friendly.

Lights – Lights as they relate to personal defense and the use of firearms typically take one of two forms, a traditional hand-held flashlight, and a light source, conventional or laser, mounted directly on the weapon.

In most civilian defensive situations, a traditional battery-operated flashlight can prove more than sufficient. Obviously, such a hand-held light should be bright enough to adequately illuminate objects at an anticipated distance, be that the length or breath of an interior

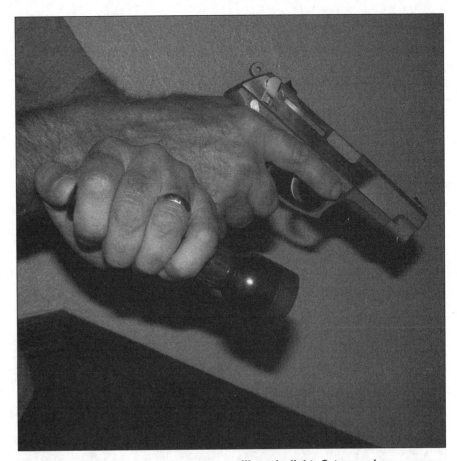

In most cases, when you need a gun, you will need a light. Get a good one.

room, or the width of a commercial storage facility. Again, and obviously, batteries should of the highest quality, and should be checked frequently. And replaced, if necessary

Two variables present themselves when discussing illumination for defense purposes, a.k.a. tactical lighting. The physical weight of the light source is one concern, one which in recent years has been addressed by those manufacturers using technologically advanced – lightweight – polymer materials in the construction of these flashlights. The weight of these modern hand-held lights has decreased, while the light (candlepower) generated has, in many cases, increased dramatically, thanks to improved power sources and better bulb/filament combinations. NOTE – These modern

lightweight, or rather, *lighter weight* flashlights, like the heavy-duty four-cell and six-cell Mag-Lites®, can also serve as very effective weapons should the situation dictate.

The second consideration is one of inconvenience. Or rather, learning to accurately shoot with one hand while holding a tactical flashlight in the other. Some suggest using a light that offers a thumb-operated pulse switch located on the butt-end. With the firearm in the strong hand, the fingers of the OFF hand are wrapped around the light, thumb on the pulse switch. This is known as the Harries technique. As such, the hands can still be used in conjunction to stabilize both the weapon and the light. One can use the light to illuminate the target and, with enough practice, search with the light without pointing the gun directly at the center of the beam of light. The goal here is to keep the light and the gun close enough to each other to properly index the pistol if you need to, but also allow you to search without pointing the gun at what might be an innocent bystander in a dark room. Too, the light can be operated as the switch intends, in pulses, rather than in a continuous, "Here I am, Bad Guy" beam. Simply explained, perhaps, but performing this feat requires both manual dexterity *and* practice.

Gun-mounted lights come in two basic forms – a traditional flashlight in miniature that is affixed to the frame beneath the barrel using a special bracket or rail, and a laser unit that actually projects a small, often red, light onto the target. This laser light, or dot, coincides with the weapon's point of impact. Both have their pros and cons. The traditional mini-light, when operated continuously as is often the case, can reveal your position; however, this same light, detached, can be operated in the same pulse manner as is any hand-held. The laser, on the other hand, simplifies aiming, yet can be alarmingly ineffective in bright light situations. Here, as in many cases, it becomes a matter of personal preference, and then, familiarity.

Sights – Like lights, sights for the defensive pistol are largely a matter of personal preference. Condensed, there are four options:

Iron, traditional – These are the unpainted/unaltered out-of-the-box iron sights with which many of us grew up. They're simple, can be adjustable or fixed, and allow for quick and easy target acquisition. Their downfall, however, comes in the dark, where they have a tendency to disappear.

You must practice holding the gun and the light at the same time, so when the moment of truth arrives you are up to the task.

Iron, colored – Here, several options, all revolving around the colors of the front sight and rear blade are available. There is the traditional and well-known "red ramp" where a portion of the front sight is milled away and filled in with color epoxy. Three-dot sights allow the shooter to simply line up the dots. They can be all white or a combination with the dots on the left and right of the rear blade one color and the front sight another color – white-green-white is common. There is the U/dot. Simply put the dot of the front sight inside the white U of the rear sight and you're in business. SIG-Sauer has made famous the dash and dot system with the vertical dash on the rear blade. Simply "dot the i" and you have your sight picture. For low light shooting, you can have glow-in-the-dark paint or Tritium inserts. Tritium is a radioactive isotope of hydrogen that glows in the dark. It is commonly used to illuminate the hands and markers of modern analog watch faces. Because it does glow, tritium makes for an excellent choice in low and no-light situations. And because it requires no batteries…well, that's just one less thing you have to worry about, isn't it? The options are almost endless and there is an entire market for optional sights that shooters can explore.

Electronic – Optical electronic sights have come a long way in recent years. While these mini marvels were once restricted to rifles or carbines, the size of the sights has dropped while the durability has improved. The optical electronic sight is now a realistic option for defensive handgun use. A couple of different styles from several makers are available. They are easy to use and quite accurate.

Laser or illuminating – The aforementioned laser sights, those which project a beam of red light onto the target, complete the more common choices. It should be noted that laser sights are not a cure-all, and should be employed in lieu of practice and familiarization with the firearm of your choice.

Grips – It's essential that the pistol you choose for defense (1) fit, (2) be comfortable, and (3) be manageable from a recoil standpoint. Fortunately, all three of these points can be addressed simply by changing the grips.

Grips, for those unfamiliar with the nomenclature, are those pieces located on either side of the firearm's frame and around which the hand is wrapped. Traditionally, grips were made of wood, hard plastic, ivory, staghorn, or other natural materials; however, in recent decades, high-tech rubber grips have very much come into their own.

In the case of most firearms and their shooters, the choice concerning grips is as individual a decision as is the make and model of handgun itself. The key, then, is personal fit, a variable which can only be determined by a trial. Sometimes you can grab the grip and know if it feels good or bad. But a true test can only be made by firing live rounds – the more the better. If, as was mentioned previously, the factory grips provide the performance you expect and need, don't change them. If they don't and you opt for aftermarket grips, install them yourself or have them installed by a competent gunsmith, and then try the piece on the range. What you are looking for in a good grip is what some people call "full engagement." Your hand is, to use the industrial term, the control surface. You must be able to get a firm hold on the gun and keep that hold regardless of stress, perspiration, sudden violent movement or anything else that may try to separate the gun from your hand. The grip also has to be the right size to allow you to fully reach the trigger of the pistol.

Combat trigger control is different than that of the target shooter. You should be able to reach the trigger with the first joint of the index finger. Target shooters will use just the tip of the finger. Remember too, that if the gun doesn't fit, the problem may be that the frame is too large or too small. Look carefully and asked a qualified instructor if you have questions. ✪

Beretta
Model 76
Model 81
Model 81BB
Model 82
Model 84 Cheetah
Model 84F
Model 85 Cheetah
Model 85F
Model 86 Cheetah
Model 87 Cheetah
Model 87 Target
Model 89
Model 89 Gold Standard
Pistol

MODERN GUN VALUES

Beretta Model 76

Beretta Model 84 Cheetah

Beretta Model 85F

Beretta Model 89

Beretta Model 84F

BERETTA MODEL 76
Semi-automatic; single action; 22 LR only; 10-shot magazine; 6" barrel; 9 1/2" overall length; adjustable rear sight, interchangeable blade front; non-glare, ribbed slide; heavy barrel; external hammer; checkered wrap-around plastic (76P) or wood (76W) grips; blued. Also known as New Sable. Introduced 1971; dropped 1985.

Perf.: $350	Exc.: $300	VGood: $275

With wood grips

Perf.: $400	Exc.: $350	VGood: $325

BERETTA MODEL 81
Semi-automatic; double action; 32 ACP; 12-shot magazine; 3 13/16" barrel; 6 13/16" overall length; blued finish; fixed sights; plastic or wood stocks. Introduced 1976; dropped 1981.

Perf.: $375	Exc.: $250	VGood: $200

Nickel finish

Perf.: $350	Exc.: $300	VGood: $250

With wood grips

Perf.: $300	Exc.: $275	VGood: $225

Beretta Model 81BB

Perf.: $300	Exc.: $275	VGood: $225

BERETTA MODEL 82
Semi-automatic; double action; 32 ACP; 9-shot straightline magazine; 3 13/16" barrel; 6 13/16" overall length; weighs 17 oz.; non-reversible magazine release; blued finish; fixed sights; wood grips. Introduced 1977; dropped 1984.

Perf.: $275	Exc.: $250	VGood: $200

Nickel finish

Perf.: $350	Exc.: $300	VGood: $250

BERETTA MODEL 84 CHEETAH
Semi-automatic; double action; 380 ACP; 10-shot magazine; 3 7/8" barrel; 6 13/16" overall length; weighs 23 oz.; black plastic (84P) or wood (84W) grips; fixed front sight, drift-adjustable rear; blue finish; squared trigger guard; exposed hammer. Imported from Italy by Beretta U.S.A. Introduced 1977.

Perf.: $400	Exc.: $325	VGood: $275

Blue, wood grips

Perf.: $375	Exc.: $350	VGood: $300

Nickel, wood grips

Perf.: $475	Exc.: $400	VGood: $325

Beretta Model 84F
Same specs as Model 84 except combat-style frame; grooved triggerguard; plastic grips; manual safety; decocking device; matte finish. Made in Italy. Introduced 1990; still in production.

Perf.: $350	Exc.: $325	VGood: $275

BERETTA MODEL 85 CHEETAH
Semi-automatic; double action; 380 ACP; 8-shot straightline magazine; 3 7/8" barrel; 6 13/16" overall length; weighs 23 oz.; black plastic (85P) or wood (85W) grips; fixed front sight, drift-adjustable rear; non-reversible magazine release; blue finish; squared triggerguard; exposed hammer. Imported from Italy by Beretta U.S.A. Introduced 1977; still imported.

Perf.: $350	Exc.: $300	VGood: $250

Blue, wood grips

Perf.: $375	Exc.: $325	VGood: $275

Nickel, wood grips

Perf.: $425	Exc.: $375	VGood: $325

Beretta Model 85F
Same specs as Model 85 except combat-type frame; grooved triggerguard; plastic grips; matte black finish; manual safety; decocking device. Made in Italy. Introduced 1990; dropped 1990.

Perf.: $375	Exc.: $325	VGood: $275

BERETTA MODEL 86 CHEETAH
Semi-automatic; double action; 22 LR; 8-shot magazine; 4 7/16" barrel; 7 5/16" overall length; weighs 23 1/2 oz.; fixed sights; tip-up barrel; checkered walnut grips; matte finish; gold trigger. Importation began 1991.

Perf.: $450	Exc.: $375	VGood: $300

BERETTA MODEL 87 CHEETAH
Semi-automatic; double action; 22 LR; 7-shot magazine; 3 7/8" barrel; 6 13/16" overall length; weighs 21 oz.; black plastic grips; fixed front sight, drift-adjustable rear; blue finish; squared trigger guard; exposed hammer. Imported from Italy by Beretta U.S.A. Introduced 1977; still imported.

Perf.: $450	Exc.: $375	VGood: $300

Beretta Model 87 Target
Same specs as Model 87 except single action; 6" barrel with counterweight; wood grips. Made in Italy. Introduced 1977; importation began in 1986; still imported.

Perf.: $500	Exc.: $425	VGood: $350

BERETTA MODEL 89
Semi-automatic; single-action only; 22 LR; 8-shot magazine; 6" barrel; 9 1/2" overall length; weighs 41 oz.; interchangeable front sight, fully-adjustable rear; semi-anatomical walnut grips; fixed monoblock barrel machined from forged steel block; aluminum alloy frame; manual safety on either side. Made in Italy. Introduced 1977. Importation began 1986; still imported.

Perf.: $600	Exc.: $500	VGood: $400

BERETTA MODEL 89 GOLD STANDARD PISTOL
Caliber: 22 LR, 8-shot magazine. Barrel: 6. Weight: 41 oz. Length: 9.5 overall. Stocks: Target-type walnut with thumbrest. Sights: Interchangeable blade front, fully adjustable rear. Features: Single action target pistol. Matte black, Bruniton finish. Imported from Italy by Beretta U.S.A.

Perf.: $525	Exc.: $400	VGood: $325

HANDGUNS

Beretta
Model 90
Model 92
Model 92S (Second Issue)
Model 92SB-P (Third Issue)
Model 92SB-P Compact
Model 92D
Model 92FS
M9 Special Edition Pistol
Model 92F Compact
Model 92FCM
Model 92FS Centurion
Model 92FS Stainless
Model 92F-EL
Model 96
Model 96 Brigadier

Beretta Model 90

Beretta Model 92

Beretta Model 92FS

Beretta M9 Special Edition Pistol

Beretta Model 96 Brigadier

BERETTA MODEL 90
Semi-automatic; double action; 32 ACP; 8-shot magazine; 3 5/8" barrel; 6 3/4" overall length; fixed sights, matted rib on slide; chamber-loaded indicator; external hammer; stainless steel barrel; moulded plastic wrap-around grips; blued. Introduced 1969; dropped 1982.
Perf.: $250   Exc.: $200   VGood: $150

BERETTA MODEL 92
Semi-automatic, double action; 9mm Para.; 15-shot magazine; 5" barrel; 8 1/2" overall length; blued finish; fixed sights; plastic grips. Updated version of the Model 951. Introduced 1976; dropped 1981.
Perf.: $600   Exc.: $500   VGood: $425

BERETTA MODEL 92S (SECOND ISSUE)
Semi-automatic; double action; 9mm Para.; 15-shot magazine; 5" barrel; 8 1/2" overall length; fixed sights; plastic grips. Variant of Model 92 with safety catch on side. Discontinued.
Perf.: $550   Exc.: $500   VGood: $400

BERETTA MODEL 92SB-P (THIRD ISSUE)
Automatic; double action; 9mm Para.; 16-shot magazine; 5" barrel; 8 1/2" overall length; weighs 34 1/2 oz.; blade front sight, windage-adjustable rear; black plastic or wood grips. Developed for U.S. Army pistol trials of 1979-1980. Introduced 1979; dropped 1985.
Perf.: $450   Exc.: $400   VGood: $350
Wood grips
Perf.: $500   Exc.: $450   VGood: $400

Beretta Model 92SB-P Compact
Same specs as Model 92SB-P except 4 5/16" barrel, 14-shot magazine; plastic grips. Introduced 1977; dropped 1985.
Perf.: $500   Exc.: $450   VGood: $400
Wood grips
Perf.: $525   Exc.: $475   VGood: $425

BERETTA MODEL 92D
Semi-automatic; double-action only; 9mm Para.; 10-shot magazine; 5" barrel; 8 1/2" overall length; weighs 34 oz.; bobbed hammer; no external safety; plastic grips; three-dot sights. Also offered with Trijicon sights. From Beretta U.S.A. Introduced 1992.
New: $450   Perf.: $400   Exc.: $350

BERETTA MODEL 92FS
Semi-automatic; double action; 9mm Para.; 15-shot magazine; 5" barrel; 8 1/2" overall length; matte black finish; squared triggerguard; grooved front backstraps; inertia firing pin; extractor acts as chamber loaded indicator; wood or plastic grips. Adopted 1985 as official U.S. military sidearm. Introduced 1984; still imported by Beretta USA.
Perf.: $550   Exc.: $500   VGood: $450
Stainless steel barrel and slide (92F)
Perf.: $600   Exc.: $550   VGood: $400

Beretta M9 Special Edition Pistol
Copy of the U.S. M9 military pistol. Similar to the Model 92FS except has special M9 serial number range; one 15-round (pre-ban) magazine; dot-and-post sight system; special M9 military packaging; Army TM 9-1005-317-10 operator's manual; M9 Special Edition patch; certificate of authenticity; Bianchi M12 holster, M1025 magazine pouch, and M1015 web pistol belt. Introduced 1998. From Beretta U.S.A.
Perf.: $700   Exc.: $550   VGood: $400

Beretta Model 92F Compact
Same specs as Beretta Model 92FS except cut down frame; 4 3/8" barrel; 7 7/8" overall length; 13-shot magazine; weighs 31/2 oz.; Trijicon sights and wood grips optionally available. From Beretta U.S.A. Introduced 1989; no longer in production.
Perf.: $500   Exc.: $450   VGood: $400
Wood grips
Perf.: $525   Exc.: $475   VGood: $425

Beretta Model 92FCM
Same specs as Model 92F Compact except thinner grip; straightline 8-shot magazine; weighs 31 oz.; 1 1/4" overall width; plastic grips. From Beretta U.S.A. Introduced 1989; no longer in production.
Perf.: $500   Exc.: $450   VGood: $400

Beretta Model 92FS Centurion
Same specs as Model 92 FS except 4 3/8" barrel shorter slide; Trijicon or three-dot sights; plastic or wood grips; 9mm Para. only. From Beretta U.S.A. Introduced 1992.
With plastic grips, three-dot sights
New: $550   Perf.: $500   Exc.: $450
With wood grips
New: $575   Perf.: $525   Exc.: $475

Beretta Model 92FS Stainless
Same specs as Model 92FS except for stainless steel satin finish; groove in slide rail; larger hammer pin head; modified to meet special-use military specs. Introduced 1990; still produced.
Perf.: $550   Exc.: $500   VGood: $450

Beretta Model 92F-EL
Same specs as Model 92FS Stainless except gold trim on safety levers, magazine release, trigger and grip screws; gold inlaid Beretta logo top of barrel; P. Beretta signature inlaid in gold on slide; contoured walnut grips with Beretta logo engraved; high-polish blued finish on barrel, frame, slide. Introduced 1991.
Perf.: $650   Exc.: $600   VGood: $500

BERETTA MODEL 96
Semi-automatic; double action; 40 S&W; 10-shot magazine; 5" barrel; 8 1/2" overall length; weighs 34 oz.; ambidextrous triple safety with passive firing pin catch; slide safety/decocking lever; trigger bar disconnect; plastic grips; blued finish. Introduced 1992.
New: $550   Perf.: $500   Exc.: $400

Beretta Model 96 Brigadier
Same specs as Model 96 except removable front sight; reconfigured high slide wall profile; 10-shot magazine; three-dot sights system; 4 15/16" barrel; weighs 35 oz.; matte black Bruniton finish. From Beretta U.S.A. Introduced 1995; still in production.
New: $600   Perf.: $550   Exc.: $450

Beretta
Model 1931
Model 1934
Model 1935
Model 3032 Tomcat
Model 8000 Cougar
Model 8000 Cougar
Model 8000D Cougar
Model 8040 Cougar
Model 8040D Cougar
New Puma (See Beretta Model 70)
New Sable (See Beretta Model 76)
Panther (See Beretta Model 318)
Plinker (See Beretta Model 948)

Bergmann
Model 1903 "Mars"
Special
Vest Pocket Models

Bergmann Vest Pocket

Beretta Model 1931

Bergmann Model 1903 "Mars"

Beretta Model 3032 Tomcat

Beretta Model 8000 Cougar

Bernardelli Vest Pocket Model

Bergmann Special

BERETTA MODEL 1931
Semi-automatic; double-action; 32 ACP; 8-shot magazine; 3 1/2" barrel; 6" overall length; weighs 22 1/2 oz.; fixed sights; walnut grips; blued finish. Italian Navy issue bears medallion with "R/Anchor/M" emblem. Commercial issue has standard "PB" embossed black plastic grips.
Exc.: $750   **VGood:** $600   **Good:** $400

BERETTA MODEL 1934
Semi-automatic; 380 ACP; 7-shot magazine; 3 3/8" barrel; 5 7/8" overall length; weighs 28 1/8 oz.; fixed sights; plastic grips; thumb safety; blued or chrome finish. Official Italian service sidearm in WWII; military versions marked "RE", "RA" or "RM" for the army, air force and navy respectively. Police versions marked "PS" on rear of frame. Wartime version lacks quality of commercial model. Introduced 1934; no longer legally importable; still in production.
Exc.: $350   **VGood:** $300   **Good:** $200

BERETTA MODEL 1935
Semi-automatic; double action; 32 ACP; 7-shot magazine; 3 3/8" barrel; 5 7/8" overall length; fixed sights; plastic grips; thumb safety; blued or chrome finish. Italian service pistol during WWII; frame markings "RA" or "RM" on frame for the air force and navy respectively. Commercial version after 1945 known as Model 935.
Exc.: $300   **VGood:** $275   **Good:** $200

BERETTA MODEL 3032 TOMCAT
Semi-automatic; 32 ACP, 7-shot magazine. Barrel: 2.45". Weight: 14.5 oz. Length: 5" overall. Stocks: Checkered black plastic. Sights: Blade front, drift-adjustable rear. Features: Double action with exposed hammer; tip-up barrel for direct loading/unloading; thumb safety; polished or matte blue finish. Imported from Italy by Beretta U.S.A. Introduced 1996.
Perf.: $200   **Exc.:** $175   **VGood:** $150

BERETTA MODEL 8000 COUGAR
Semi-automatic; double action; 9mm Para.; 10-shot magazine; 3 1/2" barrel; 7" overall length; weighs 33 1/2 oz.; textured composition grips; blade front sight, drift-adjustable rear; slide-mounted safety; exposed hammer; matte black Bruniton finish. Imported from Italy by Beretta U.S.A. Introduced 1994; still imported.
New: $525   **Perf.:** $450   **Exc.:** $375

Beretta Model 8000/8040 Mini Cougar
Similar to the Model 8000/8040 Cougar except has shorter grip frame and weighs 27.6 oz. Introduced 1998. Imported from Italy by Beretta U.S.A.
Perf.: $600   **Exc.:** $550   **VGood:** $400

Beretta Model 8000D Cougar
Same specs as Model 8000 except double-action-only trigger mechanism. Imported from Italy by Beretta U.S.A. Introduced 1994; still imported.
New: $550   **Perf.:** $500   **Exc.:** $400

BERETTA MODEL 8040 COUGAR
Semi-automatic; double action; 40 S&W; 10-shot magazine; 3 1/2" barrel; 7" overall length; weighs 33 1/2 oz.; textured composition grips; blade front sight, drift-adjustable rear; slide-mounted safety; exposed hammer; matte black Bruniton finish. Imported from Italy by Beretta U.S.A. Introduced 1994; still imported.
New: $575   **Perf.:** $550   **Exc.:** $525

Beretta Model 8040D Cougar
Same specs as Model 8040 except double-action-only trigger mechanism. Imported from Italy by Beretta U.S.A. Introduced 1994; still imported.
New: $550   **Perf.:** $525   **Exc.:** $500

BERGMANN MODEL 1903 "MARS"
Semi-automatic; 9mm Bergmann-Bayard; 6-, 10-shot magazine; 4" barrel; 10" overall length; checkered wood grips. Marked "Bergmann Mars Pat. Brev. S.G.D.G." on locking block top. About 1,000 made in Germany before rights were sold to Pieper in Belguim where, with a few minor changes, it was made as the Bergmann-Bayard.
Exc.: $5000   **VGood:** $3500   **Good:** $2250

BERGMANN SPECIAL
Semi-automatic; double action; 32 ACP; 8-shot magazine; 3 7/16" barrel; 6 3/16" overall length; checkered plastic wrap-around grips. Rare double-action competitor to Walther's Model PP, actually made by Menz but sold under Bergmann's name.
Exc.: $1200   **VGood:** $850   **Good:** $500

BERGMANN VEST POCKET MODELS
Semi-automatic; 25 ACP; 6-, 9-shot magazine; 2 1/8" barrel; 4 3/4" overall length; checkered hard rubber or wood (rare) grips. Both conventional and one-hand-cocked ("Einhand") models later marketed under the Lignose name (see Lignose).
Conventional
Exc.: $300   **VGood:** $200   **Good:** $125
"Einhand"
Exc.: $400   **VGood:** $250   **Good:** $150
32 or 380 "Einhand"
Catalogued but apparently never made.

Bernardelli
Model USA

Bersa Model 23

Bersa Model 225

Bersa Model 95
Series

Bersa Model 83

Bersa Model 223

HANDGUNS

Bernardelli
Model USA
P. One
P. One Practical VG Pistol
Standard
Vest Pocket Model

Bersa
Model 23
Model 83
Model 85
Model 86
Model 95 Series
Model 223
Model 224
Model 225

BERNARDELLI MODEL USA
Semi-automatic; 22 LR, 380 ACP; 10-shot (22 LR), 7-shot (380 ACP) magazine; 3 1/2" barrel, 6 1/2" overall length; weighs 26 1/2 oz.; ramp front sight; fully-adjustable white-outline rear; checkered plastic stocks, thumbrest; serrated trigger; inertia-type firing pin; hammer-block safety; loaded chamber indicator. Made in Italy. Introduced 1989; was imported by Armsport and by Magnum Research, Inc.; no longer imported.

Perf.: $350   **Exc.:** $300   **VGood:** $275

BERNARDELLI P. ONE
Semi-automatic; double action; 9mm Para., 40 S&W; 16-shot (9mm), 10-shot (40 S&W) magazine; 4 7/8" barrel; 8 3/8" overall length; weighs 34 oz.; checkered black plastic grips; blade front sight, fully adjustable rear; three-dot system; forged steel frame and slide; full-length slide rails; reversible magazine release; thumb safety/decocker; squared triggerguard; blue/black finish. Imported from Italy by Armsport. Introduced 1994; no longer imported.

Perf.: $550   **Exc.:** $450   **VGood:** $400
Chrome finish
Perf.: $575   **Exc.:** $500   **VGood:** $450

Bernardelli P. One Practical VB Pistol
Same specs as P. One except 9x21mm; two- or four-port compensator; straight trigger; micro-adjustable rear sight. Imported from Italy by Armsport. Introduced 1994.

New: $1300   **Perf.:** $1200   **Exc.:** $1100

BERNARDELLI STANDARD
Semi-automatic; 22 LR; 10-shot magazine; 6", 8", 10" barrel; 13" overall length (10" barrel); target sights; adjustable sight ramp; walnut target grips; blued. Simply the Pocket Model adapted for 22 LR cartridge. Introduced 1949; no longer imported.

Perf.: $225   **Exc.:** $200   **VGood:** $175

BERNARDELLI VEST POCKET MODEL
Semi-automatic; 25 ACP; 5-shot; 8-shot extension magazine also available; 2 1/8" barrel; 4 1/8" overall length; no sights, but sighting groove milled in slide; plastic grips; blued finish. Introduced 1948; U.S. importation dropped 1968.

Exc.: $200   **VGood:** $175   **Good:** $135

BERSA MODEL 23
Semi-automatic; double action; 22 LR; 10-shot magazine; 3 1/2" barrel; 6 1/2" overall length; weighs 24 1/2 oz.; walnut grips with stippled panels; blade front sight, notch windage-adjustable rear; three-dot system; firing pin, magazine safeties; blue or nickel finish. Made in Argentina; distributed by Eagle Imports, Inc. Introduced 1989; dropped 1994.
Blue finish
Perf.: $200   **Exc.:** $175   **VGood:** $150
Nickel finish
Perf.: $225   **Exc.:** $200   **VGood:** $175

BERSA MODEL 83
Semi-automatic; double action; 380 ACP; 7-shot magazine; 3 1/2" barrel; 6 1/2" overall length; weighs 25 3/4 oz.; stippled walnut grips; blade front sight, notch windage-adjustable rear; three-dot system; firing pin, magazine safety systems; blue or nickel finish. Imported from Argentina; distributed by Eagle Imports, Inc. Introduced 1989; dropped 1994.
Blue finish
Perf.: $200   **Exc.:** $175   **VGood:** $150
Nickel finish
Perf.: $225   **Exc.:** $200   **VGood:** $175

BERSA MODEL 85
Semi-automatic; double action; 380 ACP; 13-shot magazine; 3 1/2" barrel; 6 1/2" overall length; weighs 25 3/4 oz.; stippled walnut grips; blade front sight, notch windage-adjustable rear; three-dot system; firing pin, magazine safety systems; blue or nickel finish. Imported from Argentina; distributed by Eagle Imports, Inc. Introduced 1989; dropped 1994.
Blue finish
Perf.: $250   **Exc.:** $225   **VGood:** $200
Nickel finish
Perf.: $300   **Exc.:** $275   **VGood:** $250

BERSA MODEL 86
Semi-automatic; double action; 380 ACP; 13-shot magazine; 3 1/2" barrel; 6 1/2" overall length; weighs 22 oz.; wrap-around textured rubber grips; blade front sight, windage-adjustable rear; three-dot system; firing pin, magazine safeties; combat-style triggerguard; matte blue or satin nickel finish. Imported from Argentina; distributed by Eagle Imports, Inc. Introduced 1992; dropped 1994.
Blue finish
Perf.: $275   **Exc.:** $225   **VGood:** $175
Nickel finish
Perf.: $300   **Exc.:** $250   **VGood:** $200

BERSA MODEL 95 SERIES
Semi-automatic; double action; 380 ACP; 7-shot magazine; 3 1/2" barrel; 6 1/2" overall length; weighs 22 oz.; blade front sight, windage-adjustable rear; three-dot system; firing pin and magazine safeties; combat-style triggerguard; wrap-around textured rubber grips; matte blue or satin nickel. Imported from Argentina; distributed by Eagle Imports, Inc. Introduced 1992.
Matte blue finish
New: $175   **Perf.:** $175   **Exc.:** $150
Satin nickel finish
New: $225   **Perf.:** $200   **Exc.:** $175

BERSA MODEL 223
Semi-automatic; double action; 22 LR; 11-shot magazine; 3 1/2" barrel; weighs 24 1/2 oz; blade front sight, square-notch windage-adjustable rear; checkered target-type nylon stocks; thumbrest; blowback action; squared-off triggerguard; magazine safety; blued finish. Made in Argentina. Introduced 1984; dropped 1987.
Perf.: $200   **Exc.:** $175   **VGood:** $150

BERSA MODEL 224
Semi-automatic; single action; 22 LR; 11-shot magazine; 4" barrel; weighs 26 oz; blade front sight, square-notch windage-adjustable rear; checkered target-type nylon stocks; thumbrest; blowback action; combat-type triggerguard; magazine safety; blued finish. Made in Argentina. Introduced 1984; no longer dropped 1987.
Perf.: $200   **Exc.:** $175   **VGood:** $150

BERSA MODEL 225
Semi-automatic; single action; 22 LR; 10-shot magazine; 5" barrel; weighs 26 oz.; blade front sight, square-notch windage-adjustable rear; checkered target-type nylon stocks; thumbrest; blowback action; combat-type triggerguard; magazine safety; blued finish. Made in Argentina. Introduced 1984; dropped 1987.
Perf.: $175   **Exc.:** $150   **VGood:** $135

Browning

25 "Baby"
25 Lightweight
380 Standard
380 Renaissance
BDA
BDM
Buck Mark Unlimited Match
Buck Mark Varmint
Challenger
Challenger II
Challenger III
Challenger III Sporter
Challenger Gold Model
Challenger Renaissance Model
Hi-Power
Hi-Power 40 S&W Mark III
Hi-Power Capitan
Hi-Power HP-Practical

Browning 380 Standard

Browning BDA 380

Browning Hi-Power
40 S&W Mark III

Browning Hi-Power
HP-Practical

Browning Hi-Power

Browning Hi-Power
Capitan

BROWNING 25 "BABY"
Semi-automatic; 25 ACP; 6-shot magazine; 2 1/8" barrel; 4" overall length; fixed sights, hard rubber grips; blued finish. Introduced ca. 1936; dropped, not importable, 1968.
    Perf.: $350   **Exc.:** $300   **VGood:** $250

Browning 25 Lightweight
Same specs as Browning 25 except chrome-plated; polyester pearl grips; alloy frame. Introduced 1954; dropped 1968.
    Perf.: $325   **Exc.:** $275   **VGood:** $250

BROWNING 380 STANDARD
Semi-automatic; 380 ACP, 32 ACP; 9-shot magazine; 3 7/16" barrel; 6" overall length; pre-'68 models have fixed sights, later adjustable; hard rubber grips; blued finish. Redesigned 1968; dropped 1974. Last models had 41/2" barrel; 7" overall length.
    Perf.: $300   **Exc.:** $250   **VGood:** $200

Browning 380 Renaissance
Same specs as standard Browning 380 Standard except chrome-plated finish; full engraving; polyester pearl grips. Introduced 1954; dropped 1981.
    Perf.: $900   **Exc.:** $800   **VGood:** $700

BROWNING BDA
Semi-automatic; 9mm Para., 38 Super, 45 ACP; 9-shot magazine (9mm, 38 Super), 7-shot (45 ACP); 4 7/16" barrel; 7 13/16" overall length; fixed sights; plastic stocks; blued finish. Manufactured by Sauer; same as SIG-Sauer P220. Imported 1977 to 1981.
9mm, 45 ACP
    Perf.: $500   **Exc.:** $450   **VGood:** $350
38 Super
    Perf.: $600   **Exc.:** $550   **VGood:** $450

BROWNING BDA 380
Semi-automatic; 380 Auto; 12-shot magazine; 3 13/16" barrel; 6 3/4" overall length; blade front sight, windage-adjustable rear; combination safety; de-cocking lever; inertia firing pin; uncheckered walnut grips. Manufactured in Italy. Introduced 1978; dropped 1997.
    Perf.: $400   **Exc.:** $350   **VGood:** $300

BROWNING BDM
Semi-automatic; double action; 9mm Para.; 15-shot magazine; 4 3/4" barrel; 7 7/8" overall length; weighs 31 oz; low-profile removable blade front sight, windage-adjustable rear; checkered black moulded composition grips, thumbrest on both sides; all-steel frame; matte black finish; two safety systems; mode selector for switching from DA auto to "revolver" mode. Introduced 1991; dropped 1997.
    Perf.: $450   **Exc.:** $400   **VGood:** $350

Browning Buck Mark Unlimited Silhouette
Same as the Buck Mark Silhouette except has 14 heavy barrel. Conforms to IHMSA 15 maximum sight radius rule. Introduced 1991.
    New: $450   **Per.:** $400   **Exc.:** $350

Browning Buck Mark Varmint
Same specs as Buck Mark except 9 7/8" heavy barrel; full-length scope base; no sights; black laminated wood stocks, optional forend; weighs 48 oz. Introduced 1987; still in production.
    Perf.: $300   **Exc.:** $250   **VGood:** $200

BROWNING CHALLENGER
Semi-automatic; 22 LR; 10-shot magazine; 4 1/2", 6 3/4" barrels; overall length 11 7/16" (6 3/4" barrel); screw-adjustable rear sight, removable blade front; hand-checkered walnut grips; gold-plated trigger; blued finish. Introduced 1962; dropped 1974.
    Perf.: $350   **Exc.:** $300   **VGood:** $275

Browning Challenger II
Same specs as Challenger except changed grip angle; impregnated hardwood stocks. Introduced 1975; replaced by Challenger III, 1982.
    Perf.: $225   **Exc.:** $200   **VGood:** $175

Browning Challenger III
Same specs as Challenger except 5 1/2" heavy bull barrel; 9 1/2" overall length; weighs 35 oz.; lightweight alloy frame; improved sights; smooth impregnated hardwood grips; gold-plated trigger. Introduced 1982; dropped 1985.
    Perf.: $200   **Exc.:** $175   **VGood:** $165

Browning Challenger III Sporter
Same specs as Challenger III except 6 3/4" barrel; 10 7/8" overall length; weighs 29 oz.; all-steel construction; blade ramped front sight, screw-adjustable rear, drift-adjustable front. Introduced 1982; dropped 1985.
    Perf.: $200   **Exc.:** $175   **VGood:** $165

Browning Challenger Gold Model
Same specs as Challenger except gold wire inlays in metal; figured hand-carved, checkered walnut grips. Introduced 1971; dropped 1974.
    Perf.: $1200   **Exc.:** $1000   **VGood:** $750

Browning Challenger Renaissance Model
Same specs as Challenger except satin nickel finish; full engraving; top-grade hand-carved, figured walnut grips. Introduced 1971; dropped 1974.
    Perf.: $1200   **Exc.:** $1000   **VGood:** $750

BROWNING HI-POWER
Semi-automatic; 9mm Para.; 13-shot magazine; 4 5/8" barrel; fixed sights; checkered walnut (pre-1986) or moulded grips; ambidextrous safety added in '80s; blued finish. Introduced 1954; still in production.
    Perf.: $500   **Exc.:** $450   **VGood:** $350

Browning Hi-Power 40 S&W Mark III
Same specs as standard Hi-Power except 40 S&W; 10-shot magazine; weighs 35 oz.; 4 3/4" barrel; matte blue finish; low profile front sight blade, drift-adjustable rear; ambidextrous safety; moulded polyamide grips with thumbrest. Imported from Belgium by Browning. Introduced 1993; still imported.
    New: $500   **Perf.:** $450   **Exc.:** $350

Browning Hi-Power Capitan
Same specs as standard Hi-Power except adjustable tangent rear sight authentic to early-production model; Commander-style hammer; checkered walnut grips; polished blue finish. Imported from Belgium by Browning. Reintroduced 1993; still imported.
    New: $550   **Perf.:** $500   **Exc.:** $400

Browning Hi-Power HP-Practical
Same specs as standard Hi-Power except silver-chromed frame, blued slide; wrap-around Pachmayr rubber grips; round-style serrated hammer; removable front sight, windage-adjustable rear. Introduced 1981; still in production.
    Perf.: $600   **Exc.:** $550   **VGood:** $450

Charter Arms
Bulldog

Charter Arms
Police Bulldog

Charter Arms
Magnum Pug

Charter Arms
Pit Bull

HANDGUNS

Charter Arms
Bulldog
Bulldog Pug
Bulldog Tracker
Explorer II
Lady On Duty
Magnum Pug
Model 40
Model 79K
Off-Duty
Pathfinder
Pit Bull
Police Bulldog
Police Bulldog Stainless

Charter Arms
Off-Duty

Charter Arms
Model 40

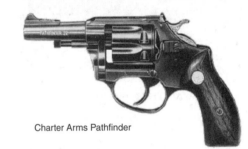

Charter Arms Pathfinder

CHARTER ARMS BULLDOG
Revolver; double action; 44 Spl.; 5-shot cylinder; 2 1/2", 3" barrel; 7 1/2" overall length; weighs 19 oz.; square notch fixed rear sight, Patridge-type front; checkered walnut or neoprene grips; chrome-moly steel frame; wide trigger and hammer, or spurless pocket hammer; blued or stainless finish. Introduced 1973; dropped 1996.

    Perf.: $200   **Exc.:** $175   **VGood:** $150
Stainless Bulldog
    Perf.: $175   **Exc.:** $165   **VGood:** $135

Charter Arms Bulldog Pug
Same specs as Bulldog except 2 1/2" shrouded barrel; 7 1/4" overall length; weighs 19 oz.; notch rear sight, ramp front; wide trigger and hammer spur; shrouded ejector rod; blued or stainless steel finish. Introduced 1986; reintroduced 1993; dropped 1993.

    Perf.: $225   **Exc.:** $200   **VGood:** $165
Stainless Bulldog Pug
    Perf.: $225   **Exc.:** $200   **VGood:** $175

Charter Arms Bulldog Tracker
Same specs as Bulldog except 357 Mag.; 2 1/2", 4", or 6" bull barrel; adjustable rear sight, ramp front; checkered walnut or Bulldog-style neoprene grips; square butt on 4" and 6" models; blued finish. Introduced 1986.

    Perf.: $175   **Exc.:** $150   **VGood:** $135

CHARTER ARMS EXPLORER II
Semi-automatic; 22 LR; 8-shot magazine; 6", 8" or 10" barrel; 15 1/2" overall length; blade front sight, open elevation-adjustable rear; serrated simulated walnut stocks; action adapted from Explorer AR-7 carbine; black, camo, gold or silver finish. Introduced 1980; discontinued 1986.

    Perf.: $100   **Exc.:** $85   **VGood:** $75

CHARTER ARMS LADY ON DUTY
Revolver; double action; 22 LR, 22 WMR, 38 Spl.; 6-shot (22LR, 22 WMR), 5-shot (38 Spl.); 2" barrel; 6 1/4" overall length; weighs 17 oz.; rosewood-color checkered plastic grips; ramp-style front sight, fixed rear; comes with lockable plastic case, trigger lock; choice of spur, pocket or double-action hammer; blue or nickel finish. Made in U.S. by Charco, Inc. Introduced 1995; dropped 1996.

    New: $175   **Perf.:** $165   **Exc.:** $150

CHARTER ARMS MAGNUM PUG
Revolver; double action; 357 Mag.; 5-shot; 2 1/4" barrel; weighs 18 oz.; Bulldog or neoprene combat grips; ramp-style front sight, fixed rear; fully shrouded barrel; pocket or spur hammer; blue finish. Made in U.S. by Charco, Inc. Introduced 1995; dropped 1996.

    New: $200   **Perf.:** $175   **Exc.:** $165

CHARTER ARMS MODEL 40
Semi-automatic; double action; 22 LR; 8-shot; 3 5/16" barrel; weighs 2 11/2 oz.; fixed sights; stainless steel finish. Introduced 1984; discontinued 1986.

    Perf.: $250   **Exc.:** $200   **VGood:** $185

CHARTER ARMS MODEL 79K
Semi-automatic; double action; 32 ACP, 380 ACP; 7-shot; 3 5/8" barrel; 6 1/2" overall length; weighs 24 1/2 oz.; fixed sights; hammer block; firing pin, magazine safeties; stainless steel finish. Imported from West Germany. Introduced 1984; no longer imported.

    Perf.: $300   **Exc.:** $275   **VGood:** $225

CHARTER ARMS OFF-DUTY
Revolver; double action; 22 LR, 38 Spl.; 5-shot (38 Spl.); 2" barrel; 6 3/4" overall length; fixed sights; choice of smooth or checkered walnut, neoprene grips; all steel; matte black finish. Introduced 1984; reintroduced 1993; dropped 1996.

    New: $165   **Perf.:** $150   **Exc.:** $135
Stainless Off-Duty
    New: $225   **Perf.:** $200   **Exc.:** $175

CHARTER ARMS PATHFINDER
Revolver; double action; 22 LR, 22 WMR; 6-shot; 2", 3", 6" barrels; 7 3/8 " overall length; weighs 18 1/2 oz.; adjustable rear sight, ramp front; round butt; wide hammer spur and trigger; blued finish. Introduced 1971; dropped 1990.

    Perf.: $175   **Exc.:** $165   **VGood:** $150
Square butt Pathfinder
    Perf.: $175   **Exc.:** $165   **VGood:** $150
Stainless Pathfinder with 3 1/2" shrouded barrel
    Perf.: $175   **Exc.:** $165   **VGood:** $150

CHARTER ARMS PIT BULL
Revolver; double action; 9mm Federal, 38 Spl., 357 Mag.; 5-shot; 2 1/2", 3 1/2", 4" barrels; 7 1/4" overall length; weighs 24 1/2 oz. (2 1/2" barrel); blade front sight, fixed rear on 2 1/2", adjustable on others; checkered neoprene grips; blued finish. Introduced 1989; discontinued 1991.

    Perf.: $225   **Exc.:** $200   **VGood:** $165
Stainless Pit Bull
    Perf.: $225   **Exc.:** $200   **VGood:** $175

CHARTER ARMS POLICE BULLDOG
Revolver; double action; 32 H&R, 38 Spl., 44 Spl.; 5-shot (44) or 6-shot; 3 1/2", 4" barrel; fixed sights; neoprene grips; square butt (44 Spl.); blued finish. Introduced 1976; dropped 1991.

    Perf.: $200   **Exc.:** $175   **VGood:** $150

Charter Arms Police Bulldog Stainless
Same specs as Police Bulldog except also offered in 357 Mag. (5-shot); shrouded barrel; square butt; stainless finish.

    Perf.: $200   **Exc.:** $175   **VGood:** $150

Colt Semi-Automatic Pistols

Combat Elite MKIV Series 80
Combat Government MKIV Series 70
Combat Government MKIV Series 80
Commander Lightweight MKIV Series 80
Defender
Delta Elite
Delta Gold Cup
Double Eagle Combat Commander MKII Series 90
Double Eagle MKII Series 90
Combat Commander MKIV Series 70
Double Eagle Officer's Model MKIV Series 90

Colt Delta Elite

Colt Double Eagle Combat Commander MKII Series 90

Colt Combat Commander MKIV Series 70

Colt Defender

Colt Combat Elite MKIV Series 80

COLT COMBAT ELITE MKIV SERIES 80
Semi-automatic; single action; 38 Super, 45 ACP; 7-, 8-shot magazine; 5" barrel; 8 1/2" overall length; weighs 39 oz.; high profile sights with 3-dot system; checkered rubber combat grips; stainless steel frame; ordnance steel slide, internal parts; beveled magazine well; extended grip safety. Introduced, 1986; still in production.

Perf.: $700	Exc.: $600	VGood: $500

COLT COMBAT GOVERNMENT MKIV SERIES 70
Semi-automatic; single action; 45 ACP; 8-shot magazine; 5" barrel; 8 3/8" overall length; weighs 40 oz. Similar to Government Model except higher undercut front sight, white outlined rear; flat mainspring housing; longer trigger; beveled magazine well; angled ejection port; Colt/Pachmayr wrap-around grips; internal firing pin safety. Introduced 1973; dropped 1983.

Perf.: $650	Exc.: $550	VGood: $450

COLT COMBAT GOVERNMENT MKIV SERIES 80
Semi-automatic; single action; 45 ACP; 5-shot magazine; 5" barrel; 8 1/2" overall length; weighs 39 oz. Similar to Combat Government MKIV Series 70 with higher undercut front sight, white outlined rear; flat mainspring housing; longer trigger beveled magazine well; angled ejection port; Colt/Pachmayr wrap-around grips; internal firing pin safety; 45 with blue, satin or stainless finish; 9mm, 38 blue only. Introduced 1983; dropped 1996.

Perf.: $600	Exc.: $500	VGood: $400

COLT COMMANDER LIGHTWEIGHT MKIV SERIES 80
Semi-automatic; 45 ACP, 38 Super, 9mm Para.; 4 1/4" barrel, 8" overall length; 7-shot magazine (45 ACP), 9-shot (38 Super, 9mm); weighs 26 1/2 oz.; basic design of Government Model auto, but of lightweight alloy, reducing weight; checkered walnut grips; fixed sights; rounded hammer spur; blued, nickel finish. Introduced 1983; still in production.

Perf.: $600	Exc.: $500	VGood: $400

COLT DEFENDER
Semi-automatic; 45 ACP, 7-shot magazine. Barrel: 3". Weight: 22-1/2 oz. Length: 6-3/4" overall. Stocks: Pebble-finish rubber wraparound with finger grooves. Sights: White dot front, snag-free Colt competition rear. Features: Stainless finish; aluminum frame; combat-style hammer; Hi Ride grip safety, extended manual safety, magazine disconnect safety. Introduced 1998.

Perf.: $600	Exc.: $500	VGood: $400

COLT DELTA ELITE
Semi-automatic; 10mm Auto; 8-shot; 5" barrel; 8 1/2" overall length; weighs 38 oz.; same general design as Government Model; 3-dot high profile combat sights; rubber combat stocks; internal firing pin safety; new recoil spring/buffer system; blued or matte stainless finish. Introduced 1987; still in production.

Perf.: $700	Exc.: $550	VGood: $450

Matte stainless
Perf.: $750	Exc.: $600	VGood: $500

Colt Delta Gold Cup
Same specs as Delta Elite except Accro adjustable rear sight; adjustable trigger; wrap-around grips; stainless steel finish. Introduced 1989; still in production.

Perf.: $850	Exc.: $700	VGood: $600

COLT DOUBLE EAGLE COMBAT COMMANDER MKII SERIES 90
Semi-automatic; double action; 40 S&W, 45 ACP; 8-shot magazine; 4 1/4" barrel; 7 3/4" overall length; weighs 36 oz.; blade front sight, windage-adjustable rear; 3-dot system; Colt Accro adjustable sight optional; stainless steel; checkered, curved extended triggerguard; wide steel trigger; decocking lever; traditional magazine release; beveled magazine well; grooved frontstrap; extended grip guard; combat-type hammer. Introduced 1991; still in production in 45 ACP.

Perf.: $600	Exc.: $500	VGood: $400

Accro sight
Perf.: $650	Exc.: $550	VGood: $450

COLT DOUBLE EAGLE MKII SERIES 90
Semi-automatic; double action; 45 ACP; 8-shot magazine; 4 1/2", 5" barrel; 8 1/2" overall length; weighs 39 oz.; blade front sight, windage-adjustable rear; black checkered thermoplastic grips; stainless steel construction; matte finish; extended triggerguard; decocking lever; grooved frontstrap; beveled magazine well; rounded hammer; extended grip guard. Introduced 1989; dropped 1996.

Perf.: $600	Exc.: $500	VGood: $400

Exc.: $800	VGood: $600	Good: $400

9mm
Exc.: $600	VGood: $450	Good: $300

COLT COMBAT COMMANDER MKIV SERIES 70
Semi-automatic; single action; 45 ACP, 38 Super, 9mm Para.; 7-shot (45 ACP), 9-shot (38 Super, 9mm); 4 1/4" barrel; 7 7/8" overall length; weighs 36 oz.; fixed blade front sight; square notch rear; all steel frame; grooved trigger; lanyard-style hammer; checkered walnut grips; blue or nickel finish. Introduced, 1970; dropped 1983.

Perf.: $750	Exc.: $600	VGood: $400

Nickel finish
Perf.: $800	Exc.: $650	VGood: $450

COLT DOUBLE EAGLE OFFICER'S MODEL MKIV SERIES 90
Semi-automatic; double action; 45 ACP; 8-shot magazine; 3 1/2" barrel; 7 1/4" overall length; weighs 35 oz.; stainless steel construction; blade front, windage-adjustable rear sight with 3-dot system; black checkered thermoplastic grips; matte finish; extended trigger guard; decocking lever; grooved frontstrap; beveled magazine well; rounded hammer; extended grip guard. Introduced 1989; dropped 1996.

Perf.: $600	Exc.: $500	VGood: $400

Lightweight model (25 oz.)
Perf.: $600	Exc.: $500	VGood: $400

Colt Huntsman

Colt Gold Cup Naional
Match MKIV Series 80

Colt Junior

Colt Government
Model MKIV Series 80

Colt Semi-Automatic Pistols

Gold Cup National Match MKIII
Gold Cup National Match MKIV Series 70
Gold Cup National Match MKIV Series 80
Gold Cup Trophy
Government Model MKIV Series 70
Government Model MKIV Series 80
Government Model 380 MKIV Series 80
Huntsman, Targetsman
Junior
Model 1900
Model 1900 Army

Colt Government
Model 380 MKIV
Series 80

Colt Gold Cup Trophy

COLT GOLD CUP NATIONAL MATCH MKIII
Semi-automatic; 45 ACP, 38 Spl.; 5" match barrel; 8 1/2" overall length; weighs 37 oz.; Patridge front sight, Colt Elliason adjustable rear; arched or flat housing; wide, grooved trigger with adjustable stop; ribbed top slide; hand-fitted with improved ejection port. Introduced 1959; dropped 1970.
45 ACP
   Exc.: $1000   **VGood:** $800   **Good:** $650
38 Spl.
   Exc.: $1100   **VGood:** $850   **Good:** $700

COLT GOLD CUP NATIONAL MATCH MKIV SERIES 70
Semi-automatic; 45 ACP; 7-shot magazine; 5" barrel; 8 3/8" overall length; weighs 38 1/2 oz; undercut front sight, Colt Elliason adjustable rear; match-grade barrel, bushing; long, wide grooved trigger; flat grip housing; hand-fitted slide; checkered walnut grips; blued finish. Introduced 1970; dropped 1983.
   Exc.: $850   **VGood:** $750   **Good:** $600

COLT GOLD CUP NATIONAL MATCH MKIV SERIES 80
Semi-automatic; single action; 45 ACP; 8-shot magazine; 5" barrel; 8 1/2" overall length; weighs 39 oz.; Patridge front sight, Colt-Elliason adjustable rear; match-grade barrel, bushing; long, wide trigger adjustable trigger stop; flat mainspring housing; hand-fitted slide; wider ejection port; checkered walnut grips; blue, stainless, bright stainless finish. Introduced 1983; dropped 1996.
   Perf.: $700   **Exc.:** $600   **VGood:** $500
Stainless finish
   Perf.: $750   **Exc.:** $650   **VGood:** $550
Bright stainless
   Perf.: $800   **Exc.:** $700   **VGood:** $600

COLT GOLD CUP TROPHY
Semi-automatic: 45 ACP, 8-shot magazine. Barrel: 5, with new design bushing. Weight: 39 oz. Length: 8-1/2. Stocks: Checkered rubber composite with silver-plated medallion. Sights: Patridge-style front, Colt-Elliason rear adjustable for windage and elevation, sight radius 6-3/4. Features: Arched or flat housing; wide, grooved trigger with adjustable stop; ribbed-top slide, hand fitted, with improved ejection port.
   Perf.: $900   **Exc.:** $800   **VGood:** $600

COLT GOVERNMENT MODEL MKIV SERIES 70
Semi-automatic; single action; 45 ACP, 38 Super, 9mm Para.; 7-shot magazine; 5" barrel; 8 3/8" overall length; weighs 40 oz; ramp front sight, fixed square notch rear; grip, thumb safeties; grooved trigger; accurizor barrel, bushing; blue or nickel (45 only) finish. Redesigned, redesignated Colt Model 1911A1. Introduced 1970; dropped 1983.
   Perf.: $500   **Exc.:** $450   **VGood:** $400
Nickel finish
   Perf.: $550   **Exc.:** $500   **VGood:** $400

COLT GOVERNMENT MODEL MKIV SERIES 80
Semi-automatic; single action; 45 ACP, 38 Super, 9mm Para.; 7-, 8-shot magazine; 5" barrel; 8 1/2" overall length; weighs 38 oz.; ramp front sight, fixed square notch rear; grip and thumb safeties; internal firing pin safety; grooved trigger; accurizor barrel bushing; checkered walnut grips; blue, nickel, satin nickel, bright stainless, stainless steel finish. Introduced 1983; still in production.
Blue, nickel, satin nickel finish
   Perf.: $600   **Exc.:** $500   **VGood:** $425
Stainless steel, bright stainless finish
   Perf.: $650   **Exc.:** $550   **VGood:** $475

COLT GOVERNMENT MODEL 380 MKIV SERIES 80
Semi-automatic; 380 ACP; 7-shot magazine; 3" barrel; 6" overall length; weighs 21 3/4 oz.; checkered composition stocks; ramp front sight, fixed square-notch rear; thumb and internal firing pin safeties; blue, nickel, satin nickel or stainless steel finish. Introduced 1983; dropped 1997.
   Perf.: $375   **Exc.:** $325   **VGood:** $275
Nickel, satin nickel finish
   Perf.: $400   **Exc.:** $325   **VGood:** $275
Stainless steel finish
   Perf.: $425   **Exc.:** $375   **VGood:** $325

COLT HUNTSMAN, TARGETSMAN
Semi-automatic; 22 LR; 4 1/2", 6" barrel; 9" overall length; checkered plastic grips; no hold-open device; fixed sights (Huntsman), adjustable sights and 6" barrel only (Targetsman). Introduced 1955; dropped 1977.
Huntsman
   Exc.: $350   **VGood:** $275   **Good:** $225
Targetsman
   Exc.: $450   **VGood:** $350   **Good:** $275

COLT JUNIOR
Semi-automatic; 22 Short, 25 ACP; 6-shot magazine; 2 1/4" barrel; 4 3/8" overall length; exposed hammer with round spur; checkered walnut stocks; fixed sights; blued. Initially produced in Spain by Astra, with early versions having Spanish markings as well as Colt identity; parts were assembled in U.S., sans Spanish identification after GCA '68 import ban. Introduced 1968; dropped 1973.
Spanish model
   Exc.: $300   **VGood:** $250   **Good:** $200
U.S.-made model
   Exc.: $325   **VGood:** $275   **Good:** $200

COLT MODEL 1900
Semi-automatic; 38 ACP; 7-shot magazine; 6" barrel; 9" overall length; spur hammer; plain walnut stocks; blued finish. Dangerous to fire modern high-velocity ammo. Was made in several variations. Introduced 1900; dropped 1903. Collector value.
Standard model
   Exc.: $5000   **VGood:** $3500 **Good:** $2500
Altered sight safety
   Exc.: $2200   **VGood:** $1400 **Good:** $1000

Colt Model 1900 Army
Same specs as Model 1900. Marked U.S. on left side of triggerguard bow, with inspector markings.
   Exc.: $7500   **VGood:** $5500 **Good:** $4500

HANDGUNS

Colt Semi-Automatic Pistols

Model 1911 British 455
Model 1911 Military
Model 1911 Russian
Model 1911A1
Colt National Match
Super 38
Super 38 National Match
Model 1991A1
Model 1991A1 Commander
Model 1991A1 Compact
Mustang

Colt National Match

Colt National Match

Colt Model 1911 Military
(Springfield Armory)

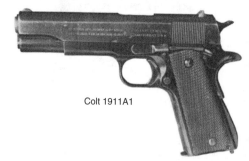

Colt 1911A1

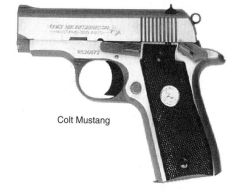

Colt Mustang

Colt Model 1911 British 455
Same specs as standard model but carries "Calibre 455" on right side of slide and may have broad arrow British ordnance stamp; made 1915-1916; 11,000 manufactured. Collector value.

    Exc.: $2000   **VGood:** $1600   **Good:** $1250

Colt Model 1911 Military
Same specs as the civilian version except serial numbers not preceded by the letter C; produced from 1912 to 1924; bright blue finish, early production; duller blue during war. Parkerized finish indicates post-war reworking and commands lesser value than original blue finish. Navy issue marked "Model of 1911 U.S. Navy" on slide.
Standard

    Exc.: $2000   **VGood:** $1400   **Good:** $850
U.S. Navy marked

    Exc.: $3750   **VGood:** $2500   **Good:** $1800
Remington-UMC (21,676)

    Exc.: $2200   **VGood:** $1700   **Good:** $950
Springfield Armory (25,767)

    Exc.: $2500   **VGood:** $2000   **Good:** $950

Colt Model 1911 Russian
Same specs as the standard version except Russian characters ANGLOZAKAZIVAT stamped on the slide. All were in 45 ACP, carrying serial numbers C-50000 through C-85000. This is an exceedingly rare collector item.

    Exc.: $3000   **VGood:** $2250   **Good:** $1650

COLT MODEL 1911A1
Semi-automatic; single action; 45 ACP, 7-shot magazine; 5" barrel; 8 1/2" overall length; weighs 38 oz.; checkered walnut (early production) or brown composition (military version) grips; ramped blade front sight, fixed high-profile square notch rear; Parkerized finish. Same specs as Model 1911 except longer grip safety spur; arched mainspring housing; finger relief cuts in frame behind trigger; plastic grips. During WWII other firms produced the 1911A1 under Colt license, including Remington-Rand, Ithaca Gun Co., and Union Switch & Signal Co. These government models bear imprint of licensee on slide. In 1970, this model was redesigned and redesignated as Government Model MKIV Series 70; approximately 850 1911A1 guns were equipped with split-collet barrel bushing and BB prefix serial number which adds to the value. Modern version (marked "Colt M1911A1(tm)") continues serial number range used on original G.I. 1911A1 guns and comes with one magazine and moulded carrying case. Introduced 1923; still produced.

Commercial model ("C" s/n)

    Exc.: $850   **VGood:** $700   **Good:** $500
BB s/n prefix

    Exc.: $950   **VGood:** $800   **Good:** $600
Military model

    Exc.: $950   **VGood:** $650   **Good:** $500
Singer Mfg. Co. (500)

    Exc.: $15,000   **VGood:** $12,000   **Good:** $8500
Union Switch & Signal (55,000)

    Exc.: $1250   **VGood:** $850   **Good:** $700
Remington-Rand (1,000,000)

    Exc.: $700   **VGood:** $600   **Good:** $500
Ithaca Gun Co. (370,000)

    Exc.: $700   **VGood:** $600   **Good:** $500
45/22 conversion unit

    Exc.: $650   **VGood:** $550   **Good:** $400
22/45 conversion unit

    Exc.: $1500   **VGood:** $1000   **Good:** $800

COLT NATIONAL MATCH
Semi-automatic; 45 ACP; 7-shot; 5" barrel; 8 1/2" overall length; weighs 37 oz.; adjustable rear, ramp front target sight; match-grade barrel; hand-honed action. Also available with fixed sights. Introduced 1933; dropped 1941.
Fixed sights

    Exc.: $2750   **VGood:** $2000   **Good:** $1600
Target sights

    Exc.: $3250   **VGood:** $2500   **Good:** $1850

COLT SUPER 38
Semi-automatic; double action; 38 Colt Super; 9-shot magazine; fixed sights standard, adjustable rear sights available. Same frame as 1911 commercial until 1970. Introduced in 1929. In 1937, the design of the firing pin, safety, hammer, etc. were changed and the model renamed the New Style Super 38. Still in production as Government Model Mark IV/Series 80.

    Exc.: $750   **VGood:** $600   **Good:** $500
Pre-WWI

    Exc.: $2500   **VGood:** $2000   **Good:** $1500

Colt Super 38 National Match
Same specs as Colt Super 38 except hand-honed action; adjustable target sights; match-grade barrel. Manufactured from 1935 to 1941.

    Exc.: $4500   **VGood:** $3500   **Good:** $2500

COLT MODEL 1991A1
Semi-automatic; 45 ACP; 7-shot magazine; 5" barrel; 8 1/2" overall length; weighs 38 oz.; ramped blade front sight, fixed square notch high-profile rear; checkered black composition grips; Parkerized finish; continuation of serial number range used on original G.I. 1911A1 guns. Introduced 1991; still in production.

    New: $500   **Perf.:** $450   **Exc.:** $400

Colt Model 1991A1 Commander
Same specs as the Model 1991A1 except 4 1/4" barrel; Parkerized finish. Comes in moulded case. Made in U.S. by Colt's Mfg. Co. Introduced 1993; still in production.

    New: $500   **Perf.:** $450   **Exc.:** $400

Colt Model 1991A1 Compact
Same specs as the Model 1991A1 except 3 1/2" barrel; 7" overall length; 3/8" shorter height. Comes with one 6-shot magazine, moulded case. Made in U.S. by Colt's Mfg. Co. Introduced 1993; still produced.

    New: $500   **Perf.:** $450   **Exc.:** $400

COLT MUSTANG
Semi-automatic; 380 ACP; 5-, 6-shot magazine; 2 3/4" barrel; 5 1/2" overall length; weighs 18 1/2 oz.; steel frame; stainless, blued or nickel finish. Similar to Colt Government Model 380. Introduced 1987; dropped 1997.

    Perf.: $350   **Exc.:** $300   **VGood:** $250
Nickel finish

    Perf.: $375   **Exc.:** $325   **VGood:** $275
Stainless finish

    Perf.: $375   **Exc.:** $325   **VGood:** $275

Colt Detective Special
(Second Issue)

Colt Detective Special
(Third Issue)

Colt Diamondback

Colt Frontier Scout

Colt Detective Special
(Fourth Issue)

Colt National Match

Colt Lawman MKIII

HANDGUNS

Colt Revolvers & Single Shots

Detective Special
(Second Issue)
Detective Special
(Third Issue)
Detective Special
(Fourth Issue)
Diamondback
Frontier Scout
Frontier Scout Buntline
King Cobra
Magnum Carry
Lawman MKIII
Lawman MKV
Metropolitan MKIII
Model 1877 Lightning
Model 1877 Thunderer
Model 1878 Frontier

COLT DETECTIVE SPECIAL (FIRST ISSUE)
Revolver; double action; 38 Spl.; 6-shot swing-out cylinder; 2", 3" barrels; 6 3/4" overall length; rounded butt introduced in 1934; blue or nickel finish. Introduced 1927; dropped 1936.

Exc.: $575   **VGood:** $475   **Good:** $350
Nickel finish
Exc.: $600   **VGood:** $500   **Good:** $375

Colt Detective Special (Second Issue)
Same specs as First Issue except 32 New Police, 38 New Police; heavier barrel; integral protective shroud enclosing ejector rod; frame, sideplate, cylinder, barrel, internal parts of high-tensile alloy steel; plastic or walnut Bulldog-type grips; fixed rear sight; notch milled in topstrap, serrated ramp front; checkered hammer spur; blue or nickel finish. Introduced 1947; dropped 1972.

Perf.: $450   **Exc.:** $350   **VGood:** $275
Nickel finish
Perf.: $475   **Exc.:** $375   **VGood:** $300

Colt Detective Special (Third Issue)
Same specs as Second Issue except 38 Spl.; shrouded ejector rod; wrap-around walnut grips. Introduced 1973; dropped 1986.

Perf.: $400   **Exc.:** $325   **VGood:** $275

Colt Detective Special (Fourth Issue)
Same specs as Third Issue except 2" barrel only; weighs 22 oz.; 6 5/8" overall length; black composition grips; ramp front sight, fixed square notch rear; glare-proof sights; grooved trigger; Colt blue finish. Made in U.S. by Colt's Mfg. Reintroduced 1993; still produced.

New: $350   **Perf.:** $290   **Exc.:** $250

COLT DIAMONDBACK
Revolver; double action; 38 Spl., 22 LR; 6-shot swing-out cylinder; 2 1/2", 4" (22 LR), 6" barrel; vent-rib barrel; scaled-down version of Python; target-type adjustable rear sight, ramp front; full checkered walnut grips; integral rounded rib beneath barrel shrouds, ejector rod; broad checkered hammer spur. Introduced 1966; dropped 1986.

Perf.: $450   **Exc.:** $350   **VGood:** $275
Nickel finish
Perf.: $500   **Exc.:** $400   **VGood:** $325
22 LR
Perf.: $525   **Exc.:** $425   **VGood:** $350

COLT FRONTIER SCOUT
Revolver; single action; 22 LR, 22 Long, 22 Short; interchangeable cylinder for 22 WMR; 4 1/2" barrel; 9 15/16" overall length; originally introduced with alloy frame; steel frame, blue finish introduced in 1959; fixed sights; plastic or wooden grips. Introduced 1958; dropped 1971.
Alloy frame
Perf.: $425   **Exc.:** $375   **VGood:** $225
Blue finish, plastic grips
Perf.: $600   **Exc.:** $400   **VGood:** $300
Nickel finish, wood grips
Perf.: $450   **Exc.:** $375   **VGood:** $250
With 22 WMR cylinder
Perf.: $450   **Exc.:** $400   **VGood:** $275

Colt Frontier Scout Buntline
Same specs as Frontier Scout except 9 1/2" barrel. Introduced 1959; dropped 1971.
Perf.: $500   **Exc.:** $425   **VGood:** $325

COLT KING COBRA
Revolver; double action; 357 Mag.; 6-shot cylinder; 2 1/2", 4", 6" barrels; 9" overall length (4" barrel); weighs 42 oz.; adjustable white outline rear sight, red insert ramp front; full-length contoured ejector rod housing, barrel rib; matte finish; stainless steel construction. Introduced 1986; still in production.
Perf.: $350   **Exc.:** $250   **VGood:** $225

COLT MAGNUM CARRY REVOLVER
Caliber: 357 Mag., 6-shot. Barrel: 2". Weight: 21 oz. Length: NA. Stocks: Combat-style rubber. Sights: Ramp front, fixed notch rear. Features: Stainless steel construction. Smooth combat trigger. Introduced 1998.
New: $400   **Perf.:** $350   **Exc.:** $250

COLT LAWMAN MKIII
Revolver; double action; 357 Mag.; also chambers 38 Spl.; 2", 4" barrels; 9 3/8" overall length (4" barrel); choice of square, round butt walnut grips; fixed sights; blued, nickel finish. Introduced 1969; dropped 1983.
Perf.: $300   **Exc.:** $225   **VGood:** $175
Nickel finish
Perf.: $325   **Exc.:** $250   **VGood:** $200

Colt Lawman MKV
Same specs as Lawman MKIII except redesigned lockwork to reduce double-action trigger pull; faster lock time; redesigned grips; shrouded ejector rod (2" barrel); fixed sights; solid rib. Introduced 1984; dropped 1985.
Perf.: $325   **Exc.:** $250   **VGood:** $200

COLT METROPOLITAN MKIII
Revolver; double action; 38 Spl.; 6-shot swing-out cylinder; 4" barrel; designed for urban law enforcement; fixed sights; choice of service, target grips of checkered walnut; blued finish, standard; nickel, optional. Introduced 1969; dropped 1972.
Perf.: $350   **Exc.:** $300   **VGood:** $200

COLT MODEL 1877 LIGHTNING
Revolver; double action; 32 Colt, 38 Colt; 6-shot cylinder; 4 1/2" - 10" barrels with ejector; 1 1/2", 2 1/2", 3 1/2", 4 1/2", 6" sans ejector; fixed sights; blued or nickel finish; hard rubber grips. Manufactured 1877 to 1909.
Exc.: $2200   **VGood:** $1850   **Good:** $1200

COLT MODEL 1877 THUNDERER
Revolver; double action; 41 Colt; 6-shot cylinder; 4 1/2"-10" barrels with ejector; 1 1/2", 2 1/2", 3 1/2", 4 1/2", 6" sans ejector; blued or nickel finish; hard rubber grips. Manufactured 1877 to 1909.
Exc.: $2500   **VGood:** $1750   **Good:** $1350

COLT MODEL 1878 FRONTIER
Revolver; double action; 32-20, 38-40, 44-40, 45 Colt, 450, 455, 476 Eley; 6-shot cylinder; 4 3/4", 5 1/2", 7 1/2" barrels with ejector; 3 1/2", 4" sans ejector; similar to Lightning model but with heavier frame; lanyard ring in butt; hard rubber grips; fixed sights; blued or nickel finish. Manufactured 1878 to 1905.
Exc.: $3500   **VGood:** $2500   **Good:** $1750

HANDGUNS

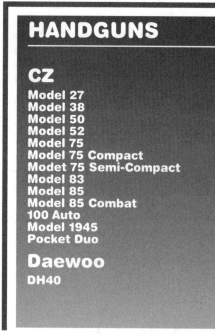

CZ
Model 27
Model 38
Model 50
Model 52
Model 75
Model 75 Compact
Model 75 Semi-Compact
Model 83
Model 85
Model 85 Combat
100 Auto
Model 1945
Pocket Duo

Daewoo
DH40

CZ Model 27

CZ Model 38

CZ Model 83

CZ Model 1945

CZ Pocket Model

CZ Model 75

CZ MODEL 27

Semi-automatic; 32 ACP; 8-shot magazine; 3 13/16" barrel; 6 1/2" overall length; weighs 25 oz.; vertical retracting grooves on slide; fixed sights; plastic grips; blued finish. Commercial and non-commercial models made until 1939 marked on top rib and left side of frame; post-1941 omit top rib marking; post-war models made until 1951 marked on slide. Manufactured from 1927 to 1951.

Pre-war
   Exc.: $350   **VGood:** $250   **Good:** $200
Post-1941
   Exc.: $325   **VGood:** $275   **Good:** $225
Post-war
   Exc.: $300   **VGood:** $250   **Good:** $200

CZ MODEL 38

Semi-automatic; double-action-only; 380 ACP; 8-shot magazine; 4 5/8" barrel; 8 1/8" overall length; weighs 32 oz.; plastic grips; fixed sights; blued finish. Also listed as CZ Pistole 39(t) during German occupation. Manufactured 1939 to 1945.
   Exc.: $375   **VGood:** $275   **Good:** $200

CZ MODEL 50

Semi-automatic; double action; 32 ACP; 8-shot; 3 3/4" barrel; 6 1/2" overall length; weighs 24 3/4 oz.; frame mounted safety catch; loaded chamber indicator. Issued to Czech police as Model VZ50. Manufactured from 1951 to approximately 1967.
   Exc.: $135   **VGood:** $110   **Good:** $100

CZ MODEL 52

Semi-automatic; 7.62 Tokarev; 8-shot; 4 3/4" barrel; 8 1/4" overall length; weighs 40 oz.; complex roller locking breech system. Manufactured from 1952 to approximately 1956.
   Exc.: $150   **VGood:** $125   **Good:** $100

CZ MODEL 75

Semi-automatic; double action or double-action-only; 9mm Para., 40 S&W; 15-shot magazine; 4 3/4" barrel; 8" overall length; weighs 35 oz.; all-steel frame; adjustable rear sight, square post front; checkered plastic; black polymer, matte or high-polish blued finish. Imported from the Czech Republic by CZ-USA.
   Perf.: $400   **Exc.:** $350 **VGood:** $300

CZ MODEL 75 Compact

Same specs as Model 75 except 10-shot magazine; 3 15/16" barrel; weighs 32 oz.; removable front sight; non-glare ribbed slide top; squared and serrated triggerguard; combat hammer. Introduced 1993; imported from the Czech Republic by CZ-USA.
   Perf.: $400   **Exc.:** $350 **VGood:** $300

CZ Model 75 Semi-Compact

Same specs as Model 75 Compact with shorter slide and barrel on full-size CZ 75 frame; 10-shot magazine; 9mm Para. only. Introduced 1994; imported from the Czech Republic by CZ-USA.
   Perf.: $400   **Exc.:** $350   **VGood:** $300

CZ MODEL 83

Semi-automatic; double action; 32 ACP, 380 ACP; 3 13/16" barrel; 6 15/16" overall length; weighs 26 1/4 oz; adjustable rear, removable square post front sight; ambidextrous magazine release and safety; non-glare ribbed slide top; high-impact checkered plastic grips; blue finish.
   Perf.: $300   **Exc.:** $250   **VGood:** $200

CZ MODEL 85

Semi-automatic; double action or double-action-only; 9mm Para., 40 S&W; 15-shot magazine; 4 3/4" barrel; 8" overall length; weighs 35 oz.; all-steel frame; ambidextrous slide release and safety levers; non-glare ribbed slide top; squared, serrated trigger- guard; trigger stop to prevent overtravel; adjustable rear sight, square post front; checkered plastic; black polymer, matte or high-polish blued finish. Introduced 1986; imported from the Czech Republic by CZ-USA.
   Perf.: $450   **Exc.:** $400   **VGood:** $350

CZ Model 85 Combat

Same specs as the Model 85 except walnut grips; round combat hammer; fully-adjustable rear sight; extended magazine release; trigger parts coated with friction-free beryllium copper. Introduced 1992; imported from the Czech Republic by CZ-USA.
   Perf.: $500   **Exc.:** $450   **VGood:** $400

CZ 100 AUTO PISTOL

Caliber: 9mm Para., 40 S&W, 10-shot magazine. Barrel: 3.7". Weight: 24 oz. Length: 6.9" overall. Stocks: Grooved polymer. Sights: Blade front with dot, white outline rear drift adjustable for windage. Features: Double action only with firing pin block; polymer frame, steel slide; has laser sight mount. Introduced 1996. Imported from the Czech Republic by CZ-USA.
   Price: 9mm Para.$389.00
   Price: 40 S&W $399.00

CZ MODEL 1945

Semi-automatic; double action; 25 ACP; 8-shot magazine; 2" barrel; 5" overall length; plastic grips; fixed sights; blued finish. Manufactured from 1945 to approximately 1960.
   Exc.: $225   **VGood:** $175   **Good:** $145

CZ POCKET DUO

Semi-automatic; 25 ACP; 6-shot magazine; 2 1/8" barrel; 4 1/2" overall length; fixed sights; plastic grips; manufactured in Czechoslovakia; blue or nickel finish. Manufactured 1926 to 1960.
   Exc.: $175   **VGood:** $150   **Good:** $125

DAEWOO DH40

Semi-automatic; double action; 40 S&W; 10-shot magazine; 4 1/8" barrel; 7 1/2" overall length; weighs 28 1/4 oz.; checkered composition grips; 1/8" blade front sight, adjustable rear; three-dot system; fast-fire mechanism; ambidextrous manual safety with internal firing pin lock; no magazine safety; alloy frame; squared triggerguard; matte black finish. Imported from Korea by Nationwide Sports Distributors. Introduced 1991; still imported.
   New: $350   **Perf.:** $275   **Exc.:** $225

Desert Industries
War Eagle

Davis D-Series
D-38 Derringer

Detonics Combat
Master Mark V

Davis P-32

Desert Industries
Double Deuce

HANDGUNS

Dakota
**Old Model Single Action
Sheriff's Model**

Davis
**Big-Bore Derringers
D-Series Derringers
Long-Bore Derringers
P-32
P-380**

Desert Eagle
**(See Magnum Research
Desert Eagle)**

Desert Industries
**Double Deuce
Two-Bit Special
War Eagle**

Detonics
**Combat Master Mark I
Combat Master Mark V
Combat Master Mark VI
Combat Master Mark VII
Compmaster**

DAKOTA OLD MODEL SINGLE ACTION
Revolver; single action; 22 LR, 32-20, 357 Mag., 38-40, 44 Spl., 44-40, 45 Colt; 6-shot cylinder; 4 5/8", 5 1/2", 7 1/2" barrel; blade front, fixed rear sight; one-piece walnut stocks; color case-hardened frame; brass grip frame, triggerguard; blued barrel cylinder; also available in nickel finish. Made in Italy. Introduced 1967; sporadic production. Was imported by EMF.
   Perf.: $275   **Exc.:** $225   **VGood:** $200
Nickel finish
   Perf.: $325   **Exc.:** $275   **VGood:** $225

DAKOTA SHERIFF'S MODEL
Revolver; single action; 32-20, 357 Mag., 38-40, 44 Spl., 44-40, 45 Colt; 6-shot; 3 1/2" barrel; blade front, fixed rear sight; one-piece walnut stock; blued finish. Made in Italy. Introduced 1994; was imported by EMF.
   Perf.: $350   **Exc.:** $300   **VGood:** $250

DAVIS BIG-BORE DERRINGERS
Derringer; over/under; 22 WMR, 32 H&R Mag., 38 Spl., 9mm Para.; 2-shot; 2 3/4" barrels; 4 9/16" overall length; weighs about 14 oz.; textured black synthetic grips; fixed sights; chrome or black teflon finish. Larger than the Davis D-Series models. Made in U.S. by Davis Industries. Introduced 1995; still produced.
   Perf.: $60   **Exc.:** $45   **VGood:** $35

DAVIS D-SERIES DERRINGERS
Derringer over/under; 22 WMR, 32 H&R, 38 Spl; 2-shot; 2 3/8" barrels; 4" overall length; weighs about 11 1/2 oz.; textured black synthetic grips; blade front, fixed notch rear sight; alloy frame; steel-lined barrels; steel breechblock; plunger-type safety with integral hammer block; chrome or black Teflon finish. Made in U.S. by Davis Industries. Introduced 1992; still produced.
   Perf.: $60   **Exc.:** $45   **VGood:** $35

DAVIS LONG-BORE DERRINGERS
Derringer over/under; 22 WMR, 32 H&R Mag., 38 Spl., 9mm Para.; 2-shot; 3 1/2" barrels; 5 3/8" overall length; weighs 16 oz.; textured black synthetic grips; fixed sights; chrome or black teflon finish. Larger than the Davis D-Series models. Made in U.S. by Davis Industries. Introduced 1995; still produced.
   Perf.: $75   **Exc.:** $60   **VGood:** $50

DAVIS P-32
Semi-automatic; double action; 32 ACP; 6-shot magazine; 2 13/16" barrel; 5 3/8" overall length; weighs 22 oz.; laminated wood stocks; fixed sights; chrome or black Teflon finish. Introduced 1986; still in production.
   Perf.: $70   **Exc.:** $60   **VGood:** $50

DAVIS P-380
Semi-automatic; double action; 380 ACP; 5-shot magazine; 2 13/16" barrel; 5 7/16" overall length; weighs 22 oz.; fixed sights; black composition grips; chrome or black Teflon finish. Introduced 1991; still in production.
   Perf.: $80   **Exc.:** $60   **VGood:** $50

DESERT INDUSTRIES DOUBLE DEUCE
Semi-automatic; double action; 22 LR; 6-shot; 2 1/2" barrel; 5 1/2" overall length; weighs 15 oz.; fixed groove sights; smooth rosewood grips; ambidextrous slide-mounted safety; stainless steel construction; matte finish. Introduced 1991; still in production by Steel City Arms.
   Perf.: $325   **Exc.:** $275   **VGood:** $225

DESERT INDUSTRIES TWO-BIT SPECIAL
Semi-automatic; double action; 25 ACP; 5-shot; 2 1/2" barrel; 5 1/2" overall length; weighs 15 oz.; fixed groove sights; smooth rosewood grips; ambidextrous slide-mounted safety; stainless steel construction; matte finish. Introduced 1991; still in production.
   Perf.: $325   **Exc.:** $275   **VGood:** $225

DESERT INDUSTRIES WAR EAGLE
Semi-automatic; double action; 380 ACP, 9mm Para., 40 S&W, 10mm Auto, 45 ACP; 10-shot, 14-shot (9mm), 8-shot (380 ACP); 4" barrel; fixed sights; rosewood grips; stainless steel construction; matte finish. Introduced 1991; still in production.
   Perf.: $700   **Exc.:** $650   **VGood:** $550

DETONICS COMBAT MASTER MARK I
Semi-automatic; 9mm Para., 38 Super, 45 ACP; 6-shot magazine (45 ACP); 3 1/2" barrel; 6 3/4" overall length; weighs 28 oz.; fixed or adjustable combat-type sights; checkered walnut stocks; throated barrel; polished feed ramp; self-adjusting cone barrel centering system; beveled magazine inlet; full-clip indicator; two-tone matte blue and stainless finish. Introduced 1977; discontinued 1992.
   Perf.: $700   **Exc.:** $600   **VGood:** $500

Detonics Combat Master Mark V
Same specs as Combat Master I except all matte stainless finish. Introduced 1977; discontinued 1985.
   Perf.: $650   **Exc.:** $550   **VGood:** $500

Detonics Combat Master Mark VI
Same specs as Combat Master Mark I except 451 Detonics Mag.; adjustable sights; polished stainless steel slide. Introduced 1977; discontinued 1989.
   Perf.: $950   **Exc.:** $750   **VGood:** $600

Detonics Combat Master Mark VII
Same specs as Combat Master Mark VI except no sights as special order option. Introduced 1977; discontinued 1982.
   Perf.: $850   **Exc.:** $750   **VGood:** $650

DETONICS COMPMASTER
Semi-automatic; 45 ACP; 7-, 8-shot magazine; 5", 6" barrel; Millet adjustable sights; checkered Pachmayr stocks; matching mainspring housing; Detonics recoil system; extended grip safety; ambidextrous safety; extended magazine release; stainless steel. Introduced 1988; discontinued 1992.
   Perf.: $1800   **Exc.:** $1400   **VGood:** $1200

HANDGUNS

E.A.A.
Witness Silver Team

EMF
1894 Target Bisley
Dakota 1875 Outlaw
Dakota 1890 Police
Dakota New Model
Hartford
Hartford Pinkerton Model

Entrèprise
Elite P500
Tactical P500
Medalist P500
Boxer P500
Tournament Shooter Model I

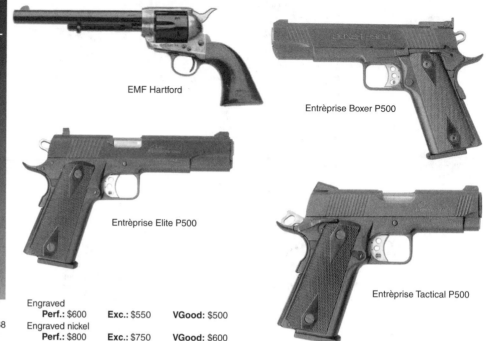

EMF Hartford

Entrèprise Boxer P500

Entrèprise Elite P500

Entrèprise Tactical P500

E.A.A. WITNESS SILVER TEAM
Semi-automatic; single action; 9mm Para., 9x21, 38 Super, 10mm, 40 S&W, 45 ACP; 10-shot magazine; 5 1/8" barrel; 9 5/8" overall length; weighs 41 1/2 oz.; black rubber grips; square post front sight, fully-adjustable rear; double-chamber compensator; competition SA trigger; extended safety; oval magazine release; competition hammer; beveled magazine well; beavertail grip; hand-fitted major components; match-grade barrel; double-dip blue finish. Comes with Super Sight and drilled and tapped for scope mount. Built for the intermediate competition shooter. From E.A.A. Custom Shop. Marketed by European American Armory Corp. Introduced 1992; still offered.

Perf.: $850   **Exc.:** $750   **VGood:** $650

EMF 1894 TARGET BISLEY
Revolver; single action; 45 Colt; 5 1/2", 7 1/2" barrel; 11" overall length (5 1/2" barrel); weighs about 45 oz.; blade front, fixed rear sight; smooth walnut grips, specially shaped grips frame and triggerguard; wide spur hammer; blue or nickel finish. Imported by E.M.F. Introduced 1995; still imported.

Blue finish
New: $600   **Perf.:** $525   **Exc.:** $475
Nickel finish
New: $675   **Perf.:** $600   **Exc.:** $550

EMF DAKOTA 1875 OUTLAW
Revolver; single action; 357, 44-40, 45 Colt; 7 1/2" barrel; 13 1/2" overall length; weighs 46 oz.; smooth walnut grips; blade front, fixed groove rear sight; authentic copy of 1875 Remington with firing pin in hammer; color case-hardened frame, blue cylinder, barrel; steel backstrap and brass triggerguard. Also offered in nickel finish, factory engraved. Imported by E.M.F.; still imported.

New: $400   **Perf.:** $350   **Exc.:** $300
Nickel finish
New: $450   **Perf.:** $400   **Exc.:** $375
Engraved
New: $500   **Perf.:** $450   **Exc.:** $400
Engraved nickel
New: $700   **Perf.:** $650   **Exc.:** $600

EMF DAKOTA 1890 POLICE
Revolver; single action; 357, 44-40, 45 Colt; 5 1/2" barrel; 12 1/2" overall length; weighs 40 oz.; smooth walnut grips; blade front, fixed groove rear sight; authentic copy of 1875 Remington with firing pin in hammer; color case-hardened frame, blue cylinder, barrel; steel backstrap and brass triggerguard; lanyard ring in butt. Also offered in nickel finish, factory engraved. Imported by E.M.F.; still imported.

Perf.: $400   **Exc.:** $350   **VGood:** $300
Nickel finish
Perf.: $550   **Exc.:** $500   **VGood:** $375

Engraved
Perf.: $600   **Exc.:** $550   **VGood:** $500
Engraved nickel
Perf.: $800   **Exc.:** $750   **VGood:** $600

EMF DAKOTA NEW MODEL
Revolver; single action; 357 Mag., 44-40, 45 Colt; 6-shot cylinder; 3 1/2", 4 3/4", 5 1/2", 7 1/2" barrel; 13" overall length (7 1/2" barrel); weighs 45 oz.; blade front, fixed rear sight; smooth walnut grips; color case-hardened frame, black nickel backstrap and triggerguard; also offered nickel plated. Imported by E.M.F.; still imported.

Perf.: $350   **Exc.:** $300   **VGood:** $250
Nickel-plated
Perf.: $450   **Exc.:** $375   **VGood:** $300

EMF HARTFORD
Revolver; single action; 22 LR, 357 Mag., 32-20, 38-40, 44-40, 44 Spec., 45 Colt; 6-shot cylinder; 4 3/4", 5 1/2", 7 1/2" barrel; 13" overall length (7 1/2" barrel); weighs 45 oz.; blade front, fixed rear sight; identical to the original Colts with inspector cartouche on left grip, original patent dates and U.S. markings; all major parts serial numbered using original Colt-style lettering, numbering; bullseye ejector head and color case-hardening on frame and hammer. Imported by E.M.F. Introduced 1990; still imported.

Perf.: $450   **Exc.:** $375   **VGood:** $300
Cavalry or Artillery model
Perf.: $450   **Exc.:** $375   **VGood:** $300
Nickel-plated
Perf.: $550   **Exc.:** $475   **VGood:** $400
Engraved, nickel-plated
Perf.: $700   **Exc.:** $650   **VGood:** $550

EMF HARTFORD PINKERTON MODEL
Revolver; single action; 45 Colt; 6-shot cylinder; 4" barrel; 10" overall length; weighs 40 oz.; smooth walnut grips; blade front, fixed rear sight; bird's-head grip; identical to the original Colts with original patent dates and markings; all major parts serial numbered using original Colt-style lettering, numbering; bullseye ejector head and color case-hardening on frame and hammer. Imported by E.M.F. Introduced 1990; still imported.

Perf.: $400   **Exc.:** $350   **VGood:** $300

ENTRÈPRISE ELITE P500
Semi-automatic; 45 ACP, 10-shot magazine. Barrel: 5". Weight: 40 oz. Length: 8.5" overall. Stocks: Black ultra-slim, double diamond, checkered synthetic. Sights: Dovetailed blade front, rear adjustable for windage; three-dot system. Features: Reinforced dust cover; lowered and flared ejection port; squared trigger guard; adjustable match trigger; bolstered front strap; high grip cut; high ride beavertail grip safety; steel flat mainspring housing; extended thumb lock;

skeletonized hammer, match grade sear, disconnector; Wolff springs. Introduced 1998. Made in U.S. by Entrèprise Arms.

Perf.: $600   **Exc.:** $550   **VGood:** $475

Entrèprise Tactical P500
Similar to the Elite model except has Tactical2 Ghost Ring sight or Novak lo-mount sight; ambidextrous thumb safety; front and rear slide serrations; full-length guide rod; throated barrel, polished ramp; tuned match extractor; fitted barrel and bushing; stainless firing pin; slide lapped to frame; dehorned. Introduced 1998. Made in U.S. by Entrèprise Arms.

Perf.: $750   **Exc.:** $650   **VGood:** $575

Entrèprise Medalist P500
Similar to the Elite model except has adjustable Competizione "melded" rear sight with dovetailed Patridge front; machined slide parallel rails with polished breech face and barrel channel; front and rear slide serrations; lowered and flared ejection port; full-length one-piece guide rod with plug; National Match barrel and bushing; stainless firing pin; tuned match extractor; oversize firing pin stop; throated barrel and polished ramp; slide lapped to frame. Introduced 1998. Made in U.S. by Entrèprise Arms.

Perf.: $800   **Exc.:** $650   **VGood:** $575

Entrèprise Boxer P500
Similar to the Medalist model except has adjustable Competizione "melded" rear sight with dovetailed Patridge front; high mass chiseled slide with sweep cut; machined slide parallel rails; polished breech face and barrel channel. Introduced 1998. Made in U.S. by Entrèprise Arms.

Perf.: $850   **Exc.:** $750   **VGood:** $650

ENTRÈPRISE TOURNAMENT SHOOTER MODEL I
Semi-automatic; 45 ACP, 10-shot magazine. Barrel: 5". Weight: 40 oz. Length: 8.5" overall. Stocks: Black ultra-slim double diamond checkered synthetic. Sights: Dovetailed Patridge front, adjustable Competizione "melded" rear. Features: Oversized magazine release button; flared magazine well; fully machined parallel slide rails; polished barrel channel and breech face; front and rear slide serrations; serrated top of slide; stainless ramped bull barrel with fully supported chamber; full-length guide rod with plug; stainless firing pin; match extractor; polished ramp; tuned match extractor; hard chrome finish. Introduced 1998. Made in U.S. by Entrèprise Arms.

Perf.: $1850   **Exc.:** $1600   **VGood:** $1450

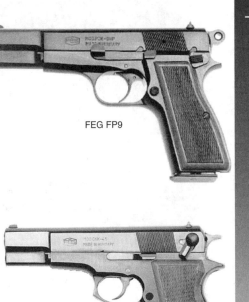

FEG B9R

FEG FP9

FEG PJK-9HP

FEG GKK-45C

FEG P9R

HANDGUNS

FEG

B9R
FP9
GKK-40C
GKK-45C
GKK-92C
Mark II AP
Mark II AP22
MBK-9HP
MBK-9HPC
P9R
PJK-9HP
PMK-380
SMC-22

FEG B9R
Semi-automatic; 380 ACP; 10-shot magazine; 4" barrel; 7" overall length; weighs 25 oz.; blade front, drift-adjustable rear sight; hand-checkered walnut grips; hammer drop safety; grooved backstrap; squared trigger guard. Introduced 1993; still imported.
New: $290   **Perf.:** $250   **Exc.:** $200

FEG FP9
Semi-automatic; single action; 9mm Para.; 10-shot magazine; 5" barrel; 7 7/8" overall length; weighs 35 oz.; checkered walnut grips; blade front sight, windage-adjustable rear; full-length ventilated rib; polished blue finish; comes with extra magazine. Imported from Hungary by Century International Arms. Introduced 1993; still imported.
New: $225   **Perf.:** $200   **Exc.:** $175

FEG GKK-40C
Semi-automatic; double action; 40 S&W; 9-shot magazine; 4 1/8" barrel; 7 3/4" overall length; weighs 36 oz.; hand-checkered walnut grips; blade front sight, windage-adjustable rear; three-dot system; combat-type trigger guard; polished blue finish; comes with two magazines, cleaning rod. Imported from Hungary by K.B.I., Inc. Introduced 1995; no longer imported.
New: $300   **Perf.:** $250   **Exc.:** $200

FEG GKK-45C
Semi-automatic; double action; 45 ACP; 8-shot magazine; 4 1/8" barrel; 7 3/4" overall length; weighs 36 oz.; hand-checkered walnut grips; blade front sight, windage-adjustable rear; three-dot system; combat-type trigger guard; polished blue finish; comes with two magazines, cleaning rod. Imported from Hungary by K.B.I., Inc. Introduced 1995; no longer imported.
New: $300   **Perf.:** $250   **Exc.:** $200

FEG GKK-92C
Semi-automatic; double action; 9mm Para.; 14-shot magazine; 4" barrel; 7 3/8" overall length; weighs 34 oz.; hand-checkered walnut grips; blade front sight, windage-adjustable rear; slide-mounted safety; hooked trigger guard; finger-grooved frontstrap; polished blue finish. Imported from Hungary by K.B.I., Inc. Introduced 1992; no longer imported.
Perf.: $300   **Exc.:** $250   **VGood:** $200

FEG MARK II AP PISTOL
Semi-automatic; double action; 380 ACP, 7-shot magazine. Barrel: 3.9". Weight: 27 oz. Length: 6.9" overall. Stocks: Checkered black composition. Sights: Blade front, rear adjustable for windage. Features: Double action. All-steel construction. Polished blue finish. Comes with two magazines. Introduced 1997. Imported from Hungary by Interarms.
Perf.: $225   **Exc.:** $200   **VGood:** $1755

FEG MARK II AP22 PISTOL
Semi-automatic; double action; 22 LR, 8-shot magazine. Barrel: 3.4". Weight: 23 oz. Length: 6.3" overall. Stocks: Checkered black composition. Sights: Blade front, rear adjustable for windage. Features: Double action. All-steel construction. Polished blue finish. Introduced 1997. Imported from Hungary by Interarms.
Perf.: $275   **Exc.:** $250   **VGood:** $225

FEG MBK-9HP
Semi-automatic; double action; 9mm Para.; 14-shot magazine; 4 5/8" barrel; 7 3/8" overall length; weighs 34 oz.; hand-checkered walnut grips; blade front sight, windage-adjustable rear; slide-mounted safety; hooked trigger guard; smooth frontstrap; polished blue finish. Imported from Hungary by K.B.I., Inc. Introduced 1992; no longer imported.
Perf.: $275   **Exc.:** $250   **VGood:** $225

FEG MBK-9HPC
Semi-automatic; double action; 9mm Para.; 14-shot magazine; 4" barrel; 7 1/4" overall length; weighs 34 oz.; hand-checkered walnut grips; blade front sight, windage-adjustable rear; slide-mounted safety; hooked trigger guard; smooth frontstrap; polished blue finish. Imported from Hungary by K.B.I., Inc. Introduced 1992; no longer imported.
Perf.: $275   **Exc.:** $250   **VGood:** $225

FEG P9R
Semi-automatic; double action; 9mm Para.; 10-shot magazine; 4 5/8" barrel; 7 15/16" overall length; weighs 35 oz.; checkered walnut grips; blade front sight, windage-adjustable rear; slide-mounted safety; all-steel construction with polished blue finish; comes with extra magazine. Imported from Hungary by Century International Arms. Introduced 1993; still imported.
New: $225   **Perf.:** $200   **Exc.:** $185

FEG PJK-9HP
Semi-automatic; single action; 9mm Para.; 10-shot magazine; 4 3/4" barrel; 8" overall length; weighs 32 oz.; hand-checkered walnut grips; blade front sight, windage-adjustable rear; three-dot system; polished blue or hard chrome finish; rounded combat-style serrated hammer; comes with two magazines and cleaning rod. Imported from Hungary by K.B.I., Inc. Introduced 1992; still imported.
New: $225   **Perf.:** $200   **Exc.:** $175

FEG PMK-380
Semi-automatic; double action; 380 ACP; 7-shot magazine; 4" barrel; 7" overall length; weighs 21 oz.; checkered black nylon thumbrest grips; blade front sight, windage-adjustable rear; anodized aluminum frame; polished blue slide; comes with two magazines, cleaning rod. Imported from Hungary by K.B.I., Inc. Introduced 1992; no longer imported.
Perf.: $200   **Exc.:** $175   **VGood:** $150

FEG SMC-22
Semi-automatic; double action; 22 LR; 8-shot magazine; 3 1/2" barrel; 6 1/8" overall length; weighs 18 1/2 oz.; checkered composition thumbrest grips; blade front sight, windage-adjustable rear; alloy frame, steel slide; blue finish; comes with two magazines, cleaning rod. Patterned after the PPK pistol. Imported from Hungary by K.B.I., Inc. Introduced 1994; still imported.
New: $200   **Perf.:** $175   **Exc.:** $150

HANDGUNS

Freedom Arms
Boot Gun
FA-S-22LR
FA-S-22M
Mini Revolver
Model 252 Silhouette
Model 97 Mid Frame
Model 252 Varmint
Model 353
Model 353 Silhouette
Model 555

Frommer
Baby Pocket Model
Liliput Pocket Model
Stop Pocket Model

FTL
Auto Nine
Pocket Partner

Gal
Compact Auto Pistol

Galesi
Model 6
Model 9

Frommer Liliput Pocket Model

FTL Auto Nine

Galesi Model 9

FREEDOM ARMS BOOT GUN
Revolver; single action; 22 LR, 22 WMR; 3" barrel; 5 7/8" overall length; weighs 5 oz.; oversize grips; floating firing pin; stainless steel construction. Introduced 1982; dropped 1990.

Perf.: $225   **Exc.:** $200   **VGood:** $175
22 WMR
Perf.: $250   **Exc.:** $200   **VGood:** $175

FREEDOM ARMS FA-S-22LR
Revolver; 22 LR; 5-shot; 1", 1 3/4", 3" barrels; blade front, notched rear sights; black ebonite grips; stainless steel construction; partial high polish finish; simulated ivory or ebony grips.

Perf.: $225   **Exc.:** $200   **VGood:** $165

FREEDOM ARMS FA-S-22M
Revolver; 22 WMR; 4-shot; 1", 1 3/4", 3" barrels; stainless steel construction; blade front, notched rear sights; simulated ivory or ebony grips.

Perf.: $75   **Exc.:** $225   **VGood:** $200

FREEDOM ARMS MINI REVOLVER
Revolver; single action; 22 LR, 22 WMR; 5-shot; 4" (22 WMR), 1", 1 3/4" barrel (22 LR); 4" overall length; blade front sight, notched rear; black ebonite grips; stainless steel construction; marketed in presentation case. Introduced 1978; dropped 1990.

Exc.: $200   **Perf.:** $175   **VGood:** $165

FREEDOM ARMS MODEL 252 SILHOUETTE
Revolver; single action; 22 LR; 5-shot cylinder, 10" barrel; weighs 63 oz.; Patridge-type front sight, click-adjustable rear; Western-style black Micarta grips; constructed of stainless steel on 454 Casull frame; lightened hammer; two-point firing pin; extra 22 WMR cylinder available. Introduced 1991; still in production.
LMSR: $1432

Perf.: $1000   **Exc.:** $850   **VGood:** $750
With extra WMR cylinder
Perf.: $1200   **Exc.:** $1000   **VGood:** $900

FREEDOM ARMS MODEL 97 MID FRAME REVOLVER
Caliber: 357 Mag., 6-shot cylinder. Barrel: 5-1/2", 7-1/2". Weight: 40 oz. (5-1/2"barrel). Length: 10-3/4"overall (5-1/2"barrel). Stocks: Wine wood. Sights: Blade on ramp front, fixed or fully adjustable rear. Features: Made of stainless steel; polished cylinder, matte frame. Introduced 1997.

New: $1250   **Perf.:** $1000   **Exc.:** $850

Freedom Arms Model 252 Varmint
Same specs as Model 252 Silhouette except 7 1/2" barrel; weighs 59 oz.; black/green laminated hardwood grips; brass bead front sight, fully-adjustable rear; extra 22 WMR cylinder available. Introduced 1991; still produced.

Perf.: $1000   **Exc.:** $800   **VGood:** $700

FREEDOM ARMS MODEL 353
Revolver; single action; 5-shot; 4 3/4", 6", 7 1/2", 9" barrel; 14" overall length (7 1/2" barrel); weighs about 59 oz.; blade front sight on ramp, fully-adjustable rear; Pachmayr rubber grips (Field Grade), impregnated hardwood grips (Premier Grade); Field Grade with matte stainless finish; Premier Grade with brush stainless finish. Introduced 1992; still in production.
Field Grade
New: $1000   **Perf.:** $900   **Exc.:** $700
Premier Grade
New: $1300   **Perf.:** $1000   **Exc.:** $800

Freedom Arms Model 353 Silhouette
Same specs as Model 353 except 9" barrel; silhouette competition sights; Field Grade finish and grips; trigger over-travel screw; front sight hood. Introduced 1992; still in production.

New: $1100   **Perf.:** $1000   **Exc.:** $850

FREEDOM ARMS MODEL 555
Revolver; single action; 50 AE; 5-shot cylinder; 4 3/4", 6", 71/2", 10" barrel; 14" overall length (71/2" barrel); weighs 50 oz.; removable blade front sight on ramp, adjustable rear; Pachmayr rubber grips on Field Grade; impregnated hardwood on Premier Grade; Field Grade with matte stainless finish; Premier Grade with brushed stainless finish. Introduced 1994; still produced.
Field Grade
New: $1100   **Perf.:** $1000   **Exc.:** $850
Premier Grade
New: $1300   **Perf.:** $1250   **Exc.:** $1000

FROMMER BABY POCKET MODEL
Semi-automatic; 32 ACP; 6-shot magazine; smaller version of Stop Pocket Model with 2" barrel; 4 3/4" overall length. Manufactured from 1919 to approximately 1922.

Exc.: $350   **VGood:** $275   **Good:** $200

FROMMER LILIPUT POCKET MODEL
Semi-automatic; blowback action; 25 ACP; 6-shot magazine; 2 1/8" barrel; 4 5/16" overall length; hard rubber stocks; fixed sights; blued finish. Manufactured 1921 to 1924.

Exc.: $250   **VGood:** $200   **Good:** $150

FROMMER STOP POCKET MODEL
Semi-automatic; 32 ACP, 380 ACP; 6-shot (380 ACP), 7-shot (32 ACP) magazine; 3 7/8" barrel; 6 1/2" overall length; external hammer; grooved wood or checkered hard rubber stocks; fixed sights; blued finish. Manufactured in Hungary, 1912 to 1920.

Exc.: $325   **VGood:** $250   **Good:** $175

FTL AUTO NINE
Semi-automatic; single action; 22 LR; 8-shot magazine; 2 1/8" barrel; 4 5/16" overall length; weighs 9 1/4 oz.; blade front sight, fixed notch rear; checkered black plastic grips; manual push-button safety; alloy frame; hard chromed slide and magazine; barrel support bushing. Made by Auto Nine Corp. Marketed by FTL Marketing Corp. Introduced 1985; no longer in production.

Perf.: $175   **Exc.:** $150   **VGood:** $125

FTL POCKET PARTNER
Semi-automatic; 22 LR; 8-shot magazine; 2 1/4" barrel; 4 3/4" overall length; weighs 10 oz.; internal hammer; fixed sights; checkered plastic stocks; all-steel construction; brushed blue finish. Introduced 1985; no longer in production.

Perf.: $125   **Exc.:** $100   **VGood:** $85

GAL COMPACT AUTO PISTOL
Caliber: 45 ACP, 8-shot magazine. Barrel: 4.25". Weight: 36 oz. Length: 7.75" overall. Stocks: Rubberized wrap-around. Sights: Low profile, fixed, three-dot system. Features: Forged steel frame and slide; competition trigger, hammer, slide stop magazine release, beavertail grip safety; front and rear slide grooves; two-tone finish. Introduced 1996. Imported from Israel by J.O. Arms, Inc.

Perf.: $425   **Exc.:** $375   **VGood:** $300

GALESI MODEL 6
Semi-automatic; 25 ACP; 6-shot magazine; 2 1/2" barrel; 4 3/8" overall length; plastic stocks; slide-top groove sights; blued finish. Manufactured in Italy. Introduced 1930; no longer in production.

Exc.: $250   **VGood:** $150   **Good:** $125

GALESI MODEL 9
Semi-automatic; 22 LR, 32 ACP, 380 ACP; 7-shot magazine; 3 1/4" barrel; plastic stocks; fixed sights; blued finish. Introduced 1930; no longer in production.

Exc.: $300   **VGood:** $250   **Good:** $175

Glock Model 24
Competition

Grendel P-10

Great Western Frontier

Glock 26

Glock 27

Glock 29

HANDGUNS

Glock
Model 24 Competition
Glock 26, 27
Glock 29, 30

Golan

Great Western
Derringer
Frontier

Grendel
P-10
P-12
P-30
P-30L
P-30M
P-31

Guardian
Guardian-SS

Glock 30 Auto Pistols

GLOCK MODEL 24 COMPETITION
Semi-automatic; double action; 40 S&W; 10-shot magazine; 6" barrel; 8 1/2" overall length; weighs 29 1/2 oz.; black polymer grips; blade front sight with dot, white outline windage-adjustable rear; long-slide competition model available as compensated or non-compensated; factory-installed competition trigger; drop-free magazine. Imported from Austria by Glock, Inc. Introduced 1994; still imported.

New: $650   **Perf.:** $525   **Exc.:** $450
Compensated barrel
New: $700   **Perf.:** $575   **Exc.:** $500

GLOCK 26, 27
Semi-automatic; 9mm Para. (M26), 10-shot magazine; 40 S&W (M27), 9-shot magazine. Barrel: 3.47". Weight: 21.75 oz. Length: 6.3" overall. Stocks: Integral. Stippled polymer. Sights: Dot on front blade, fixed or fully adjustable white outline rear. Features: Sub-compact size. Polymer frame, steel slide; double-action trigger with "Safe Action" system, three safeties. Matte black Tenifer finish. Hammer-forged barrel. Imported from Austria by Glock, Inc. Introduced 1996.

Perf.: $500   **Exc.:** $450   **VGood:** $400
Adjustable sight
Perf.: $525   **Exc.:** $475   **VGood:** $425

GLOCK 29, 30
Caliber: 10mm (M29), 45 ACP (M30), 10-shot magazine. Barrel: 3.78". Weight: 24 oz. Length: 6.7" overall. Stocks: Integral. Stippled polymer. Sights: Dot on front, fixed or fully adjustable white outline rear. Features: Compact size. Polymer frame steel slide; double-recoil spring reduces recoil; Safe Action system with three safeties; Tenifer finish. Two magazines supplied. Introduced 1997. Imported from Austria by Glock, Inc.

Perf.: $550   **Exc.:** $475   **VGood:** $425
Adjustable sight
Perf.: $575   **Exc.:** $500   **VGood:** $450

GOLAN
Semi-automatic; 9mm Para., 40 S&W, 10-shot magazine. Barrel: 3.9". Weight: 34 oz. Length: 7" overall. Stocks: Textured composition. Sights: Fixed. Features: Fully ambidextrous double/single action; forged steel slide, alloy frame; matte blue finish. Introduced 1994. Imported from Israel by J.O. Arms, Inc.

Perf.: $550   **Exc.:** $450   **VGood:** $400

GREAT WESTERN DERRINGER
Derringer; over/under; 38 S&W; 2-shot; 3" barrels; 5" overall length; checkered black plastic grips; fixed sights; blued finish. Replica of Remington Double Derringer. Manufactured 1953 to 1962.

Exc.: $275   **VGood:** $200   **Good:** $150

GREAT WESTERN FRONTIER
Revolver; single action; 22 LR, 22 Hornet, 38 Spl., 357 Mag., 44 Spl., 44 Mag., 45 Colt; 6-shot cylinder; 4 3/4", 5 1/2", 7 1/2" barrel lengths; grooved rear sight, fixed blade front; imitation stag grips; blued finish. Was sold primarily by mail order. Manufactured 1951 to 1962.

Exc.: $350   **VGood:** $300   **Good:** $250

GRENDEL P-10
Semi-automatic; double action; 380 ACP; 10-shot magazine; 3" barrel; 5 5/16" overall length; weighs 15 oz.; checkered polycarbonate metal composite grips; fixed sights; inertia safety hammer system; magazine loads from top; matte black, electroless nickel or green finish. Made in U.S. by Grendel, Inc. Introduced 1987; discontinued 1991.

Perf.: $110   **Exc.:** $90   **VGood:** $75

GRENDEL P-12
Semi-automatic; double action; 380 ACP; 10-shot magazine; 3" barrel; 5 5/16" overall length; weighs 13 oz.; checkered DuPont ST-800 polymer grips; fixed sights; inertia safety hammer system; all-steel frame; grip forms magazine well and trigger guard; blue finish. Made in U.S. by Grendel, Inc. Introduced 1992; still produced.

New: $150   **Perf.:** $125   **Exc.:** $110
Electroless nickel finish
New: $170   **Perf.:** $150   **Exc.:** $135

GRENDEL P-30
Semi-automatic; double action; 22 WMR; 30-shot magazine; 5", 8" barrel; 8 1/2" overall length (5" barrel); weighs 21 oz. (5" barrel); checkered Zytel grips;

blade front sight, fixed rear; blowback action with fluted chamber; ambidextrous safety; reversible magazine catch. Made in U.S. by Grendel, Inc. Introduced 1990; dropped 1994.

Perf.: $175   **Exc.:** $150   **VGood:** $135

Grendel P-30L
Same specs as the P-30 except 8" barrel only. Made in U.S. by Grendel, Inc. Introduced 1990; dropped 1994.

Perf.: $200   **Exc.:** $175   **VGood:** $165

Grendel P-30M
Same specs as the P-30 except removable muzzle-brake. Made in U.S. by Grendel, Inc. Introduced 1990; dropped 1994.

Perf.: $200   **Exc.:** $175   **VGood:** $150

GRENDEL P-31
Semi-automatic; 22 WMR; 30-shot magazine; 11" barrel; 17 1/2" overall length; 48 oz.; adjustable blade front, fixed rear; blowback action with fluted chamber; ambidextrous safety; muzzlebrake; scope mount optional; checkered black Zytel grip and forend; matte black finish. Made in U.S. by Grendel, Inc. Introduced 1991; dropped 1995.

Perf.: $300   **Exc.:** $250   **VGood:** $225

GUARDIAN-SS
Semi-automatic; double action; 380 ACP; 6-shot magazine; 3 1/4" barrel; 6" overall length; weighs 20 oz.; checkered walnut stocks; ramp front sight, windage-adjustable combat rear; narrow polished trigger; Pachmayr grips; blue slide; hand-fitted barrel; polished feed ramp; funneled magazine well; stainless steel. Introduced 1982; dropped 1985. Marketed by Michigan Armament, Inc.

Exc.: $300   **VGood:** $250   **Good:** $200

HANDGUNS

Hawes
Medallion Model
Trophy Model

Hawes/SIG-Sauer
P220

Heckler & Koch
HK4
Mark 23
P7 K3
P7 M8
P7 M10
P7 M13
P7 PSP
P9S
P9S Competition Kit
P9S Target
SP 89

H&K HK4

H&K P9S

H&K P7 M8

H&K P7 M13

H&K Mark 23

HAWES MEDALLION MODEL
Revolver; double action; 22 LR, 38 Spl.; 6-shot; 3", 4", 6" barrel; fixed sights; swing-out cylinder; blued finish. No longer in production.

Exc.: $135   **VGood:** $125   **Good:** $100

HAWES TROPHY MODEL
Revolver; double action; 22 LR, 38 Spl.; 6-shot; 6" barrel; adjustable sights; swing-out cylinder; blued finish. No longer in production.

Exc.: $135   **VGood:** $125   **Good:** $100

HAWES/SIG-SAUER P220
Semi-automatic; 9mm Para., 38 Super, 45 ACP; 7-shot magazine (45 ACP), 9-shot (9mm, 38); 4 3/8" barrel; 7 3/4" overall length; checkered European walnut or black plastic stocks; windage-adjustable rear sight, blade front; square combat triggerguard. Manufactured in Germany. Introduced 1977; still in production; dropped by Hawes in 1980. Also known as Browning BDA, SIG/Sauer P220.

Exc.: $450   **VGood:** $400   **Good:** $350

HECKLER & KOCH HK4
Semi-automatic; double action; 22 LR, 25 ACP, 32 ACP, 380 ACP; 8-shot magazine; 3 1/2" barrel; 6" overall length; windage-adjustable rear sight, fixed front; checkered black plastic grips; blued finish. Early version available with interchangeable barrels, magazines for four calibers. Imported from Germany originally by Harrington & Richardson, then by Heckler & Koch; importation dropped 1984.

Exc.: $350   **VGood:** $275   **Good:** $200

Four caliber set

Exc.: $750   **VGood:** $650   **Good:** $500

HECKLER & KOCH MARK 23
Semi-automatic; 45 ACP, 10-shot magazine. Barrel: 5.87". Weight: 43 oz. Length: 9.65" overall. Stocks: Integral with frame; black polymer. Sights: Blade front, rear drift adjustable for windage; three-dot. Features: Polymer frame; double action; exposed hammer; short recoil, modified Browning action. Civilian version of the SOCOM pistol. Introduced 1996. Imported from Germany by Heckler & Koch, Inc.

Exc.: $1850   **VGood:** $1500   **Good:** $1200

HECKLER & KOCH P7 K3
Semi-automatic; single action; 22 LR, 380 ACP; 8-shot magazine; 3 13/16" barrel; 26 1/2 oz.; fixed sights; black plastic grips; cocked by pressure on frontstrap; large triggerguard with heat shield; oil-filled buffer to decrease recoil; blue or nickel finish. Introduced 1988; no longer imported.

Exc.: $850   **VGood:** $700   **Good:** $600

22 LR conversion unit

Exc.: $600   **VGood:** $500   **Good:** $400

32 ACP conversion unit

Exc.: $300   **VGood:** $200   **Good:** $150

HECKLER & KOCH P7 M8
Semi-automatic; 9mm Para.; 8-shot magazine; 4 1/8" barrel; 6 3/4" overall length; weighs 29 oz.; blade front, adjustable rear sight with three-dot system; unique "squeeze cocker" system in frontstrap; gas-retarded action; squared combat-type triggerguard; stippled black plastic grips; blue finish. Imported from Germany by Heckler & Koch, Inc.

Perf.: $850   **Exc.:** $750   **VGood:** $650

HECKLER & KOCH P7 M10
Semi-automatic; 40 S&W; 10-shot magazine; 4 1/8" barrel; 7" overall length; weighs 43 oz.; blade front, adjustable rear sight with three-dot system; unique "squeeze cocker" system in frontstrap; gas-retarded action; squared combat-type triggerguard; stippled black plastic grips; blue finish. Imported from Germany by Heckler & Koch, Inc. Introduced 1992; no longer in production.

Perf.: $1000   **Exc.:** $900   **VGood:** $750

HECKLER & KOCH P7 M13
Semi-automatic; 9mm Para.; 13-shot magazine; 4 1/8" barrel; 6 1/2" overall length; 30 oz.; fixed sights; black plastic grips; cocked by pressure on frontstrap; large triggerguard with heat shield; ambi-

dextrous magazine release; blue or nickel finish. Introduced 1986; importation discontinued 1994.

Perf.: $1250   **Exc.:** $1100   **VGood:** $1000

Nickel finish

Perf.: $1350   **Exc.:** $1150   **VGood:** $1000

HECKLER & KOCH P7 PSP
Semi-automatic; single action; 9mm Para; 8-shot magazine; 4 1/8" barrel; 6 1/2" overall length; weighs 29 oz.; fixed sights; black plastic grips; cocked by pressure on frontstrap; squared combat triggerguard; blued finish. Imported from West Germany. Introduced 1982; discontinued 1986.

Perf.: $800   **Exc.:** $700   **VGood:** $600

HECKLER & KOCH P9S
Semi-automatic; double action; 9mm Para., 45 ACP; 9-shot magazine (9mm), 7-shot (45 ACP); 4" barrel; 5 7/16" overall length; fixed sights; checkered plastic grips; loaded/cocked indicators; hammer cocking lever; phosphated finish. Originally imported from Germany by Gold Rush Gun Shop in 1977, then by Heckler & Koch, Inc.; importation dropped 1984.

Exc.: $800   **VGood:** $700   **Good:** $500

Heckler & Koch P9S Competition Kit
Same specs as P9S except 9mm Para.; additional 5 1/2" barrel with weight; additional slide; adjustable sights, trigger; walnut stock. Introduced 1977; discontinued 1984.

Exc.: $1300   **VGood:** $950   **Good:** $750

Heckler & Koch P9S Target
Same specs as P9S except adjustable sights, trigger. Introduced 1977; discontinued 1984.

Exc.: $900   **VGood:** $750   **Good:** $650

HECKLER & KOCH SP 89
Semi-automatic; single action; 9mm Para.; 15-, 30-shot magazine; 4 1/2" barrel; 12 7/8" overall length; weighs 4 1/2 lbs.; black high-impact plastic grip; post front sight, fully-adjustable diopter rear; design inspired by the HK94 rifle; has special flash-hider forend. Imported from Germany by Heckler & Koch, Inc. Introduced 1989; no longer imported.

Perf.: $3500   **Exc.:** $3000   **VGood:** $2500

Price: Blue	$685.00
Price: Blue with control lever on right	$706.00
Price: Stainless steel	$731.00
Price: Stainless steel with control lever on right	$752.00

HANDGUNS
Heckler & Koch
USP 9/USP 40
USP Compact Auto Pistol
USP 45
USP45 Compact
USP45 Match
USP45 Tactical
VP 70Z

H&K USP 9mm

H&K P9S
Competition Kit

H&K P7 PSB

H&K SP 89

H&K VP 70Z

Helwan 9mm

H&K USP Compact
Auto Pistol

H&K USP45 Tactical

H&K USP45
Compact

HECKLER & KOCH USP 9/USP 40

Semi-automatic; single action/double action or double-action-only; 9mm Para., 40 S&W; 16-shot magazine (9mm), 13-shot (40 S&W); 4 1/4" barrel; 6 15/16" overall length; weighs 28 oz. (USP40); non-slip stippled black polymer grips; blade front sight, windage-adjustable rear; polymer frame; modified Browning action with recoil reduction system; single control lever; special "hostile environment" finish on all metal parts; available in SA/DA, DAO, left- and right-hand versions. Imported from Germany by Heckler & Koch, Inc. Introduced 1993; still imported.

Right-hand

New: $575	**Perf.:**$500	**Exc.:** $450

Left-hand

New: $595	**Perf.:**$550	**Exc.:** $500

Heckler & Koch USP Compact Auto Pistol

Similar to the USP except has 3.58" barrel, measures 6.81" overall, and weighs 1.60 lbs. (9mm). Available in 9mm Para. or 40 S&W with 10-shot magazine. Introduced 1996. Imported from Germany by Heckler & Koch, Inc.

Right-hand

New: $575	**Perf.:**$500	**Exc.:** $450

Left-hand

New: $595	**Perf.:**$550	**Exc.:** $500

Heckler & Koch USP 45

Same specs as USP 9/USP 40 except 45 ACP; 10-shot magazine; 4 1/8" barrel; 7 7/8" overall length; weighs 30 oz.; adjustable three-dot sight system; available in SA/DA, DAO; left- and right-hand versions. Imported from Germany by Heckler & Koch, Inc. Introduced 1995; still imported.

Right-hand

New: $625	**Perf.:** $500	**Exc.:** $450

Left-hand

New: $650	**Perf.:** $550	**Exc.:** $500

Heckler & Koch USP45 Compact

Similar to the USP45 except has stainless slide; 8-shot magazine; modified and contoured slide and frame; extended slide release; 3.80" barrel, 7.09" overall length, weighs 1.75 lbs.; adjustable three-dot sights. Introduced 1998. Imported from Germany by Heckler & Koch, Inc.

Right-hand

New: $625	**Perf.:**$500	**Exc.:** $450

Left-hand

New: $650	**Perf.:**$550	**Exc.:** $500

HECKLER & KOCH USP45 MATCH

Semi-automatic; 45 ACP, 10-shot magazine. Barrel: 6.02. Weight: 2.38 lbs. Length: 9.45. Stocks: Textured polymer. Sights: High profile target front, fully adjustable target rear. Features: Adjustable trigger stop. Polymer frame, blue or stainless steel slide. Introduced 1997. Imported from Germany by Heckler & Koch, Inc.

Blue

New: $1200	**Perf.:**$1000	**Exc.:** $850

Stainless

New: $1250	**Perf.:**$1050	**Exc.:** $900

HECKLER & KOCH USP45 TACTICAL

Semi-automatic; 45 ACP, 10-shot magazine. Barrel: 4.92". Weight: 2.24 lbs. Length: 8.64" overall. Stocks: Non-slip stippled polymer. Sights: Blade front, fully adjustable target rear. Features: Has extended threaded barrel with rubber O-ring; adjustable trigger; extended magazine floorplate; adjustable trigger stop; polymer frame. Introduced 1998. Imported from Germany by Heckler & Koch, Inc.

New: $850	**Perf.:**$750	**Exc.:** $650

HECKLER & KOCH VP 70Z

Semi-automatic; double-action-only; 9mm Para.; 18-shot magazine; 4 1/2" barrel; 8" overall length; ramp front sight, channeled rear on slide; stippled black plastic stocks; recoil-operated; only four moving parts; double-column magazine; phosphated finish. Manufactured in West Germany. Introduced 1976; importation dropped 1989.

Perf.:$450	**Exc.:** $400	**VGood:** $300

HANDGUNS

Jennings
Model J-25
Model M-38
Model M-48

Jericho
Model 941

JSL
Spitfire

Kahr
K9
K9, K40
KS40 Small Frame
MK9 Micro-Compact

Kareen
MKII Auto
MKII Compact

Kassnar
M-100D
Model M-100TC

Kahr MK9 Micro Compact Pistol

Kahr K9

Jericho Model 941

Kareen MKII Auto Pistol

Jennings Model J-25

Kassnar M-100D

JENNINGS MODEL J-25
Semi-automatic; 25 ACP; 6-shot magazine; 2 1/2" barrel; weighs 12 oz.; 4 15/16" overall length; fixed sights; synthetic walnut or black combat-style grips. Introduced 1981; still in production.
    Perf.: $65   **Exc.:** $50   **VGood:** $40

JENNINGS MODEL M-38
Semi-automatic; 22 LR, 32 ACP, 380 ACP; 2 13/16" barrel; weighs 16 oz.; non-ferrous alloy construction; black grips; chrome or blue finish.
    Perf.: $75   **Exc.:** $60   **VGood:** $50

JENNINGS MODEL M-48
Semi-automatic; 22 LR, 32 ACP, 380 ACP; 4" barrel; weighs 24 oz.; non-ferrous alloy construction; black grips; chrome or blue finish. dropped 1995.
    Perf.: $75   **Exc.:** $60   **VGood:** $50

JERICHO MODEL 941
Semi-automatic; double action; 9mm Para.; 16-shot magazine; 4 3/8" barrel; 8 1/8" overall length; weighs 33 oz.; high impact black polymer grips; blade front sight, windage-adjustable rear; three tritium dots; all steel construction; polygonal rifling; ambidextrous safety. Produced in Israel by Israel Military Industries; distributed by K.B.I., Inc. Introduced 1990; dropped 1991.
    Perf.: $450   **Exc.:** $375   **VGood:** $300

JSL SPITFIRE
Semi-automatic; double action; 9mm Para.; 15-shot magazine; 4 3/8" barrel; 8 7/8" overall length; weighs 40 oz.; textured composition grips; blade front sight, fully-adjustable rear; stainless steel construction; ambidextrous safety. Imported from England by Rogers Ltd. International. Introduced 1992; importation dropped 1993.
    Perf.: $1200   **Exc.:** $900   **VGood:** $750

KAHR K9
    Semi-automatic; double action; 9mm Para.; 7-shot magazine; 3 1/2" barrel; 6" overall length; weighs 25 oz.; wrap-around textured soft polymer grips; blade front sight, windage drift-adustable rear; bar-dot combat style; passive firing pin block; made of 4140 ordnance

steel; matte black finish. Made in U.S. by Kahr Arms. Introduced 1994; still produced. LMSR: $595
    New: $500   **Perf.:** $425   **Exc.:** $350

KAHR K9, K40
Semi-automatic; double action; 9mm Para.; 7-shot magazine; 40 S&W; 6-shot magazine; 3 1/2" barrel; 6" overall length; weighs 25 oz.; wrap-around textured soft polymer grips; blade front sight, windage drift-adustable rear; bar-dot combat style; passive firing pin block; made of 4140 ordnance steel; matte black finish. Made in U.S. by Kahr Arms. Many sight, finish options. Introduced 1994; still produced.
    New: $500   **Perf.:** $425   **Exc.:** $350

Kahr KS40 Small Frame
Same as standard K40 except 1/2" shorter grip. Comes with one 5-shot, one 6-shot magazine. Introduced 1998. Made in U.S. by Kahr Arms.
    New: $550   **Perf.:** $475   **Exc.:** $400
    With night sights. $677.00
    New: $600   **Perf.:** $525   **Exc.:** $450

Kahr MK9 Micro-Compact
Similar to the K9 except is 5.5" overall, 4" high, has a 3" barrel. Weighs 22 oz. Has snag-free bar-dot sights, polished feed ramp, dual recoil spring system, DA-only trigger. Comes with 6- and 7-shot magazines. Introduced 1998.
Matte stainless
    New: $550   **Perf.:** $475   **Exc.:** $400
Matte stainless, tritium night sights
    New: $650   **Perf.:** $575   **Exc.:** $500
    Duo-Tone (stainless frame, Black-T slide)
        $749.00
    New: $700   **Perf.:** $600   **Exc.:** $500

    Duo-Tone with tritium night sights $$836.00
    New: $775   **Perf.:** $675   **Exc.:** $600

KAREEN MKII AUTO
Semi-automatic; single action; 9mm Para.; 13 (now 10)-shot magazine; 4 3/4" barrel; 8" overall length; weighs 32 oz.; blade front sight, windage-adjustable rear; checkered European walnut grips (early model), rubberized grips (later versions); blued finish, two-tone or matte black finish, optional. Made in Israel. Introduced 1969 by Century International Arms, Inc.; still imported by J.O. Arms.
    Perf.: $350   **Exc.:** $275   **VGood:** $225

Kareen MKII Compact
Same specs as MKII except 3 1/4" barrel; 6 1/2" overall length; weighs 28 oz.; rubber grips. Introduced 1995; still in production.
    New: $350   **Exc.:** $300   **VGood:** $275

KASSNAR M-100D
Revolver; double action; 22 LR, 22 WMR, 38 Spl.; 6-shot cylinder; 3", 4", 6" barrels; target-style checkered hardwood stocks; elevation-adjustable rear sight, ramp front; vent-rib barrel. Manufactured in the Philippines by Squires Bingham; imported by Kassnar. Introduced 1977; no longer imported.
    Exc.: $125   **VGood:** $110   **Good:** $100

KASSNAR MODEL M-100TC
Revolver; double action; 22 LR, 22 WMR, 38 Spl.; 6-shot cylinder; 3", 4", 6" barrels; full ejector rod shroud; target-style checkered hardwood stocks; elevation-adjustable rear sight, ramp front; vent-rib barrel. Manufactured in the Philippines by Squires Bingham; imported by Kassnar. Introduced 1977; no longer imported.
    Exc.: $135   **VGood:** $125   **Good:** $110

HANDGUNS

Kassnar
PJK-9HP
KBI
PSP-25
KEL-TEC
P-11
Kimber
Classic 45 Custom
Classic 45 Gold Match
Classic 45 Polymer Frame
Classic 45 Royal
Compact 45
Custom Target

Kassnar PJK-9HP

Kel-Tec P-11

Kimber Classic 45 Custom

KBI PSP-25

Kimber Classic 45 Polymer Frame

Kimber Classic 45

Kimber Classic 45 Gold Match

Kimber Custom Target

KASSNAR PJK-9HP
Semi-automatic; single action; 9mm Para.; 13-shot magazine; 4 3/4" barrel; 8" overall length; weighs 32 oz.; adjustable rear sight, ramp front; checkered European walnut stocks; with or without full-length vent rib. Made in Hungary. Introduced 1986; no longer imported.
    Perf.: $225   **Exc.:** $175   **VGood:** $165

KBI PSP-25
Semi-automatic; single action; 25 ACP; 6-shot magazine; 2 1/8" barrel; 4 1/8" overall length; weighs 9 1/2 oz.; fixed sights; checkered black plastic grips; all-steel construction; polished blue or chrome finish. Close copy of Browning Baby 25 made under F.N. license. Introduced 1990; no longer in production.
    Perf.: $180   **Exc.:** $160   **VGood:** $140

KEL-TEC P-11
Semi-automatic; double-action-only; 9mm Para.; 10-shot magazine; 3 1/8" barrel; 5 9/16" overall length; weighs 14 oz.; checkered black polymer grips; blade front sight, windage-adjustable rear; ordnance steel slide, aluminum frame; blue finish. Made in U.S. by Kel-Tec CNC Industries, Inc. Introduced 1995; still produced.
    New: $250   **Perf.:** $225   **Exc.:** $200
Electroless nickel finish
    New: $350   **Perf.:** $300   **Exc.:** $235
Gray finish
    New: $280   **Perf.:** $250   **Exc.:** $200

KIMBER CLASSIC 45 CUSTOM
Semi-automatic; single action; 45 ACP; 8-shot magazine; 5" barrel; 8 1/2" overall length; weighs 38 oz.; checkered hard synthetic grips; McCormick dovetailed front sight, low combat rear; Chip McCormick Corp. forged frame and slide; match barrel; extended combat thumb safety; high beavertail grip safety; skeletonized lightweight composite trigger; skeletonized

Commander-type hammer; elongated Commander ejector; bead-blasted black oxide finish; flat mainspring housing; short guide rod; lowered and flared ejection port; serrated front and rear of slide; relief cut under trigger guard; Wolff spring set; beveled magazine well. Made in U.S. by Kimber of America, Inc. Introduced 1995; still produced.
    New: $550   **Perf.:** $500   **Exc.:** $425
Custom stainless
    New: $700   **Perf.:** $650   **Exc.:** $500

Kimber Classic 45 Gold Match
Same specs as Custom except long guide rod; polished blue finish; Bo-Mar BMCS low-mount adjustable rear sight; fancy walnut grips; tighter tolerances; comes with one 10-shot and one 8-shot magazine, factory proof target. Made in U.S. by Kimber of America, Inc. Introduced 1995; still produced.
    New: $900   **Perf.:** $800   **Exc.:** $700

Kimber Classic 45 Polymer Frame
Similar to the Classic 45 Custom except has black polymer frame with stainless steel insert, hooked trigger guard, checkered front strap. Weighs 34.4 oz., overall length 8.75". Introduced 1997.
    New: $750   **Perf.:** $675   **Exc.:** $600
Polymer Stainless $948.00
    New: $850   **Perf.:** $675   **Exc.:** $650
Polymer Target $957.00
    New: $850   **Perf.:** $675   **Exc.:** $650
Polymer Stainless Target $1,036.00
    New: $900   **Perf.:** $800   **Exc.:** $700

Kimber Classic 45 Royal
Same specs as the Custom model except has checkered diamond-pattern walnut grips; long guide rod; polished blue finish; comes with two 8-shot maga-

zines. Made in U.S. by Kimber of America, Inc. Introduced 1995; still produced.
    New: $650   **Perf.:** $600   **Exc.:** $500

Kimber Compact 45
Similar to the Classic Custom except has 4" barrel fitted directly to the slide with no bushing; full-length guide rod; 7-shot magazine; grip is .400" shorter than full-size guns. Weighs 34 oz.; Compact Aluminum weighs 28 oz. Introduced 1998.
    New: $600   **Perf.:** $500   **Exc.:** $400
Compact Stainless
    New: $700   **Perf.:** $600   **Exc.:** $500
Compact Aluminum
    New: $600   **Perf.:** $500   **Exc.:** $400

KIMBER CUSTOM TARGET
Caliber: 45 ACP, 7-shot magazine. Barrel: 5. Weight: 38 oz. Length: 8.7 overall. Stocks: Black synthetic. Sights: Blade front, Kimber fully adjustable rear; dovetailed. Features: Match trigger; beveled front and rear slide serrations; lowered, flared ejection port; full-length guide rod; Wolff springs. Introduced 1996.
Custom Target
    New: $650   **Perf.:** $600   **Exc.:** $500
Stainless Target
    New: $800   **Perf.:** $700   **Exc.:** $625

HANDGUNS

Korth
Semi-Automatic
Semi-Auto

Lahti
Finnish Model L-35
Swedish Model 40

L.A.R.
Grizzly Win. Mag. Mark I
Grizzly Win. Mag. Mark I, 8≤, 10≤
Grizzly Win. Mag. Mark II
Grizzly 44 Mag. Mark IV
Grizzly 50 Mark V

Laseraim Arms
Series I
Series II
Series III

Lahti Swedish Model 40

Lahti Finnish Model L-35

L.A.R. Grizzly Win. Mag. Mark I

L.A.R. Grizzly 50 Mark V

Laseraim Arms Series III

Korth Semi-Auto

KORTH SEMI-AUTOMATIC
Semi-automatic; double-action; 9mm Para., 9x21; 10-shot; 4", 5", 6" barrel; 10 1/2" overall length; weighs 35 oz.; forged, machined frame and slide; adjustable combat sights; checkered walnut stocks; matte or polished finish. Introduced 1985; dropped 1989. Now imported from Germany Korth U.S.A.
   Perf.: $2750   **Exc.:** $2500   **VGood:** $2000

KORTH SEMI-AUTO
Semi-automatic; double action; 9mm Para. (10-shot), 40 S&W (9-shot). Barrel: 4", 5". Weight: NA. Length: NA. Stocks: Checkered walnut. Sights: Ramped front, fully adjustable rear. Features: Forged steel construction; double action; locked breech; recoil operated. Imported from Germany by Korth U.S.A.
High-polish blued finish
   New: $6000   **Perf.:** $5500   **Exc.:** $4500
Plasma-coated matte silver finish
   New: $7000   **Perf.:** $6500   **Exc.:** $6000
Plasma-coated high-polish silver finish
   New: $7500   **Perf.:** $7000   **Exc.:** $6500

LAHTI FINNISH MODEL L-35
Semi-automatic; 9mm Para.; 8-shot magazine; 4 3/4" barrel; fixed sights; checkered plastic stocks; blued finish. Manufactured on a limited basis in Finland from 1935 to 1954.
   Exc.: $1200   **VGood:** $950   **Good:** $800

LAHTI SWEDISH MODEL 40
Semi-automatic; 9mm Para.; 8-shot magazine; 4 3/4" barrel; fixed sights; checkered plastic stocks; blued finish. Manufactured in Sweden by Husqvarna. Manufactured 1942 to 1946.
   Exc.: $375   **VGood:** $300   **Good:** $250

L.A.R. GRIZZLY WIN. MAG. MARK I
Semi-automatic; single action; 30 Mauser, 357 Mag., 357/45 Grizzly Win. Mag., 10mm, 45 ACP, 45 Win. Mag.; 7-shot magazine; 5 1/2", 6 1/2" barrel; 10 5/8" overall length; weighs 51 oz.; ramped blade front, adjustable rear sight; no-slip rubber combat grips; ambidextrous safeties; conversion units 45 to 357 Mag., 45 ACP, 10mm, 45 Win. Mag. available; phosphated finish. Introduced 1984; dropped 1999.
   Perf.: $850   **Exc.:** $750   **VGood:** $575

L.A.R. Grizzly Win. Mag. Mark I, 8", 10"
Same specs as Mark I standard except 8", 10" barrel; lengthened slide. Introduced 1984; dropped 1999.
   Perf.: $1200   **Exc.:** $1000   **VGood:** $900
10" barrel
   Perf.: $1250   **Exc.:** $1100   **VGood:** $950

L.A.R. Grizzly Win. Mag. Mark II
Same specs as the Grizzly Win. Mag. Mark I except fixed sights; standard safeties. Introduced 1986; discontinued 1986.
   Perf.: $550   **Exc.:** $450   **VGood:** $400

L.A.R. GRIZZLY 44 MAG. MARK IV
Semi-automatic; single action; 44 Mag.; 7-shot magazine; 5 1/2", 6 1/2" barrel; 10 5/8" overall length; weighs 51 oz.; ramped blade front, adjustable rear sight; no-slip rubber combat grips; beavertail grip safety; matte blue, hard chrome, chrome or nickel finish. Introduced 1991; dropped 1999.
   Perf.: $750   **Exc.:** $650   **VGood:** $575
Hand chrome, chrome or nickel finish
   Perf.: $850   **Exc.:** $750   **VGood:** $650

L.A.R. GRIZZLY 50 MARK V
Semi-automatic; single action; 50 AE; 6-shot magazine; 5 1/2", 6 1/2" barrel; 10 5/8" overall length; weighs 56 oz.; ramped blade front, adjustable rear sight; no-slip rubber combat grips; ambidextrous safeties; conversion units available; phosphated finish. Made in U.S. by L.A.R. Mfg., Inc. Introduced, 1993; dropped 1999.
   New: $900   **Perf.:** $850   **Exc.:** $750

LASERAIM ARMS SERIES I
Semi-automatic; single action; 10mm Auto, 45 ACP; 8-shot magazine (10mm), 7-shot (45 ACP); 4 3/8", 6" barrel, with compensator; 9 3/4" overall length (6" barrel); weighs 46 oz.; pebble-grained black composite grips; blade front sight, fully-adjustable rear; barrel compensator; stainless steel construction; ambidextrous safety-levers; extended slide release; integral mount for laser sight; matte black Teflon finish. Made in U.S. by Emerging Technologies, Inc. Introduced 1993; dropped 1999.
   New: $400   **Perf.:** $350   **Exc.:** $300
With adjustable sight
   New: $450   **Perf.:** $400   **Exc.:** $350

With fixed sight and Auto Illusion red dot sight system
   New: $650   **Perf.:** $600   **Exc.:** $550
With fixed sight and Laseraim Laser with Hotdot
   New: $750   **Perf.:** $700   **Exc.:** $650

LASERAIM ARMS SERIES II
Semi-automatic; single action; 10mm Auto, 45 ACP, 40 S&W; 8-shot magazine (10mm), 7-shot (45 ACP); 3 3/8", 5" barrel without compensator; weighs 43 oz. (5"), 37 oz. (3 3/8"); pebble-grained black composite grips; blade front sight, fixed or windage-adjustable rear; stainless steel construction; ambidextrous safety-levers; extended slide release; integral mount for laser sight; matte stainless finish. Made in U.S. by Emerging Technologies, Inc. Introduced 1993; dropped 1999.
   New: $450   **Perf.:** $400   **Exc.:** $350
With adjustable sight (5" barrel)
   New: $475   **Perf.:** $425   **Exc.:** $375
With fixed sight and Auto Illusion red dot sight
   New: $500   **Perf.:** $425   **Exc.:** $400
With fixed sight and Laseraim Laser with Hotdot
   New: $550   **Perf.:** $475   **Exc.:** $450

LASERAIM ARMS SERIES III
Semi-automatic; single action; 10mm Auto, 45 ACP; 8-shot magazine (10mm), 7-shot (45 ACP); 5" barrel with dual-port compensator; 7 5/8" overall length; weighs 43 oz.; pebble-grained black composite grips; blade front sight, fixed or windage-adjustable rear; stainless steel construction; ambidextrous safety-levers; extended slide release; integral mount for laser sight; matte stainless finish. Made in U.S. by Emerging Technologies, Inc. Introduced 1994; dropped 1999.
With fixed sight
   New: $500   **Perf.:** $450   **Exc.:** $400
With adjustable sight
   New: $525   **Perf.:** $475   **Exc.:** $425
With fixed sight and Dream Team Laseraim laser sight
   New: $600   **Perf.:** $550   **Exc.:** $500

Liberty Mustang

Les Incorporated
Rogak P-18

Le Francais
Pocket Model

Le Francais
Policeman Model

Le Francais
Army Model

Lignose Model 3A
Einhand

HANDGUNS

Laseraim Arms
Series IV
Le Francais
Army Model
Pocket Model
Policeman Model

Les Incorporated
Rogak P-18

Liberty
Mustang

Lignose
Model 2 Pocket
Model 2A Einhand
Model 3 Pocket
Model 3A Einhand

Liliput
4.25
25 ACP

Ljutic
LJ II
Space Pistol

Llama
IIIA Small Frame

Liliput 4.25

LASERAIM ARMS SERIES IV
Semi-Automatic; 45 ACP; 7-shot magazine; 3 3/8", 5" barrel; weighs 37 oz.; full serrated slide; diamond wood grips; stainless steel construction; blade front, fully-adjustable rear sight; ambidextrous safety levers; integral mount for laser sight. Made in U.S. by Emerging Technologies, Inc. Introduced 1996; dropped 1999.

New: $600   **Perf.:** $550   **Exc.:** $500

LE FRANCAIS ARMY MODEL
Semi-automatic; double action; 9mm Browning Long; 8-shot magazine; 5" flip up barrel; 7 3/4" overall length; fixed sights; checkered European walnut stocks; blued finish. Manufactured 1928 to 1938.

Exc.: $1200   **VGood:** $1000   **Good:** $700

LE FRANCAIS POCKET MODEL
Semi-automatic; double action; 32 ACP; 7-shot magazine; 3 1/2" flip-up barrel; 6" overall length; fixed sights; checkered hard rubber stocks; blued finish. Manufactured in France. Introduced 1950; discontinued 1965. Rare in the U.S.

Exc.: $750   **VGood:** $600   **Good:** $450

LE FRANCAIS POLICEMAN MODEL
Semi-automatic; double action; 25 ACP; 7-shot magazine; 2 1/2", 3 1/2" flip up barrel; fixed sights; hard rubber stocks; blued finish. Introduced 1914; discontinued about 1960.

Exc.: $250   **VGood:** $225   **Good:** $185

LES INCORPORATED ROGAK P-18
Semi-automatic; double action; 9mm Para.; 18-shot magazine; 5 1/2" barrel; post front sight, V-notch rear, drift adjustable for windage; checkered resin stocks; stainless steel; matte or deluxe high gloss finishes. Introduced 1977; discontinued 1981.

Exc.: $400   **VGood:** $350   **Good:** $300

Deluxe high gloss finish

Exc.: $450   **VGood:** $400   **Good:** $350

LIBERTY MUSTANG
Revolver; single action; 22 LR, 22 WMR or combo; 8-shot cylinder; 5" barrel; 10 1/2" overall length; weighs 34 oz.; blade front, adjustable rear sight; smooth rosewood grips; side ejector rod; blued finish. Imported from Italy by Liberty. Introduced 1976; discontinued 1980.

Exc.: $150   **VGood:** $135   **Good:** $110

LIGNOSE MODEL 2 POCKET
Semi-automatic; 25 ACP; 6-shot magazine; 2" barrel; 4 1/2" overall length; checkered hard rubber stocks; blued finish. Manufactured in Germany from 1920 first under Bergmann name, then Lignose to late 1920s.

Exc.: $200   **VGood:** $175   **Good:** $150

Lignose Model 2A Einhand
Same specs as Model 2 Pocket except sliding trigger guard allows slide retraction with trigger finger.

Exc.: $350   **VGood:** $250   **Good:** $200

LIGNOSE MODEL 3 POCKET
Semi-automatic; 25 ACP; 9-shot magazine; 2" barrel; 4 1/2" overall length; checkered hard rubber stocks; blued finish. Manufactured in Germany.

Exc.: $225   **VGood:** $200   **Good:** $150

Lignose Model 3A Einhand
Same specs as Model 3 Pocket except sliding trigger guard allows slide retraction with trigger finger.

Exc.: $350   **VGood:** $300   **Good:** $250

LILIPUT 4.25
Semi-automatic; 4.25mm; 6-shot; 1 13/16" barrel; 3 1/2" overall length; weighs 8 oz.; blue or nickel finish. Made by August Menz, Suhl, Germany. Introduced 1920.

Exc.: $800   **VGood:** $700   **Good:** $550

LILIPUT 25 ACP
Semi-automatic; 25 ACP; 6-shot; 2" barrel; 4 1/8" overall length; weighs 10 oz.; blue or nickel finish.

Made by August Menz, Suhl Germany. Introduced 1925.

Exc.: $250   **VGood:** $200   **Good:** $150

LJUTIC LJ II
Derringer; double action; 22 WMR; 2-shot; 2 3/4" side-by-side barrels; fixed sights; checkered walnut stocks; vent rib; positive safety; stainless steel construction. Introduced 1981; dropped 1989. About 1000 produced.

Perf.: $1500   **Exc.:** $1200   **VGood:** $1000

LJUTIC SPACE PISTOL
Single shot; bolt action; 22 WMR, 357 Mag., 44 Mag., 308 Win.; 13 1/2" barrel; scope mounts; American walnut grip, forend; button trigger; Introduced 1981; prototype only.

LLAMA IIIA SMALL FRAME
Semi-automatic; single action; 380 ACP, 32 ACP (disc. 1993); 7-shot magazine; 3 11/16" barrel; 6 1/2" overall length; weighs 23 oz.; adjustable target sights; checkered thumbrest plastic grips; vent rib; grip safety; loaded chamber indicator; blued, chrome engraved, blue engraved or gold engraved finishes. Early versions were sans vent rib, had lanyard ring, no thumbrest on grips. Introduced 1951; still in production.

HANDGUNS

Llama

VIII
IX Large Frame
IX-A Large Frame
IX-B Compact Frame
IX-C New Generation Large Frame
IX-D New Generation Compact Frame
XA Small Frame
XI
XV Small Frame

Llama IIIA Small Frame

Llama IX-C New Generation Large Model

Llama VIII

Ljutic LJII

Llama XI Large Frame

Llama Comanche

Llama XV Small Frame

Llama XV Small Frame

Blued finish
 Perf.: $250 **Exc.:** $200 **VGood:** $175
Chrome engraved
 Perf.: $275 **Exc.:** $225 **VGood:** $200
Blue engraved
 Perf.: $275 **Exc.:** $225 **VGood:** $200
Gold engraved
 Perf.: $500 **Exc.:** $450 **VGood:** $400

LLAMA VIII
Semi-automatic; 38 Super; 9-shot magazine; 5" barrel; 8 1/2" overall length; fixed sights; hand-checkered walnut grips; vent rib; grip safety; blued, chrome, chrome engraved or blued engraved finishes. Imported by Stoeger. Introduced 1952; no longer in production.
 Perf.: $275 **Exc.:** $250 **VGood:** $225
Chrome finish
 Perf.: $300 **Exc.:** $275 **VGood:** $250
Chrome engraved
 Perf.: $325 **Exc.:** $300 **VGood:** $275
Blue engraved
 Perf.: $300 **Exc.:** $250 **VGood:** $225

LLAMA IX LARGE FRAME
Semi-automatic; single action; 9mm, 38 Super, 45 ACP; 9-shot magazine (9mm, 38 Super), 7-shot (45 ACP); 5 1/8" barrel; 41 oz.; adjustable sights; black plastic grips; blued or satin chrome finish. Introduced 1936; no longer imported.
 Perf.: $325 **Exc.:** $275 **VGood:** $225
Satin chrome finish
 Perf.: $350 **Exc.:** $300 **VGood:** $250

LLAMA IX-A LARGE FRAME
Semi-automatic; 45 ACP; 7-shot magazine; 5 1/8" barrel; 8 1/2" overall length; weighs 36 oz.; hand-checkered walnut grips; vent rib; fixed sights; grip safety; loaded chamber indicator; blue, chrome, chrome engraved or blue engraved finishes. Introduced 1952; still imported as IX-C New Generation Large Frame.
 Perf.: $375 **Exc.:** $325 **VGood:** $275
Chrome finish
 Perf.: $400 **Exc.:** $350 **VGood:** $300
Chrome engraved
 Perf.: $450 **Exc.:** $400 **VGood:** $350
Blue engraved
 Perf.: $400 **Exc.:** $350 **VGood:** $300

LLAMA IX-B COMPACT FRAME
Semi-automatic; single action; 45 ACP; 7-shot magazine; 4 1/4" barrel; 7 7/8" overall length; weighs 34 oz.; checkered polymer grips; blade front sight, fully-adjustable rear; scaled-down version of Llama Large Frame; locked breech mechanism; manual and grip safeties; blue or chrome finish. Imported from Spain by SGS Importers Int'l., Inc. Introduced 1985; still imported as IX-D model.
 Perf.: $300 **Exc.:** $250 **VGood:** $225
Chrome finish
 Perf.: $325 **Exc.:** $275 **VGood:** $250

LLAMA IX-C NEW GENERATION LARGE FRAME
Semi-automatic; single action; 45 ACP; 13-shot magazine; 5 1/8" barrel; 8 1/2" overall length; 41 oz.; three-dot combat sights; military-style hammer; loaded chamber indicator; anatomically designed rubber grips; non-glare matte finish. Introduced 1994; Converted to 10-shot magazine 1995; still in production.
 New: $350 **Perf.:** $300 **Exc.:** $250

LLAMA IX-D NEW GENERATION COMPACT FRAME
Semi-automatic; single action; 45 ACP; 13-shot; 4 1/4" barrel; 7 7/8" overall length; weighs 39 oz.; three-dot combat sights; rubber grips; non-glare matte finish. Converted to 10-shot 1995; still in production.
 New: $350 **Perf.:** $300 **Exc.:** $250

LLAMA XA SMALL FRAME
Semi-automatic; 32 ACP; 7-shot magazine; 3 11/16" barrel; 6 1/2" overall length; checkered thumbrest plastic grips; grip safety; blued, chrome engraved or blue engraved finishes; successor to Llama X which had no grip safety. Imported by Stoeger. Introduced 1951; no longer in production.
 Exc.: $200 **VGood:** $175 **Good:** $150
Chrome engraved
 Exc.: $225 **VGood:** $200 **Good:** $150
Blue engraved
 Exc.: $225 **VGood:** $200 **Good:** $175

LLAMA XI
Semi-automatic; 9mm Para.; 8-shot magazine; 5" barrel; 8 1/2" overall length; adjustable sights; checkered thumbrest; plastic grips; vent rib; blued, chrome, chrome engraved or blued engraved finishes. Imported by Stoeger Arms. Introduced 1954; no longer in production.
 Perf.: $275 **Exc.:** $250 **VGood:** $200
Chrome finish
 Perf.: $300 **Exc.:** $275 **VGood:** $250
Chrome engraved
 Perf.: $325 **Exc.:** $300 **VGood:** $275
Blue engraved
 Perf.: $325 **Exc.:** $300 **VGood:** $275

LLAMA XV SMALL FRAME
Semi-automatic; 22 LR; 8-shot magazine; 3 11/16" barrel; 6 1/2" overall length; weighs 23 oz.; adjustable target sights; checkered thumbrest plastic grips; vent rib; grip safety; blued, chrome engraved or blue engraved finishes. Introduced 1951; no longer in production.
 Perf.: $225 **Exc.:** $200 **VGood:** $175
Chrome engraved
 Perf.: $250 **Exc.:** $225 **VGood:** $200
Blue engraved
 Perf.: $250 **Exc.:** $225 **VGood:** $200

HANDGUNS
Llama
Comanche
Comanche I
Comanche II
Comanche III
Martial
Martial Deluxe
Max-I Auto Pistols
Max-I New Generation
Max-I New Generation Compact Frame
Micromax 380 Auto Pistol
Minimax Series
Minimax-II Auto Pistol
Model 82

Llama Martial

Llama Minimax Series

Llama Max-I

Llama IIIA Small Frame

Llama IIIA Small Frame

Llama IIIA Small Frame

LLAMA COMANCHE
Revolver; double action; 22 LR, 357 Mag.; 6-shot cylinder; 4", 6" barrel; 9 1/4" overall length (4" barrel); weighs 28 oz.; blade front sight, fully-adjustable rear; checkered walnut stocks; ventilated rib; wide spur hammer; blue finish. Was imported from Spain by SGS Importers International, Inc. No longer imported.

Exc.: $200   **VGood:** $175   **Good:** $150

LLAMA COMANCHE I
Revolver; double action; 22 LR; 6-shot cylinder; 6" barrel; 11 1/4" overall length; target-type sights; checkered walnut stocks; blued finish. Introduced in 1977, replacing Martial 22 model; discontinued 1982.

Exc.: $200   **VGood:** $175   **Good:** $150

Llama Comanche II
Same specs as Comanche I except 38 Spl.; 4" barrel. Introduced 1977; discontinued 1982.

Exc.: $175   **VGood:** $150   **Good:** $135

Llama Comanche III
Same specs as Comanche I except 22 LR, 357 Mag.; 4", 6", 8 1/2" barrel; 9 1/4" overall length; ramp front, adjustable rear sight; blued, satin chrome or gold finish. Introduced in 1977 as "Comanche"; renamed 1977; no longer in production.

Perf.: $250   **Exc.:** $225   **VGood:** $200

Satin chrome finish
Perf.: $275   **Exc.:** $250   **VGood:** $225

Gold finish
Perf.: $750   **Exc.:** $650   **VGood:** $500

LLAMA MARTIAL
Revolver; double action; 22 LR, 38 Spl.; 6-shot cylinder; 4" barrel (38 Spl.), 6" (22 LR); 11 1/4" overall length (6" barrel); target sights; hand-checkered walnut grips; blued finish. Imported by Stoeger. Introduced 1969; discontinued 1976.

Exc.: $200   **VGood:** $175   **Good:** $150

Llama Martial Deluxe
Same specs as Martial model except choice of satin chrome, chrome engraved, blued engraved, gold engraved finishes; simulated pearl stocks.

Satin chrome finish
Exc.: $250   **VGood:** $200   **Good:** $150

Chrome engraved
Exc.: $275   **VGood:** $225   **Good:** $175

Blue engraved
Exc.: $275   **VGood:** $225   **Good:** $175

Gold engraved
Exc.: $750   **VGood:** $600   **Good:** $500

LLAMA MAX-I NEW GENERATION LARGE FRAME
Semi-automatic; single action; 9mm Para., 45 ACP; 9-shot magazine (9mm), 7-shot (45 ACP); 5 1/8" barrel; 8 1/2" overall length; weighs 36 oz.; blade front sight, windage-adjustable rear; black rubber grips; three-dot system; skeletonized combat-style hammer; steel frame; extended manual and grip safeties; blue or duo-tone finish. Imported from Spain by Import Sports, Inc. Introduced 1995; still imported.

New: $250   **Perf.:** $200   **Exc.:** $175

Duo-tone finish
New: $325   **Perf.:** $300   **Exc.:** $250

Llama Max-I New Generation Compact Frame
Same specs as the Max-I except 7-shot; 4 1/4" barrel; 7 7/8" overall length; weighs 34 oz. Imported from Spain by Import Sports, Inc. Introduced 1995; still imported.

New: $300   **Perf.:** $275   **Exc.:** $225

Duo-tone finish
New: $350   **Perf.:** $325   **Exc.:** $300

LLAMA MICROMAX 380 AUTO
Semi-automatic; 380 ACP, 7-shot magazine. Barrel: 3-11/16". Weight: 23 oz. Length: 6-1/2" overall. Stocks: Checkered high impact polymer. Sights: 3-dot combat. Features: Single action design. Mini custom

extended slide release; mini custom extended beaver-tail grip safety; combat-style hammer. Introduced 1997. Imported from Spain by Import Sports, Inc.

New: $200   **Perf.:** $175   **Exc.:** $150

Satin chrome $281.95
New: $225   **Perf.:** $250   **Exc.:** $225

LLAMA MINIMAX SERIES
Semi-automatic; 9mm Para., 8-shot; 40 S&W, 7-shot; 45 ACP, 6-shot magazine. Barrel: 3-1/2". Weight: 35 oz. Length: 7-1/3" overall. Stocks: Checkered rubber. Sights: Three-dot combat. Features: Single action, skeletonized combat-style hammer, extended slide release, cone-style barrel, flared ejection port. Introduced 1996. Imported from Spain by Import Sports, Inc.

New: $250   **Perf.:** $225   **Exc.:** $175

Duo-tone finish (45 only) or satin chrome
New: $275   **Perf.:** $250   **Exc.:** $200

Llama Minimax-II Auto
Same as the Minimax except in 45 ACP only, with 10-shot staggered magazine. Introduced 1997. Imported from Spain by Import Sports, Inc.

New: $300   **Perf.:** $275   **Exc.:** $225

Satin chrome
New: $325   **Perf.:** $300   **Exc.:** $250

LLAMA MODEL 82
Semi-automatic; double action; 9mm Para.; 15-shot magazine; 4 1/4" barrel; 8" overall length; weighs 39 oz.; blade-type front sight, drift-adjustable rear; 3-dot system; matte black polymer stocks; ambidextrous safety; blued finish. Made in Spain. Introduced 1987; discontinued 1993.

Perf.: $650   **Exc.:** $600   **VGood:** $550

HANDGUNS

Llama
Model 87 Competition Model
Omni
Super Comanche IV
Super Comanche V

Lorcin
L-9mm
L-22
L-25
L-32
L-380
LH-380
LT-25

Luger
Model 1900 Commercial
Model 1900 Swiss

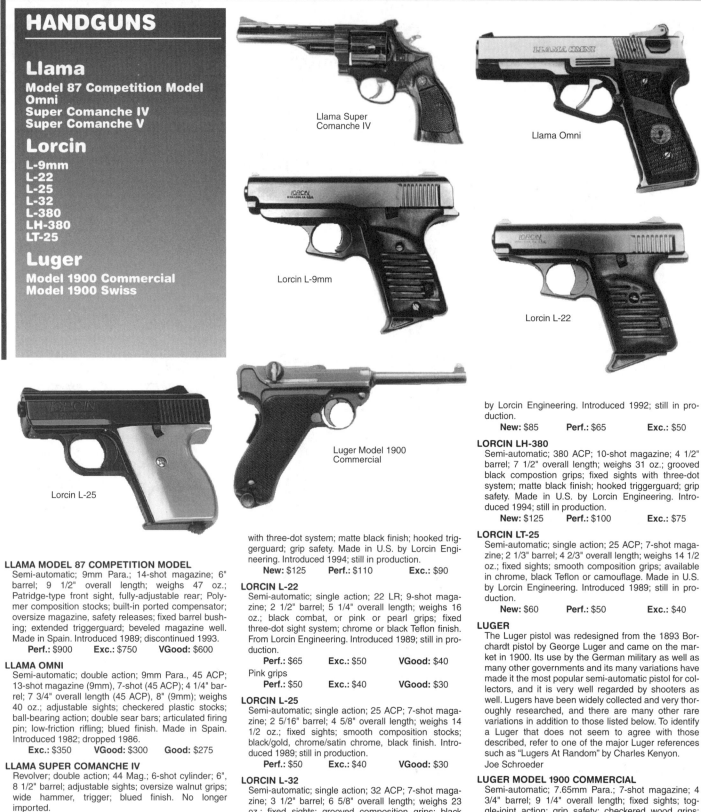

Llama Super Comanche IV

Llama Omni

Lorcin L-9mm

Lorcin L-22

Lorcin L-25

Luger Model 1900 Commercial

LLAMA MODEL 87 COMPETITION MODEL
Semi-automatic; 9mm Para.; 14-shot magazine; 6" barrel; 9 1/2" overall length; weighs 47 oz.; Patridge-type front sight, fully-adjustable rear; Polymer composition stocks; built-in ported compensator; oversize magazine, safety releases; fixed barrel bushing; extended triggerguard; beveled magazine well. Made in Spain. Introduced 1989; discontinued 1993.
Perf.: $900   **Exc.:** $750   **VGood:** $600

LLAMA OMNI
Semi-automatic; double action; 9mm Para., 45 ACP; 13-shot magazine (9mm), 7-shot (45 ACP); 4 1/4" barrel; 7 3/4" overall length (45 ACP), 8" (9mm); weighs 40 oz.; adjustable sights; checkered plastic stocks; ball-bearing action; double sear bars; articulated firing pin; low-friction rifling; blued finish. Made in Spain. Introduced 1982; dropped 1986.
Exc.: $350   **VGood:** $300   **Good:** $275

LLAMA SUPER COMANCHE IV
Revolver; double action; 44 Mag.; 6-shot cylinder; 6", 8 1/2" barrel; adjustable sights; oversize walnut grips; wide hammer, trigger; blued finish. No longer imported.
Perf.: $325   **Exc.:** $275   **VGood:** $250

Llama Super Comanche V
Same specs as Super Comanche IV except 357 Mag. only; 4" barrel also available. Discontinued 1988.
Perf.: $300   **Exc.:** $250   **VGood:** $200

LORCIN L-9MM
Semi-automatic; single action; 9mm Para.; 10-shot magazine; 4 1/2" barrel; 7 1/2" overall length; weighs 31 oz.; grooved black composition grips; fixed sights with three-dot system; matte black finish; hooked triggerguard; grip safety. Made in U.S. by Lorcin Engineering. Introduced 1994; still in production.
New: $125   **Perf.:** $110   **Exc.:** $90

LORCIN L-22
Semi-automatic; single action; 22 LR; 9-shot magazine; 2 1/2" barrel; 5 1/4" overall length; weighs 16 oz.; black combat, or pink or pearl grips; fixed three-dot sight system; chrome or black Teflon finish. From Lorcin Engineering. Introduced 1989; still in production.
Perf.: $65   **Exc.:** $50   **VGood:** $40
Pink grips
Perf.: $50   **Exc.:** $40   **VGood:** $30

LORCIN L-25
Semi-automatic; single action; 25 ACP; 7-shot magazine; 2 5/16" barrel; 4 5/8" overall length; weighs 14 1/2 oz.; fixed sights; smooth composition stocks; black/gold, chrome/satin chrome, black finish. Introduced 1989; still in production.
Perf.: $50   **Exc.:** $40   **VGood:** $30

LORCIN L-32
Semi-automatic; single action; 32 ACP; 7-shot magazine; 3 1/2" barrel; 6 5/8" overall length; weighs 23 oz.; fixed sights; grooved composition grips; black Teflon or chrome finish with black grips. Made in U.S. by Lorcin Engineering. Introduced 1992; still in production.
New: $70   **Perf.:** $65   **Exc.:** $50

LORCIN L-380
Semi-automatic; single action; 380 ACP; 7-shot magazine; 3 1/2" barrel; 6 5/8" overall length; weighs 23 oz.; fixed sights; grooved composition grips; black Teflon or chrome finish with black grips. Made in U.S. by Lorcin Engineering. Introduced 1992; still in production.
New: $85   **Perf.:** $65   **Exc.:** $50

LORCIN LH-380
Semi-automatic; 380 ACP; 10-shot magazine; 4 1/2" barrel; 7 1/2" overall length; weighs 31 oz.; grooved black compostion grips; fixed sights with three-dot system; matte black finish; hooked triggerguard; grip safety. Made in U.S. by Lorcin Engineering. Introduced 1994; still in production.
New: $125   **Perf.:** $100   **Exc.:** $75

LORCIN LT-25
Semi-automatic; single action; 25 ACP; 7-shot magazine; 2 1/3" barrel; 4 2/3" overall length; weighs 14 1/2 oz.; fixed sights; smooth composition grips; available in chrome, black Teflon or camouflage. Made in U.S. by Lorcin Engineering. Introduced 1989; still in production.
New: $60   **Perf.:** $50   **Exc.:** $40

LUGER
The Luger pistol was redesigned from the 1893 Borchardt pistol by George Luger and came on the market in 1900. Its use by the German military as well as many other governments and its many variations have made it the most popular semi-automatic pistol for collectors, and it is very well regarded by shooters as well. Lugers have been widely collected and very thoroughly researched, and there are many other rare variations in addition to those listed below. To identify a Luger that does not seem to agree with those described, refer to one of the major Luger references such as "Lugers At Random" by Charles Kenyon.
Joe Schroeder

LUGER MODEL 1900 COMMERCIAL
Semi-automatic; 7.65mm Para.; 7-shot magazine; 4 3/4" barrel; 9 1/4" overall length; fixed sights; toggle-joint action; grip safety; checkered wood grips; blued finish. Toggle marked in script "DWM" for Deutsche Waffen und Munitionsfabrik. Distinguished by dished toggle knobs with a lock, recessed breechblock.
Exc.: $3250   **VGood:** $2750   **Good:** $2000

Luger Model 1900 Swiss
Same specs as Model 1900 Comercial except Swiss cross on chamber.
Exc.: $3750   **VGood:** $2750   **Good:** $2000

Rossi Model
511 Sportsman

Rossi Model 68

HANDGUNS

Rossi

**Model 89 Stainless
Model 94
Model 511 Sportsman
Model 515
Model 518
Model 720
Model 720C
Model 851
877 Revolver
Model 941
Model 951
Model 971
Model 971 Comp Gun
Model 971 Stainless
Model 971` VRC Revolver**

Rossi Lady Rossi

Rossi Model 518

Rossi Model 720C

Rossi Model 971
Comp Gun

Rossi Model 951

Rossi Model 851

ROSSI MODEL 89 STAINLESS
Revolver; double action; 32 S&W; 6-shot; 3" barrel; 8 3/4" overall length; weighs 21 oz.; ramp front sight, drift-adjustable square notch rear; checkered wood or rubber stocks; stainless steel; matte finish. Introduced 1985; discontinued 1986; reintroduced 1989; no longer imported.
    Exc.: $160   **VGood:** $150   **Good:** $125

ROSSI MODEL 94
Revolver; double action; 38 Spl.; 6-shot; 3", 4" barrel; 27 1/2 oz.; ramp front sight; adjustable rear; checkered wood stocks; blued finish. Introduced 1985; discontinued 1988.
    Exc.: $175   **VGood:** $150   **Good:** $135

ROSSI MODEL 511 SPORTSMAN
Revolver; double action; 22 LR; 6-shot; 4" barrel; 9" overall length; weighs 30 oz.; adjustable square-notch rear sight, orange-insert ramp front; checkered wood stocks; heavy barrel; integral sight rib; shrouded ejector rod; stainless steel construction. Made in Brazil. Introduced 1986; discontinued 1990.
    Exc.: $150   **VGood:** $135   **Good:** $125

ROSSI MODEL 515
Revolver; double action; 22 WMR; 6-shot cylinder; 4" barrel; 9" overall length; weighs 30 oz.; checkered wood and finger-groove wrap-around rubber grips; blade front sight with red insert, fully-adjustable rear; small frame; stainless steel construction; solid integral barrel rib. Imported from Brazil by Interarms. Introduced 1994; still imported.
    New: $200   **Perf.:** $175   **Exc.:** $150

ROSSI MODEL 518
Revolver; double action; 22 LR; 6-shot cylinder; 4" barrel; 9" overall length; weighs 30 oz.; checkered wood and finger-groove wrap-around rubber grips; blade front sight with red insert, fully-adjustable rear; small frame; stainless steel construction; solid integral barrel rib. Imported from Brazil by Interarms. Introduced 1994; no longer imported.
    New: $200   **Perf.:** $185   **Exc.:** $160

ROSSI MODEL 720
Revolver; double action; 44 Spl.; 5-shot cylinder; 3" barrel; 8" overall length; weighs 27 1/2 oz.; checkered rubber, combat-style grips; red insert front sight on ramp, fully-adjustable rear; all stainless steel construction; solid barrel rib; full ejector rod shroud. Imported from Brazil by Interarms. Introduced 1992.
    New: $225   **Perf.:** $175   **Exc.:** $150

Rossi Model 720C
Same specs as the Model 720 except spurless hammer; double-action only. Imported from Brazil by Interarms. Introduced 1992; no longer imported.
    New: $200   **Perf.:** $165   **Exc.:** $135

ROSSI MODEL 851
Revolver; double action; 38 Spl.; 6-shot; 3", 4" barrel; 8" overall length (3" barrel); weighs 27 1/2 oz.; red-insert blade front sight, windage-adjustable rear; checkered Brazilian hardwood grips; medium-size frame; stainless steel construction; vent rib. Introduced 1991; no longer imported.
    New: $200   **Perf.:** $175   **Exc.:** $135

ROSSI MODEL 877 REVOLVER
Caliber: 357 Mag., 6-shot cylinder. Barrel: 2". Weight: 26 oz. Length: NA. Stocks: Stippled synthetic. Sights: Blade front, fixed groove rear. Features: Stainless steel construction; fully enclosed ejector rod. Introduced 1996. no longer imported.
    Perf.: $200   **Exc.:** $165   **VGood:** $140

ROSSI MODEL 941
Revolver; double action; 38 Spl.; 6-shot; 4" solid rib barrel; 9" overall length; weighs 30 oz.; colored insert front sight, adjustable rear; checkered hardwood combat stocks; shrouded ejector rod; blued finish. Made in Brazil. Introduced 1985; discontinued 1990.
    Exc.: $175   **VGood:** $150   **Good:** $125

ROSSI MODEL 951
Revolver; double action; 38 Spl.; 6-shot; 4" vent-rib barrel; 9" overall length; weighs 30 oz.; colored insert front sight, adjustable rear; checkered hardwood combat stocks; shrouded ejector rod; blued finish. Made in Brazil. Introduced 1985; discontinued 1990.
    Exc.: $175   **VGood:** $150   **Good:** $125

ROSSI MODEL 971
Revolver; double action; 357 Mag.; 6-shot; 2 1/2", 4", 6" heavy barrel; 9" overall length; weighs 36 oz.; blade front sight, fully-adjustable rear; checkered Brazilian hardwood grips; matted sight rib; target trigger; wide checkered hammer spur; full-length ejector rod shroud; blued (4" only) or stainless finish. Made in Brazil. Introduced 1988; no longer imported.
    New: $200   **Perf.:** $175   **Exc.:** $150

Rossi Model 971 Comp Gun
Same specs as Model 971 except stainless finish; 3 1/4" barrel with integral compensator; overall length 9"; weighs 32 oz.; red insert front sight, fully-adjustable rear; checkered, contoured rubber grips. Imported from Brazil by Interarms. Introduced 1993; no longer imported
    New: $225   **Perf.:** $200   **Exc.:** $175

Rossi Model 971 Stainless
Same general specs as Model 971 except 2 1/2", 4", 6" barrel; rubber grips; stainless steel construction. Introduced 1989; no longer imported.
    New: $225   **Perf.:** $200   **Exc.:** $175

Rossi Model 971 VRC Revolver
Similar to the Model 971 except has Rossi's 8-port Vented Rib Compensator; checkered finger-groove rubber grips; stainless steel construction. Available with 2.5", 4", 6" barrel; weighs 30 oz. with 2-5/8" barrel. Introduced 1996. No longer imported.
    Perf.: $275   **Exc.:** $235   **VGood:** $200

SIG Sauer
P220 "American"
P225
P226
P228
P229
P229 S Auto Pistol
P230
P230 SL Stainless
P232
P239 Pistol

SIG Sauer P232

SIG Sauer P220 "American"

SIG Sauer P226

SIG Sauer P228

SIG Sauer P230

SIG SAUER P220 "AMERICAN"
Semi-automatic; double action; 38 Super, 45 ACP; 9-shot (38 Super), 7-shot (45 ACP) magazine; 4 3/8" barrel; 7 3/4" overall length; weighs 28 1/4 oz. (9mm); checkered black plastic grips; blade front sight, drift-adjustable rear; squared combat-type trigger guard; side-button magazine release. Im ported from Germany by SIGARMS, Inc. Still imported but only in 45 ACP.

New: $650	**Perf.:** $600	**Exc.:** $500

With Siglite night sights

New: $750	**Perf.:** $700	**Exc.:** $575

With K-Kote finish

New: $675	**Perf.:** $625	**Exc.:** $525

With K-Kote finish, Siglite night sights

New: $800	**Perf.:** $750	**Exc.:** $600

SIG SAUER P225
Semi-automatic; double action, DA-only; 9mm Para.; 8-shot; 3 7/8" barrel; 7 3/32" overall length; weighs 26 oz.; blade-type front sight, windage-adjustable rear; checkered black plastic grips; squared combat-type trigger guard; shorter, lighter version of P220; blued finish. Made in Germany. Introduced 1985, dropped 1998.

New: $600	**Perf.:** $550	**Exc.:** $450

K-Kote finish

New: $650	**Perf.:** $600	**Exc.:** $500

Nickel finish

New: $650	**Perf.:** $600	**Exc.:** $500

Siglite night sights

New: $700	**Perf.:** $650	**Exc.:** $525

SIG SAUER P226
Semi-automatic; double action, DA-only; 9mm Para.; 15-, 20-shot; 4 3/8" barrel; weighs 26 1/2 oz.; high contrast sights; black plastic checkered stocks; blued finish. Made in Germany. Introduced 1983; still imported.

New: $700	**Perf.:** $600	**Exc.:** $500

K-Kote finish

New: $750	**Perf.:** $650	**Exc.:** $550

Nickel finish

New: $750	**Perf.:** $650	**Exc.:** $550

Siglite night sights

New: $800	**Perf.:** $700	**Exc.:** $575

SIG SAUER P228
Semi-automatic; double action, DA-only; 9mm Para.; 10-shot; 3 7/8" barrel; 7" overall length; weighs 29 oz.; three-dot sights; black plastic grips; blued finish. Made in Germany. Introduced 1989; dropped 1997.

New: $650	**Perf.:** $550	**Exc.:** $475

K-Kote finish

New: $700	**Perf.:** $600	**Exc.:** $500

Nickel finish

New: $700	**Perf.:** $600	**Exc.:** $500

Siglite night sights

New: $750	**Perf.:** $650	**Exc.:** $550

SIG SAUER P229
Semi-automatic; double action, DA-only; 9mm Para., 40 S&W, 357 SIG; 12-shot; 3 7/8" barrel; 7" overall length; 30 1/2 oz.; three-dot sights; checkered black plastic grips; aluminum alloy frame; blued slide. Made in Germany. Introduced 1991; still produced.

New: $700	**Perf.:** $600	**Exc.:** $500

Siglite night sights

New: $800	**Perf.:** $700	**Exc.:** $575

Nickel

New: $850	**Perf.:** $750	**Exc.:** $650

SIG Sauer P229 S Auto Pistol
Similar to the P229 except available in 357 SIG only; 4.8" heavy barrel; 8.6" overall length; weighs 40.6 oz.; vented compensator; adjustable target sights; rubber grips; extended slide latch and magazine release. Made of stainless steel. Introduced 1998.

New: $1100	**Perf.:** $950	**Exc.:** $750

SIG SAUER P230
Semi-automatic; double action; 22 LR, 32 ACP, 380 ACP, 9mm Ultra; 10-shot (22 LR), 8-shot (32 ACP), 7-shot (380 ACP, 9mm); 3 3/4" barrel; 6 1/2" overall length; weighs 16 oz.; fixed sights; checkered black plastic stocks; blued finish. Introduced 1977; dropped 1996. Manufactured in Germany.

New: $400	**Perf.:** $350	**Exc.:** $300

SIG Sauer P230 SL Stainless
Same specs as P230 except stainless steel; 22 oz.

New: $450	**Perf.:** $400	**Exc.:** $350

SIG SAUER P232
Semi-automatic; double action. Improved version of P230; 32 ACP, 380 ACP, 8-shot (32 ACP), 7-shot (380 ACP); 3 3/4" barrel; 6 1/2" overall length; weighs 16 oz.; fixed sights; checkered black plastic stocks; blued finish. Introduced 1997. Imported from Germany by SIGARMS, Inc.

New: $500	**Perf.:** $600	**Exc.:** $500

SIG SAUER P239
Semi-automatic; double action; 9mm Para., 8-shot, 357 SIG, 40 S&W, 7-shot magazine. Barrel: 3.6" Weight: 25.2 oz. Length: 6.6" overall. Stocks: Checkered black composite. Sights: Blade front, rear adjustable for windage. Optional Siglite night sights. Features: SA/DA or DAO; blackened stainless steel slide, aluminum alloy frame. Introduced 1996.

New: $600	**Perf.:** $500	**Exc.:** $450

With Siglite night sights

New: $675	**Perf.:** $550	**Exc.:** $500

SMITH & WESSON
The section on Smith & Wesson handguns has been reorganized to make it easier to use and understand. First, it has been divided into revolvers and semi-automatics with revolvers listed first.

Second, these two major areas are delineated further with revolvers divided into four distinct groups: Early Models, Small (I and J) Frames, Medium (K and L) Frames, Large (N) Frames; and semi-automatics divided into five groups: Pre-WWII, Post-WWII, 2nd Generation, 3rd Generation and Rimfire Target.

Today's Smith & Wessons all bear a model number and serial number. However, prior to 1958, S&W handguns bore only a serial number along with the specific name of that model, e.g. 38 Military & Police. In 1958, the factory began using a model numbering system. On revolvers, the model designation is stamped in the yoke cut in the frame and covered by the cylinder arm when the cylinder is in the closed postion. The official serial number can be found on the butt of the gun. For revolvers factory-issued with target stocks that cover the butt, the serial number is

Smith & Wesson
Bodyguard (Model 649)

Smith & Wesson
Centennial (Model 40)

Smith & Wesson 1977 22/32
Kit Gun M.R.F. (Model 63)

Smith & Wesson
Centennial (Model 640)

Smith & Wesson Chief's
Special (Model 36)

HANDGUNS

Smith & Wesson Revolvers

1960 22/32 Kit Gun M.R.F.
(Model 51)
1977 22/32 Kit Gun M.R.F.
(Model 63)
Airweight Kit Gun (Model 43)
Bodyguard (Model 49)
Bodyguard (Model 649)
Bodyguard Airweight
(Model 38)
Centennial (Model 40)
Centennial (Model 640)
Centennial (Model 940)
Centennial Airweight
(Model 42)
Centennial Airweight
(Model 442)
Centennial Airweight
(Model 642)
Chief's Special (Model 36)

also stamped on the frame in the area under the yoke. Serial numbers that begin with a letter indicate post-World War II manufacture. The new triple-alpha/four-numeric system began in 1980. Caution:

1. There is also a number stamped on the yoke which is called the work number. There is no relationship between this number and the serial number.

2. Handguns are classified by basic model numbers. The number following the model number is called the dash number and is necessary only when ordering parts.

On semi-automatics, the serial number can be found on the left side of the frame along with the model designation.

Roy Jinks

SMITH & WESSON 1960 22/32 KIT GUN M.R.F. (MODEL 51)

Revolver; 22 WMR; 3 1/2" barrel; 8" overall length; weighs 24 oz.; all steel frame and cylinder; fixed 1/10" serrated front ramp, micro-click adjustable rear; checkered walnut, round or square-butt stocks; blue or nickel finish. Introduced 1960; dropped 1974.

   Exc.: $325   **VGood:** $275   **Good:** $225

Nickel finish

   Exc.: $350   **VGood:** $300   **Good:** $250

SMITH & WESSON 1977 22/32 Kit Gun M.R.F. (MODEL 63)

Revolver; 22 LR; 6-shot; 2", 4" barrel; 8" overall length (4" barrel); weighs 24 1/4 oz.; stainless steel construction; fixed 1/10" serrated front ramp sight, micro-click adjustable rear; round butt soft rubber or checkered walnut square-butt stocks with medallion; satin finish. Introduced 1977; still in production.

   New: $375   **Perf.:** $325   **Exc.:** $250

SMITH & WESSON AIRWEIGHT KIT GUN (MODEL 43)

Revolver; 22 LR; 3 1/2" barrel; 8" overall length; weighs 14 1/4" oz.; alloy aluminum frame and cylinder; fixed 1/10" serrated front ramp, micro-click adjustable rear; checkered walnut, round or square-butt stocks; blue or nickel finish. Introduced 1955; dropped 1974.

   Exc.: $350   **VGood:** $300   **Good:** $250

SMITH & WESSON BODYGUARD (MODEL 49)

Revolver; double action; 38 Spl.; 5-shot; 2" barrel; 6 5/16" overall length; steel construction; weighs 20 1/2 oz.; fixed 1/10" serrated front ramp, square notch rear; features shrouded hammer that can be cocked manually for single-action firing. Introduced 1955; dropped 1996.

   Perf.: $250   **Exc.:** $200   **VGood:** $175

SMITH & WESSON BODYGUARD (MODEL 649)

Revolver; double action; 38 Spl.; 5-shot; 2" barrel; 6 5/16" overall length; weighs 20 1/2 oz.; stainless steel construction; fixed 1/10" serrated front ramp, square notch rear; satin finish; features shrouded hammer that can be cocked manually for single-action firing. Introduced 1955; still in production.

   Perf.: $375   **Exc.:** $325   **VGood:** $250

SMITH & WESSON BODYGUARD AIRWEIGHT (MODEL 38)

Revolver; double action; 38 Spl.; 5-shot; 2" barrel; 6 5/16" overall length; weighs 14 1/2 oz.; fixed 1/10" serrated front ramp, square notch rear; blue or nickel finish; features shrouded hammer that can be cocked manually for single-action firing. Introduced 1955; dropped 1998.

   Perf.: $350   **Exc.:** $250   **VGood:** $200

SMITH & WESSON CENTENNIAL (MODEL 40)

Revolver; double action; 38 Spl; 5-shot; 2" barrel; 6 1/2" overall length; weighs 19 oz.; concealed hammer; fixed 1/10" serrated front ramp, square notch rear. Swing-out version of earlier top-break design with grip safety. Introduced 1953; dropped 1974. Collector value.

   Exc.: $400   **VGood:** $350   **Good:** $275

SMITH & WESSON CENTENNIAL (MODEL 640)

Revolver; double action; 38 Spl.; 5-shot; 2", 3" barrel; 6 5/16" overall length; weighs 20 oz.; serrated ramp front, fixed notch rear sight; Goncalo Alves round-butt grips; stainless steel version of the Model 40 sans grip safety; concealed hammer; smoothed edges. Introduced 1990; still in production.

   New: $375   **Perf.:** $325   **Exc.:** $275

SMITH & WESSON CENTENNIAL (MODEL 940)

Revolver; double action; 9mm Para.; 5-shot; 2", 3" barrel; 6 5/16" overall length; weighs 20 oz.; serrated ramp front, fixed notch rear sight; rubber grips; stainless steel version of the Model 40 sans grip safety; concealed hammer; smoothed edges. Introduced 1990; dropped 1998.

   New: $375   **Perf.:** $325   **Exc.:** $275

SMITH & WESSON CENTENNIAL AIRWEIGHT (MODEL 42)

Revolver; double action; 38 Spl; 5-shot; 2" barrel; 6 1/2" overall length; concealed hammer; aluminum alloy frame and cylinder; fixed 1/10" serrated front ramp, square notch rear. Lightweight version of Model 40. Introduced 1953; dropped 1974. Collector value.

Blue

   Exc.: $400   **VGood:** $350   **Good:** $250

Nickel

   Exc.: $950   **VGood:** $750   **Good:** $450

SMITH & WESSON CENTENNIAL AIRWEIGHT (MODEL 442)

Revolver; double action; 38 Spl.; 5-shot cylinder; 2" barrel; weighs 15 3/4 oz.; 6 5/8" overall length; Uncle Mike's Custom Grade Santoprene grips; serrated ramp front sight, fixed notch rear; alloy frame; carbon steel barrel and cylinder; concealed hammer. Made in U.S. by Smith & Wesson. Introduced 1993; still produced.

   New: $350   **Perf.:** $300   **Exc.:** $250

Nickel finish

   New: $375   **Perf.:** $325   **Exc.:** $275

SMITH & WESSON CENTENNIAL AIRWEIGHT (MODEL 642)

Revolver; double action; 38 Spl.; 5-shot; 2" carbon steel barrel; 6 5/16" overall length; anodized alloy frame; weighs 15 oz.; serrated ramp front, fixed notch rear sight; Uncle Mike's Custom Grade Santoprene grips; same as the Model 40 sans grip safety; concealed hammer; smoothed edges. Introduced 1990; still in production.

   Perf.: $400   **Exc.:** $350   **VGood:** $250

SMITH & WESSON CHIEF'S SPECIAL (MODEL 36)

Revolver; double action; 38 Spl.; 5-shot; 2", 3" barrel; 7 3/8" overall length (3" barrel); weighs 21 1/2 oz.; fixed 1/10" serrated front ramp, square notch rear; all steel frame and cylinder; checkered round butt soft rubber grips most common; square-butt available; blue or nickel finish. Dropped 1999.

   New: $275   **Perf.:** $225   **Exc.:** $175

HANDGUNS

Smith & Wesson

Chief's Special Airweight (Model 37)
Model 637 Airweight Revolver
Chief's Special Stainless (Model 60)
Model 60 357 Magnum Chiefs Special
Ladysmith (Model 36-LS)
Ladysmith (Model 60-LS)
Model 60 3≤ Full Lug
Model 651
Target Model 1953 (Model 35)
Terrier (Model 32)
K and L Medium Frame Revolvers
32-20 Hand Ejector
38 Military & Police

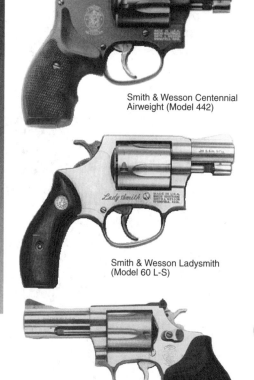

Smith & Wesson Centennial Airweight (Model 442)

Smith & Wesson Chief's Special Airweight (Model 37)

Smith & Wesson Ladysmith (Model 60 L-S)

Smith & Wesson Model 637 Airweight Revolver

Smith & Wesson Target Model 1953 (Model 35)

Smith & Wesson Model 60 357 Mangum Chief's Special

Smith & Wesson Model 651

SMITH & WESSON CHIEF'S SPECIAL AIRWEIGHT (MODEL 37)
Revolver; double action; 38 Spl.; 5-shot; 2" barrel; 6 1/2" overall length; weighs 19 1/2 oz.; lightweight version of Model 36, incorporating aluminum alloy frame; weighs 14 1/2 oz.; fixed 1/10" serrated front ramp, square notch rear; all steel frame and cylinder; checkered round butt grips most common; square-butt available; blue or nickel finish. Still in production.
New: $350   **Perf:** $275   **Exc.:** $225

Smith & Wesson Model 637 Airweight Revolver
Similar to the Model 37 Airweight except has alloy frame, stainless steel barrel, cylinder and yoke; rated for 38 Spec. +P; Uncle Mike's Boot Grip. Weighs 15 oz. Introduced 1996.
New: $375   **Perf.:** $300   **Exc.:** $225

SMITH & WESSON CHIEF'S SPECIAL STAINLESS (MODEL 60)
Revolver; double action; 38 Spl.; 5-shot; 2" barrel; 6 1/2" overall length; weighs 19 oz.; stainless steel construction; fixed 1/10" serrated front ramp, square notch rear; checkered walnut round butt grips. Dropped 1996.
New: $300   **Perf.:** $250   **Exc.:** $225

Smith & Wesson Model 60 357 Magnum Chiefs Special
Similar to the Model 60 in 38 Special except is 357 Magnum; 2-1/8" or 3" barrel. Weighs 24 oz.; 7-1/2" overall length (3" barrel). Has Uncle Mike's Combat grips.
New: $400   **Perf.:** $350   **Exc.:** $275

SMITH & WESSON LADYSMITH (MODEL 36-LS)
Revolver; double action; 38 Spl.; 5-shot; 2" barrel; 6 5/16" overall length; weighs 20 oz.; carbon steel construction; serrated front ramp, square notch rear; rosewood laminate grips; comes in fitted carry/storage case; blue finish. Introduced 1989; still in production.
New: $350   **Perf.:** $300   **Exc.:** $225

SMITH & WESSON LADYSMITH (MODEL 60-LS)
Revolver; double action; 38 Spl.; 5-shot; 2" barrel; 6 5/16" overall length; weighs 20 oz.; stainless steel construction; serrated front ramp, square notch rear; rosewood laminate grips; stainless satin finish. Introduced 1989; still in production.
New: $350   **Perf.:** $300   **Exc.:** $250

SMITH & WESSON MODEL 60 3" FULL LUG
Revolver; double action; 38 Spl.; 5-shot; 3" full lug barrel; 7 1/2" overall length; weighs 24 1/2 oz.; stainless steel construction; fixed pinned black ramp front sight, adjustable black blade rear; rubber combat grips. Introduced 1991; Still in production.
New: $350   **Perf.:** $300   **Exc.:** $250

SMITH & WESSON MODEL 651
Revolver; double action; 22 WMR; 6-shot cylinder; 4" heavy barrel; 8 11/16" overall length; weighs 24 1/2 oz.; stainless steel construction; ramp front, adjustable micrometer-click rear; semi-target hammer; combat trigger; soft rubber or checkered walnut square-butt stocks with medallion; satin finish. Introduced 1983; dropped 1998.
Exc.: $300   **VGood:** $250   **Good:** $150

SMITH & WESSON TARGET MODEL 1953 (MODEL 35)
Revolver; 22 LR; 6-shot; 6" barrel; 10 1/2" overall length; weighs 25 oz.; ribbed barrel; micrometer rear sight; Magna-type stocks; flattened cylinder latch; blue finish. A redesign of the 22/32 Target model. Introduced 1953; dropped 1974.
Exc.: $300   **VGood:** $200   **Good:** $175

SMITH & WESSON TERRIER (MODEL 32)
Revolver; 38 S&W, 38 Colt New Police; 5-shot; 2" barrel; 6 1/4" overall length; weighs 17 oz.; fixed sights with 1/10" serrated ramp front, square notch rear; round butt checkered walnut stocks with medallion; blue or nickel finish. Introduced 1936; dropped 1974.
Exc.: $250   **VGood:** $175   **Good:** $125

K AND L MEDIUM FRAME REVOLVERS
Smith & Wesson's original medium-frame revolver was the "K" frame introduced in 1899. In 1980, S&W offered an improved medium frame revolver for the 357 Magnum cartridge and this new frame was called the "L" frame.

SMITH & WESSON 32-20 HAND EJECTOR
Revolver; 32 Winchester; 6-shot; 4", 5", 6", 6 1/2" barrels; fixed or adjustable sights (rare); hard black rubber round or checkered walnut square-butt grips; caliber marking on early models, 32 Winchester; late models, 32 W.C.F., marked 32/20.
Exc.: $400   **VGood:** $325   **Good:** $175

SMITH & WESSON 38 MILITARY & POLICE
Revolver; double action; 38 Spl.; 6-shot; 4", 5", 6", 6 1/2" barrels; hard rubber round butt (early models) or checkered walnut square-butt grips; blue or nickel finish. The first S&W K-frame was the 38 Hand Ejector which later became known as the 38 Military & Police. This model was introduced in 1899 and has been in continuous production. During the last 96 years, S&W has produced over 5 million of these revolvers, resulting in numerous variations which affect values only slightly. The most collectable of these, the 38 Hand Ejector First Model, can be easily recognized by the lack of a locking lug located on the underside of the barrel and the serial number 1 through 20,975. Between 1899 and 1940 this model was available with both fixed sights and an adjustable target sight. The target model, referred to as the 38 Military and Police Target Model, brings a premium price and was the predecessor to all K-frame target models.
38 Hand Ejector First Model
Exc.: $450   **VGood:** $300   **Good:** $150
Standard models
Exc.: $300   **VGood:** $225   **Good:** $135

Smith & Wesson
Model 469

Smith & Wesson
Model 645

Smith & Wesson
Model 745

Smith & Wesson
Model 669

Smith & Wesson
Model 910

Smith & Wesson
Model 410 DA

HANDGUNS
Smith & Wesson Semi-Automatic Pistols
Model 459
Model 469
Model 539
Model 559
Model 639
Model 645
Model 659
Model 669
Model 745
Third Generation Models (1988-1995)
Model 356 TSW Limited
Model 356 TSW Compact
Model 410 DA
Model 411

SMITH & WESSON MODEL 459

Semi-automatic; double-action; 9mm Para.; 14-shot magazine; 4" barrel; 7 7/16" overall length; weighs 27 1/2 oz. sans magazine; has same general specs as Model 439, except for increased magazine capacity, straighter, longer grip frame; blued or nickel finish. Introduced 1980; dropped 1989.

Blue finish

Exc.: $350   **VGood:** $300   **Good:** $250

Nickel finish

Exc.: $375   **VGood:** $325   **Good:** $275

SMITH & WESSON MODEL 469

Semi-automatic; 9mm Para.; 3 1/2" barrel; 12-shot magazine; accepts 14-shot 459 magazine; 6 7/8" overall length; weighs 26 oz.; cut-down version of Model 459; cross-hatching on front of trigger guard, backstrap; plastic pebble-grain grips; curved finger-extension magazine; bobbed hammer; sandblasted blued finish. Introduced 1983; dropped 1988.

Exc.: $300   **VGood:** $250   **Good:** $225

SMITH & WESSON MODEL 539

Semi-automatic; double action; 9mm Para.; 8-shot magazine; 4" barrel; 7 7/16" overall length; weighs 36 oz.; carbon steel construction; trigger-actuated firing pin lock; magazine disconnector; 1/8" serrated ramp front, windage-adjustable square notch rear and protective shield on both sides of blade; checkered high-impact moulded nylon; bright blue or nickel finish. Approximately 10,000 manufactured. Introduced 1981; dropped 1984.

Exc.: $400   **VGood:** $350   **Good:** $300

SMITH & WESSON MODEL 559

Semi-automatic; double action; 9mm Para.; 14-shot magazine; 4" barrel; 7 7/16" overall length; weighs 40 oz. sans magazine; has same general specs as Model 459, except carbon steel construction; blue or nickel finish. Approximately 10,000 manufactured. Introduced 1981; dropped 1984.

Exc.: $450   **VGood:** $400   **Good:** $350

SMITH & WESSON MODEL 639

Semi-automatic; double action; 9mm Para.; 8-shot magazine; 4" barrel; 7 7/16" overall length; weighs 27 1/2 oz. sans magazine; stainless steel construction; trigger-actuated firing pin lock; magazine disconnector; 1/8" serrated ramp front, windage-adjustable square notch rear with protective shield on both sides of blade; checkered high-impact moulded nylon; bright blue or nickel finish. Introduced 1981; dropped 1988.

Exc.: $350   **VGood:** $300   **Good:** $250

SMITH & WESSON MODEL 645

Semi-automatic; double action; 45 ACP; 8-shot magazine; 5" barrel; 8 3/4" overall length; weighs 37 5/8 oz.; red ramp front sight, drift-adjustable rear; checkered nylon stocks; stainless steel construction; cross-hatch knurling on recurved front trigger guard, backstrap; beveled magazine well. Introduced 1985; dropped 1988.

Exc.: $450   **VGood:** $400   **Good:** $350

SMITH & WESSON MODEL 659

Semi-automatic; double action; 9mm Para.; 14-shot magazine; 4" barrel; 7 7/16" overall length; weighs 27 1/2 oz. sans magazine; has same general specs as Model 439, except stainless steel construction. Introduced 1981; dropped 1988.

Exc.: $350   **VGood:** $300   **Good:** $225

SMITH & WESSON MODEL 669

Semi-automatic; 9mm Para.; 3 1/2" barrel; 12-shot magazine; accepts 14-shot 459 magazine; 6 7/8" overall length; weighs 26 oz.; same specs as Model 469 except slide and barrel manufactured of stainless steel; aluminum alloy frame finished in natural finish. Introduced 1985; dropped 1988.

Exc.: $350   **VGood:** $300   **Good:** $250

SMITH & WESSON MODEL 745

Semi-automatic; 45 ACP; 8-shot magazine; 5" barrel; 8 5/8" overall length; weighs 38 3/4 oz.; fixed Novak rear sight, serrated ramp front; blued slide, trigger, hammer, sights. Marketed with two magazines. Introduced 1987; dropped 1990.

Exc.: $450   **VGood:** $400   **Good:** $350

THIRD GENERATION MODELS (1988-1995)
SMITH & WESSON MODEL 356 TSW LIMITED

Semi-automatic; single action; 356 TSW; 15-shot magazine; 5" barrel; weighs 44 oz.; 8 1/2" overall length; checkered black composition grips; blade front sight drift adjustable for windage, fully-adjustable Bo-Mar rear; stainless steel frame and slide; hand-fitted titaniumcoated stainless steel bushing; match grade barrel; extended magazine well and oversize release; magazine pads; extended safety. Checkered front strap. Made in U.S. by Smith & Wesson; available through Lew Horton Dist. Introduced 1993; no longer in production.

Exc.: $1200   **VGood:** $850   **Good:** $750

Smith & Wesson Model 356 TSW Compact

Same specs as the 356 TSW Limited except has 3 1/2" barrel; 12-shot magazine; Novak LoMount combat sights; 7" overall length; weighs 37 oz. Made in U.S. by Smith & Wesson; available from Lew Horton Dist. Introduced 1993; no longer in production.

Exc.: $850   **VGood:** $725   **Good:** $550

SMITH & WESSON MODEL 410 DA

Semi-automatic; double action; 40 S&W; 10-shot magazine. Barrel: 4". Weight: 28.5 oz. Length: 7.5 oz. Stocks: One-piece Xenoy, wrap-around with straight backstrap. Sights: Post front, fixed rear; three-dot system. Features: Aluminum alloy frame; blued carbon steel slide; traditional double action with left-side slide-mountd decocking lever. Introduced 1996.

New: $425   **Perf.:** $375   **Exc.:** $300

SMITH & WESSON MODEL 411

Semi-automatic; double action; 40 S&W; 10-shot magazine; 4" barrel; weighs 28 oz.; 7 3/8" overall length; one-piece Xenoy wrap-around grips with straight backstrap; post front sight with white dot, fixed two-dot rear; alloy frame, blue carbon steel slide; slide-mounted decocking lever. Made in U.S. by Smith & Wesson. Introduced 1994; still produced.

New: $450   **Perf.:** $400   **Exc.:** $325

HANDGUNS

Smith & Wesson Semi-Automatic Pistols

Model 908
Model 909
Model 910
Model 915
Model 1006
Model 1026
Model 1046
Model 1066
Model 1066-NS
Model 1076
Model 1086
Model 3904
Model 3906
Model 3913

Smith & Wesson
Model 915

Smith & Wesson
Model 1066

Smith & Wesson
Model 1026

Smith & Wesson
Model 1086

Smith & Wesson
Model 3904

Smith & Wesson
Model 908

Smith & Wesson
Model 3913

SMITH & WESSON MODEL 908

Caliber: 9mm Para., 8-shot magazine. Barrel: 3-1/2". Weight: 26 oz. Length: 6-13/16". Stocks: One-piece Xenoy, wrap-around with straight backstrap. Sights: Post front, fixed rear, three-dot system. Features: Aluminum alloy frame, matte blue carbon steel slide; bobbed hammer; smooth trigger. Introduced 1996.

New: $425   **Perf.:** $375   **Exc.:** $300

SMITH & WESSON MODEL 909

Semi-automatic; double action; 9mm Para.; 9-shot magazine; 4" barrel; weighs 27 oz.; 7 3/8" overall length; one-piece Xenoy wrap-around grips with curved backstrap; post front sight with white dot, fixed two-dot rear; alloy frame, blue carbon steel slide; slide mounted decocking lever. Made in U.S. by Smith & Wesson. Introduced 1995; still produced.

New: $350   **Perf.:** $300   **Exc.:** $250

SMITH & WESSON MODEL 910

Semi-automatic; double action; 9mm Para.; 10-shot magazine; 4" barrel; weighs 27 oz.; 7 3/8" overall length; one-piece Xenoy wrap-around grips with curved backstrap; post front sight with white dot, fixed two-dot rear; alloy frame, blue carbon steel slide; slide mounted decocking lever. Introduced 1995; still produced.

New: $375   **Perf.:** $325   **Exc.:** $275

SMITH & WESSON MODEL 915

Semi-automatic; double action; 9mm Para.; 15-shot magazine; 4" barrel; 7 1/2" overall length; weighs 28 1/2 oz.; one-piece Xenoy wrap-around grips with straight backstrap; post front sight with white dot, fixed rear; alloy frame, blue carbon steel slide; slide-mounted decocking lever. Made in U.S. by Smith & Wesson. Introduced 1992; dropped 1995.

New: $350   **Perf.:** $300   **Exc.:** $250

SMITH & WESSON MODEL 1006

Semi-automatic; double action; 10mm auto; 9-shot magazine; 5" barrel; weighs 38 oz.; one-piece Xenoy wrap-around grips with straight backstrap; rounded trigger guard; choice of Novak LoMount Carry fixed rear sight with two white dots or adjustable micro-click rear with two white dots; stainless steel construction; satin stainless finish. Introduced 1990; dropped 1993.

Perf.: $550   **Exc.:** $475   **VGood:** $400

SMITH & WESSON MODEL 1026

Semi-automatic; double action; 10mm auto; 9-shot magazine; 5" barrel; weighs 38 oz.; frame mounted decocking lever, fixed sights; one-piece Delrin grips; rounded trigger guard. Introduced 1990; dropped 1992.

Exc.: $550   **VGood:** $500   **Good:** $400

SMITH & WESSON MODEL 1046

Semi-automatic; double-action-only; 10mm auto; 9-shot magazine; 5" barrel; weighs 38 oz.; rounded trigger guard; fixed sights; wrap-around grips with straight backstrap; stainless steel with satin finish. Introduced 1990; dropped 1992.

Exc.: $525   **VGood:** $450   **Good:** $375

SMITH & WESSON MODEL 1066

Semi-automatic; double action; 10mm auto; 9-shot magazine; 4 1/4" barrel; fixed sights; wrap-around grips with straight backstrap; ambidextrous safety. Introduced 1990; dropped 1992.

Exc.: $500   **VGood:** $400   **Good:** $350

Smith & Wesson Model 1066-NS

Same specs as Model 1066 except Tritium night sights.

Exc.: $550   **VGood:** $450   **Good:** $40

SMITH & WESSON MODEL 1076

Semi-automatic; double action; 10mm auto; 9-shot magazine; 4 1/4" barrel; frame mounted decocking lever; wrap-around grips with straight backstrap; fixed sights. Introduced 1990; dropped 1993.

Exc.: $500   **VGood:** $400   **Good:** $350

SMITH & WESSON MODEL 1086

Semi-automatic; double-action-only; 10mm auto; 9-shot magazine; 4 1/4" barrel; wrap-around grips with straight backstrap; fixed sights; ambidextrous safety. Introduced 1990; dropped 1993.

Perf.: $700   **Exc.:** $600   **VGood:** $450

SMITH & WESSON MODEL 3904

Semi-automatic; double action; 9mm Para.; 8-shot magazine; 4" barrel; 7 1/2" overall length; weighs 28 oz.; one-piece wrap-around Delrin stocks; post front sight with white dot, fixed or fully-adjustable two-dot rear; blued finish; smooth trigger; serrated hammer. Introduced 1989; dropped 1991.

Exc.: $400   **VGood:** $350   **Good:** $300

SMITH & WESSON MODEL 3906

Semi-automatic; double action; 9mm Para.; 8-shot magazine; 4" barrel; 7 5/8" overall length; weighs 28 oz.; stainless steel construction; one-piece wrap-around Delrin stocks; post front sight with white dot, fixed or fully-adjustable two-dot rear; blued finish; smooth trigger; serrated hammer. Introduced 1989; dropped 1991.

Exc.: $450   **VGood:** $400   **Good:** $350

SMITH & WESSON MODEL 3913

Semi-automatic; double action; 9mm Para.; 8-shot magazine; 3 1/2" barrel; 6 13/16" overall length; weighs 26 oz.; post white-dot front sight, two-dot windage-adjustable Novak LoMount Carry rear; aluminum alloy frame; stainless steel slide; bobbed hammer; no half-cock notch; smooth trigger; straight backstrap. Introduced 1990; dropped 1999.

New: $500   **Perf.:** $450   **Exc.:** $350

Smith & Wesson
Model 3914

Smith & Wesson
Model 4006

Smith & Wesson
Model 4053

Smith & Wesson
Model 3914
Ladysmith

HANDGUNS

Smith & Wesson Semi-Automatic Pistols

Model 3913 LadySmith
Model 3913-NL
Model 3913TSW/3953TSW
Model 3914
Model 3914 LadySmith
Model 3914-NL
Model 3953
Model 3954
Model 4006
Model 4043
Model 4013
Model 4053
Model 4014
Model 4046
Model 4053
Model 4054

Smith & Wesson
Model 3913
Ladysmith

SMITH & WESSON MODEL 3913 LADYSMITH
Semi-automatic; double action; 9mm Para.; 8-shot magazine; 3 1/2" barrel; 6 13/16" overall length; weighs 26 oz.; post white-dot front sight, two-dot windage-adjustable Novak LoMount Carry rear; upswept frame at front; rounded trigger guard; frosted stainless steel finish; gray ergonomic grips designed for smaller hands. Introduced 1990; still produced.
New: $575   **Perf.:** $500   **Exc.:** $400

Smith & Wesson Model 3913-NL
Same specs as Model 3913 except without LadySmith logo; slightly modified frame design; right-hand safety only; stainless slide in alloy frame. Introduced 1990; dropped 1994.
Perf.: $450   **Exc.:** $350   **VGood:** $275

Smith & Wesson Model 3913TSW/3953TSW
Similar to the Model 3913 and 3953 except TSW guns have tighter tolerances, ambidextrous manual safety/decocking lever, flush-fit magazine, delayed-unlock firing system. DAO Model 3953 has magazine disconnector. Compact alloy frame, stainless steel slide. Straight backstrap. Introduced 1998.
New: $600   **Perf.:** $525   **Exc.:** $450

SMITH & WESSON MODEL 3914
Semi-automatic; double action; 9mm Para.; 8-shot magazine; 3 1/2" barrel; 6 13/16" overall length; weighs 26 oz.; post white-dot front sight, two-dot windage-adjustable Novak LoMount Carry rear; aluminum alloy frame; blued steel slide; bobbed hammer; no half-cock notch; smooth trigger straight backstrap. Introduced 1990; dropped 1995.
New: $400   **Perf.:** $325   **Exc.:** $250

SMITH & WESSON MODEL 3914 LADYSMITH
Semi-automatic; double action; 9mm Para.; 8-shot magazine; 3 1/2" barrel; 6 13/16" overall length; weighs 26 oz.; post white-dot front sight, two-dot windage-adjustable Novak LoMount Carry rear; same specs as standard 3913, except slide is of blued steel. Introduced 1990; dropped 1992.
Perf.: $450   **Exc.:** $375   **VGood:** $275

Smith & Wesson Model 3914-NL
Same specs as 3914 except without LadySmith logo; slightly modified frame design; right-hand safety only; blued finish, black grips. Introduced 1990; dropped 1991.
Perf.: $400   **Exc.:** $300   **VGood:** $250

SMITH & WESSON MODEL 3953
Semi-automatic; double-action-only; 9mm Para.; 8-shot magazine; 3 1/2" barrel; 7" overall length;

weighs 25 1/2 oz.; post white-dot front sight, two-dot windage-adjustable Novak LoMount Carry rear; aluminum alloy frame; stainless steel slide; bobbed hammer; no half-cock notch; smooth trigger straight backstrap. Introduced 1990; dropped 1999.
New: $500   **Perf.:** $450   **Exc.:** $350

SMITH & WESSON MODEL 3954
Semi-automatic; double-action-only; 9mm Para.; 8-shot magazine; 3 1/2" barrel; 7" overall length; weighs 25 1/2 oz.; post white-dot front sight, two-dot windage-adjustable Novak LoMount Carry rear; aluminum alloy frame; blued steel slide; alloy frame; bobbed hammer; no half-cock notch; smooth trigger straight backstrap. Introduced 1990; dropped 1992.
Perf.: $400   **Exc.:** $350   **VGood:** $275

SMITH & WESSON MODEL 4006
Semi-automatic; 40 S&W; 11-shot magazine; 4" barrel; 7 1/2" overall length; weighs 38 oz.; replaceable white-dot post front sight, Novak two-dot fixed rear or two-dot micro-click adjustable rear; Xenoy wrap-around grips, checkered panels; straight backstrap; made of stainless steel; non-reflective finish. Introduced 1991.
New: $650   **Perf.:** $600   **Exc.:** $500
Tritium night sights
New: $725   **Perf.:** $675   **Exc.:** $575

Smith & Wesson Model 4043
Similar to the Model 4006 except is double-action-only. Has a semi-bobbed hammer, smooth trigger, 4" barrel; Novak LoMount Carry rear sight, post front with white dot. Overall length is 7 1/2", weighs 28 oz. Alloy frame. Extra magazine included. Introduced 1991; dropped 1999.
New: $700   **Perf.:** $600   **Exc.:** $500

SMITH & WESSON MODEL 4013
Semi-automatic; double action; 40 S&W; 7-shot magazine; 3 1/2" barrel; 7" overall length; weighs 26 oz.; white-dot post front sight, two-dot Novak LoMount Carry rear; one-piece Xenoy wrap-around grip; straight backstrap; alloy frame; stainless steel slide. Introduced 1991; dropped 1996.
New: $550   **Perf.:** $500   **Exc.:** $425

SMITH & WESSON MODEL 4053 TSW
Semi-automatic; double action; 40 S&W; 9-shot magazine. Barrel: 3 1/2". Weight: 26.4 oz. Length: 6 7/8" overall. Stocks: Checkered black polymer. Sights: Novak three-dot system. Features: double-action only system; stainless slide, alloy frame; fixed barrel bush-

ing; ambidextrous decocker; reversible magazine catch. Introduced 1997.
New: $725   **Perf.:** $625   **Exc.:** $550

SMITH & WESSON MODEL 4014
Semi-automatic; double action; 40 S&W; 7-shot magazine; 3 1/2" barrel; 7" overall length; weighs 26 oz.; blued steel slide; white-dot post front sight, two-dot Novak LoMount Carry rear; one-piece Xenoy wrap-around grip; straight backstrap; alloy frame; stainless steel slide. Introduced 1991; dropped 1993
Perf.: $500   **Exc.:** $450   **VGood:** $350

SMITH & WESSON MODEL 4046
Semi-automatic; double-action-only; 40 S&W; 11-shot; 4" barrel; 7 1/2" overall length; weighs 38 oz.; smooth trigger; semi-bobbed hammer; post white-dot front sight, Novak LoMount Carry rear. Introduced 1991; dropped 1999.
Perf.: $550   **Exc.:** $475   **VGood:** $350

SMITH & WESSON MODEL 4053
Semi-automatic; double-action-only; 40 S&W; 7-shot magazine; 3 1/2" barrel; 7" overall length; weighs 26 oz.; white-dot post front sight, two-dot Novak LoMount Carry rear; one-piece Xenoy wrap-around grip; straight backstrap; alloy frame; stainless steel slide. Introduced 1991; dropped 1997.
New: $600   **Perf.:** $550   **Exc.:** $450

SMITH & WESSON MODEL 4054
Semi-automatic; double-action-only; 40 S&W; 7-shot magazine; 3 1/2" barrel; 7" overall length; weighs 26 oz.; blued steel slide; white-dot post front sight, two-dot Novak LoMount Carry rear; one-piece Xenoy wrap-around grip; straight backstrap; alloy frame; stainless steel slide. Introduced 1991; dropped 1992.
Perf.: $475   **Exc.:** $400   **VGood:** $300

HANDGUNS

Smith & Wesson Semi-Automatic Pistols

Model 4505
Model 4506
Model 4513TSW/4553TSW
Model 4516
Model 4526
Model 4536
Model 4546
Model 4556
Model 4566
Model 4567-NS
Model 4576
Model 4586
Model 5903
Model 5904

Smith & Wesson
Model 5904

Smith & Wesson
Model 5903

Smith & Wesson
Model 4586

Smith & Wesson
Model 4516

Smith & Wesson
Model 4506

Smith & Wesson
Model 5906

SMITH & WESSON MODEL 4505
Semi-automatic; 45 ACP; 8-shot magazine; 5" barrel; one-piece wrap-around Delrin stock; arched or straight backstrap; post front sight with white dot, fixed or adjustable rear; blued finish. Introduced 1990; dropped 1991.

Perf: $550	**Exc.:** $425	**VGood:** $325

SMITH & WESSON MODEL 4506
Semi-automatic; 45 ACP; 8-shot magazine; 5" barrel; one-piece, wrap-around Xenoy stocks; arched or straight backstrap; post front sight with white dot, fixed or adjustable Novak LoMount Carry rear; serrated hammer spur; stainless steel construction. Introduced 1989; dropped 1999.

New: $650	**Perf:** $550	**Exc.:** $475

SMITH & WESSON MODEL 4513TSW/4553TSW
Semi-automatic; double action; 45 ACP, 6-shot magazine. Barrel: 3 3/4". Weight: 28 oz. (M4513TSW). Length: 6 7/8" overall. Stocks: Checkered Xenoy; straight backstrap. Sights: White dot front, Novak Lo Mount Carry 2-Dot rear. Features: Model 4513TSW is traditional double action, Model 4553TSW is double action only. TSW series has tighter tolerances, ambidextrous manual safety/decocking lever, flush-fit magazine, delayed-unlock firing system. DAO has magazine disconnector. Compact alloy frame, stainless steel slide. Introduced 1998.
Model 4513TSW

New: $675	**Perf.:** $575	**Exc.:** $450

Model 4553TSW

New: $675	**Perf.:** $575	**Exc.:** $450

SMITH & WESSON MODEL 4516
Semi-automatic; 45 ACP; 7-shot magazine; 3 3/4" barrel; one-piece wrap-around Xenoy stock; straight backstrap; post front sight with white dot; fixed Novak rear sight; bobbed hammer. Introduced 1989; dropped 1997.

New: $600	**Perf:** $500	**Exc.:** $400

SMITH & WESSON MODEL 4526
Semi-automatic; 45 ACP; 8-shot magazine; 5" barrel; decocking lever; one-piece wrap-around Delrin stock; arched or straight backstrap; post front sight with white dot, fixed or adjustable rear; serrated hammer spur; stainless steel construction. Introduced 1991; dropped 1993.

Perf: $575	**Exc.:** $425	**VGood:** $350

SMITH & WESSON MODEL 4536
Semi-automatic; 45 ACP; 8-shot magazine; 3 3/4" barrel; decocking lever; one-piece wrap-around Delrin stock; arched or straight backstrap; post front sight with white dot, fixed or adjustable rear; serrated ham-

mer spur; stainless steel construction. Introduced 1990; dropped 1991.

Perf: $575	**Exc.:** $425	**VGood:** $350

SMITH & WESSON MODEL 4546
Semi-automatic; double-action-only; 45 ACP; 8-shot magazine; 5" barrel; decocking lever; stainless steel construction; one-piece wrap-around Delrin stock; arched or straight backstrap; post front sight with white dot, fixed or adjustable rear; serrated hammer spur; stainless steel construction. Introduced 1990; dropped 1991.

Perf: $600	**Exc.:** $525	**VGood:** $400

SMITH & WESSON MODEL 4556
Semi-automatic; double-action-only; 45 ACP; 8-shot magazine; 3 3/4" barrel; decocking lever; stainless steel construction; one-piece wrap-around Delrin stock; arched or straight backstrap; post front sight with white dot, fixed or adjustable rear; serrated hammer spur; stainless steel construction. Introduced 1990; dropped 1991.

Perf: $600	**Exc.:** $500	**VGood:** $425

SMITH & WESSON MODEL 4566
Semi-automatic; double-action-only; 45 ACP; 8-shot magazine; 4 1/4" barrel; ambidextrous safety; decocking lever; stainless steel construction; one-piece wrap-around Delrin stocks; arched or straight backstrap; fixed sights; serrated hammer spur; stainless steel construction. Introduced 1990; dropped 1999.

New: $650	**Perf:** $600	**Exc.:** $500

SMITH & WESSON MODEL 4567-NS
Semi-automatic; 45 ACP; 4 1/4" barrel; stainless steel slide; blued steel frame; bobbed hammer; one-piece wrap-around grip; straight, blued backstrap; rounded

edges; Novak sights with tritium inserts. Introduced 1991; dropped 1991.

Perf: $550	**Exc.:** $450	**VGood:** $350

SMITH & WESSON MODEL 4576
Semi-automatic; double action; 45 ACP; 8-shot magazine; 4 1/4" barrel; ambidextrous safety; decocking lever; stainless steel construction; one-piece wrap-around Delrin stocks; arched or straight backstrap; fixed sights; serrated hammer spur made of stainless steel. Introduced 1990; no longer produced.

Perf: $600	**Exc.:** $550	**VGood:** $450

SMITH & WESSON MODEL 4586
Semi-automatic; double-action-only; 45 ACP; 8-shot magazine; 4 1/4" barrel; ambidextrous safety; decocking lever; stainless steel construction; one-piece wrap-around Xenoy stock; arched or straight backstrap; fixed sights; serrated hammer spur. Introduced 1990; dropped 1999.

New: $650	**Perf:** $600	**Exc.:** $500

SMITH & WESSON MODEL 5903
Semi-automatic; double action; 9mm Para.; 14-, 10-shot magazine; 4" barrel; 7 1/2" overall length; weighs 28-37 oz.; stainless steel alloy frame; ambidextrous safety; one-piece wrap-around Xenoy stocks; fixed sights; blued finish; smooth trigger; serrated hammer. Introduced 1989; dropped 1997.

New: $550	**Perf:** $500	**Exc.:** $425

SMITH & WESSON MODEL 5904
Semi-automatic; double action; 9mm Para.; 14-, 10-shot magazine; 4" barrel; 7 1/2" overall length; weighs 28-37 oz.; one-piece wrap-around Xenoy stocks; fixed or adjustable sights; blued finish; smooth trigger; serrated hammer. Introduced 1989; dropped 1998.

New: $550	**Perf:** $500	**Exc.:** $400

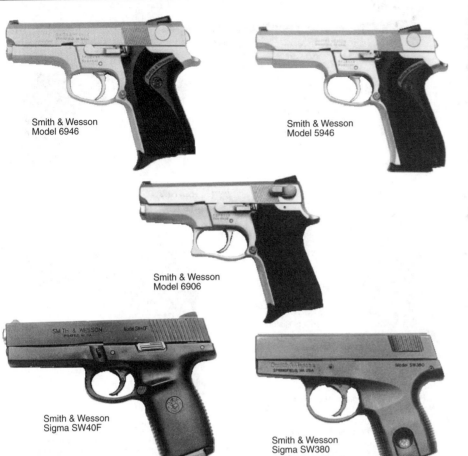

Smith & Wesson
Model 6946

Smith & Wesson
Model 5946

Smith & Wesson
Model 6906

Smith & Wesson
Sigma SW40F

Smith & Wesson
Sigma SW380

Smith & Wesson Semi-Automatic Pistols

Model 5905
Model 5906
Model 5924
Model 5926
Model 5943
Model 5943-SSV
Model 5944
Model 5946
Model 6904
Model 6906
Model 6926
Model 6944
Model 6946
Sigma SW9F
Sigma SW9C

SMITH & WESSON MODEL 5905
Semi-automatic; double action; 9mm Para.; 14-shot magazine; 4" barrel; 7 5/8" overall length; weighs 30 oz.; blued frame, slide; ambidextrous safety; one-piece wrap-around Delrin stocks; adjustable sights; blued finish; smooth trigger; serrated hammer. Introduced 1989; dropped 1992.

Perf: $650   **Exc.:** $600   **VGood:** $550

SMITH & WESSON MODEL 5906
Semi-automatic; double action; 9mm Para.; 14-, 10-shot magazine; 4" barrel; 7 1/2" overall length; weighs 28-38 oz.; stainless steel construction; ambidextrous safety; one-piece wrap-around Xenoy stock; fixed or adjustable sights; blued finish; smooth trigger; serrated hammer. Introduced 1989; dropped 1999.

New: $600   **Perf:** $525   **Exc.:** $425

SMITH & WESSON MODEL 5924
Semi-automatic; double action; 9mm Para.; 14-shot magazine; 4" barrel; 7 1/2" overall length; weighs 30 oz.; blue frame; frame mounted decocking lever; ambidextrous safety; one-piece wrap-around Delrin stocks; fixed sights; blued finish; smooth trigger; serrated hammer. Introduced 1989; dropped 1992.

Perf: $450   **Exc.:** $350   **VGood:** $300

SMITH & WESSON MODEL 5926
Semi-automatic; double action; 9mm Para.; 14-shot magazine; 4" barrel; 7 1/2" overall length; weighs 30 oz.; stainless steel construction; frame mounted decocking lever; ambidextrous safety; one-piece wrap-around Delrin stocks; fixed sights; blued finish; smooth trigger; serrated hammer. Introduced 1989; dropped 1992.

Perf: $550   **Exc.:** $450   **VGood:** $375

SMITH & WESSON MODEL 5943
Semi-automatic; double-action-only; 9mm Para.; 14-shot magazine; 4" barrel; 7 1/2" overall length; weighs 30 oz.; stainless alloy frame; frame mounted decocking lever; ambidextrous safety; one-piece wrap-around Delrin stocks; fixed sights; blued finish; smooth trigger; serrated hammer. Introduced 1989; dropped 1992.

Perf: $500   **Exc.:** $450   **VGood:** $350

SMITH & WESSON Model 5943-SSV
Same specs as 5943 except 3 1/2" barrel; bobbed hammer; short slide; double-action-only; alloy frame; blued slide, slide stop, magazine release, trigger, hammer; black post front sight, Novak fixed rear tritium inserts; black curved backstrap grips. Introduced 1990; dropped 1992.

Perf: $525   **Exc.:** $475   **VGood:** $350

SMITH & WESSON MODEL 5944
Semi-automatic; double-action-only; 9mm Para.; 14-shot magazine; 4" barrel; 7 1/2" overall length; weighs 30 oz.; blue alloy frame; frame mounted decocking lever; ambidextrous safety; one-piece wrap-around Delrin stocks; fixed sights; blued finish; smooth trigger; serrated hammer. Introduced 1989; dropped 1992.

Perf: $450   **Exc.:** $400   **VGood:** $325

SMITH & WESSON MODEL 5946
Semi-automatic; double-action-only; 9mm Para.; 14-shot magazine; 4" barrel; 7 5/8" overall length; weighs 30 oz.; stainless steel construction; frame mounted decocking lever; ambidextrous safety; one-piece wrap-around Delrin stocks; fixed sights; blued finish; smooth trigger; serrated hammer. Introduced 1989; dropped 1999.

New: $600   **Perf:** $550   **Exc.:** $450

SMITH & WESSON MODEL 6904
Semi-automatic; double action; 9mm Para.; 12-, 10-shot magazine; 3 1/2" barrel; weighs 26 1/2 oz.; fixed rear sight; .260" bobbed hammer; blue finish. Introduced 1989; dropped 1997.

New: $500   **Perf:** $450   **Exc.:** $375

SMITH & WESSON MODEL 6906
Semi-automatic; double action; 9mm Para.; 12-, 10-shot magazine; 3 1/2" barrel; weighs 261/2 oz.; stainless steel construction; fixed rear sight; .260" bobbed hammer. Introduced 1989; dropped 1999.

New: $550   **Perf:** $500   **Exc.:** $400

With night sights

New: $650   **Perf:** $600   **Exc.:** $500

SMITH & WESSON MODEL 6926
Semi-automatic; double action; 9mm Para.; 12-shot magazine; 3 1/2" barrel; weighs 261/2 oz.; aluminum alloy frame; stainless slide; decocking lever; fixed sights; bobbed hammer. Introduced 1990; dropped 1992.

Perf: $500   **Exc.:** $450   **VGood:** $350

SMITH & WESSON MODEL 6944
Semi-automatic; double-action-only; 9mm Para.; 12-shot magazine; 3 1/2" barrel; weighs 26 1/2 oz.; aluminum alloy frame; blued steel slide; decocking lever; fixed sights; bobbed hammer. Introduced 1990; dropped 1992.

Perf: $450   **Exc.:** $400   **VGood:** $300

SMITH & WESSON MODEL 6946
Semi-automatic; double-action-only; 9mm Para.; 12-, 10-shot magazine; 3 1/2" barrel; weighs 26 1/2 oz.; aluminum alloy frame; stainless steel slide; decocking lever; fixed sights or night sights; .260" bobbed hammer. Introduced 1990; dropped 1999.

New: $550   **Perf:** $500   **Exc.:** $400

With night sights

New: $625   **Perf:** $575   **Exc.:** $475

SMITH & WESSON SIGMA SW9F
Semi-automatic; double action; 9mm Para.; 10-shot magazine; 4 1/2" barrel; 7 1/2" overall length; weighs 26 oz.; integral polymer grips; post front sight with white dot, fixed rear with two dots; tritium night sights optional; ergonomic polymer frame; internal striker firing system; corrosion-resistant slide; Teflon-filled, electroless-nickel coated magazine. Introduced 1994; dropped 1996.

New: $500   **Perf:** $450   **Exc.:** $375

With fixed tritium night sights

New: $575   **Perf:** $525   **Exc.:** $450

Smith & Wesson Sigma SW9C
Same specs as the SW9F except 4" barrel; weighs 24 1/2 oz. Introduced 1995; dropped 1998.

New: $500   **Perf:** $450   **Exc.:** $375

With fixed tritium night sights

New: $575   **Perf:** $525   **Exc.:** $450

Springfield Armory
Model 1911-A1 Defender
Model 1911-A1 Distinguished
Model 1911-A1 Expert Pistol
Model 1911-A1 Factory Comp
Model 1911-A1 High Capacity
Mocel V10 Ultra Compact
  Pistol
Armoury TRP Pistols
Model 1911-A1 N.M. Hardball
Model 1911-A1 N.R.A. PPC
Model 1911-A1 Product
  Improved Defender
Model 1911-A1 Trophy Master
  Competition Pistol
Model 1911-A1 Trophy Master
  Competition Expert Pistol
Model 1911-A1 Trophy Match

Springfield Armory Model
1911-A1 High Capacity

Springfield Armory
Model 1911-A1 Defender

Springfield Armoury
Model V10 Ultra
Compact Pistol

Springfield Armoury
TRP

Springfield Armory Model 1911-A1 Defender
Same specs as Model 1911-A1 except 45 ACP only; fixed combat-type sights; beveled magazine well; bobbed hammer; extended thumb safety; serrated frontstrap; walnut stocks; marketed with two stainless steel magazines; phosphated finish. Introduced 1988; discontinued 1990.

Perf.: $450   **Exc.:** $400   **VGood:** $325
Blued finish
Perf.: $475   **Exc.:** $425   **VGood:** $350

Springfield Armory Model 1911-A1 Distinguished
Same specs as the 1911-A1 except full-house pistol with match barrel with compensator; Bo-Mar low-mounted adjustable rear sight; full-length recoil spring guide rod and recoil spring retainer; beveled and polished magazine well; walnut grips; hard chrome finish; 45 ACP; comes with two magazines with slam pads, plastic carrying case. From Springfield, Inc. Introduced 1992.

New: $2200   **Perf.:** $1850   **Exc.:** $1500

Springfield Armory Model 1911-A1 Expert Pistol
Same specs as Model 1911-A1 except triple-chamber tapered cone compensator on match barrel with dovetailed front sight; lowered and flared ejection port; fully tuned for reliability; bobbed hammer; match trigger; Duotone finish; comes with two magazines, plastic carrying case. From Springfield, Inc. Introduced 1992.

New: $1600   **Perf.:** $1250   **Exc.:** $1000

Springfield Armory Model 1911-A1 Factory Comp
Same specs as the standard 1911-A1 except bushing-type dual-port compensator; adjustable rear sight; extended thumb safety; Videcki speed trigger; beveled magazine well; checkered walnut grips standard. Available in 38 Super or 45 ACP, blue only. From Springfield, Inc. Introduced 1992.

New: $750   **Perf.:** $650   **Exc.:** $500

Springfield Armory Model 1911-A1 High Capacity
Same specs as the Model 1911-A1 except 45 ACP, 9mm; 10-shot magazine; Commander-style hammer; walnut grips; ambidextrous thumb safety; beveled magazine well; plastic carrying case. From Springfield, Inc. Introduced 1993; still produced.
45 ACP
New: $600   **Perf.:** $500   **Exc.:** $350
9mm Para.
New: $500   **Perf.:** $450   **Exc.:** $375
45 ACP Factory Comp
New: $700   **Perf.:** $600   **Exc.:** $500

45 ACP Comp Lightweight, matte finish
New: $700   **Perf.:** $600   **Exc.:** $500
45 ACP Compact, blued
New: $550   **Perf.:** $475   **Exc.:** $350
45 ACP Compact, stainless steel
New: $650   **Perf.:** $550   **Exc.:** $450

Springfield Armoury Model V10 Ultra Compact Pistol
Similar to the 1911A1 Compact except has shorter slide, 3.5" barrel, recoil reducing compensator built into the barrel and slide. Beavertail grip safety, beveled magazine well, "hi-viz" combat sights, Videcki speed trigger, flared ejection port, stainless steel frame, blued slide, match grade barrel, walnut grips. Introduced 1996. From Springfield, Inc.
New: $550   **Perf.:** $475   **Exc.:** $400

Springfield Armoury TRP Pistols
Similar to the 1911A1 except 45 ACP only; has checkered front strap and mainspring housing; Novak combat rear sight and matching dovetailed front sight; tuned, polished extractor; oversize barrel link; lightweight speed trigger and combat action job; match barrel and bushing; extended thumb safety and fitted beavertail grip safety; Carry bevel on entire pistol; checkered cocobolo wood grips; comes with two Wilson 8-shot magazines. Frame is engraved "Tactical," both sides of frame with "TRP." Introduced 1998.
Standard with Armory Kote finish
New: $950   **Perf.:** $800   **Exc.:** $700
Standard, stainless steel
New: $1000   **Perf.:** $850   **Exc.:** $750
Price: Champion, Armory Kote
New: $1100   **Perf.:** $950   **Exc.:** $800

Springfield Armory Model 1911-A1 N.M. Hardball
Same specs as Model 1911-A1 except Bo-Mar adjustable rear sight with undercut front blade; fitted match Videcki trigger with 4-lb. pull; fitted slide to frame; throated National Match barrel and bushing; polished feed ramp; recoil buffer system; tuned extractor; Herrett walnut grips; comes with two magazines, plastic carrying case, test target. From Springfield, Inc. Introduced 1992.
New: $1000   **Perf.:** $850   **Exc.:** $650

Springfield Armory Model 1911-A1 N.R.A. PPC
Specifically designed to comply with NRA rules for PPC competition; custom slide-to-frame fit; polished feed ramp; throated barrel; total internal honing; tuned

extractor; recoil buffer system; fully checkered walnut grips; two fitted magazines; factory test target; custom carrying case. From Springfield, Inc. Introduced 1995; still produced.
New: $1350   **Perf.:** $1100   **Exc.:** $900

Springfield Armory Model 1911-A1 Product Improved Defender
Same specs as Model 1911-A1 except 4 1/4" slide; low-profile three-dot sight system; tapered cone dual-port compensator system; rubberized grips; reverse recoil plug; full-length recoil spring guide; serrated frontstrap; extended thumb safety; skeletonized hammer with modified grip safety to match; Videcki speed trigger; Bi-Tone finish. From Springfield, Inc. Introduced 1991.
New: $800   **Perf.:** $700   **Exc.:** $600

Springfield Armory Model 1911-A1 Trophy Master Competition Pistol
Same specs as Model 1911-A1 except combat-type sights; Pachmayr wrap-around grips; ambidextrous safety; match trigger; bobbed hammer. Introduced 1988; discontinued 1990.
Perf.: $1450   **Exc.:** $1200   **VGood:** $950

Springfield Armory Model 1911-A1 Trophy Master Competition Expert Pistol
Same specs as Model 1911-A1 except match barrel with compensator; wrap-around Pachmayer grips; ambidextrous thumb safety; lowered, flared ejection port; blued finish. Introduced 1988; discontinued 1990.
Perf.: $1600   **Exc.:** $1350   **VGood:** $1000

Springfield Armory Model 1911-A1 Trophy Match
Same specs as Model 1911-A1 except factory accurized; 4- to 5 1/2-lb. trigger pull; click-adjustable rear sight; match-grade barrel and bushing; checkered walnut grips. From Springfield, Inc. Introduced 1994; still produced.
Blue finish
New: $800   **Perf.:** $700   **Exc.:** $600
Stainless steel
New: $825   **Perf.:** $725   **Exc.:** $650
High Capacity (stainless steel, 10-shot magazine, front slide serrations, checkered slide serrations)
New: $950   **Perf.:** $800   **Exc.:** $700

Springfield Armory Panther

Springfield Armory Omega Match

Star Firestar

Springfield Armory Omega

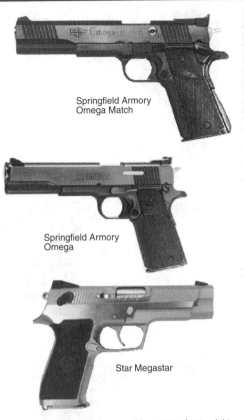

Star Megastar

Star Firestar Plus

HANDGUNS

Springfield Armory
Model P9 Factory Comp
Model P9 Subcompact
Model P9 Ultra LSP
Omega
Omega Match
Panther

Stallard
JS-9

Star
Firestar
Firestar M45
Firestar Plus
Megastar
Model 28

Star Model 28

Springfield Armory P9 Factory Comp
Same specs as the standard P9 except comes with dual-port compensator system; extended sear safety; extended magazine release; fully-adjustable rear sight; extra-slim competition wood grips; stainless or bi-tone (stainless and blue) finish; overall length is 9 1/2" with 5 1/2" barrel; weighs 34 oz. From Springfield, Inc. Introduced 1992; dropped 1993.
9mm Para., bi-tone finish or stainless
Perf.: $550   **Exc.:** $450   **VGood:** $350
40 S&W, bi-tone finish
Perf.: $575   **Exc.:** $475   **VGood:** $375
40 S&W, stainless, 45 ACP bi-tone finish
Perf.: $600   **Exc.:** $500   **VGood:** $400
45 ACP, stainless
Perf.: $550   **Exc.:** $500   **VGood:** $450

Springfield Armory Model P9 Subcompact
Same specs as Model P9 except 9mm Para., 40 S&W; 12-shot (9mm), 9-shot (40 S&W); 3 1/2" barrel; weighs 32 oz.; compact slide frame; squared trigger-guard; extended magazine floorplate. Introduced 1990; discontinued 1992.
Perf.: $350   **Exc.:** $300   **VGood:** $250

Springfield Armory Model P9 Ultra LSP
Same specs as Model P9 except 5" barrel; 8 3/8" overall length; weighs 34 1/4 oz.; long slide ported; rubber or walnut stocks; blued, Parkerized or blue/stainless finish. Introduced 1991; discontinued 1993.
Perf.: $550   **Exc.:** $450   **VGood:** $350
Phosphated finish
Perf.: $575   **Exc.:** $475   **VGood:** $375
Stainless steel
Perf.: $600   **Exc.:** $500   **VGood:** $450
Stainless frame/matte black slide
Perf.: $600   **Exc.:** $525   **VGood:** $450

SPRINGFIED ARMORY OMEGA
Semi-automatic; single action; 38 Super, 10mm, 40 S&W, 45 ACP; 5-shot (10mm, 40 S&W), 7-shot (45 ACP), 9-shot (38 Super) magazine; 5", 6" barrel; weighs 46 oz.; polygonal rifling; rubberized wrap-around grips; removable ramp front sight, fully-adjustable rear. Convertible between calibers; double serrated slide; built on 1911-A1 frame. Made in U.S. by Springfield Armory; now Springfield, Inc. Introduced 1987; discontinued 1990.
Exc: $650   **VGood:** $500   **Good:** $350

Springfield Armory Omega Match
Same specs as Omega except adjustable breech face; new extractor system; low profile combat sights; double serrated slide. Introduced 1991; discontinued 1992.
Perf.: $750   **Exc.:** $650   **VGood:** $500

SPRINGFIELD ARMORY PANTHER
Semi-automatic; double action; 9mm Para., 40 S&W, 45 ACP; 15-shot (9mm Para.), 11-shot (40 S&W), 9-shot (45 ACP); 40 S&W, 11-shot; 45 ACP, 9-shot magazine; 3 3/4" barrel; 7" overall length; weighs 29 oz.; narrow profile checkered walnut grips; low profile blade front sight, windage-adjustable rear; three-dot system; hammer drop and firing pin safeties; serrated front and rear straps; serrated slide top; Commander hammer; frame-mounted slide stop; button magazine release; matte blue finish. From Springfield Armory; now Springfield, Inc. Introduced 1991; dropped 1992.
Perf.: $500   **Exc.:** $400   **VGood:** $350

STALLARD JS-9
Semi-automatic; single action; 9mm Para.; 8-shot; 4 1/2" barrel; 7 3/4" overall length; weighs 48 oz.; low-profile fixed sights; textured plastic grips; non-glare blued finish. Introduced 1990; still in production.
New: $120   **Perf.:** $100   **Exc.:** $80

STAR FIRESTAR
Semi-automatic; single action; 9mm Para., 40 S&W; 7-shot (9mm), 6-shot (40 S&W); 3 3/8" barrel; 6 1/2" overall length; weighs 30 oz.; blade front sight, fully-adjustable three-dot rear; ambidextrous safety; blued or Starvel finish. Introduced 1990. Dropped 1993.
New: $275   **Perf.:** $250   **Exc.:** $200

Star Firestar M45
Same specs as Firestar except 45 ACP; 6-shot magazine; 3 1/2" barrel; 6 13/16" overall length; weighs 35 oz.; reverse-taper Acculine barrel. Imported from Spain by Interarms. Introduced 1992. Production ended when Star went out of business in 1997.

Blue finish
New: $300   **Perf.:** $250   **Exc.:** $200
Starvel finish
New: $325   **Perf.:** $275   **Exc.:** $225

Star Firestar Plus
Same specs as Firestar except 10-shot (9mm) magazine; also available in 40 S&W and 45 ACP. Imported from Spain by Interarms. Introduced 1994. Production ended 1997.
Blue finish, 9mm
New: $300   **Perf.:** $250   **Exc.:** $200
Starvel finish, 9mm
New: $325   **Perf.:** $275   **Exc.:** $225
Blue finish, 40 S&W
New: $350   **Perf.:** $300   **Exc.:** $250
Starvel finish, 40 S&W
New: $375   **Perf.:** $325   **Exc.:** $300
Blue finish, 45 ACP
New: $375   **Perf.:** $325   **Exc.:** $300
Starvel finish, 45 ACP
New: $400   **Perf.:** $350   **Exc.:** $375

STAR MEGASTAR
Semi-automatic; double action; 10mm, 45 ACP; 14-shot (10mm), 12-shot (45 ACP) magazine; 4 9/16" barrel; 8 1/2" overall length; weighs 47 1/2 oz.; checkered composition grips; blade front sight, adjustable rear; steel frame and slide; reverse-taper Acculine barrel. Imported from Spain by Interarms. Introduced 1992. Production ended 1992.
Blue finish, 10mm, 45 ACP
Perf.: $400   **Exc.:** $350   **VGood:** $275
Starvel finish, 10mm, 45 ACP
Perf.: $425   **Exc.:** $375   **VGood:** $300

STAR MODEL 28
Semi-automatic; double action; 9mm Para.; 15-shot; 4 1/4" barrel; 8" overall length; weighs 40 oz.; square blade front sight, square-notch click-adjustable rear; grooved triggerguard face, front and backstraps; checkered black plastic stocks; ambidextrous safety; blued finish. Introduced 1983; discontinued 1984; replaced by Model 30M.
Exc.: $400   **VGood:** $350   **Good:** $300

HANDGUNS

Sturm Ruger Semi-Automatics

Government Model Stainless
Mark II Target
P85 Mark II
MK-4B Compact Pistol
P89 DAO
Ruger P89
Ruger P89D Decocker
P90
P91 DC Decocker
P93 Compact
P94
P94L

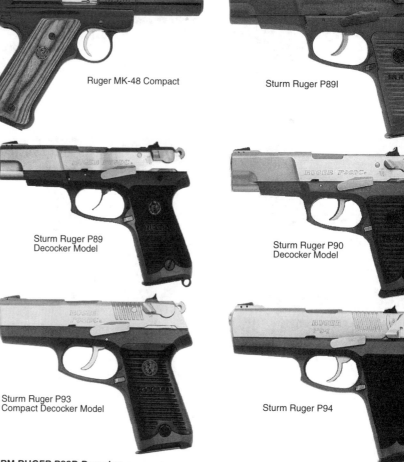

Ruger MK-48 Compact

Sturm Ruger P89I

Sturm Ruger P89 Decocker Model

Sturm Ruger P90 Decocker Model

Sturm Ruger P93 Compact Decocker Model

Sturm Ruger P94

STURM RUGER MARK II GOVERNMENT MODEL STAINLESS

Semi-automatic; 22 LR; 10-shot magazine; 6 7/8" slab-sided barrel; receiver drilled, tapped for Ruger scope base adaptor; checkered walnut grip panels; right-hand thumb rest; blued open sights. Marketed with 1" stainless scope rings, integral base. Introduced 1991; still in production.

New: $350   **Perf.:** $300   **Exc.:** $250

Sturm Ruger Mark II Target

Same specs as standard model except 5 1/4", 6 7/8" barrel; 11 1/8" overall length; weighs 42 oz.; .125" blade front sight, adjustable micro-click rear; sight radius 93/8". Introduced 1982; still in production.

New: $250   **Perf.:** $200   **Exc.:** $165
Stainless steel finish
New: $300   **Perf.:** $250   **Exc.:** $200

Ruger MK-4B Compact

Similar to the Mark II Standard pistol except has 4" bull barrel, Patridge-type front sight, fully adjustable rear, and smooth laminated hardwood thumbrest stocks. Weighs 38 oz., overall length of 8-3/16". Comes with extra magazine, plastic case, lock. Introduced 1996.

New: $300   **Perf.:** $250   **Exc.:** $200

STURM RUGER P85 MARK II

Semi-automatic; double action, DAO; 9mm Para.; 15-shot magazine; 4 1/2" barrel; 7 13/16" overall length; weighs 32 oz.; windage-adjustable square-notch rear sight, square post front; ambidextrous slide-mounted safety levers; 4140 chome-moly steel slide; aluminum alloy frame; grooved Xenoy composition stocks; ambidextrous magazine release; blue or stainless finish. Decocker version also available. Introduced 1986; dropped 1992.

New: $325   **Perf.:** $300   **Exc.:** $250
Stainless finish
New: $375   **Perf.:** $325   **Exc.:** $275

STURM RUGER P89

Semi-automatic; double action; 9mm Para., 10-shot magazine. Barrel: 4.50". Weight: 32 oz. Length: 7.84" overall. Stocks: Grooved black Xenoy composition. Sights: Square post front, square notch rear adjustable for windage, both with white dot inserts. Features: Double action with ambidextrous slide-mounted safety-levers. Slide is 4140 chrome-moly steel or 400-series stainless steel, frame is a lightweight aluminum alloy. Ambidextrous magazine release. Blue or stainless steel. Introduced 1986; stainless introduced 1990.

New: $325   **Perf.:** $300   **Exc.:** $250
Stainless finish
New: $375   **Perf.:** $325   **Exc.:** $275

STURM RUGER P89D Decocker

Similar to the standard P89 except has ambidextrous decocking levers in place of the regular slide-mounted safety. The decocking levers move the firing pin inside the slide where the hammer can not reach it, while simultaneously blocking the firing pin from forward movement-allows shooter to decock a cocked pistol without manipulating the trigger. Conventional thumb decocking procedures are therefore unnecessary. Blue or stainless steel. Introduced 1990.

New: $325   **Perf.:** $300   **Exc.:** $250
Stainless finish
New: $375   **Perf.:** $325   **Exc.:** $275

STURM RUGER P89/DAO

Semi-automatic; double action, double-action-only; 9mm Para.; 15-shot magazine; 4 1/2" barrel; 7 13/16" overall length; weighs 32 oz.; improved version of P85 Mark II; windage-adjustable square-notch rear sight, square post front; internal safety; bobbed, spurless hammer; gripping grooves on rear of slide; stainless steel construction. Decocker model also available at no extra cost; blue or stainless (DAO) finish. Marketed with plastic case, extra magazine, loading tool. Introduced 1991; still in production.

New: $325   **Perf.:** $300   **Exc.:** $250
Stainless
New: $400   **Perf.:** $350   **Exc.:** $300

STURM RUGER P90

Semi-automatic; double action; 45 ACP; 7-shot magazine; 4 1/2" barrel; 7 15/16" overall length; weighs 33 1/2 oz.; aluminum frame; stainless steel slide; ambidextrous slide-mounted safety levers; square post front, square notch windage-adjustable rear; stainless steel only. Decocker model also available at no extra cost. Introduced 1991; still in production.

New: $400   **Perf.:** $350   **Exc.:** $300

STURM RUGER P91 DC DECOCKER

Semi-automatic; double action, double-action-only; 40 S&W; 11-shot magazine; 4 1/2" barrel; 7 15/16" over-all length; weighs 33 oz.; ambidextrous slide-mounted safety levers; square post front, windage-adjustable square notch rear with white dot inserts; grooved black Xenoy composition grips; stainless finish. Marketed with plastic case, extra magazine, loading tool. Introduced 1991; dropped 1994.

New: $400   **Perf.:** $350   **Exc.:** $300

STURM RUGER P93 COMPACT

Semi-automatic; double action; 9mm Para.; 10-shot magazine; 3 15/16" barrel; 7 5/16" overall length; weighs 31 oz.; grooved black Xenoy composition grips; square post front sight, square notch windage-adjustable rear with white dot inserts; forward third of the slide tapered and polished to the muzzle; front of the slide crowned with a convex curve; seven finger grooves on slide; 400-series stainless steel slide; lightweight alloy frame. Available as decocker-only or double-action-only. Introduced 1993; still produced.

New: $425   **Perf.:** $375   **Exc.:** $325

STURM RUGER P94

Semi-automatic; double-action-only, decock only, or manual safety; 9mm Para., 40 S&W; 10-shot magazine; 4 1/4" barrel; 7 1/2" overall length; weighs 33 oz.; grooved Xenoy grips; square post front sight, windage-adjustable rear; three-dot system; slide gripping grooves roll over top of slide; ambidextrous safety-levers; ambidextrous decocking levers; matte finish stainless slide and barrel, alloy frame; frame size between full-size P-Series and compact P93. Introduced 1994; still produced.

New: $350   **Perf.:** $300   **Exc.:** $275

Sturm Ruger P94L

Same specs as the KP94 except laser sight mounts in housing cast integrally with frame; Allen-head screws control windage and elevation adjustments. Made in U.S. by Sturm, Ruger. Introduced 1994; still produced for law enforcement only.

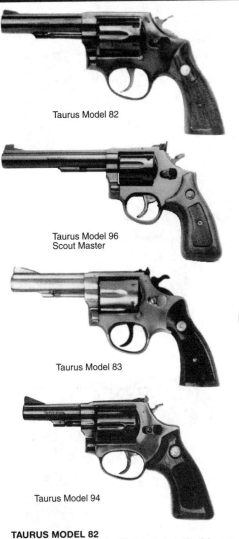

Taurus Model 82

Taurus Model 96
Scout Master

Taurus Model 83

Taurus Model 94

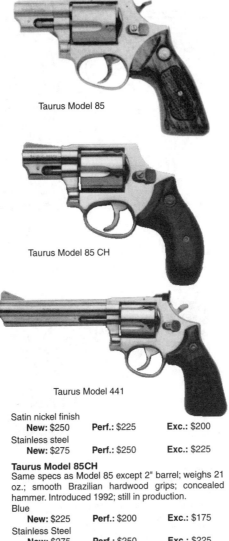

Taurus Model 85

Taurus Model 85 CH

Taurus Model 441

HANDGUNS

Taurus

Model 82
Model 83
Model 84
Model 85
Model 85CH
Model 86 Target Master
Model 94
Model 96 Scout Master
Model 431
Model 441
Model 445, 445CH

Taurus Model 431

Taurus Model 445, 445CH

Satin nickel finish
New: $250   **Perf.:** $225   **Exc.:** $200
Stainless steel
New: $275   **Perf.:** $250   **Exc.:** $225

Taurus Model 85CH
Same specs as Model 85 except 2" barrel; weighs 21 oz.; smooth Brazilian hardwood grips; concealed hammer. Introduced 1992; still in production.
Blue
New: $225   **Perf.:** $200   **Exc.:** $175
Stainless Steel
New: $275   **Perf.:** $250   **Exc.:** $225

TAURUS MODEL 86 TARGET MASTER
Revolver; double action; 38 Spl.; 6-shot cylinder; 6" barrel; 11 1/4" overall length; weighs 34 oz.; oversize target-type grips of checkered Brazilian hardwood; Patridge front sight, micro-click fully-adjustable rear; blue finish with non-reflective finish on barrel. Imported from Brazil by Taurus International. Dropped 1994.
Perf.: $275   **Exc.:** $225   **VGood:** $200

TAURUS MODEL 94
Revolver; double action; 22 LR; 9-shot; 3", 4" barrel; weighs 25 oz.; serrated ramp front sight, click-adjustable rear; checkered Brazilian hardwood stocks; color case-hardened hammer, trigger; floating firing pin; blued or stainless finish. Introduced 1988; still imported.
New: $225   **Perf.:** $200   **Exc.:** $165
Stainless steel
New: $250   **Perf.:** $225   **Exc.:** $200

TAURUS MODEL 94
Revolver, double action; 22 LR, 9-shot cylinder. Barrel: 2", 4", 5". Weight: 25 oz. Stocks: Soft black rubber. Sights: Serrated ramp front, click-adjustable rear for windage and elevation. Features: Floating firing pin, color case-hardened hammer and trigger. Introduced 1989. Imported by Taurus International.
New: $225   **Perf.:** $175   **Exc.:** $150
Stainless finish
New: $275   **Perf.:** $200   **Exc.:** $175

TAURUS MODEL 96 SCOUT MASTER
Revolver; double action; 22 LR; 6-shot; 6" barrel; weighs 34 oz.; heavy solid barrel rib; adjustable target

TAURUS MODEL 82
Revolver; double action; 38 Spl.; 6-shot; 3", 4" heavy barrel; 9 1/4" overall length; weighs 34 oz.; fixed sights; checkered Brazilian hardwood grips; blue, satin nickel or stainless steel finish. Introduced 1971; still in production.
New: $200   **Perf.:** $150   **Exc.:** $125
Satin nickel finish
New: $225   **Perf.:** $165   **Exc.:** $135
Stainless steel
New: $225   **Perf.:** $175   **Exc.:** $150
Price: Blue $296.00
Price: Stainless $344.00

TAURUS MODEL 83
Revolver; double action; 38 Spl.; 6-shot; 4" heavy barrel; 9 1/2" overall length; weighs 34 oz.; adjustable rear sight, ramp front; hand-checkered oversize Brazilian hardwood grips; blue or stainless steel finish. Introduced 1977; still in production.
New: $200   **Perf.:** $150   **Exc.:** $125
Stainless steel
New: $225   **Perf.:** $185   **Exc.:** $150

TAURUS MODEL 84
Revolver; double action; 38 Spl.; 6-shot; 4" barrel; 9 1/2" overall length; adjustable rear sight, ramp front; checkered wood grips; blued finish. Introduced 1971; discontinued 1978.
Exc.: $135   **VGood:** $115   **Good:** $100

TAURUS MODEL 85
Revolver; double action; 38 Spl.; 5-shot; 2", 3" barrel; weighs 21 oz.; ramp front sight, square-notch rear; checkered Brazilian hardwood grips; blued, satin nickel or stainless finish. Introduced 1980; still imported.
New: $225   **Perf.:** $200   **Exc.:** $175

trigger; Patridge type front, micrometer click-adjustable rear; checkered Brazilian hardwood grips; blued finish. Introduced 1971; still in production.
New: $275   **Perf.:** $225   **Exc.:** $175\

TAURUS MODEL 431
Revolver; double action; 44 Spl.; 5-shot; 3", 4", 6" barrel; weighs 40 1/2 oz. (6" barrel); checkered Brazilian hardwood grips; serrated ramp front sight, fixed rear; heavy barrel with solid rib and full-length ejector shroud; blue or stainless finish. Imported by Taurus International. Introduced 1992; still imported.
Blue finish
New: $200   **Perf.:** $175   **Exc.:** $135
Stainless steel
New: $275   **Perf.:** $225   **Exc.:** $185

TAURUS MODEL 441
Revolver; double action; 44 Spl.; 5-shot cylinder; 3", 4", 6" barrel; weighs 40 1/2 oz. (6" barrel); checkered Brazilian hardwood grips; serrated ramp front sight, micrometer click fully-adjustable rear; heavy barrel with solid rib and full-length ejector shroud; blue or stainless finish. Imported by Taurus International. Introduced 1992; still imported.
Blue finish
New: $225   **Perf.:** $185   **Exc.:** $150
Stainless steel
New: $300   **Perf.:** $250   **Exc.:** $200

TAURUS MODEL 445, 445CH
Revolver; double action; 44 Special, 5-shot. Barrel: 2". Weight: 28.25 oz. Length: 6-3/4" overall. Stocks: Soft black rubber. Sights: Serrated ramp front, notch rear. Features: Blue or stainless steel. Standard or concealed hammer. Introduced 1997. Imported by Taurus International.

Taurus
Model PT 22
Model PT 25
Model PT 58
Model PT 91AF
Model PT 92AF
Model PT 92AFC
Model PT 99AF
Model PT 100
Model PT 101
Model PT-111 Millennium
Model PT 908
Model PT-911

Taurus Model PT 101

Taurus Model PT 92AF

Taurus Model PT 22

Taurus Model PT 58

Taurus Model PT-911

Blue finish
> **New:** $250   **Perf.:** $200   **Exc.:** $175

Stainless steel
> **New:** $300   **Perf.:** $250   **Exc.:** $200

TAURUS MODEL PT 22
Semi-automatic; double action; 22 LR; 9-shot magazine; 2 3/4" barrel; 5 1/4" overall length; weighs 12 1/2 oz.; smooth Brazilian hardwood grips; blade front sight, fixed rear; tip-up barrel for loading, cleaning. Made in U.S. by Taurus International. Introduced 1992; still produced.

Blue finish
> **New:** $165   **Perf.:** $135   **Exc.:** $110

Stainless steel
> **New:** $175   **Perf.:** $150   **Exc.:** $135

TAURUS MODEL PT 25
Semi-automatic; double action; 25 ACP; 8-shot magazine; 2 3/4" barrel; 5 1/4" overall length; weighs 12 1/2 oz.; smooth Brazilian hardwood grips; blade front sight, fixed rear; tip-up barrel for loading, cleaning. Made in U.S. by Taurus International. Introduced 1992; still produced.

Blue finish
> **New:** $150   **Perf.:** $125   **Exc.:** $110

Stainless steel
> **New:** $175   **Perf.:** $150   **Exc.:** $135

TAURUS MODEL PT 58
Semi-automatic; double action; 380 ACP; 12-, 10-shot; 4" barrel; weighs 30 oz.; integral blade front sight, notch rear with three-dot system; Brazilian hardwood stocks; exposed hammer; inertia firing pin; blued finish. Introduced 1988; still imported.

> **New:** $325   **Perf.:** $300   **Exc.:** $250

Stainless steel
> **New:** $400   **Perf.:** $350   **Exc.:** $300

TAURUS MODEL PT 91AF
Semi-automatic; double action; 41 AE; 10-shot; 5" barrel; weighs 34 oz.; fixed sights; smooth wood grips; exposed hammer; blued finish. Introduced 1990; discontinued 1991.

> **Perf.:** $350   **Exc.:** $300   **VGood:** $250

Satin nickel finish
> **Perf.:** $375   **Exc.:** $325   **VGood:** $275

TAURUS MODEL PT 92AF
Semi-automatic; double action; 9mm Para.; 15-, 10-shot; 5" barrel; 8 1/2" overall length; weighs 34 oz.; fixed sights; black plastic stocks; exposed hammer; chamber loaded indicator; inertia firing pin; blued, nickel or stainless finish. Introduced 1983; still imported.

Blue, nickel finish
> **New:** $425   **Perf.:** $375   **Exc.:** $325

Stainless steel (PT 92SS)
> **New:** $450   **Perf.:** $425   **Exc.:** $375

Taurus Model PT 92AFC
Same specs as PT 92AF except 4" barrel; 13-, 10-shot; 7 1/2" overall length; weighs 31 oz. Introduced 1991; still imported.

> **New:** $350   **Perf.:** $325   **Exc.:** $275

Stainless steel
> **New:** $400   **Perf.:** $350   **Exc.:** $300

TAURUS MODEL PT 99AF
Semi-automatic; double action; 9mm Para.; 15-, 10-shot; 5" barrel; 8 1/2" overall length; adjustable sights; uncheckered Brazilian walnut stocks; exposed hammer; chamber-loaded indicator; inertia firing pin; blue, satin nickel or stainless steel finish. Introduced 1983; still in production.

Blue
> **New:** $450   **Perf.:** $375   **Exc.:** $300

Stainless steel
> **New:** $475   **Perf.:** $425   **Exc.:** $375

TAURUS MODEL PT 100
Semi-automatic; double action; 40 S&W; 11-, 10-shot; 5" barrel; fixed sights; three-dot combat system; uncheckered Brazilian hardwood grips; ambidextrous hammer-drop safety; exposed hammer; chamber-loaded indicator; inertia firing pin; blue or stainless steel finish. Introduced 1991; still imported.

Blue
> **New:** $450   **Perf.:** $400   **Exc.:** $325

Stainless steel
> **New:** $475   **Perf.:** $425   **Exc.:** $375

TAURUS MODEL PT 101
Semi-automatic; double action; 40 S&W; 11-, 10-shot; 5" barrel; 34 oz.; adjustable sights; uncheckered Brazilian hardwood grips; ambidextrous hammer-drop safety; exposed hammer; chamber-loaded indicator; inertia firing pin; blue or stainless steel finish. Introduced 1992; still imported.

Blue
> **New:** $450   **Perf.:** $375   **Exc.:** $300

Stainless steel
> **New:** $475   **Perf.:** $425   **Exc.:** $375

TAURUS MODEL PT-111 MILLENNIUM
Semi-automatic; double action only; 9mm Para.; 10-shot magazine. Barrel: 3.30". Weight: 19 oz. Length: 6.0" overall. Stocks: Polymer. Sights: Fixed.

Low profile, three-dot combat. Features: Double action only. Firing pin lock; polymer frame; striker fired; push-button magazine release. Introduced 1998. Imported by Taurus International.

Blue finish
> **New:** $275   **Perf.:** $225   **Exc.:** $185

Stainless steel
> **New:** $300   **Perf.:** $250   **Exc.:** $200

TAURUS MODEL PT 908
Semi-automatic; double action; 9mm Para.; 8-shot magazine; 3 13/16" barrel; 7" overall length; weighs 30 oz.; checkered black composition grips; drift-adjustable front and rear sights, three-dot combat; exposed hammer; manual ambidextrous hammer-drop; inertia firing pin; chamber loaded indicator; blue or stainless steel finish. Imported by Taurus International. Introduced 1993; still imported.

Blue
> **New:** $325   **Perf.:** $300   **Exc.:** $250

Stainless steel
> **New:** $375   **Perf.:** $350   **Exc.:** $300

TAURUS MODEL PT-911
Semi-automatic; double action; 9mm Para., 10-shot magazine. Barrel: 3.85". Weight: 28.2 oz. Length: 7.05" overall. Stocks: Black rubber. Sights: Fixed. Low profile, three-dot combat. Features: Double action, exposed hammer; ambidextrous hammer drop; chamber loaded indicator. Introduced 1997. Imported by Taurus International.

Blue finish
> **New:** $375   **Perf.:** $325   **Exc.:** $275

Stainless steel
> **New:** $400   **Perf.:** $350   **Exc.:** $325

Walther Model 7

Walther Model 8

Walther Model 4

Walther Model 9

Walther Model HP

Walther Model PP

HANDGUNS

Walther
Model 4
Model 5
Model 6
Model 7
Model 8
Model 8 Lightweight
Model 9
Model HP
Model PP
Model PP Lightweight
Model PP Mark II
Model PP Post-WWII
Model PPK
Model PPK American

32 caliber
    Exc.: $400   **VGood:** $300   **Good:** $225
380 caliber
    Exc.: $1000   **VGood:** $750   **Good:** $500
22 caliber
    Exc.: $850   **VGood:** $650   **Good:** $450
25 caliber
    Exc.: $3000   **VGood:** $2500   **Good:** $2000

Walther Model PP Lightweight
Same specs as Model PP except aluminum alloy frame. Introduced 1929; dropped 1945.
32 caliber
    Exc.: $750   **VGood:** $450   **Good:** $375
380 caliber
    Exc.: $1200   **VGood:** $950   **Good:** $700

Walther Model PP Mark II
Same specs as pre-WWII model. Currently manufactured in France by Manufacture De Machines Du Haut-Rhin. Introduced 1953; still in production, but not imported.
    Exc.: $250   **VGood:** $200   **Good:** $175

Walther Model PP Post-WWII
Same specs as pre-war except not made in 25-caliber. Currently manufactured by Carl Walther Waffenfabrik, Ulm/Donau, West Germany. Still in production. Imported by Interarms.
    Exc.: $350   **VGood:** $275   **Good:** $200

WALTHER MODEL PPK
Semi-automatic; 22 LR, 25 ACP, 32 ACP, 380 ACP; 7-shot magazine; 3 1/4" barrel; 5 7/8" overall length; the Kurz (short) version of the PP; checkered plastic grips; fixed sights; blued finish. WWII production has less value due to poorer workmanship. Introduced 1931; dropped 1945. RZM, PDM and other special markings bring a premium.
Wartime models
    Exc.: $350   **VGood:** $300   **Good:** $250
32 caliber
    Exc.: $450   **VGood:** $375   **Good:** $325
380 caliber
    Exc.: $1250   **VGood:** $950   **Good:** $650
22 caliber
    Exc.: $900   **VGood:** $700   **Good:** $500
25 caliber
    Exc.: $4500   **VGood:** $4000   **Good:** $3500

Walther Model PPK American
Same specs as PPK except 6-shot magazine; 3 7/8" barrel; 6 5/16" overall length; weighs 21 oz.; 380 ACP only; blued or stainless finish. Made in U.S. Introduced 1986; still marketed by Interarms.
    New: $575   **Perf.:** $500   **Exc.:** $400

WALTHER MODEL 4
Semi-automatic; 32 ACP; 8-shot magazine; 3 1/2" barrel; 5 7/8" overall length; checkered hard rubber stocks; fixed sights; blued finish. Manufactured 1910 to 1920.
    Exc.: $250   **VGood:** $150   **Good:** $100

WALTHER MODEL 5
Semi-automatic; 25 ACP; 6-shot magazine; 2" barrel; 4 7/16" overall length; checkered hard rubber stocks; fixed sights; blued finish. Same specs as Model 2 except better workmanship; improved finish. Manufactured 1913 to 1918; collector value.
    Exc.: $350   **VGood:** $250   **Good:** $200

WALTHER MODEL 6
Semi-automatic; 9mm Para.; 8-shot magazine; 4 3/4" barrel; 8 1/4" overall length; checkered hard rubber stocks; fixed sights; blued finish. Manufactured 1915 to 1917. Rare.
    Exc.: $4500 **VGood:** $3500 **Good:** $2750

WALTHER MODEL 7
Semi-automatic; 25 ACP; 8-shot magazine; 3" barrel; 5 5/16" overall length; checkered hard rubber stocks; fixed sights; blued finish. Manufactured 1917 to 1918.
    Exc.: $500   **VGood:** $425   **Good:** $350

WALTHER MODEL 8
Semi-automatic; 25 ACP; 8-shot magazine; 2 7/8" barrel; 5 1/8" overall length; fixed sights; checkered plastic grips; blued. Manufactured by Waffenfabrik Walther, Zella-Mehlis, Germany. Introduced 1920; dropped 1945.
    Exc.: $400   **VGood:** $325   **Good:** $275

Walther Model 8 Lightweight
Same specs as Model 8, except aluminum alloy. Introduced 1927; dropped about 1935.
    Exc.: $1000   **VGood:** $750   **Good:** $600

WALTHER MODEL 9
Semi-automatic; 25 ACP; 6-shot magazine; 2" barrel; 3 15/16" overall length; checkered plastic grips; fixed sights; blued. Introduced 1921; dropped 1945.
    Exc.: $450   **VGood:** $375   **Good:** $325

WALTHER MODEL HP
Semi-automatic; 9mm, 7.65mm Para. (very rare); 10-shot magazine; 5" barrel; 8 3/8" overall length; checkered (early) or grooved plastic or checkered wood (rare) grips; fixed sights; blued. Early examples have rectangular firing pin. Introduced 1939; dropped 1945.
Rectangular firing pin
    Exc.: $2250 **VGood:** $1850 **Good:** $1200
Round firing pin
    Exc.: $1500   **VGood:** $950   **Good:** $700

WALTHER MODEL PP
Semi-automatic; 22 LR, 25 ACP, 32 ACP, 380 ACP; 8-shot magazine; 3 7/8" barrel; 6 5/16" overall length; designed as law-enforcement model; fixed sights; checkered plastic grips; blued. WWII production has less value because of poorer workmanship. Introduced 1929; dropped 1945. RZM, PDM and other special markings bring a premium.
Wartime models
    Exc.: $350   **VGood:** $300   **Good:** $250

Includes models suitable for several forms of competition and other sporting purposes.

Accu-Tek HC-380

Accu-Tek XL-9

Auto-Ordnance 1911A1 Standard

Baer Custom Carry

Auto-Ordnance Deluxe

Baer Premium II

ACCU-TEK MODEL HC-380 AUTO PISTOL

Caliber: 380 ACP, 10-shot magazine. **Barrel:** 2.75". **Weight:** 26 oz. **Length:** 6" overall. **Grips:** Checkered black composition. **Sights:** Blade front, rear adjustable for windage. **Features:** External hammer; manual thumb safety with firing pin and trigger disconnect; bottom magazine release. Stainless steel construction. Introduced 1993. Price includes cleaning kit and gun lock. Made in U.S.A. by Accu-Tek.
Price: Satin stainless $249.00

ACCU-TEK XL-9 AUTO PISTOL

Caliber: 9mm Para., 5-shot magazine. **Barrel:** 3". **Weight:** 24 oz. **Length:** 5.6" overall. **Grips:** Black pebble composition. **Sights:** Three-dot system; rear adjustable for windage. **Features:** Stainless steel construction; double-action-only mechanism. Introduced 1999. Price includes cleaning kit and gun lock, two magazines. Made in U.S.A. by Accu-Tek.
Price: $267.00

AMERICAN DERRINGER LM-5 AUTOMATIC PISTOL

Caliber: 25 ACP, 5-shot magazine. **Barrel:** 2-1/4". **Weight:** 15 oz. **Length:** NA. **Grips:** Wood. **Sights:** Fixed. **Features:** Compact, stainless, semi-auto, single-action hammerless design. Hand assembled and fitted.
Price: $425.00

AUTO-ORDNANCE 1911A1 AUTOMATIC PISTOL

Caliber: 45 ACP, 7-shot magazine. **Barrel:** 5". **Weight:** 39 oz. **Length:** 8-1/2" overall. **Grips:** Checkered plastic with medallion. **Sights:** Blade front, rear adjustable for windage. **Features:** Same specs as 1911A1 military guns-parts interchangeable. Frame and slide blued; each radius has nonglare finish. Made in U.S.A. by Auto-Ordnance Corp.
Price: 45 ACP, blue $511.00
Price: 45 ACP, Parkerized $515.00
Price: 45 ACP Deluxe (three-dot sights, textured rubber
  wraparound grips) $525.00

AUTAUGA 32 AUTO PISTOL

Caliber: 32 ACP, 6-shot magazine. **Barrel:** 2". **Weight:** 11.3 oz. **Length:** 4.3" overall. **Grips:** Black polymer. **Sights:** Fixed. **Features:** Double-ac-

tion-only mechanism. Stainless steel construction. Uses Winchester Silver Tip ammunition.
Price: . . . . NA

BAER 1911 CUSTOM CARRY AUTO PISTOL

Caliber: 45 ACP, 7- or 10-shot magazine. **Barrel:** 5". **Weight:** 37 oz. **Length:** 8.5" overall. **Grips:** Checkered walnut. **Sights:** Baer improved ramp-style dovetailed front, Novak low-mount rear. **Features:** Baer forged NM frame, slide and barrel with stainless bushing; fitted slide to frame; double serrated slide (full-size only); Baer speed trigger with 4-lb. pull; Baer deluxe hammer and sear, tactical-style extended ambidextrous safety, beveled magazine well; polished feed ramp and throated barrel; tuned extractor; Baer extended ejector, checkered slide stop; lowered and flared ejection port, full-length recoil guide rod; recoil buff. Partial listing shown. Made in U.S.A. by Les Baer Custom, Inc.
Price: Standard size, blued $1,640.00
Price: Standard size, stainless $1,690.00
Price: Comanche size, blued $1,640.00
Price: Comanche size, stainless $1,690.00
Price: Comanche size, aluminum frame, blued slide $1,923.00
Price: Comanche size, aluminum frame, stainless slide $1,995.00

BAER 1911 PREMIER II AUTO PISTOL

Caliber: 9x23, 38 Super, 400 Cor-Bon, 45 ACP, 7- or 10-shot magazine. **Barrel:** 5". **Weight:** 37 oz. **Length:** 8.5" overall. **Grips:** Checkered rosewood, double diamond pattern. **Sights:** Baer dovetailed front, low-mount Bo-Mar rear with hidden leaf. **Features:** Baer NM forged steel frame and barrel with stainless bushing; slide fitted to frame; double serrated slide; lowered, flared ejection port; tuned, polished extractor; Baer extended ejector, checkered slide stop, aluminum speed trigger with 4-lb. pull, deluxe Commander hammer and sear, beavertail grip safety with pad, beveled magazine well, extended ambidextrous safety; flat mainspring housing; polished feed ramp and throated barrel; 30 lpi checkered front strap. Made in U.S.A. by Les Baer Custom, Inc.
Price: Blued $1,428.00
Price: Stainless $1,558.00
Price: 6" model, blued, from $1,595.00

Beretta M8000/8040 Cougar

Beretta 96

Bersa Thunder 380

BAER 1911 S.R.P. PISTOL

Caliber: 45 ACP. **Barrel:** 5". **Weight:** 37 oz. **Length:** 8.5" overall. **Grips:** Checkered walnut. **Sights:** Trijicon night sights. **Features:** Similar to the F.B.I. contract gun except uses Baer forged steel frame. Has Baer match barrel with supported chamber, Wolff springs, complete tactical action job. All parts Magna-fluxed; deburred for tactical carry. Has Baer Ultra Coat finish. Tuned for reliability. Contact Baer for complete details. Introduced 1996. Made in U.S.A. by Les Baer Custom, Inc.

Price: Government or Comanche length $2,240.00

BERETTA MODEL 92FS PISTOL

Caliber: 9mm Para., 10-shot magazine. **Barrel:** 4.9". **Weight:** 34 oz. **Length:** 8.5" overall. **Grips:** Checkered black plastic. **Sights:** Blade front, rear adjustable for windage. Tritium night sights available. **Features:** Double action. Extractor acts as chamber loaded indicator, squared trigger guard, grooved front and backstraps, inertia firing pin. Matte or blued finish. Introduced 1977. Made in U.S.A. and imported from Italy by Beretta U.S.A.

Price: With plastic grips $712.00
Price: Vertec with access rail $751.00
Price: Vertec Inox $801.00

Beretta Model 92FS/96 Brigadier Pistols

Similar to the Model 92FS/96 except with a heavier slide to reduce felt recoil and allow mounting removable front sight. Wrap-around rubber grips. Three-dot sights dovetailed to the slide, adjustable for windage. Weighs 35.3 oz. Introduced 1999.

Price: 9mm or 40 S&W, 10-shot $772.00
Price: Inox models (stainless steel) $822.00

Beretta Model 96 Pistol

Same as the Model 92FS except chambered for 40 S&W. Ambidextrous safety mechanism with passive firing pin catch, slide safety/decocking lever, trigger bar disconnect. Has 10-shot magazine. Available with three-dot sights. Introduced 1992.

Price: Model 96, plastic grips $712.00
Price: Stainless, rubber grips $772.00
Price: Vertec with access rail $751.00
Price: Vertec Inox $801.00

BERETTA MODEL 80 CHEETAH SERIES DA PISTOLS

Caliber: 380 ACP, 10-shot magazine (M84); 8-shot (M85); 22 LR, 7-shot (M87). **Barrel:** 3.82". **Weight:** About 23 oz. (M84/85); 20.8 oz. (M87). **Length:** 6.8" overall. **Grips:** Glossy black plastic (wood optional at extra cost). **Sights:** Fixed front, drift-adjustable rear. **Features:** Double action, quick takedown, convenient magazine release. Introduced 1977. Imported from Italy by Beretta U.S.A.

Price: Model 84 Cheetah, plastic grips $615.00
Price: Model 85 Cheetah, plastic grips, 8-shot $579.00
Price: Model 87 Cheetah, wood, 22 LR, 7-shot $615.00
Price: Model 87 Target, plastic grips $708.00

Beretta Model 86 Cheetah

Similar to the 380-caliber Model 85 except has tip-up barrel for first-round loading. Barrel length is 4.4", overall length of 7.33". Has 8-shot magazine, walnut grips. Introduced 1989.

Price: $615.00

Beretta Model 21 Bobcat Pistol

Similar to the Model 950 BS. Chambered for 22 LR or 25 ACP. Both double action. Has 2.4" barrel, 4.9" overall length; 7-round magazine on 22 cal.; 8 rounds in 25 ACP, 9.9 oz., available in nickel, matte, engraved or blue finish. Plastic grips. Introduced in 1985.

Price: Bobcat, 22 or 25, blue $300.00
Price: Bobcat, 22, stainless $329.00
Price: Bobcat, 22 or 25, matte $265.00

BERETTA MODEL 3032 TOMCAT PISTOL

Caliber: 32 ACP, 7-shot magazine. **Barrel:** 2.45". **Weight:** 14.5 oz. **Length:** 5" overall. **Grips:** Checkered black plastic. **Sights:** Blade front, drift-adjustable rear. **Features:** Double action with exposed hammer; tip-up barrel for direct loading/unloading; thumb safety; polished or matte blue finish. Imported from Italy by Beretta U.S.A. Introduced 1996.

Price: Blue $393.00
Price: Matte $358.00
Price: Stainless $443.00
Price: With Tritium sights $436.00

BERETTA MODEL 8000/8040/8045 COUGAR PISTOL

Caliber: 9mm Para., 10-shot, 40 S&W, 10-shot magazine; 45 ACP, 8-shot. **Barrel:** 3.6". **Weight:** 33.5 oz. **Length:** 7" overall. **Grips:** Checkered plastic. **Sights:** Blade front, rear drift adjustable for windage. **Features:** Slide-mounted safety; rotating barrel; exposed hammer. Matte black Bruniton finish. Announced 1994. Imported from Italy by Beretta U.S.A.

Price: 8000 and 8000L $729.00
Price: D model, 9mm, 40 S&W $729.00
Price: D model, 45 ACP $779.00
Price: Inox $794.00

BERETTA MODEL 9000S COMPACT PISTOL

Caliber: 9mm Para., 40 S&W; 10-shot magazine. **Barrel:** 3.4". **Weight:** 26.8 oz. **Length:** 6.6". **Grips:** Soft polymer. **Sights:** Windage-adjustable white-dot rear, white-dot blade front. **Features:** Glass-reinforced polymer frame; patented tilt-barrel, open-slide locking system; chrome-lined barrel; external serrated hammer; automatic firing pin and manual safeties. Introduced 2000. Imported from Italy by Beretta USA.

Price: 9000S Type F (single and double action, external hammer) $472.00

BERSA THUNDER LITE 380 AUTO PISTOLS

Caliber: 380 ACP, 7-shot (Thunder 380 Lite), 9-shot magazine (Thunder 380 DLX). **Barrel:** 3.5". **Weight:** 23 oz. **Length:** 6.6" overall. **Grips:** Black polymer. **Sights:** Blade front, notch rear adjustable for windage; three-dot system. **Features:** Double action; firing pin and magazine safeties. Available in blue, nickel, or duo tone. Introduced 1995. Distributed by Eagle Imports, Inc.

Price: Thunder 380, 7-shot, deep blue finish $266.95
Price: Thunder 380 Deluxe, 9-shot, satin nickel $299.95
Price: Thunder 380 Gold, 7-shot $299.95

Charles Daly M-1911-A1P

Cobra FS380

Cobra CA32

Bersa Thunder 45 Ultra Compact Pistol

Similar to the Bersa Thunder 380 except in 45 ACP. Available in three finishes. Introduced 2003. Imported from Argentina by Eagle Imports, Inc.
Price: Thunder 45, matte blue **$400.95**
Price: Thunder 45, Duotone **$424.95**
Price: Thunder 45, Satin nickel **$441.95**

BLUE THUNDER/COMMODORE 1911-STYLE AUTO PISTOLS

Caliber: 45 ACP, 7-shot magazine. **Barrel:** 4-1/4", 5". **Weight:** NA. **Length:** NA. **Grips:** Checkered hardwood. **Sights:** Blade front, drift-adjustable rear. **Features:** Extended slide release and safety, spring guide rod, skeletonized hammer and trigger, magazine bumper, beavertail grip safety. Imported from the Philippines by Century International Arms Inc.
Price: . . . . **$464.80 to $484.80**

BROWNING HI-POWER 9MM AUTOMATIC PISTOL

Caliber: 9mm Para.,10-shot magazine. **Barrel:** 4-21/32". **Weight:** 32 oz. **Length:** 7-3/4" overall. **Grips:** Walnut, hand checkered, or black Polyamide. **Sights:** 1/8" blade front; rear screw-adjustable for windage and elevation. Also available with fixed rear (drift-adjustable for windage). **Features:** External hammer with half-cock and thumb safeties. A blow on the hammer cannot discharge a cartridge; cannot be fired with magazine removed. Fixed rear sight model available. Includes gun lock. Imported from Belgium by Browning.
Price: Fixed sight model, walnut grips **$680.00**
Price: Fully adjustable rear sight, walnut grips **$730.00**
Price: Mark III, standard matte black finish, fixed sight, moulded grips, ambidextrous safety **$662.00**

Browning Hi-Power Practical Pistol

Similar to the standard Hi-Power except has silver-chromed frame with blued slide, wrap-around Pachmayr rubber grips, round-style serrated hammer and removable front sight, fixed rear (drift-adjustable for windage). Available in 9mm Para. Includes gun lock. Introduced 1991.
Price: **$717.00**

BROWNING PRO-9

Caliber: 9mm Luger, 10-round magazine. **Barrel:** 4". **Weight:** 30 oz. **Overall length:** 7 1/4". **Features:** Double-action, ambidextrous decocker and safety. Fixed, three-dot-style sights, 6" sight radius. Molded composite grips with interchangeable backstrap inserts.
Price: **$628.00**

BROWNING HI-POWER

Caliber: 9mm, 40 S&W. **Barrel:** 4 3/4". **Weight:** 32 to 35 oz. **Overall length:** 7 3/4". **Features:** Blued, matte, polymer or silver-chromed frame; molded, wraparound Pachmayr or walnut grips; Commander-style or spur-type hammer.
Price: Practical model, fixed sights **$791.00**
Price: Mark II model, epoxy finish **$730.00**
Price: HP Standard, blued, fixed sights, walnut grips **$751.00**
Price: HP Standard, blued, adj. sights **$805.00**

CHARLES DALY M-1911-A1P AUTOLOADING PISTOL

Caliber: 45 ACP, 7- or 10-shot magazine. **Barrel:** 5". **Weight:** 38 oz. **Length:** 8-3/4" overall. **Grips:** Checkered. **Sights:** Blade front, rear drift adjustable for windage; three-dot system. **Features:** Skeletonized combat hammer and trigger; beavertail grip safety; extended slide release; oversize thumb safety; Parkerized finish. Introduced 1996. Imported from the Philippines by K.B.I., Inc.
Price: **$469.95**

COBRA ENTERPRISES FS380 AUTO PISTOL

Caliber: 380 ACP, 7-shot magazine. **Barrel:** 3.5". **Weight:** 2.1 lbs. **Length:** 6-3/8" overall. **Grips:** Black composition. **Sights:** Fixed. **Features:** Choice of bright chrome, satin nickel or black finish. Introduced 2002. Made in U.S.A. by Cobra Enterprises.
Price: **$130.00**

COBRA ENTERPRISES FS32 AUTO PISTOL

Caliber: 32 ACP, 8-shot magazine. **Barrel:** 3.5". **Weight:** 2.1 lbs. **Length:** 6-3/8" overall. **Grips:** Black composition. **Sights:** Fixed. **Features:** Choice of black, satin nickel or bright chrome finish. Introduced 2002. Made in U.S.A. by Cobra Enterprises.
Price: **$130.00**

COBRA INDUSTRIES PATRIOT PISTOL

Caliber: 380ACP, 9mm Luger, 10-shot magazine. **Barrel:** 3.3". **Weight:** 20 oz. **Length:** 6" overall. **Grips:** Checkered polymer. **Sights:** Fixed. **Features:** Stainless steel slide with load indicator; double-action-only trigger system. Introduced 2002. Made in U.S.A. by Cobra Enterprises, Inc.
Price: **$279.00**

COBRA INDUSTRIES CA32, CA380

Caliber: 32ACP, 380 ACP. **Barrel:** 2.8" **Weight:** 22 oz. **Length:** 5.4". **Grips:** Laminated wood (CA32); Black molded synthetic (CA380). **Sights:** Fixed. **Features:** True pocket pistol size and styling without bulk. Made in U.S.A. by Cobra Enterprises.
Price: . . . . **NA**

COLT MODEL 1991 MODEL O AUTO PISTOL

Caliber: 45 ACP, 7-shot magazine. **Barrel:** 5". **Weight:** 38 oz. **Length:** 8.5" overall. **Grips:** Checkered black composition. **Sights:** Ramped blade front, fixed square notch rear, high profile. **Features:** Matte finish. Continuation of serial number range used on original G.I. 1911 A1 guns. Comes with one magazine and moulded carrying case. Introduced 1991.
Price: **$645.00**
Price: Stainless **$800.00**

Colt Model 1991 Model O Commander Auto Pistol

Similar to the Model 1991 A1 except has 4-1/4" barrel. Overall length is 7-3/4". Comes with one 7-shot magazine, molded case.
Price: Blue **$645.00**
Price: Stainless steel **$800.00**

Colt 1991 Model O

Colt 1991 Model O Commander

Colt XSE Model O Commander

Colt XSE Lightweight Commander

Colt Defender

Colt Series 70

Colt 38 Super

Colt Gunsite

Price: **$773.00**
Price: 41 Magnum Model, from **$825.00**

COLT XSE SERIES MODEL O AUTO PISTOLS
Caliber: 45 ACP, 8-shot magazine. **Barrel:** 4.25", 5". **Grips:** Checkered, double diamond rosewood. **Sights:** Drift-adjustable three-dot combat. **Features:** Brushed stainless finish; adjustable, two-cut aluminum trigger; extended ambidextrous thumb safety; upswept beavertail with palm swell; elongated slot hammer; beveled magazine well. Introduced 1999. From Colt's Manufacturing Co., Inc.
Price: XSE Government (5" barrel) **$950.00**
Price: XSE Commander (4.25" barrel) **$950.00**

COLT XSE LIGHTWEIGHT COMMANDER AUTO PISTOL
Caliber: 45 ACP, 8-shot. **Barrel:** 4-1/4". **Weight:** 26 oz. **Length:** 7-3/4" overall. **Grips:** Double diamond checkered rosewood. **Sights:** Fixed, glare-proofed blade front, square notch rear; three-dot system. **Features:** Brushed stainless slide, nickeled aluminum frame; McCormick elongated-slot enhanced hammer, McCormick two-cut adjustable aluminum hammer. Made in U.S.A. by Colt's Mfg. Co., Inc.
Price: 45, stainless **$950.00**

COLT DEFENDER
Caliber: 40 S&W, 45 ACP, 7-shot magazine. **Barrel:** 3". **Weight:** 22-1/2 oz. **Length:** 6-3/4" overall. **Grips:** Pebble-finish rubber wraparound with finger grooves. **Sights:** White dot front, snag-free Colt competition rear. **Features:** Stainless finish; aluminum frame; combat-style hammer; Hi Ride grip safety, extended manual safety, disconnect safety. Introduced 1998. Made in U.S.A. by Colt's Mfg. Co.

COLT SERIES 70
Caliber: 45 ACP. **Barrel:** 5". **Weight:** NA. **Length:** NA. **Grips:** Rosewood with double diamond checkering pattern. **Sights:** Fixed. **Features:** A custom replica of the Original Series 70 pistol with a Series 70 firing system, original rollmarks. Introduced 2002. Made in U.S.A. by Colt's Manufacturing.
Price: .... **NA**

COLT 38 SUPER
Caliber: 38 Super. **Barrel:** 5". **Weight:** NA. **Length:** 8-1/2". **Grips:** Checkered rubber (stainless and blue models); wood with double diamond checkering pattern (bright stainless model). **Sights:** 3-dot. **Features:** Beveled magazine well, standard thumb safety and service-style grip safety. Introduced 2003. Made in U.S.A. by Colt's Mfg. Co.
Price: .... (Blue) **$864.00** (Stainless steel) **$943.00**
Price: .... (Bright stainless steel) **$1,152.00**

COLT GUNSITE PISTOL
Caliber: 45 ACP. **Barrel:** 5". **Weight:** NA. **Length:** NA. **Grips:** Rosewood. **Sights:** Heinie, front; Novak, rear. **Features:** Contains most all of the Gunsite school recommended features such as Series 70 firing system, Smith & Alexander metal grip safety w/palm swell, serrated flat mainspring housing, dehorned all around. Available in blue or stainless steel. Introduced 2003. Made in U.S.A. by Colt's Mfg. Co.
Price: .... **NA**

CZ 75B 9mm

CZ 75B Decocker

CZ 85

CZ 97B

CZ 100

CZ 75B AUTO PISTOL
Caliber: 9mm Para., 40 S&W, 10-shot magazine. **Barrel:** 4.7". **Weight:** 34.3 oz. **Length:** 8.1" overall. **Grips:** High impact checkered plastic. **Sights:** Square post front, rear adjustable for windage; three-dot system. **Features:** Single action/double action design; firing pin block safety; choice of black polymer, matte or high-polish blue finishes. All-steel frame. Imported from the Czech Republic by CZ-USA.
Price: Black polymer **$529.00**
Price: Glossy blue **$559.00**
Price: Dual tone or satin nickel **$559.00**
Price: 22 LR conversion unit **$399.00**

CZ 75B Decocker
Similar to the CZ 75B except has a decocking lever in place of the safety lever. All other specifications are the same. Introduced 1999. Imported from the Czech Republic by CZ-USA.
Price: 9mm, black polymer **$559.00**
Price: 40 S&W **$569.00**

CZ 75B Compact Auto Pistol
Similar to the CZ 75 except has 10-shot magazine, 3.9" barrel and weighs 32 oz. Has removable front sight, non-glare ribbed slide top. Trigger guard is squared and serrated; combat hammer. Introduced 1993. Imported from the Czech Republic by CZ-USA.
Price: 9mm, black polymer **$559.00**
Price: Dual tone or satin nickel **$569.00**
Price: D Compact, black polymer **$569.00**
Price: CZ2075 Sub-compact RAMI **$559.00**

CZ 75M IPSC Auto Pistol
Similar to the CZ 75B except has a longer frame and slide, slightly larger grip to accommodate new heavy-duty magazine. Ambidextrous thumb safety, safety notch on hammer; two-port in-frame compensator; slide racker; frame-mounted Firepoint red dot sight. Introduced 2001. Imported from the Czech Republic by CZ USA.
Price: 40 S&W, 10-shot mag. **$1,551.00**
Price: CZ 75 Standard IPSC (40 S&W, adj. sights) **$1,038.00**

CZ 85B Auto Pistol
Same gun as the CZ 75 except has ambidextrous slide release and safety-levers; non-glare, ribbed slide top; squared, serrated trigger guard; trigger stop to prevent overtravel. Introduced 1986. Imported from the Czech Republic by CZ-USA.

Price: Black polymer **$483.00**
Price: Combat, black polymer **$540.00**
Price: Combat, dual tone **$487.00**
Price: Combat, glossy blue **$499.00**

CZ 85 Combat
Similar to the CZ 85B (9mm only) except has an adjustable rear sight, adjustable trigger for overtravel, free-fall magazine, extended magazine catch. Does not have the firing pin block safety. Introduced 1999. Imported from the Czech Republic by CZ-USA.
Price: 9mm, black polymer **$540.00**
Price: 9mm, glossy blue **$566.00**
Price: 9mm, dual tone or satin nickel **$586.00**

CZ 83B DOUBLE-ACTION PISTOL
Caliber: 9mm Makarov, 32 ACP, 380 ACP, 10-shot magazine. **Barrel:** 3.8". **Weight:** 26.2 oz. **Length:** 6.8" overall. **Grips:** High impact checkered plastic. **Sights:** Removable square post front, rear adjustable for windage; three-dot system. **Features:** Single action/double action; ambidextrous magazine release and safety. Blue finish; non-glare ribbed slide top. Imported from the Czech Republic by CZ-USA.
Price: Blue **$378.00**
Price: Nickel **$397.00**

CZ 97B AUTO PISTOL
Caliber: 45 ACP, 10-shot magazine. **Barrel:** 4.85". **Weight:** 40 oz. **Length:** 8.34" overall. **Grips:** Checkered walnut. **Sights:** Fixed. **Features:** Single action/double action; full-length slide rails; screw-in barrel bushing; linkless barrel; all-steel construction; chamber loaded indicator; dual transfer bars. Introduced 1999. Imported from the Czech Republic by CZ-USA.
Price: Black polymer **$625.00**
Price: Glossy blue **$641.00**

CZ 100 AUTO PISTOL
Caliber: 9mm Para., 40 S&W, 10-shot magazine. **Barrel:** 3.7". **Weight:** 24 oz. **Length:** 6.9" overall. **Grips:** Grooved polymer. **Sights:** Blade front with dot, white outline rear drift adjustable for windage. **Features:** Double action only with firing pin block; polymer frame, steel slide; has laser sight mount. Introduced 1996. Imported from the Czech Republic by CZ-USA.
Price: 9mm Para **$405.00**
Price: 40 S&W **$424.00**

**Dan Wesson Firearms
Pointman Major**

**Dan Wesson Firearms
Major Aussie**

**Dan Wesson Firearms
Patriot Marksman**

DAN WESSON FIREARMS POINTMAN MAJOR AUTO PISTOL

Caliber: 45 ACP. **Barrel:** 5". **Grips:** Rosewood checkered. **Features:** Blued or stainless steel frame and serrated slide; Chip McCormick match-grade trigger group, sear and disconnect; match-grade barrel; high-ride beavertail safety; checkered slide release; **Sights:** High rib; interchangeable sight system; laser engraved. Introduced 2000. Made in U.S.A. by Dan Wesson Firearms.
Price: Model PM1-B (blued) **$799.00**
Price: Model PM1-S (stainless) **$699.00**

Dan Wesson Firearms Pointman Seven Auto Pistols

Similar to Pointman Major, dovetail adjustable target rear sight and dovetail target front sight. Available in blued or stainless finish. Introduced 2000. Made in U.S.A. by Dan Wesson Firearms.
Price: PM7 (blued frame and slide) **$999.00**
Price: PM7S (stainless finish) **$799.00**

Dan Wesson Firearms Pointman Guardian Auto Pistols

Similar to Pointman Major, more compact frame with 4.25" barrel. Available in blued or stainless finish with fixed or adjustable sights. Introduced 2000. Made in U.S.A. by Dan Wesson Firearms.
Price: PMG-FS, all new frame (fixed sights) **$769.00**
Price: PMG-AS (blued frame and slide, adjustable sights) **$799.00**
Price: PMGD-FS Guardian Duce, all new frame (stainless frame and blued slide, fixed sights) **$829.00**
Price: PMGD-AS Guardian Duce (stainless frame and blued slide, adj. sights) **$799.00**

Dan Wesson Firearms Major Tri-Ops Packs

Similar to Pointman Major. Complete frame assembly fitted to 3 match grade complete slide assemblied (9mm, 10mm, 40 S&W). Includes recoil springs and magazines that come in hard cases fashioned after high-grade European rifle case. Constructed of navy blue cordura stretched over hardwood with black leather trim and comfortable black leather wrapped handle. Brass corner protectors, dual combination locks, engraved presentation plate on the lid. Inside, the Tri-Ops Pack components are nested in precision die-cut closed cell foam and held sercurely in place by convoluted foam in the inside of the lid. Introduced 2002. Made in U.S.A. by Dan Wesson Firearms.
Price: TOP1B (blued), TOP1-S (stainless) **$2,459.00**

Dan Wesson Firearms Major Aussie

Similar to Pointman Major. Available in 45 ACP. Features Bomar-style adjustable rear target sight, unique slide top configuration exclusive to this model (features radius from the flat side surfaces of the slide to a narrow flat on top and then a small redius and reveal ending in a flat, low (1/16" high) sight rib 3/8" wide with lengthwise serrations). Clearly identified by the Southern Cross flag emblem laser engraved on the sides of the slide (available in 45 ACP only). Introduced 2002. Made in U.S.A. by Dan Wesson Firearms.
Price: PMA-B (blued) **$799.00**
Price: PMA-S (stainless) **$799.00**

Dan Wesson Firearms Pointman Minor Auto Pistol

Similar to Pointman Major. Full size (5") entry level IDPA or action pistol model with blued carbon alloy frame and round top slide, bead blast matte finish on frame and slide top and radius, satin-brushed polished finish on sides of slide, chromed barrel, dovetail mount fixed rear target sight and tactical/target ramp front sight, match trigger, skeletonized target hammer, high ride beavertail, fitted extractor, serrations on thumb safety, slide release and mag release, lowered and relieved ejection port, beveled mag well, exotic hardwood grips, serrated mainspring housing, laser engraved. Introduced 2000. Made in U.S.A. by Dan Wesson Firearms.
Price: Model PM2-P **$599.00**

Dan Wesson Firearms Pointman Hi-Cap Auto Pistol

Similar to Pointman Minor, full-size high-capacity (10-shot) magazine with 5" chromed barrel, blued finish and dovetail fixed rear sight. Match adjustable trigger, ambidextrous extended thumb safety, beavertail safety. Introduced 2001. From Dan Wesson Firearms.
Price: PMHC (Pointman High-Cap) **$689.00**

Dan Wesson Firearms Pointman Dave Pruitt Signature Series

Similar to other full-sized Pointman models, customized by Master Pistolsmith and IDPA Grand Master Dave Pruitt. Alloy carbon-steel with black oxide bluing and bead-blast matte finish. Front and rear chevron cocking serrations, dovetail mount fixed rear target sight and tactical/target ramp front sight, ramped match barrel with fitted match bushing and link, Chip McCormick (or equivalent) match grade trigger group, serrated ambidextrous tactical/carry thumb safety, high ride beavertail, serrated slide release and checkered mag release, match grade sear and hammer, fitted extractor, lowered and relieved ejection port, beveled mag well, full length 2-piece recoil spring guide rod, cocobolo double diamond checkered grips, serrated steel mainspring housing, special laser engraving. Introduced 2001. From Dan Wesson Firearms.
Price: PMDP (Pointman Dave Pruitt) **$899.00**

DAN WESSON FIREARMS PATRIOT 1911 PISTOL

Caliber: 45 ACP. **Grips:** Exotic exhibition grade cocobolo, double diamond hand cut checkering. **Sights:** New innovative combat/carry rear sight that completely encloses the dovetail. **Features:** The new Patriot Expert and Patriot Marksman are full size match grade series 70 1911s machined from steel forgings. Available in blued chome moly steel or stainless steel. Beveled mag well, lowered and flared ejection port, high sweep beavertail safety. Introduced June 2002.
Price: Model PTM-B (blued) **$797.00**
Price: Model PTM-S (stainless) **$898.00**
Price: Model PTE-B (blued) **$864.00**
Price: Model PTE-S (stainless) **$971.00**

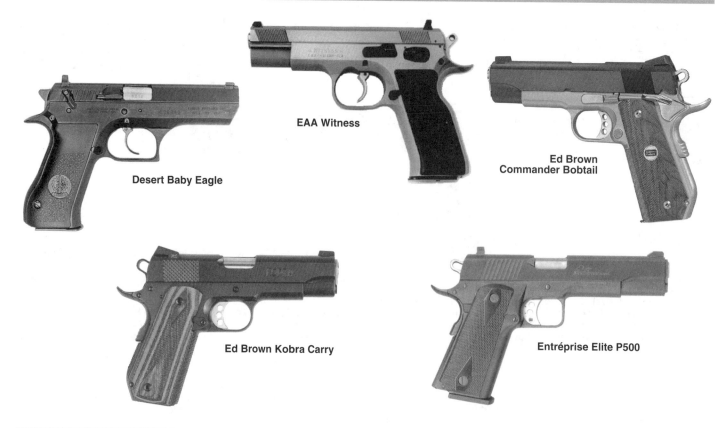

EAA Witness

Desert Baby Eagle

Ed Brown
Commander Bobtail

Ed Brown Kobra Carry

Entréprise Elite P500

DESERT BABY EAGLE PISTOLS

Caliber: 9mm Para., 40 S&W, 45 ACP, 10-round magazine. **Barrel:** 3.5", 3.7", 4.72". **Weight:** 26.8 - 39.8 oz. **Length:** 7.25" to 8.25" overall. **Grips:** Polymer. **Sights:** Drift-adjustable rear, blade front. **Features:** Steel frame and slide; polygonal rifling to reduce barrel wear; slide safety; decocker. Reintroduced in 1999. Imported from Israel by Magnum Research Inc.

Price: Standard (9mm or 40 cal.; 4.72" barrel, 8.25" overall) **$499.00**

Price: Semi-Compact (9mm, 40 or 45 cal.; 3.7" barrel, 7.75" overall) **$499.00**

Price: Compact (9mm or 40 cal.; 3.5" barrel, 7.25" overall) **$499.00**

Price: Polymer (9mm or 40 cal; polymer frame; 3.25" barrel, 7.25" overall) **$499.00**

EAA WITNESS DA AUTO PISTOL

Caliber: 9mm Para., 10-shot magazine; 38 Super, 40 S&W, 10-shot magazine; 45 ACP, 10-shot magazine. **Barrel:** 4.50". **Weight:** 35.33 oz. **Length:** 8.10" overall. **Grips:** Checkered rubber. **Sights:** Undercut blade front, open rear adjustable for windage. **Features:** Double-action trigger system; round trigger guard; frame-mounted safety. Introduced 1991. Imported from Italy by European American Armory.

Price: 9mm, blue **$449.00**
Price: 9mm, Wonder finish **$459.00**
Price: 9mm Compact, blue, 10-shot **$449.00**
Price: As above, Wonder finish. **$459.00**
Price: 38 Super, blue **$449.00**
Price: 38 Super, Wonder finish **$459.00**
Price: 40 S&W, blue **$449.00**
Price: As above, Wonder finish. **$459.00**
Price: 40 S&W Compact, 9-shot, blue **$449.00**
Price: As above, Wonder finish. **$459.00**
Price: 45 ACP, blue. **$449.00**
Price: As above, Wonder finish. **$459.00**
Price: 45 ACP Compact, 8-shot, blue. **$449.00**
Price: As above, Wonder finish. **$459.00**

ED BROWN CLASSIC CUSTOM

Caliber: 45 ACP, 7 shots. **Barrel:** 5". **Weight:** 39 oz. **Stocks:** Cocobolo wood. **Sights:** Bo-Mar adjustable rear, dovetail front. **Features:** Single-action, M1911 style, custom made to order, stainless frame and slide available.

Price: **$2,895.00**

ED BROWN COMMANDER BOBTAIL

Caliber: 45 ACP, 400 Cor-Bon, 40 S&W, 357 SIG, 38 Super, 9mm Luger, 7-shot magazine. **Barrel:** 4.25". **Weight:** 34 oz. **Grips:** Hogue exotic wood. **Sights:** Customer preference front; fixed Novak low-mount, rear. Optional night inserts available. **Features:** Checkered forestrap and bob-tailed mainspring housing. Other options available.

Price: Executive Carry **$2,295.00**
Price: Executive Elite **$2,195.00**

ED BROWN KOBRA

Caliber: 45 ACP, 7-shot magazine. **Barrel:** 5" (Kobra); 4.25" (Kobra Carry). **Weight:** 39 oz. (Kobra); 34 oz. (Kobra Carry). **Grips:** Hogue exotic wood. **Sights:** Ramp, front; fixed Novak low-mount night sights, rear. **Features:** Has snakeskin pattern serrations on forestrap and mainspring housing, denorned edges, beavertail grip safety.

Price: Kobra **$1,895.00**
Price: Kobra Carry **$1,995.00**

ENTRÉPRISE ELITE P500 AUTO PISTOL

Caliber: 45 ACP, 10-shot magazine. **Barrel:** 5". **Weight:** 40 oz. **Length:** 8.5" overall. **Grips:** Black ultra-slim, double diamond, checkered synthetic. **Sights:** Dovetailed blade front, rear adjustable for windage; three-dot system. **Features:** Reinforced dust cover; lowered and flared ejection port; squared trigger guard; adjustable match trigger; bolstered front strap; high grip cut; high ride beavertail grip safety; steel flat mainspring housing; extended thumb lock; skeletonized hammer; match grade sear, disconnector; Wolff springs. Introduced 1998. Made in U.S.A. by Entréprise Arms.

Price: **$739.90**

Entréprise
Tactical 500

FEG PJK-9HP

Felk MTF 450

Firestorm Mini

Firestorm 45 Gov't

Glock 17C

Entréprise Medalist P500 Auto Pistol

Similar to the Elite model except has adjustable Competizione "melded" rear sight with dovetailed Patridge front; machined slide parallel rails with polished breech face and barrel channel; front and rear slide serrations; lowered and flared ejection port; full-length one-piece guide rod with plug; National Match barrel and bushing; stainless firing pin; tuned match extractor; oversize firing pin stop; throated barrel and polished ramp; slide lapped to frame. Introduced 1998. Made in U.S.A. by Entréprise Arms.
Price: 45 ACP **$979.00**
Price: 40 S&W **$1,099.00**

Entréprise Tactical P500 Auto Pistol

Similar to the Elite model except has Tactical2 Ghost Ring sight or Novak lo-mount sight; ambidextrous thumb safety; front and rear slide serrations; full-length guide rod; throated barrel, polished ramp; tuned match extractor; fitted barrel and bushing; stainless firing pin; slide lapped to frame; dehorned. Introduced 1998. Made in U.S.A. by Entréprise Arms.
Price: **$979.90**
Price: Tactical Plus (full-size frame, Officer's slide). **$1,049.00**

ERMA KGP68 AUTO PISTOL

Caliber: 32 ACP, 6-shot, 380 ACP, 5-shot. **Barrel:** 4". **Weight:** 22-1/2 oz. **Length:** 7-3/8" overall. **Grips:** Checkered plastic. **Sights:** Fixed. **Features:** Toggle action similar to original "Luger" pistol. Action stays open after last shot. Has magazine and sear disconnect safety systems.
Price: **$499.95**

FEG PJK-9HP AUTO PISTOL

Caliber: 9mm Para., 10-shot magazine. **Barrel:** 4.75". **Weight:** 32 oz. **Length:** 8" overall. **Grips:** Hand-checkered walnut. **Sights:** Blade front, rear adjustable for windage; three dot system. **Features:** Single action; polished blue or hard chrome finish; rounded combat-style serrated hammer. Comes with two magazines and cleaning rod. Imported from Hungary by K.B.I., Inc.
Price: Blue **$259.95**
Price: Hard chrome. **$259.95**

FEG SMC-380 AUTO PISTOL

Caliber: 380 ACP, 6-shot magazine. **Barrel:** 3.5". **Weight:** 18.5 oz. **Length:** 6.1" overall. **Grips:** Checkered composition with thumbrest. **Sights:** Blade front, rear adjustable for windage. **Features:** Patterned after the PPK pistol. Alloy frame, steel slide; double action. Blue finish. Comes with two magazines, cleaning rod. Imported from Hungary by K.B.I., Inc.
Price: **$224.95**

FELK MTF 450 AUTO PISTOL

Caliber: 9mm Para. (10-shot); 40 S&W (8-shot); . 357 Mag, 45 ACP (9-shot magazine). **Barrel:** 3.5". **Weight:** 19.9 oz. **Length:** 6.4" overall. **Grips:** Checkered. **Sights:** Blade front; adjustable rear. **Features:** Double-action only trigger, striker fired; polymer frame; trigger safety, firing pin safety, trigger bar safety; adjustable trigger weight; fully interchangeable slide/barrel to change calibers. Introduced 1998. Imported by Felk Inc.
Price: **$395.00**
Price: 45 ACP pistol with 9mm and 40 S&W slide/barrel
assemblies **$999.00**

FIRESTORM AUTO PISTOL

Features: 7 or 10 rd. double action pistols with matte, duotone or nickel finish. Distributed by SGS Importers International.
Price: 22 LR 10 rd, 380 7 rd. matte. **$264.95**
Price: Duotone **$274.95**
Price: Mini 9mm, 40 S&W, 10 rd. matte **$383.95**
Price: Duotone **$391.95**
Price: Nickel **$408.95**
Price: Mini 45, 7 rd. matte. **$383.95**
Price: Duotone 45. . . . . **$399.95**
Price: Nickel 45 . . . . **$416.95**
Price: 45 Government, Compact, 7 rd. matte **$324.95**
Price: Duotone **$333.95**
Price: Extra magazines. **$29.95-49.95**

GLOCK 17 AUTO PISTOL

Caliber: 9mm Para., 10-shot magazine. **Barrel:** 4.49". **Weight:** 22.04 oz. (without magazine). **Length:** 7.32" overall. **Grips:** Black polymer. **Sights:** Dot on front blade, white outline rear adjustable for windage. **Features:** Polymer frame, steel slide; double-action trigger with "Safe Action" system; mechanical firing pin safety, drop safety; simple takedown without tools; locked breech, recoil operated action. Adopted by Austrian armed forces 1983. NATO approved 1984. Imported from Austria by Glock, Inc.
Price: Fixed sight, extra magazine, magazine loader, cleaning kit **$641.00**
Price: Adjustable sight **$671.00**
Price: Model 17L (6" barrel) **$800.00**
Price: Model 17C, ported barrel (compensated) **$646.00**

Glock 22

Glock 26

Glock 30

Glock 31

Glock 35

Glock 19 Auto Pistol

Similar to the Glock 17 except has a 4" barrel, giving an overall length of 6.85" and weight of 20.99 oz. Magazine capacity is 10 rounds. Fixed or adjustable rear sight. Introduced 1988.

Price: Fixed sight **$641.00**
Price: Adjustable sight **$671.00**
Price: Model 19C, ported barrel **$646.00**

Glock 20 10mm Auto Pistol

Similar to the Glock Model 17 except chambered for 10mm Automatic cartridge. Barrel length is 4.60", overall length is 7.59", and weight is 26.3 oz. (without magazine). Magazine capacity is 10 rounds. Fixed or adjustable rear sight. Comes with an extra magazine, magazine loader, cleaning rod and brush. Introduced 1990. Imported from Austria by Glock, Inc.

Price: Fixed sight **$700.00**
Price: Adjustable sight **$730.00**

Glock 21 Auto Pistol

Similar to the Glock 17 except chambered for 45 ACP, 10-shot magazine. Overall length is 7.59", weight is 25.2 oz. (without magazine). Fixed or adjustable rear sight. Introduced 1991.

Price: Fixed sight **$700.00**
Price: Adjustable sight **$730.00**

Glock 22 Auto Pistol

Similar to the Glock 17 except chambered for 40 S&W, 10-shot magazine. Overall length is 7.28", weight is 22.3 oz. (without magazine). Fixed or adjustable rear sight. Introduced 1990.

Price: Fixed sight **$641.00**
Price: Adjustable sight **$671.00**
Price: Model 22C, ported barrel **$646.00**

Glock 23 Auto Pistol

Similar to the Glock 19 except chambered for 40 S&W, 10-shot magazine. Overall length is 6.85", weight is 20.6 oz. (without magazine). Fixed or adjustable rear sight. Introduced 1990.

Price: Fixed sight **$641.00**
Price: Model 23C, ported barrel **$646.00**
Price: Adjustable sight **$671.00**

GLOCK 26, 27 AUTO PISTOLS

Caliber: 9mm Para. (M26), 10-shot magazine; 40 S&W (M27), 9-shot magazine. **Barrel:** 3.46". **Weight:** 21.75 oz. **Length:** 6.29" overall. **Grips:** Integral. Stippled polymer. **Sights:** Dot on front blade, fixed or fully adjustable white outline rear. **Features:** Subcompact size. Polymer frame, steel slide; double-action trigger with "Safe Action" system, three safeties. Matte black Tenifer finish. Hammer-forged barrel. Imported from Austria by Glock, Inc. Introduced 1996.

Price: Fixed sight **$641.00**
Price: Adjustable sight **$671.00**

GLOCK 29, 30 AUTO PISTOLS

Caliber: 10mm (M29), 45 ACP (M30), 10-shot magazine. **Barrel:** 3.78". **Weight:** 24 oz. **Length:** 6.7" overall. **Grips:** Integral. Stippled polymer. **Sights:** Dot on front, fixed or fully adjustable white outline rear. **Features:** Compact size. Polymer frame steel slide; double-recoil spring reduces recoil; Safe Action system with three safeties; Tenifer finish. Two magazines supplied. Introduced 1997. Imported from Austria by Glock, Inc.

Price: Fixed sight **$700.00**
Price: Adjustable sight **$730.00**

Glock 31/31C Auto Pistols

Similar to the Glock 17 except chambered for 357 Auto cartridge; 10-shot magazine. Overall length is 7.32", weight is 23.28 oz. (without magazine). Fixed or adjustable sight. Imported from Austria by Glock, Inc.

Price: Fixed sight **$641.00**
Price: Adjustable sight **$671.00**
Price: Model 31C, ported barrel **$646.00**

Glock 32/32C Auto Pistols

Similar to the Glock 19 except chambered for the 357 Auto cartridge; 10-shot magazine. Overall length is 6.85", weight is 21.52 oz. (without magazine). Fixed or adjustable sight. Imported from Austria by Glock, Inc.

Price: Fixed sight **$616.00**
Price: Adjustable sight **$644.00**
Price: Model 32C, ported barrel **$646.00**

Glock 33 Auto Pistol

Similar to the Glock 26 except chambered for the 357 Auto cartridge; 9-shot magazine. Overall length is 6.29", weight is 19.75 oz. (without magazine). Fixed or adjustable sight. Imported from Austria by Glock, Inc.

Price: Fixed sight **$641.00**
Price: Adjustable sight **$671.00**

Heckler & Koch
USP Compact

Heckler & Koch USP45

Heckler & Koch
USP45 Compact

Heckler & Koch
USP45 Tactical

Heckler & Koch
Elite

Heckler & Koch
Mark 23 Special Operations

GLOCK 34, 35 AUTO PISTOLS
Caliber: 9mm Para. (M34), 40 S&W (M35), 10-shot magazine. **Barrel:** 5.32". **Weight:** 22.9 oz. **Length:** 8.15" overall. **Grips:** Integral. Stippled polymer. **Sights:** Dot on front, fully adjustable white outline rear. **Features:** Polymer frame, steel slide; double-action trigger with "Safe Action" system; three safeties; Tenifer finish. Imported from Austria by Glock, Inc.
Price: Model 34, 9mm. $770.00
Price: Model 35, 40 S&W $770.00

GLOCK 36 AUTO PISTOL
Caliber: 45 ACP, 6-shot magazine. **Barrel:** 3.78". **Weight:** 20.11 oz. **Length:** 6.77" overall. **Grips:** Integral. Stippled polymer. **Sights:** Dot on front, fully adjustable white outline rear. **Features:** Polymer frame, steel slide; double-action trigger with "Safe Action" system; three safeties; Tenifer finish. Imported from Austria by Glock, Inc.
Price: Fixed sight $700.00
Price: Adj. sight $730.00

HECKLER & KOCH USP AUTO PISTOL
Caliber: 9mm Para., 10-shot magazine, 40 S&W, 10-shot magazine, 357 Mag. **Barrel:** 4.25". **Weight:** 28 oz. (USP40). **Length:** 6.9" overall. **Grips:** Non-slip stippled black polymer. **Sights:** Blade front, rear adjustable for windage. **Features:** New HK design with polymer frame, modified Browning action with recoil reduction system, single control lever. Special "hostile environment" finish on all metal parts. Available in SA/DA, DAO, left- and right-hand versions. Introduced 1993. Imported from Germany by Heckler & Koch, Inc.
Price: Right-hand $769.00
Price: Left-hand $794.00

Heckler & Koch USP Compact Auto Pistol
Similar to the USP except has 3.58" barrel, measures 6.81" overall, and weighs 1.60 lbs. (9mm). Available in 9mm Para. 357 SIG or 40 S&W with 10-shot magazine. Introduced 1996. Imported from Germany by Heckler & Koch, Inc.
Price: Blue $799.00
Price: Blue with control lever on right $824.00
Price: Same as USP Compact DAO, enhanced trigger
performance $799.00

Heckler & Koch USP45 Auto Pistol
Similar to the 9mm and 40 S&W USP except chambered for 45 ACP, 10-shot magazine. Has 4.13" barrel, overall length of 7.87" and weighs 30.4 oz. Has adjustable three-dot sight system. Available in SA/DA, DAO, left- and right-hand versions. Introduced 1995. Imported from Germany by Heckler & Koch, Inc.
Price: Right-hand $839.00
Price: Left-hand $864.00

Heckler & Koch USP45 Compact
Similar to the USP45 except has stainless slide; 8-shot magazine; modified and contoured slide and frame; extended slide release; 3.80" barrel, 7.09" overall length, weighs 1.75 lbs.; adjustable three-dot sights. Introduced 1998. Imported from Germany by Heckler & Koch, Inc.
Price: With control lever on left, stainless $909.00
Price: As above, blue $857.00
Price: With control lever on right, stainless $944.00
Price: As above, blue $892.00

HECKLER & KOCH USP45 TACTICAL PISTOL
Caliber: 45 ACP, 10-shot magazine. **Barrel:** 4.92". **Weight:** 2.24 lbs. **Length:** 8.64" overall. **Grips:** Non-slip stippled polymer. **Sights:** Blade front, fully adjustable target rear. **Features:** Has extended threaded barrel with rubber O-ring; adjustable trigger; extended magazine floorplate; adjustable trigger stop; polymer frame. Introduced 1998. Imported from Germany by Heckler & Koch, Inc.
Price: $1,115.00

HECKLER & KOCH MARK 23 SPECIAL OPERATIONS PISTOL
Caliber: 45 ACP, 10-shot magazine. **Barrel:** 5.87". **Weight:** 43 oz. **Length:** 9.65" overall. **Grips:** Integral with frame; black polymer. **Sights:** Blade front, rear drift adjustable for windage; three-dot. **Features:** Polymer frame; double action; exposed hammer; short recoil, modified Browning action. Civilian version of the SOCOM pistol. Introduced 1996. Imported from Germany by Heckler & Koch, Inc.
Price: $2,112.00

Heckler & Koch P7M8

Hi-Point 9MM Comp

Kahr K9

Heckler & Koch USP Expert Pistol

Combines features of the USP Tactical and HK Mark 23 pistols with a new slide design. Chambered for 45 ACP, .40 S&W & 9mm; 10-shot magazine. Has adjustable target sights, 5.20" barrel, 8.74" overall length, weighs 1.87 lbs. Match-grade single- and double-action trigger pull with adjustable stop; ambidextrous control levers; elongated target slide; barrel O-ring that seals and centers barrel. Suited to IPSC competition. Introduced 1999. Imported from Germany by Heckler & Koch, Inc.

Price: **$1,869.00**

Heckler & Koch Elite

A long slide version of the USP combining features found on standard-sized and specialized models of the USP. Most noteworthy is the 6.2" barrel, making it the most accurate of the USP series. In 9mm and .45 ACP. Imported from Germany by Heckler & Koch, Inc. Introduced 2003.

Price: **$1,569.00**

HECKLER & KOCH P7M8 AUTO PISTOL

Caliber: 9mm Para., 8-shot magazine. **Barrel:** 4.13". **Weight:** 29 oz. **Length:** 6.73" overall. **Grips:** Stippled black plastic. **Sights:** Blade front, adjustable rear; three dot system. **Features:** Unique "squeeze cocker" in frontstrap cocks the action. Gas-retarded action. Squared combat-type trigger guard. Blue finish. Compact size. Imported from Germany by Heckler & Koch, Inc.

Price: P7M8, blued **$1,515.00**

HECKLER & KOCH P2000 GPM PISTOL

Caliber: 9mmx19; 10-shot magazine. 13- or 16-round law enforcement/military magazines. **Barrel:** 3.62". **Weight:** 21.87 ozs. **Length:** 7". **Grips:** Interchangeable panels. **Sights:** Fixed Patridge style, drift adjustable for windage, standard 3-dot. **Features:** German Pistol Model incorporating features of the HK USP Compact such as the pre-cocked hammer system which combines the advantages of a cocked striker with the double action hammer system. Introduced 2003. Imported from Germany by Heckler & Koch, Inc.

Price: **$887.00**

HECKLER & KOCK P2000SK SUBCOMPACT

Caliber: 9mm and 40 S&W. **Barrel:** 2.48". **Weight:** 1.49 lbs. (9mm) or 1.61 lbs. (40 S&W). **Sights:** Fixed Patridge style, drift adjustable. **Features:** Standard accessory rails, ambidextrous slide release, polymer frame, polygonal bore profile.

Price: **$887.00**

HI-POINT FIREARMS 9MM COMP PISTOL

Caliber: 9mm, Para., 10-shot magazine. **Barrel:** 4". **Weight:** 39 oz. **Length:** 7.72" overall. **Grips:** Textured acetal plastic. **Sights:** Adjustable; low profile. **Features:** Single-action design. Scratch-resistant, non-glare blue finish, alloy frame. Muzzle brake/compensator. Compensator is slotted for laser or flashlight mounting. Introduced 1998. From MKS Supply, Inc.

Price: Matte black **$159.00**

HI-POINT FIREARMS MODEL 9MM COMPACT PISTOL

Caliber: 9mm Para., 8-shot magazine. **Barrel:** 3.5". **Weight:** 29 oz. **Length:** 6.7" overall. **Grips:** Textured acetal plastic. **Sights:** Combat-style adjustable three-dot system; low profile. **Features:** Single-action design; frame-mounted magazine release; polymer or alloy frame. Scratch-resistant matte finish. Introduced 1993. Made in U.S.A. by MKS Supply, Inc.

Price: Black, alloy frame **$149.00**
Price: With polymer frame (29 oz.), non-slip grips **$149.00**
Price: Aluminum with polymer frame **$149.00**

Hi-Point Firearms Model 380 Polymer Pistol

Similar to the 9mm Compact model except chambered for 380 ACP, 8-shot magazine, adjustable three-dot sights. Weighs 29 oz. Polymer frame. Introduced 1998. Made in U.S.A. by MKS Supply.

Price: **$114.00**

Hi-Point Firearms 380 Comp Pistol

Similar to the 380 Polymer Pistol except has a 4" barrel with muzzle compensator; action locks open after last shot. Includes a 10-shot and an 8-shot magazine; trigger lock. Introduced 2001. Made in U.S.A. by MKS Supply Inc.

Price: **$135.00**
Price: With laser sight **$229.00**

HI-POINT FIREARMS 45 POLYMER FRAME

Caliber: 45 ACP, 9-shot, 40 S&W . **Barrel:** 4.5". **Weight:** 35 oz. **Sights:** Adjustable 3-dot. **Features:** Last round lock-open, grip mounted magazine release, magazine disconnect safety, integrated accessory rail. Introduced 2002. Made in U.S.A. by MKS Supply Inc.

Price: **$179.00**

IAI M-2000 PISTOL

Caliber: 45 ACP, 8-shot. **Barrel:** 5", (Compact 4.25"). **Weight:** 36 oz. **Length:** 8.5", (6" Compact). **Grips:** Plastic or wood. **Sights:** Fixed. **Features:** 1911 Government U.S. Army-style. Steel frame and slide parkerized. GI grip safety. Beveled feed ramp barrel. By IAI, Inc.

Price: **$465.00**

KAHR K9, K40 DA AUTO PISTOLS

Caliber: 9mm Para., 7-shot, 40 S&W, 6-shot magazine. **Barrel:** 3.5". **Weight:** 25 oz. **Length:** 6" overall. **Grips:** Wrap-around textured soft polymer. **Sights:** Blade front, rear drift adjustable for windage; bar-dot combat style. **Features:** Trigger-cocking double-action mechanism with passive firing pin block. Made of 4140 ordnance steel with matte black finish. Contact maker for complete price list. Introduced 1994. Made in U.S.A. by Kahr Arms.

Price: E9, black matte finish **$425.00**
Price: Matte black, night sights 9mm **$668.00**
Price: Matte stainless steel, 9mm....................... **$638.00**
Price: 40 S&W, matte black **$580.00**
Price: 40 S&W, matte black,
night sights **$668.00**
Price: 40 S&W, matte stainless **$638.00**
Price: K9 Elite 98 (high-polish stainless slide flats, Kahr combat
trigger), from **$694.00**
Price: As above, MK9 Elite 98, from..................... **$694.00**
Price: As above, K40 Elite 98, from **$694.00**
Price: Covert, black, stainless slide, short grip............. **$599.00**
Price: Covert, black, tritium nite sights **$689.00**

Kahr MK40

Kel-Tec P-11

Kel-Tec P-32

Kimber Custom II

Kimber Pro Carry II

Kahr K9 9mm Compact Polymer Pistol

Similar to K9 steel frame pistol except has polymer frame, matte stainless steel slide. Barrel length 3.5"; overall length 6"; weighs 17.9 oz. Includes two 7-shot magazines, hard polymer case, trigger lock. Introduced 2000. Made in U.S.A. by Kahr Arms.

Price: **$599.00**

Kahr MK9/MK40 Micro Pistol

Similar to the K9/K40 except is 5.5" overall, 4" high, has a 3" barrel. Weighs 22 oz. Has snag-free bar-dot sights, polished feed ramp, dual recoil spring system, DA-only trigger. Comes with 6- and 7-shot magazines. Introduced 1998. Made in U.S.A. by Kahr Arms.

Price: Matte stainless **$638.00**
Price: Elite 98, polished stainless, tritium night sights **$791.00**

KAHR PM9 PISTOL

Caliber: 9x19. **Barrel:** 3", 1:10 twist. **Weight:** 15.9 oz. **Length:** 5.3" overall. **Features:** Lightweight black polymer frame, polygonal rifling, stainless steel slide, DAO with passive striker block, trigger lock, hard case, 6 and 7 rd. mags.

Price: Matte stainless slide **$622.00**
Price: Tritium night sights **$719.00**

KEL-TEC P-11 AUTO PISTOL

Caliber: 9mm Para., 10-shot magazine. **Barrel:** 3.1". **Weight:** 14 oz. **Length:** 5.6" overall. **Grips:** Checkered black polymer. **Sights:** Blade front, rear adjustable for windage. **Features:** Ordnance steel slide, aluminum frame. Double-action-only trigger mechanism. Introduced 1995. Made in U.S.A. by Kel-Tec CNC Industries, Inc.

Price: Blue **$314.00**
Price: Hard chrome **$368.00**
Price: Parkerized **$355.00**

KEL-TEC P-32 AUTO PISTOL

Caliber: 32 ACP, 7-shot magazine. **Barrel:** 2.68". **Weight:** 6.6 oz. **Length:** 5.07" overall. **Grips:** Checkered composite. **Sights:** Fixed. **Features:** Double-action-only mechanism with 6-lb. pull; internal slide stop. Textured composite grip/frame. Now available in 380 ACP. Made in U.S.A. by Kel-Tec CNC Industries, Inc.

Price: Blue **$300.00**
Price: Hard chrome **$340.00**
Price: Parkerized **$355.00**

KIMBER CUSTOM II AUTO PISTOL

Caliber: 45 ACP, 40 S&W, .38 Super, 9 mm. **Barrel:** 5", match grade; 9 mm, .40 S&W, .38 Super barrels ramped. **Weight:** 38 oz. **Length:** 8.7" overall. **Grips:** Checkered black rubber, walnut, rosewood. **Sights:** Dovetail front and rear, Kimber low profile adj. or fixed three dot (green) Meptrolight night sights. **Features:** Slide, frame and barrel machined from steel or stainless steel. Match grade barrel, chamber and trigger group. Extended thumb safety, beveled magazine well, beveled front and rear slide serrations, high ride beavertail grip safety, checkered flat mainspring housing, kidney cut under trigger guard, high cut grip, match grade stainless steel barrel bushing, polished breech face, Commander-style hammer, lowered and flared ejection port, Wolff springs, bead blasted black oxide finish. Introduced 1996. Made in U.S.A. by Kimber Mfg., Inc.

Price: Custom **$745.00**
Price: Custom Walnut (double-diamond walnut grips) **$767.00**
Price: Custom Stainless **$848.00**
Price: Custom Stainless 40 S&W **$799.00**
Price: Custom Stainless Target 45 ACP (stainless, adj. sight) ... **$989.00**
Price: Custom Stainless Target 38 Super **$994.00**

Kimber Stainless II Auto Pistol

Similar to Custom II except has stainless steel frame, 4" bbl., grip is .400" shorter than standard, no front serrations. Weighs 34 oz. 45 ACP only. Introduced in 1998. Made in U.S.A. by Kimber Mfg., Inc.

Price: **$964.00**

Kimber Pro Carry II Auto Pistol

Similar to Custom II, has aluminum frame, 4" bull barrel fitted directly to the slide without bushing. HD with stainless steel frame. Introduced 1998. Made in U.S.A. by Kimber Mfg., Inc.

Price: Pro Carry **$789.00**
Price: Pro Carry w/night sights **$893.00**
Price: Pro Carry Stainless w/night sights **$862.00**
Price: Pro Carry HD II 38 Super **$936.00**

Kimber Ultra Carry II Auto Pistol

Similar to Compact Stainless II, lightweight aluminum frame, 3" match grade bull barrel fitted to slide without bushing. Grips .400" shorter. Special slide stop. Low effort recoil. Weighs 25 oz. Introduced in 1999. Made in U.S.A. by Kimber Mfg., Inc.

Price: **$783.00**
Price: Stainless **$858.00**
Price: Stainless 40 S&W **$903.00**

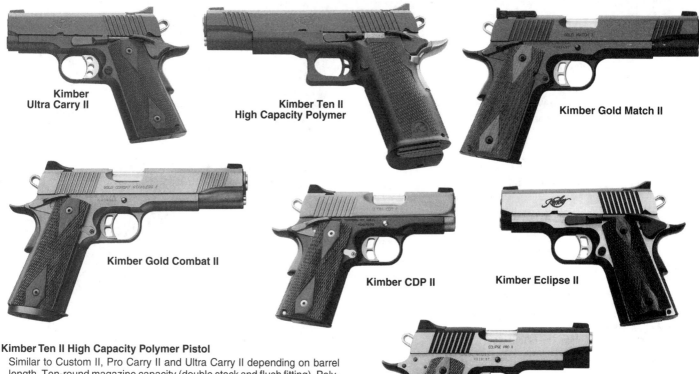

Kimber Ultra Carry II

Kimber Ten II High Capacity Polymer

Kimber Gold Match II

Kimber Gold Combat II

Kimber CDP II

Kimber Eclipse II

Kimber Eclipse Pro II

Kimber Ten II High Capacity Polymer Pistol

Similar to Custom II, Pro Carry II and Ultra Carry II depending on barrel length. Ten-round magazine capacity (double stack and flush fitting). Polymer grip frame molded over stainless steel or aluminum (BP Ten pistols only) frame insert. Checkered front strap and belly of trigger guard. All models have fixed sights except Gold Match Ten II, which has adjustable sight. Frame grip dimensions approximate that of the standard 1911 for natural aiming and better recoil control. **Weight:** 24 to 34 oz. Improved version of the Kimber Polymer series. Made in U.S.A. by Kimber Mfg., Inc.

Price: Pro Carry Ten II $828.00
Price: Stainless Ten II $812.00

Kimber Gold Match II Auto Pistol

Similar to Custom II models. Includes stainless steel barrel with match grade chamber and barrel bushing, ambidextrous thumb safety, adjustable sight, premium aluminum trigger, hand-checkered double diamond rosewood grips. Barrel hand-fitted to bushing and slide for target accuracy. Made in U.S.A. by Kimber Mfg., Inc.

Price: Gold Match II $1,192.00
Price: Gold Match Stainless II 45 ACP $1,342.00
Price: Gold Match Stainless II 40 S&W $1,373.00

Kimber Gold Match Ten II Polymer Auto Pistol

Similar to Stainless Gold Match II. High capacity polymer frame with 10-round magazine. No ambi thumb safety. Polished flats add elegant look. Introduced 1999. Made in U.S.A. by Kimber Mfg., Inc.

Price: $1,373.00

Kimber Gold Combat II Auto Pistol

Similar to Gold Match II except designed for concealed carry. Extended and beveled magazine well, Meprolight tritium night sights; premium aluminum trigger; 30 lpi front strap checkering; special Custom Shop markings; KimPro premium finish. Introduced 1999. Made in U.S.A. by Kimber Mfg., Inc.

Price: 45 ACP $1,716.00
Price: Stainless (stainless frame and slide, special markings) . . $1,657.00

Kimber CDP II Series Auto Pistol

Similar to Custom II, but designed for concealed carry. Aluminum frame. Standard features include stainless steel slide, Meprolight tritium three-dot (green) dovetail-mounted night sights, match grade barrel and chamber, 30 lpi front strap checkering, two tone finish, ambidextrous thumb

safety, hand-checkered double diamond rosewood grips. Introduced in 2000. Made in U.S.A. by Kimber Mfg., Inc.

Price: Ultra CDP II 40 S&W $1,165.00
Price: Ultra CDP II (3" barrel, short grip) $1,165.00
Price: Compact CDP II (4" barrel, short grip) $1,165.00
Price: Pro CDP II (4" barrel, full length grip) $1,165.00
Price: Custom CDP II (5" barrel, full length grip) $1,203.00

Kimber Eclipse II Series Auto Pistol

Similar to Custom II and other stainless Kimber pistols. Stainless slide and frame, black anodized, two tone finish. Gray/black laminated grips. 30 lpi front strap checkering. All have night sights, with Target versions having Meprolight adjustable Bar/Dot version. Made in U.S.A. by Kimber Mfg., Inc.

Price: Eclipse Ultra II (3" barrel, short grip) $1,074.00
Price: Eclipse Pro II (4" barrel, full length grip) $1,074.00
Price: Eclipse Pro Target II (4" barrel, full length grip,
adjustable sight) $1,177.00
Price: Eclipse Custom II (5" barrel, full length grip) $1,077.00
Price: Eclipse Target II (5" barrel, full length grip,
adjustable sight) $1,177.00

Kimber Super Match II Auto Pistol

Similar to Gold Match II. Built for target and action shooting competition. Tested for accuracy. Target included. Stainless steel barrel and chamber. KimPro finish on stainless steel slide. Stainless steel frame. 30 lpi checkered front strap, premium aluminum trigger, Kimber adjustable sight. Introduced in 1999.

Price: $1,966.00

Llama Micromax 380

Llama Minimax

Llama Max-1
Government Deluxe

North American
Arms Guardian

Para-Ordnance P12.45

Para-Ordnance LDA

KORTH PISTOL
Caliber: .40 S&W, .357 SIG (9-shot); 9mm Para, 9x21 (10-shot). **Barrel:** 4" (standard), 5" (optional). Trigger **Weight:** 3.3 lbs. (single Action), 11 lbs. (double action). **Sights:** Fully adjustable. **Features:** All parts of surface-hardened steel; recoil-operated action, mechanically-locked via large pivoting bolt block maintaining parallel positioning of barrel during the complete cycle. Accessories include sound suppressor for qualified buyers. Imported by Korth USA.
Price: **$5,602.00**

LLAMA MICROMAX 380 AUTO PISTOL
Caliber: 32 ACP, 8-shot, 380 ACP, 7-shot magazine. **Barrel:** 3-11/16". **Weight:** 23 oz. **Length:** 6-1/2" overall. **Grips:** Checkered high impact polymer. **Sights:** 3-dot combat. **Features:** Single-action design. Mini custom extended slide release; mini custom extended beavertail grip safety; combat-style hammer. Introduced 1997. Distributed by Import Sports, Inc.
Price: Matte blue. **$291.95**
Price: Satin chrome (380 only) **$308.95**

LLAMA MINIMAX SERIES
Caliber: 40 S&W, 7-shot; 45 ACP, 6-shot magazine. **Barrel:** 3-1/2". **Weight:** 35 oz. **Length:** 7-1/3" overall. **Grips:** Checkered rubber. **Sights:** Three-dot combat. **Features:** Single action, skeletonized combat-style hammer, extended slide release, cone-style barrel, flared ejection port. Introduced 1996. Distributed by Import Sports, Inc.
Price: Blue **$341.95**
Price: Duo-Tone finish (45 only) **$349.95**
Price: Satin chrome **$358.95**

Llama Minimax Sub-Compact Auto Pistol
Similar to the Minimax except has 3.14" barrel, weighs 31 oz.; 6.8" overall length; has 10-shot magazine with finger extension; beavertail grip safety. Introduced 1999. Distributed by Import Sports, Inc.
Price: 45 ACP, matte blue. **$358.95**
Price: As above, satin chrome **$374.95**
Price: Duo-Tone finish (45 only) **$366.95**

LLAMA MAX-I AUTO PISTOLS
Caliber: 45 ACP, 7-shot. **Barrel:** 5-1/8". **Weight:** 36 oz. **Length:** 8-1/2" overall. **Grips:** Polymer. **Sights:** Blade front; three-dot system. **Features:** Single-action trigger; skeletonized combat-style hammer; steel frame; extended manual and grip safeties, matte finish. Introduced 1995. Distributed by Import Sports, Inc.
Price: 45 ACP, 7-shot, Government model **$358.95**

NORTH AMERICAN ARMS GUARDIAN PISTOL
Caliber: 32 ACP, 380 ACP, 32NAA, 6-shot magazine. **Barrel:** 2.1". **Weight:** 13.5 oz. **Length:** 4.36" overall. **Grips:** Black polymer. **Sights:** Fixed. **Features:** Double-action-only mechanism. All stainless steel construction; snag-free. Introduced 1998. Made in U.S.A. by North American Arms.
Price: . . . . **$402.00 to $479.00**

PARA-ORDNANCE P-SERIES AUTO PISTOLS
Caliber: 9mm Para., 40 S&W, 45 ACP, 10-shot magazine. **Barrel:** 3", 3-1/2", 4-1/4", 5". **Weight:** From 24 oz. (alloy frame). **Length:** 8.5" overall. **Grips:** Textured composition. **Sights:** Blade front, rear adjustable for windage. High visibility three-dot system. **Features:** Available with alloy, steel or stainless steel frame with black finish (silver or stainless gun). Steel and stainless steel frame guns weigh 40 oz. (P14.45), 36 oz. (P13.45), 34 oz. (P12.45). Grooved match trigger, rounded combat-style hammer. Beveled magazine well. Manual thumb, grip and firing pin lock safeties. Solid barrel bushing. Contact maker for full details. Introduced 1990. Made in Canada by Para-Ordnance.
Price: Steel frame **$795.00**
Price: Alloy frame **$765.00**
Price: Stainless steel **$865.00**

Para-Ordnance Limited Pistols
Similar to the P-Series pistols except with full-length recoil guide system; fully adjustable rear sight; tuned trigger with overtravel stop; beavertail grip safety; competition hammer; front and rear slide serrations; ambidextrous safety; lowered ejection port; ramped match-grade barrel; dovetailed front sight. Introduced 1998. Made in Canada by Para-Ordnance.
Price: 9mm, 40 S&W, 45 ACP . . . . **$945.00 to $999.00**

Para-Ordnance LDA Auto Pistols
Similar to P-series except has double-action trigger mechanism. Steel frame with matte black finish, checkered composition grips. Available in 9mm Para., 40 S&W, 45 ACP. Introduced 1999. Made in Canada by Para-Ordnance.
Price: **$775.00**

Para-Ordnance C5 45 LDA Para Carry

Para-Ordnance C7 45 LDA Para Companion

Peters Stahl High Capacity

Peters Stahl Trophy Master

Peters Stahl Millennium

Phoenix Arms HP22

Rock River Standard Match

Para-Ordnance LDA Limited Pistols

Similar to LDA, has ambidextrous safety, adjustable rear sight, front slide serrations and full-length recoil guide system. Made in Canada by Para-Ordnance.
Price: Black finish **$975.00**
Price: Stainless **$1,049.00**

PARA-ORDNANCE C5 45 LDA PARA CARRY

Caliber: 45 ACP. **Barrel:** 3", 6+1 shot. **Weight:** 30 oz. **Length:** 6.5". **Grips:** Double diamond checkered Cocobolo. **Features:** Stainless finish and receiver, "world's smallest DAO 45 auto." Para LDA trigger system and safeties.
Price: **$899.00**

PARA-ORDNANCE C7 45 LDA PARA COMPANION

Caliber: 45 ACP. **Barrel:** 3.5", 7+1 shot. **Weight:** 32 oz. **Length:** 7". **Grips:** Double diamond checkered Cocobolo. **Features:** Para LDA trigger system with Para LDA 3 safeties (slide lock, firing pin block and grip safety). Lightning speed, full size capacity.
Price: **$899.00**

PETERS STAHL AUTOLOADING PISTOLS

Caliber: 9mm Para., 45 ACP. **Barrel:** 5" or 6". **Grips:** Walnut or walnut with rubber wrap. **Sights:** Fully adjustable rear, blade front. **Features:** Stainless steel extended slide stop, safety and extended magazine release button; speed trigger with stop and approx. 3-lb. pull; polished ramp. Introduced 2000. Imported from Germany by Phillips & Rogers.
Price: High Capacity (accepts 15-shot magazines in 45 cal.; includes 10-shot magazine) **$1,695.00**
Price: Trophy Master (blued or stainless, 7-shot in 45, 8-shot in 9mm) **$1,995.00**
Price: Millennium Model (titanium coating on receiver and slide) **$2,195.00**

PHOENIX ARMS HP22, HP25 AUTO PISTOLS

Caliber: 22 LR, 10-shot (HP22), 25 ACP, 10-shot (HP25). **Barrel:** 3". **Weight:** 20 oz. **Length:** 5-1/2" overall. **Grips:** Checkered composition. **Sights:** Blade front, adjustable rear. **Features:** Single action, exposed hammer; manual hold-open; button magazine release. Available in satin nickel, polished blue finish. Introduced 1993. Made in U.S.A. by Phoenix Arms.

Price: With gun lock and cable lanyard **$130.00**
Price: HP Rangemaster kit with 5" bbl., locking case and assessories **$171.00**
Price: HP Deluxe Rangemaster kit with 3" and 5" bbls., 2 mags., case **$210.00**

ROCK RIVER ARMS STANDARD MATCH AUTO PISTOL

Caliber: 45 ACP. **Barrel:** NA. **Weight:** NA. **Length:** NA. **Grips:** Cocobolo, checkered. **Sights:** Heine fixed rear, blade front. **Features:** Chrome-moly steel frame and slide; beavertail grip safety with raised pad; checkered slide stop; ambidextrous safety; polished feed ramp and extractor; aluminum speed trigger with 3.5 lb. pull. Made in U.S.A. From Rock River Arms.
Price: **$1,025.00**

ROCKY MOUNTAIN ARMS PATRIOT PISTOL

Caliber: 223, 10-shot magazine. **Barrel:** 7", with muzzle brake. **Weight:** 5 lbs. **Length:** 20.5" overall. **Grips:** Black composition. **Sights:** None furnished. **Features:** Milled upper receiver with enhanced Weaver base; milled lower receiver from billet plate; machined aluminum National Match handguard. Finished in DuPont Teflon-S matte black or NATO green. Comes with black nylon case, one magazine. Introduced 1993. From Rocky Mountain Arms, Inc.
Price: With A-2 handle top . . . . **$2,500.00 to $2,800.00**
Price: Flat top model . . . . **$3,000.00 to $3,500.00**

Ruger P89

Ruger P90

Ruger P93D

Ruger KP94D

Ruger KP95DAO

RUGER P89 AUTOLOADING PISTOL

Caliber: 9mm Para., 10-shot magazine. **Barrel:** 4.50". **Weight:** 32 oz. **Length:** 7.84" overall. **Grips:** Grooved black synthetic composition. **Sights:** Square post front, square notch rear adjustable for windage, both with white dot inserts. **Features:** Double action, ambidextrous slide-mounted safety-levers. Slide 4140 chrome-moly steel or 400-series stainless steel, frame lightweight aluminum alloy. Ambidextrous magazine release. Blue, stainless steel. Introduced 1986; stainless 1990.
Price: P89, blue, extra mag and mag loader, plastic case locks . **$475.00**
Price: KP89, stainless, extra mag and mag loader,
  plastic case locks **$525.00**

Ruger P89D Decocker Autoloading Pistol

Similar to standard P89 except has ambidextrous decocking levers in place of regular slide-mounted safety. Decocking levers move firing pin inside slide where hammer cannot reach, while simultaneously blocking firing pin from forward movement, allows shooter to decock cocked pistol without manipulating trigger. Conventional thumb decocking procedures are therefore unnecessary. Blue, stainless steel. Introduced 1990.
Price: P89D, blue, extra mag and mag loader, plastic case locks **$475.00**
Price: KP89D, stainless, extra mag and mag loader,
  plastic case locks **$525.00**

Ruger P89 Double-Action-Only Autoloading Pistol

Same as KP89 except operates only in double-action mode. Has spurless hammer, gripping grooves on each side of rear slide; no external safety or decocking lever. Internal safety prevents forward movement of firing pin unless trigger is pulled. Available 9mm Para., stainless steel only. Introduced 1991.
Price: Lockable case, extra mag and mag loader. **$525.00**

RUGER P90 MANUAL SAFETY MODEL AUTOLOADING PISTOL

Caliber: 45 ACP, 8-shot magazine. **Barrel:** 4.50". **Weight:** 33.5 oz. **Length:** 7.75" overall. **Grips:** Grooved black synthetic composition. **Sights:** Square post front, square notch rear adjustable for windage, both with white dot. **Features:** Double action ambidextrous slide-mounted safety-levers move firing pin inside slide where hammer can not reach, simultaneously blocking firing pin from forward movement. Stainless steel only. Introduced 1991.
Price: KP90 with extra mag, loader, case and gunlock. **$565.00**
Price: P90 (blue). **$525.00**

Ruger KP90 Decocker Autoloading Pistol

Similar to the P90 except has a manual decocking system. The ambidextrous decocking levers move the firing pin inside the slide where the hammer cannot reach it, while simultaneously blocking the firing pin from forward movement, allows shooter to decock a cocked pistol without manipulating the trigger. Available only in stainless steel. Overall length 7.75", weighs 33.5 oz. Introduced 1991.
Price: KP90D with case, extra mag and mag loading tool **$565.00**

RUGER P93 COMPACT AUTOLOADING PISTOL

Caliber: 9mm Para., 10-shot magazine. **Barrel:** 3.9". **Weight:** 31 oz. **Length:** 7.25" overall. **Grips:** Grooved black synthetic composition. **Sights:** Square post front, square notch rear adjustable for windage. **Features:** Front of slide crowned with convex curve; slide has seven finger grooves; trigger guard bow higher for better grip; 400-series stainless slide, lightweight alloy frame; also blue. Decocker-only or DAO-only. Includes hard case and lock. Introduced 1993. Made in U.S.A. by Sturm, Ruger & Co.
Price: KP93DAO, double-action-only **$575.00**
Price: KP93D ambidextrous decocker, stainless **$575.00**
Price: P93D, ambidextrous decocker, blue **$495.00**

Ruger KP94 Autoloading Pistol

Sized midway between full-size P-Series and compact P93. 4.25" barrel, 7.5" overall length, weighs about 33 oz. KP94 manual safety model; KP94DAO double-action-only (both 9mm Para., 10-shot magazine); KP94D is decocker-only in 40-caliber with 10-shot magazine. Slide gripping grooves roll over top of slide. KP94 has ambidextrous safety levers; KP94DAO has no external safety, full-cock hammer position or decocking lever; KP94D has ambidextrous decocking levers. Matte finish stainless slide, barrel, alloy frame. Also blue. Includes hard case and lock. Introduced 1994. Made in U.S.A. by Sturm, Ruger & Co.
Price: P94, P944, blue (manual safety) **$495.00**
Price: KP94 (9mm), KP944 (40-caliber) (manual
  safety-stainless) **$575.00**
Price: KP94DAO (9mm), KP944DAO (40-caliber) **$575.00**
Price: KP94D (9mm), KP944D (40-caliber)-decock only **$575.00**

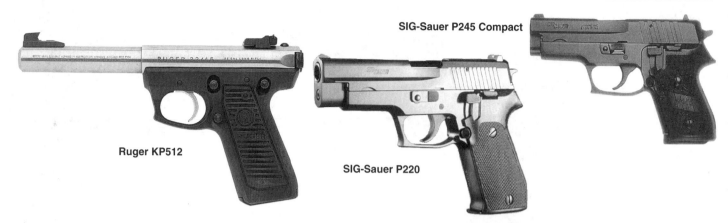

SIG-Sauer P245 Compact

Ruger KP512

SIG-Sauer P220

RUGER P95 AUTOLOADING PISTOL

Caliber: 9mm Para., 10-shot magazine. **Barrel:** 3.9". **Weight:** 27 oz. **Length:** 7.25" overall. **Grips:** Grooved; integral with frame. **Sights:** Blade front, rear drift adjustable for windage; three-dot system. **Features:** Moulded polymer grip frame, stainless steel or chrome-moly slide. Suitable for +P+ ammunition. Safety model, decocker or DAO. Introduced 1996. Made in U.S.A. by Sturm, Ruger & Co. Comes with lockable plastic case, spare magazine, loader and lock.

Price: P95 DAO double-action-only **$425.00**
Price: P95D decocker only **$425.00**
Price: KP95D stainless steel decocker only **$475.00**
Price: KP95DAO double-action only, stainless steel **$475.00**
Price: KP95 safety model, stainless steel **$475.00**
Price: P95 safety model, blued finish **$425.00**

RUGER P97 AUTOLOADING PISTOL

Caliber: 45 ACP 8-shot magazine. **Barrel:** 4-1/8". **Weight:** 30-1/2 oz. **Length:** 7-1/4" overall. Grooved: Integral with frame. **Sights:** Blade front, rear drift adjustable for windage; three dot system. **Features:** Moulded polymer grip frame, stainless steel slide. Decocker or DAO. Introduced 1997. Made in U.S.A. by Sturm, Ruger & Co. Comes with lockable plastic case, spare magazine, loading tool.

Price: KP97D decocker only **$495.00**
Price: KP97DAO double-action only **$495.00**
Price: P97D decocker only, blued **$460.00**

SAFARI ARMS ENFORCER PISTOL

Caliber: 45 ACP, 6-shot magazine. **Barrel:** 3.8", stainless. **Weight:** 36 oz. **Length:** 7.3" overall. **Grips:** Smooth walnut with etched black widow spider logo. **Sights:** Ramped blade front, LPA adjustable rear. **Features:** Extended safety, extended slide release; Commander-style hammer; beavertail grip safety; throated, polished, tuned. Parkerized matte black or satin stainless steel finishes. Made in U.S.A. by Safari Arms.

Price: **$630.00**

SAFARI ARMS GI SAFARI PISTOL

Caliber: 45 ACP, 7-shot magazine. **Barrel:** 5", 416 stainless. **Weight:** 39.9 oz. **Length:** 8.5" overall. **Grips:** Checkered walnut. **Sights:** G.I.-style blade front, drift-adjustable rear. **Features:** Beavertail grip safety; extended thumb safety and slide release; Commander-style hammer. Parkerized finish. Reintroduced 1996.

Price: **$439.00**

SAFARI ARMS CARRIER PISTOL

Caliber: 45 ACP, 7-shot magazine. **Barrel:** 6", 416 stainless steel. **Weight:** 30 oz. **Length:** 9.5" overall. **Grips:** Wood. **Sights:** Ramped blade front, LPA adjustable rear. **Features:** Beavertail grip safety; extended controls; full-length recoil spring guide; Commander-style hammer. Throated, polished and tuned. Satin stainless steel finish. Introduced 1999. Made in U.S.A. by Safari Arms, Inc.

Price: **$714.00**

SAFARI ARMS COHORT PISTOL

Caliber: 45 ACP, 7-shot magazine. **Barrel:** 3.8", 416 stainless. **Weight:** 37 oz. **Length:** 8.5" overall. **Grips:** Smooth walnut with laser-etched black widow logo. **Sights:** Ramped blade front, LPA adjustable rear. **Features:** Combines the Enforcer model, slide and MatchMaster frame. Beavertail grip safety; extended thumb safety and slide release; Commander-style hammer. Throated, polished and tuned. Satin stainless finish. Introduced 1996. Made in U.S.A. by Safari Arms, Inc.

Price: **$654.00**

SAFARI ARMS MATCHMASTER PISTOL

Caliber: 45 ACP, 7-shot. **Barrel:** 5" or 6", 416 stainless steel. **Weight:** 38 oz. (5" barrel). **Length:** 8.5" overall. **Grips:** Smooth walnut. **Sights:** Ramped blade, LPA adjustable rear. **Features:** Beavertail grip safety; extended controls; Commander-style hammer; throated, polished, tuned. Parkerized matte-black or satin stainless steel. Made in U.S.A. by Olympic Arms, Inc.

Price: 5" barrel **$594.00**
Price: 6" barrel **$654.00**

Safari Arms Carry Comp Pistol

Similar to the Matchmaster except has Wil Schueman-designed hybrid compensator system. Made in U.S.A. by Olympic Arms, Inc.

Price: **$1,067.00**

SEECAMP LWS 32 STAINLESS DA AUTO

Caliber: 32 ACP Win. Silvertip, 6-shot magazine. **Barrel:** 2", integral with frame. **Weight:** 10.5 oz. **Length:** 4-1/8" overall. **Grips:** Glass-filled nylon. **Sights:** Smooth, no-snag, contoured slide and barrel top. **Features:** Aircraft quality 17-4 PH stainless steel. Inertia-operated firing pin. Hammer fired double-action-only. Hammer automatically follows slide down to safety rest position after each shot, no manual safety needed. Magazine safety disconnector. Polished stainless. Introduced 1985. From L.W. Seecamp.

Price: **$425.00**

SEMMERLING LM-4 SLIDE-ACTION PISTOL

Caliber: 45 ACP, 4-shot magazine. **Barrel:** 2". **Weight:** 24 oz. **Length:** NA. **Grips:** NA. **Sights:** NA. **Features:** While outwardly appearing to be a semi-automatic, the Semmerling LM-4 is a unique and super compact pistol employing a thumb activated slide mechanism (the slide is manually retracted between shots). Hand-built and super reliable, it is intended for professionals in law enforcement and for concealed carry by licensed and firearms-knowledgeable private citizens. From American Derringer Corp.

Price: **$2,635.00**

SIG-SAUER P220 SERVICE AUTO PISTOL

Caliber: 45 ACP, (7- or 8-shot magazine). **Barrel:** 4-3/8". **Weight:** 27.8 oz. **Length:** 7.8" overall. **Grips:** Checkered black plastic. **Sights:** Blade front, drift adjustable rear for windage. Optional Siglite nightsights. **Features:** Double action. Decocking lever permits lowering hammer onto locked firing pin. Squared combat-type trigger guard. Slide stays open after last shot. Imported from Germany by SIGARMS, Inc.

SIG-Sauer Pro 2009

SIG-Sauer P229 Sport

SIG-Sauer P232

Smith & Wesson 457 TDA

Price: Blue SA/DA or DAO **$790.00**
Price: Blue, Siglite night sights **$880.00**
Price: K-Kote or nickel slide **$830.00**
Price: K-Kote or nickel slide with Siglite night sights. **$930.00**

SIG-Sauer P220 Sport Auto Pistol
Similar to the P220 except has 4.9" barrel, ported compensator, all-stainless steel frame and slide, factory-tuned trigger, adjustable sights, extended competition controls. Overall length is 9.9", weighs 43.5 oz. Introduced 1999. From SIGARMS, Inc.
Price: **$1,320.00**

SIG-Sauer P245 Compact Auto Pistol
Similar to the P220 except has 3.9" barrel, shorter grip, 6-shot magazine, 7.28" overall length, and weighs 27.5 oz. Introduced 1999. From SIG-ARMS, Inc.
Price: Blue **$780.00**
Price: Blue, with Siglite sights. **$850.00**
Price: Two-tone **$830.00**
Price: Two-tone with Siglite sights. **$930.00**
Price: With K-Kote finish **$830.00**
Price: K-Kote with Siglite sights **$930.00**

SIG-Sauer P229 DA Auto Pistol
Similar to the P228 except chambered for 9mm Para., 40 S&W, 357 SIG. Has 3.86" barrel, 7.08" overall length and 3.35" height. Weighs 30.5 oz. Introduced 1991. Frame made in Germany, stainless steel slide assembly made in U.S.; pistol assembled in U.S. From SIGARMS, Inc.
Price: **$795.00**
Price: With nickel slide **$890.00**
Price: Nickel slide Siglite night sights **$935.00**

SIG PRO AUTO PISTOL
Caliber: 9mm Para., 40 S&W, 10-shot magazine. **Barrel:** 3.86". **Weight:** 27.2 oz. **Length:** 7.36" overall. **Grips:** Composite and rubberized one-piece. **Sights:** Blade front, rear adjustable for windage. Optional Siglite night sights. **Features:** Polymer frame, stainless steel slide; integral frame accessory rail; replaceable steel frame rails; left- or right-handed magazine release. Introduced 1999. From SIGARMS, Inc.
Price: SP2340 (40 S&W) **$596.00**
Price: SP2009 (9mm Para.) **$596.00**
Price: As above with Siglite night sights **$655.00**

SIG-Sauer P226 Service Pistol
Similar to the P220 pistol except has 4.4" barrel, and weighs 28.3 oz. 357 SIG or 40 S&W. Imported from Germany by SIGARMS, Inc.
Price: Blue SA/DA or DAO **$830.00**
Price: With Siglite night sights **$930.00**
Price: Blue, SA/DA or DAO 357 SIG. **$830.00**
Price: With Siglite night sights **$930.00**
Price: K-Kote finish, 40 S&W only or nickel slide **$830.00**
Price: K-Kote or nickel slide Siglite night sights **$930.00**
Price: Nickel slide 357 SIG **$875.00**
Price: Nickel slide, Siglite night sights **$930.00**

SIG-Sauer P229 Sport Auto Pistol
Similar to the P229 except available in 357 SIG only; 4.8" heavy barrel; 8.6" overall length; weighs 40.6 oz.; vented compensator; adjustable target sights; rubber grips; extended slide latch and magazine release. Made of stainless steel. Introduced 1998. From SIGARMS, Inc.
Price: **$1,320.00**

SIG-SAUER P232 PERSONAL SIZE PISTOL
Caliber: 380 ACP, 7-shot. **Barrel:** 3-3/4". **Weight:** 16 oz. **Length:** 6-1/2" overall. **Grips:** Checkered black composite. **Sights:** Blade front, rear adjustable for windage. **Features:** Double action/single action or DAO. Blowback operation, stationary barrel. Introduced 1997. Imported from Germany by SIGARMS, Inc.
Price: Blue SA/DA or DAO **$505.00**
Price: In stainless steel. **$545.00**
Price: With stainless steel slide, blue frame **$525.00**
Price: Stainless steel, Siglite night sights, Hogue grips **$585.00**

SIG-SAUER P239 PISTOL
Caliber: 9mm Para., 8-shot, 357 SIG 40 S&W, 7-shot magazine. **Barrel:** 3.6". **Weight:** 25.2 oz. **Length:** 6.6" overall. **Grips:** Checkered black composite. **Sights:** Blade front, rear adjustable for windage. Optional Siglite night sights. **Features:** SA/DA or DAO; blackened stainless steel slide, aluminum alloy frame. Introduced 1996. Made in U.S.A. by SIGARMS, Inc.
Price: SA/DA or DAO **$620.00**
Price: SA/DA or DAO with Siglite night sights. **$720.00**
Price: Two-tone finish **$665.00**
Price: Two-tone finish, Siglite sights **$765.00**

SMITH & WESSON MODEL 22A SPORT PISTOL
Caliber: 22 LR, 10-shot magazine. **Barrel:** 4", 5-1/2", 7". **Weight:** 29 oz. **Length:** 8" overall. **Grips:** Two-piece polymer. **Sights:** Patridge front, fully adjustable rear. **Features:** Comes with a sight bridge with Weaver-style integral optics mount; alloy frame; .312" serrated trigger; stainless steel slide and barrel with matte blue finish. Introduced 1997. Made in U.S.A. by Smith & Wesson.
Price: 4" **$264.00**
Price: 5-1/2" **$292.00**
Price: 7" **$331.00**

SMITH & WESSON MODEL 457 TDA AUTO PISTOL
Caliber: 45 ACP, 7-shot magazine. **Barrel:** 3-3/4". **Weight:** 29 oz. **Length:** 7-1/4" overall. **Grips:** One-piece Xenoy, wrap-around with straight backstrap. **Sights:** Post front, fixed rear, three-dot system. **Features:** Aluminum alloy frame, matte blue carbon steel slide; bobbed hammer; smooth trigger. Introduced 1996. Made in U.S.A. by Smith & Wesson.
Price: **$591.00**

Smith &
Wesson 908

Smith & Wesson
4013 TSW

Smith & Wesson
410 DA

Smith & Wesson
910 DA

Smith & Wesson
3913 LadySmith

SMITH & WESSON MODEL 908 AUTO PISTOL

Caliber: 9mm Para., 8-shot magazine. **Barrel:** 3-1/2". **Weight:** 26 oz. **Length:** 6-13/16". **Grips:** One-piece Xenoy, wrap-around with straight backstrap. **Sights:** Post front, fixed rear, three-dot system. **Features:** Aluminum alloy frame, matte blue carbon steel slide; bobbed hammer; smooth trigger. Introduced 1996. Made in U.S.A. by Smith & Wesson.
Price: **$535.00**

SMITH & WESSON MODEL 4013, 4053 TSW AUTOS

Caliber: 40 S&W, 9-shot magazine. **Barrel:** 3-1/2". **Weight:** 26.4 oz. **Length:** 6-7/8" overall. **Grips:** Xenoy one-piece wrap-around. **Sights:** Novak three-dot system. **Features:** Traditional double-action system; stainless slide, alloy frame; fixed barrel bushing; ambidextrous decocker; reversible magazine catch, equipment rail. Introduced 1997. Made in U.S.A. by Smith & Wesson.
Price: Model 4013 TSW **$886.00**
Price: Model 4053 TSW, double-action-only **$886.00**

SMITH & WESSON MODEL 22S SPORT PISTOLS

Similar to the Model 22A Sport except with stainless steel frame. Available only with 5-1/2" or 7" barrel. Introduced 1997. Made in U.S.A. by Smith & Wesson.
Price: 5-1/2" standard barrel. **$358.00**
Price: 5-1/2" bull barrel, wood target stocks with thumbrest **$434.00**
Price: 7" standard barrel **$395.00**
Price: 5-1/2" bull barrel, two-piece target stocks with thumbrest . **$353.00**

SMITH & WESSON MODEL 410 DA AUTO PISTOL

Caliber: 40 S&W, 10-shot magazine. **Barrel:** 4". **Weight:** 28.5 oz. **Length:** 7.5 oz. **Grips:** One-piece Xenoy, wrap-around with straight backstrap. **Sights:** Post front, fixed rear; three-dot system. **Features:** Aluminum alloy frame; blued carbon steel slide; traditional double action with left-side slide-mounted decocking lever. Introduced 1996. Made in U.S.A. by Smith & Wesson.
Price: Model 410 . . . . **$591.00**
Price: Model 410, HiViz front sight **$612.00**

SMITH & WESSON MODEL 910 DA AUTO PISTOL

Caliber: 9mm Para., 10-shot magazine. **Barrel:** 4". **Weight:** 28 oz. **Length:** 7-3/8" overall. **Grips:** One-piece Xenoy, wrap-around with straight back-

strap. **Sights:** Post front with white dot, fixed two-dot rear. **Features:** Alloy frame, blue carbon steel slide. Slide-mounted decocking lever. Introduced 1995.
Price: Model 910 . . . . **$535.00**
Price: Model 410, HiViz front sight **$535.00**

SMITH & WESSON MODEL 3913 TRADITIONAL DOUBLE ACTION

Caliber: 9mm Para., 8-shot magazine. **Barrel:** 3-1/2". **Weight:** 26 oz. **Length:** 6-13/16" overall. **Grips:** One-piece Delrin wrap-around, textured surface. **Sights:** Post front with white dot, Novak LoMount Carry with two dots. **Features:** Aluminum alloy frame, stainless slide (M3913) or blue steel slide (M3914). Bobbed hammer with no half-cock notch; smooth .304" trigger with rounded edges. Straight backstrap. Equipment rail. Extra magazine included. Introduced 1989.
Price: **$760.00**

Smith & Wesson Model 3913-LS Ladysmith Auto

Similar to the standard Model 3913 except has frame that is upswept at the front, rounded trigger guard. Comes in frosted stainless steel with matching gray grips. Grips are ergonomically correct for a woman's hand. Novak LoMount Carry rear sight adjustable for windage, smooth edges for snag resistance. Extra magazine included. Introduced 1990.
Price: **$782.00**

Smith & Wesson Model 3953 DAO Pistol

Same as the Model 3913 except double-action-only. Model 3953 has stainless slide with alloy frame. Overall length 7"; weighs 25.5 oz. Extra magazine included. Equipment rail. Introduced 1990.
Price: **$760.00**

Smith & Wesson Model 3913TSW/3953TSW Auto Pistols

Similar to the Model 3913 and 3953 except TSW guns have tighter tolerances, ambidextrous manual safety/decocking lever, flush-fit magazine, delayed-unlock firing system; magazine disconnector. Compact alloy frame, stainless steel slide. Straight backstrap. Introduced 1998. Made in U.S.A. by Smith & Wesson.
Price: Single action/double action **$760.00**
Price: Double action only **$760.00**

Smith & Wesson 4006

Smith & Wesson
4566 TSW

Smith & Wesson
Sigma SW40V

SMITH & WESSON MODEL 4006 TDA AUTO

Caliber: 40 S&W, 10-shot magazine. **Barrel:** 4". **Weight:** 38.5 oz. **Length:** 7-7/8" overall. **Grips:** Xenoy wrap-around with checkered panels. **Sights:** Replaceable post front with white dot, Novak LoMount Carry fixed rear with two white dots, or micro. click adjustable rear with two white dots. **Features:** Stainless steel construction with non-reflective finish. Straight backstrap, quipment rail. Extra magazine included. Introduced 1990.

Price: With adjustable sights. **$944.00**
Price: With fixed sight **$907.00**
Price: With fixed night sights. **$1,040.00**
Price: With Saf-T-Trigger, fixed sights **$927.00**

SMITH & WESSON MODEL 4006 TSW

Caliber: 40, 10-shot. **Barrel:** 4". **Grips:** Straight back strap grip. **Sights:** Fixed Novak LoMount Carry. **Features:** Traditional double action, ambidextrous safety, Saf-T-Trigger, equipment rail, satin stainless.

Price: **$927.00**

Smith & Wesson Model 4043, 4046 DA Pistols

Similar to the Model 4006 except is double-action-only. Has a semi-bobbed hammer, smooth trigger, 4" barrel; Novak LoMount Carry rear sight, post front with white dot. Overall length is 7-1/2", weighs 28 oz. Model 4043 has alloy frame, equipment rail. Extra magazine included. Introduced 1991.

Price: Model 4043 (alloy frame) **$886.00**
Price: Model 4046 (stainless frame) **$907.00**
Price: Model 4046 with fixed night sights **$1,040.00**

SMITH & WESSON MODEL 4500 SERIES AUTOS

Caliber: 45 ACP, 8-shot magazine. **Barrel:** 5" (M4506). **Weight:** 41 oz. (4506). **Length:** 8-1/2" overall. **Grips:** Xenoy one-piece wrap-around, arched or straight backstrap. **Sights:** Post front with white dot, adjustable or fixed Novak LoMount Carry on M4506. **Features:** M4506 has serrated hammer spur, equipment rail. All have two magazines. Contact Smith & Wesson for complete data. Introduced 1989.

Price: Model 4566 (stainless, 4-1/4", traditional DA, ambidextrous safety, fixed sight) **$942.00**
Price: Model 4586 (stainless, 4-1/4", DA only) **$942.00**
Price: Model 4566 (stainless, 4-1/4" with Saf-T-Trigger, fixed sight) **$961.00**

SMITH & WESSON MODEL 4513TSW/4553TSW PISTOLS

Caliber: 45 ACP, 7-shot magazine. **Barrel:** 3-3/4". **Weight:** 28 oz. (M4513TSW). **Length:** 6-7/8 overall. **Grips:** Checkered Xenoy; straight backstrap. **Sights:** White dot front, Novak LoMount Carry 2-Dot rear. **Features:** Model 4513TSW is traditional double action, Model 4553TSW is double action only. TSW series has tighter tolerances, ambidextrous manual safety/decocking lever, flush-fit magazine, delayed-unlock firing system; magazine disconnector. Compact alloy frame, stainless steel slide, equipment rail. Introduced 1998. Made in U.S.A. by Smith & Wesson.

Price: Model 4513TSW. **$924.00**
Price: Model 4553TSW. **$924.00**

SMITH & WESSON MODEL 4566 TSW

Caliber: 45 ACP. **Barrel:** 4-1/4", 8-shot . **Grips:** Straight back strap grip. **Sights:** Fixed Novak LoMount Carry. **Features:** Ambidextrous safety, equipment rail, Saf-T-Trigger, satin stainless finish. Traditional double action.

Price: **$961.00**

SMITH & WESSON MODEL 5900 SERIES AUTO PISTOLS

Caliber: 9mm Para., 10-shot magazine. **Barrel:** 4". **Weight:** 28-1/2 to 37-1/2 oz. (fixed sight); 38 oz. (adjustable sight). **Length:** 7-1/2" overall. **Grips:** Xenoy wrap-around with curved backstrap. **Sights:** Post front with white dot, fixed or fully adjustable with two white dots. **Features:** All stainless, stainless and alloy or carbon steel and alloy construction. Smooth .304" trigger, .260" serrated hammer. Equipment rail. Introduced 1989.

Price: Model 5906 (stainless, traditional DA, adjustable sight, ambidextrous safety) **$904.00**
Price: As above, fixed sight. **$841.00**
Price: With fixed night sights. **$995.00**
Price: With Saf-T-Trigger. **$882.00**
Price: Model 5946 DAO (as above, stainless frame and slide). . . **$863.00**

SMITH & WESSON ENHANCED SIGMA SERIES DAO PISTOLS

Caliber: 9mm Para., 40 S&W, 10-shot magazine. **Barrel:** 4". **Weight:** 26 oz. **Length:** 7.4" overall. **Grips:** Integral. **Sights:** White dot front, fixed rear; three-dot system. Tritium night sights available. **Features:** Ergonomic polymer frame; low barrel centerline; internal striker firing system; corrosion-resistant slide; Teflon-filled, electroless-nickel coated magazine, equipment rail. Introduced 1994. Made in U.S.A. by Smith & Wesson.

Price: SW9E, 9mm, 4" barrel, black finish, fixed sights **$447.00**
Price: SW9V, 9mm, 4" barrel, satin stainless, fixed night sights. . **$447.00**
Price: SW9VE, 4" barrel, satin stainless, Saf-T-Trigger, fixed sights **$466.00**
Price: SW40E, 40 S&W, 4" barrel, black finish, fixed sights **$657.00**
Price: SW40V, 40 S&W, 4" barrel, black polymer, fixed sights . . . **$447.00**
Price: SW40VE, 4" barrel, satin stainless, Saf-T-Trigger, fixed sights **$466.00**

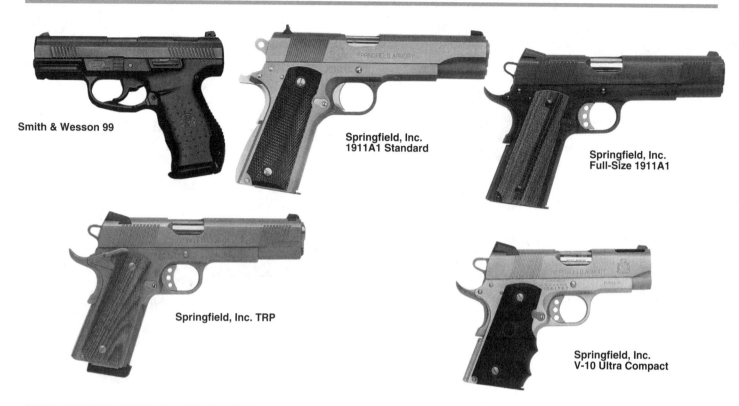

Smith & Wesson 99

Springfield, Inc.
1911A1 Standard

Springfield, Inc.
Full-Size 1911A1

Springfield, Inc. TRP

Springfield, Inc.
V-10 Ultra Compact

SMITH & WESSON MODEL CS9 CHIEF'S SPECIAL AUTO

Caliber: 9mm Para., 7-shot magazine. **Barrel:** 3". **Weight:** 20.8 oz. **Length:** 6-1/4" overall. **Grips:** Hogue wrap-around rubber. **Sights:** White dot front, fixed two-dot rear. **Features:** Traditional double-action trigger mechanism. Alloy frame, stainless or blued slide. Ambidextrous safety. Introduced 1999. Made in U.S.A. by Smith & Wesson.

Price: Blue or stainless **$680.00**

Smith & Wesson Model CS40 Chief's Special Auto

Similar to CS9, chambered for 40 S&W (7-shot magazine), 3-1/4" barrel, weighs 24.2 oz., measures 6-1/2" overall. Introduced 1999. Made in U.S.A. by Smith & Wesson.

Price: Blue or stainless **$717.00**

Smith & Wesson Model CS45 Chief's Special Auto

Similar to CS40, chambered for 45 ACP, 6-shot magazine, weighs 23.9 oz. Introduced 1999. Made in U.S.A. by Smith & Wesson.

Price: Blue or stainless **$717.00**

SMITH & WESSON MODEL 99

Caliber: 9mm Para. 4" barrel; 40 S&W 4-1/8" barrel; 10-shot, adj. sights. **Features:** Traditional double action satin stainless, black polymer frame, equipment rail, Saf-T-Trigger.

Price: 4" barrel **$648.00**
Price: 4-1/8" barrel **$648.00**

SPRINGFIELD, INC. FULL-SIZE 1911A1 AUTO PISTOL

Caliber: 9mm Para., 9-shot; 38 Super, 9-shot; 40 S&W, 9-shot; 45 ACP, 7-shot. **Barrel:** 5". **Weight:** 35.6 oz. **Length:** 8-5/8" overall. **Grips:** Cocobolo. **Sights:** Fixed three-dot system. **Features:** Beveled magazine well; lowered and flared ejection port. All forged parts, including frame, barrel, slide. All new production. Introduced 1990. From Springfield, Inc.

Price: Mil-Spec 45 ACP, Parkerized **$559.00**
Price: Standard, 45 ACP, blued, Novak sights **$824.00**
Price: Standard, 45 ACP, stainless, Novak sights. **$828.00**
Price: Lightweight 45 ACP (28.6 oz., matte finish, night sights) . . **$877.00**
Price: 40 S&W, stainless. **$860.00**
Price: 9mm, stainless **$837.00**

Springfield, Inc. TRP Pistols

Similar to 1911A1 except 45 ACP only, checkered front strap and mainspring housing, Novak Night Sight combat rear sight and matching dovetailed front sight, tuned, polished extractor, oversize barrel link; lightweight speed trigger and combat action job, match barrel and bushing, extended ambidextrous thumb safety and fitted beavertail grip safety. Carry bevel on entire pistol; checkered cocobolo wood grips, comes with two Wilson 7-shot magazines. Frame is engraved "Tactical," both sides of frame with "TRP." Introduced 1998. From Springfield, Inc.

Price: Standard with Armory Kote finish. **$1,395.00**
Price: Standard, stainless steel **$1,370.00**
Price: Standard with Operator Light Rail Armory Kote **$1,473.00**

Springfield, Inc. 1911A1 High Capacity Pistol

Similar to Standard 1911A1, available in 45 ACP with 10-shot magazine. Commander-style hammer, walnut grips, beveled magazine well, plastic carrying case. Can accept higher-capacity Para-Ordnance magazines. Introduced 1993. From Springfield, Inc.

Price: Mil-Spec 45 ACP **$756.00**
Price: 45 ACP Ultra Compact (3-1/2" bbl.) **$909.00**

Springfield, Inc. 1911A1 V-Series Ported Pistols

Similar to standard 1911A1, scalloped slides with 10, 12 or 16 matching barrel ports to redirect powder gasses and reduce recoil and muzzle flip. Adjustable rear sight, ambi thumb safety, Videki speed trigger, and beveled magazine well. Checkered walnut grips standard. Available in 45 ACP, stainless or bi-tone. Introduced 1992.

Price: V-16 Long Slide, stainless **$1,121.00**
Price: Target V-12, stainless **$878.00**
Price: V-10 (Ultra-Compact, bi-tone). **$853.00**
Price: V-10 stainless **$863.00**

Springfield, Inc. 1911A1 Champion Pistol

Similar to standard 1911A1, slide is 4". Novak Night Sights. Delta hammer and cocobolo grips. Available in 45 ACP only; Parkerized or stainless. Introduced 1989.

Price: Stainless. **$849.00**

**Springfield, Inc.
X-Treme Duty**

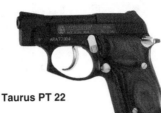

Taurus PT 22

Taurus PT-911

Springfield, Inc. Ultra Compact Pistol

Similar to 1911A1 Compact, shorter slide, 3.5" barrel, beavertail grip safety, beveled magazine well, Novak Low Mount or Novak Night Sights, Videki speed trigger, flared ejection port, stainless steel frame, blued slide, match grade barrel, rubber grips. Introduced 1996. From Springfield, Inc.

Price: Parkerized 45 ACP, Night Sights **$589.00**
Price: Stainless 45 ACP, Night Sights. **$849.00**
Price: Lightweight, 9mm, stainless **$837.00**

Springfield, Inc. Compact Lightweight

Mates a Springfield Inc. Champion length slide with the shorter Ultra-Compact forged alloy frame for concealability. In 45 ACP.

Price: **$733.00**

Springfield, Inc. Long Slide 1911 A1 Pistol

Similar to Full Size model, 6" barrel and slide for increased sight radius and higher velocity, fully adjustable sights, muzzle-forward weight distribution for reduced recoil and quicker shot-to-shot recovery. From Springfield Inc.

Price: Target, 45 ACP, stainless with Night Sights **$1,049.00**
Price: Trophy Match, stainless with adj. sights **$1,452.00**
Price: V-16 stainless steel **$1,121.00**

SPRINGFIELD, INC. MICRO-COMPACT 1911A1 PISTOL

Caliber: 45 ACP, 40 S&W 6+1 capacity. **Barrel:** 3" 1:16 LH. **Weight:** 24 oz. **Length:** 5.7". **Sights:** Novak LoMount tritium. Dovetail front. **Features:** Forged frame and slide, ambi thumb safety, extreme carry bevel treatment, lockable plastic case, 2 magazines.

Price: . . . . **$993.00 to $1,021.00**

SPRINGFIELD, INC. X-TREME DUTY

Caliber: 9mm, 40 S&W, 357 Sig. **Barrel:** 4.08". **Weight:** 22.88 oz. **Length:** 7.2". **Sights:** Dovetail front and rear. **Features:** Lightweight, ultra high-impact polymer frame. Trigger, firing pin and grip safety. Two 10-rod steel easy glide magazines. Imported from Croatia.

Price: . . . . **$489.00 to $1,099.00**

STEYR M & S SERIES AUTO PISTOLS

Caliber: 9mm Para., 40 S&W, 357 SIG; 10-shot magazine. **Barrel:** 4" (3.58" for Model S). **Weight:** 28 oz. (22.5 oz. for Model S). **Length:** 7.05" overall (6.53" for Model S). **Grips:** Ultra-rigid polymer. **Sights:** Drift-adjustable, white-outline rear; white-triangle blade front. **Features:** Polymer frame; trigger-drop firing pin, manual and key-lock safeties; loaded chamber indicator; 5.5-lb. trigger pull; 111-degree grip angle enhances natural pointing. Introduced 2000. Imported from Austria by GSI Inc.

Price: Model M (full-sized frame with 4" barrel) **$609.95**
Price: Model S (compact frame with 3.58" barrel) **$609.95**
Price: Extra 10-shot magazines (Model M or S) **$39.00**

TAURUS MODEL PT 22/PT 25 AUTO PISTOLS

Caliber: 22 LR, 8-shot (PT 22); 25 ACP, 9-shot (PT 25). **Barrel:** 2.75". **Weight:** 12.3 oz. **Length:** 5.25" overall. **Grips:** Smooth rosewood or mother-of-pearl. **Sights:** Fixed. **Features:** Double action. Tip-up barrel for

loading, cleaning. Blue, nickel, duotone or blue with gold accents. Introduced 1992. Made in U.S.A. by Taurus International.

Price: 22 LR, 25 ACP, blue, nickel or with duo-tone finish
with rosewood grips **$219.00**
Price: 22 LR, 25 ACP, blue with gold trim, rosewood grips. **$234.00**
Price: 22 LR, 25 ACP, blue, nickel or duotone finish with checkered
wood grips. **$219.00**
Price: 22 LR, 25 ACP, blue with gold trim, mother of pearl grips . **$250.00**

TAURUS MODEL PT24/7

Caliber: 9mm, 10+1 shot; .40 Cal., 10+1 shot. **Barrel:** 4". **Weight:** 27.2 oz. **Length:** 7-18". **Grips:** RIBBER rubber-finned overlay on polymer. **Sights:** Adjustable. **Features:** Accessory rail, four safeties, blue or stainless finish, consistent trigger pull weight and travel. Introduced 2003. Imported from Brazil by Taurus International.

Price: 9mm **$578.00**
Price: .40 Cal. **$594.00**

TAURUS MODEL PT92 AUTO PISTOL

Caliber: 9mm Para., 10-shot mag. **Barrel:** 5". **Weight:** 34 oz. **Length:** 8.5" overall. **Grips:** Checkered rubber, rosewood, mother-of-pearl. **Sights:** Fixed notch rear. Three-dot sight system. Also offered with micrometer-click adjustable night sights. **Features:** Double action, ambidextrous 3-way hammer drop safety, allows cocked & locked carry. Blue, stainless steel, blue with gold highlights, stainless steel with gold highlights, forged aluminum frame, integral keylock. .22 LR conversion kit available. Imported from Brazil by Taurus International.

Price: Blue . . . . **$578.00 to $672.00**

Taurus Model PT99 Auto Pistol

Similar to PT92, fully adjustable rear sight.

Price: Blue . . . . **$575.00 to $670.00**
Price: 22 Conversion kit for PT 92 and PT99 (includes barrel and slide)
. . . . **$266.00**

TAURUS MODEL PT-100/101 AUTO PISTOL

Caliber: 40 S&W, 10-shot mag. **Barrel:** 5". **Weight:** 34 oz. **Length:** 8-1/2". **Grips:** Checkered rubber, rosewood, mother-of-pearl. **Sights:** 3-dot fixed or adjustable; night sights available. **Features:** Single/double action with three-position safety/decocker. Re-introduced in 2001. Imported by Taurus International.

Price: PT100. . . . . **$578.00 to $672.00**
Price: PT101. . . . . **$594.00 to $617.00**

TAURUS MODEL PT-111 MILLENNIUM PRO AUTO PISTOL

Caliber: 9mm Para., 10-shot mag. **Barrel:** 3.25". **Weight:** 18.7 oz. **Length:** 6-1/8" overall. **Grips:** Polymer. **Sights:** Three-dot fixed; night sights available. Low profile, three-dot combat. **Features:** Double action only, polymer frame, matte stainless or blue steel slide, manual safety, integral keylock. Deluxe models with wood grip inserts. Now issued in a third generation series with many cosmetic and internal improvements.

Price: . . . . **$445.00 to $539.00**

Taurus PT-938

Taurus PT-945

Taurus PT-940

Taurus PT-957

Taurus Model PT-111 Millennium Titanium Pistol
Similar to PT-111, titanium slide, night sights.
Price: **$586.00**

TAURUS PT-132 MILLENIUM PRO AUTO PISTOL
Caliber: 32 ACP, 10-shot mag. **Barrel:** 3.25". **Weight:** 18.7 oz. **Grips:** Polymer. **Sights:** 3-dot fixed; night sights available. **Features:** Double action only, polymer frame, matte stainless or blue steel slide, manual safety, integral keylock action. Introduced 2001.
Price: .... **$445.00 to $461.00**

TAURUS PT-138 MILLENIUM PRO SERIES
Caliber: 380 ACP, 10-shot mag. **Barrel:** 3.25". **Weight:** 18.7 oz. **Grips:** Polymer. **Sights:** Fixed three-dot fixed. **Features:** Double action only, polymer frame, matte stainless or blue steel slide, manual safety, integral keylock.
Price: .... **$445.00 to $461.00**

TAURUS PT-140 MILLENIUM PRO AUTO PISTOL
Caliber: 40 S&W, 10-shot mag. **Barrel:** 3.25". **Weight:** 18.7 oz. **Grips:** Checkered polymer. **Sights:** 3-dot fixed; night sights available. **Features:** Double-action-only; matte stainless or blue steel slide, black polymer frame, manual safety, integral keylock action. From Taurus International.
Price: .... **$484.00 to $578.00**

TAURUS PT-145 MILLENIUM AUTO PISTOL
Caliber: 45 ACP, 10-shot mag. **Barrel:** 3.27". **Weight:** 23 oz. **Stock:** Checkered polymer. **Sights:** 3-dot fixed; night sights available. **Features:** Double-action only, matte stainless or blue steel slide, black polymer frame, manual safety, integral keylock. From Taurus International.
Price: .... **$484.00 to $578.00**

TAURUS MODEL PT-911 AUTO PISTOL
Caliber: 9mm Para., 10-shot mag. **Barrel:** 4". **Weight:** 28.2 oz. **Length:** 7" overall. **Grips:** Checkered rubber, rosewood, mother-of-pearl. **Sights:** Fixed, three-dot blue or stainless; night sights optional. **Features:** Double action, semi-auto ambidextrous three-way hammer drop safety, allows cocked and locked carry. Blue, stainless steel, blue with gold highlights, or stainless steel with gold highlights, forged aluminum frame, integral keylock.
Price: .... **$523.00 to $617.00**

TAURUS MODEL PT-938 AUTO PISTOL
Caliber: 380 ACP, 10-shot mag. **Barrel:** 3.72". **Weight:** 27 oz. **Length:** 6.5" overall. **Grips:** Checkered rubber. **Sights:** Fixed, three-dot. **Features:** Double action, ambidextrous three-way hammer drop allows cocked & locked carry. Forged aluminum frame. Integral keylock. Imported by Taurus International.
Price: Blue **$516.00**
Price: Stainless...................................... **$531.00**

TAURUS MODEL PT-940 AUTO PISTOL
Caliber: 40 S&W, 10-shot mag. **Barrel:** 3-5/8". **Weight:** 28.2 oz. **Length:** 7" overall. **Grips:** Checkered rubber, rosewood or mother-of-pearl. **Sights:** Fixed, three-dot blue or stainless; night sights optional. **Features:** Double action, semi-auto ambidextrous three-way hammer drop safety, allows cocked & locked carry. Blue, stainless steel, blue with gold highlights, or stainless steel with gold hightlights, forged aluminum frame, integral keylock.
Price: .... **$523.00 to $617.00**

TAURUS MODEL PT-945 SERIES
Caliber: 45 ACP, 8-shot mag. **Barrel:** 4.25". **Weight:** 28.2/29.5 oz. **Length:** 7.48" overall. **Grips:** Checkered rubber, rosewood or mother-of-pearl. **Sights:** Fixed, three-dot; night sights optional. **Features:** Double-action with ambidextrous three-way hammer drop safety allows cocked & locked carry. Forged aluminum frame, PT-945C has ported barrel/slide. Blue, stainless, blue with gold highlights, stainless with gold highlights, integral keylock. Introduced 1995. Imported by Taurus International.
Price: .... **$563.00 to $641.00**

TAURUS MODEL PT-957 AUTO PISTOL
Caliber: 357 SIG, 10-shot mag. **Barrel:** 4". **Weight:** 28 oz. **Length:** 7" overall. **Grips:** Checkered rubber, rosewood or mother-of-pearl. **Sights:** Fixed, three-dot blue or stainless; night sights optional. **Features:** Double action, blue, stainless steel, blue with gold accents or stainless with gold accents, ported barrel/slide, three-position safety with decocking lever and ambidextrous safety. Forged aluminum frame, integral keylock. Introduced 1999. Imported by Taurus International.
Price: .... **$525.00 to $620.00**
Price: Non-ported............................ **$525.00 to $535.00**

Walther PPK/S

Walther PPK

Walther P99

Walther P22

Wilkinson Sherry

with interchangeable backstrap inserts. Comes with two magazines. Introduced 1997. Imported from Germany by Carl Walther USA.
Price: **$799.00**

Walther P990 Auto Pistol
Similar to the P99 except is double-action-only. Available in blue or silver tenifer finish. Introduced 1999. Imported from Germany by Carl Walther USA.
Price: **$749.00**

WALTHER P22 PISTOL
Caliber: 22 LR. Barrel: 3.4", 5". Weight: 19.6 oz. (3.4"), 20.3 oz. (5"). Length: 6.26", 7.83". Grips: NA. Sights: Interchangeable white dot, front, two-dot adjustable, rear. Features: A rimfire version of the Walther P99 pistol, available in nickel slide with black frame, or green frame with black slide versions. Made in Germany and distributed in the U.S. by Smith & Wesson.
Price: . . . . **NA**

WILKINSON SHERRY AUTO PISTOL
Caliber: 22 LR, 8-shot magazine. Barrel: 2-1/8". Weight: 9-1/4 oz. Length: 4-3/8" overall. Grips: Checkered black plastic. Sights: Fixed, groove. Features: Cross-bolt safety locks the sear into the hammer. Available in all blue finish or blue slide and trigger with gold frame. Introduced 1985.
Price: **$280.00**

WILKINSON LINDA AUTO PISTOL
Caliber: 9mm Para. Barrel: 8-5/16". Weight: 4 lbs., 13 oz. Length: 12-1/4" overall. Grips: Checkered black plastic pistol grip, walnut forend. Sights: Protected blade front, aperture rear. Features: Fires from closed bolt. Semi-auto only. Straight blowback action. Cross-bolt safety. Removable barrel. From Wilkinson Arms.
Price: **$675.00**

TAURUS MODEL 922 SPORT PISTOL
Caliber: .22 LR, 10-shot magazine. Barrel: 6". Weight: 24.8 oz. Length: 9-1/8". Grips: Polymer. Sights: Adjustable. Features: Matte blue steel finish, machined target crown, polymer frame, single and double action, easy disassembly for cleaning.
Price: . . . . (blue) **$310.00**
Price: . . . . (stainless) **$328.00**

WALTHER PPK/S AMERICAN AUTO PISTOL
Caliber: 380 ACP, 7-shot magazine. Barrel: 3.27". Weight: 23-1/2 oz. Length: 6.1" overall. Stocks: Checkered plastic. Sights: Fixed, white markings. Features: Double action; manual safety blocks firing pin and drops hammer; chamber loaded indicator on 32 and 380; extra finger rest magazine provided. Made entirely in the United States. Introduced 1980.
Price: 380 ACP only, blue **$540.00**
Price: As above, 32 ACP or 380 ACP, stainless **$540.00**

Walther PPK American Auto Pistol
Similar to Walther PPK/S except weighs 21 oz., has 6-shot capacity. Made in the U.S. Introduced 1986.
Price: Stainless, 32 ACP or 380 ACP **$540.00**
Price: Blue, 380 ACP only **$540.00**

WALTHER P99 AUTO PISTOL
Caliber: 9mm Para., 9x21, 40 S&W,10-shot magazine. Barrel: 4". Weight: 25 oz. Length: 7" overall. Grips: Textured polymer. Sights: Blade front (comes with three interchangeable blades for elevation adjustment), micrometer rear adjustable for windage. Features: Double-action mechanism with trigger safety, decock safety, internal striker safety; chamber loaded indicator; ambidextrous magazine release levers; polymer frame

Includes models suitable for hunting and competitive courses of fire, both police and international.

Armscor M-200DC

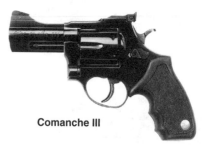

Comanche III

ARMSCOR M-200DC REVOLVER

Caliber: 38 Spec., 6-shot cylinder. **Barrel:** 2-1/2", 4". **Weight:** 22 oz. (2-1/2" barrel). **Length:** 7-3/8" overall (2-1/2" barrel). **Grips:** Checkered rubber. **Sights:** Blade front, fixed notch rear. **Features:** All-steel construction; floating firing pin, transfer bar ignition; shrouded ejector rod; blue finish. Reintroduced 1996. Imported from the Philippines by K.B.I., Inc.
Price: 2-1/2" **$199.99**
Price: 4" **$205.00**

ARMSPORT MODEL 4540 REVOLVER

Caliber: 38 Special. **Barrel:** 4". **Weight:** 32 oz. **Length:** 9" overall. **Sights:** Fixed rear, blade front. **Features:** Ventilated rib; blued finish. Imported from Argentina by Armsport Inc.
Price: **$140.00**

COMANCHE I, II, III DA REVOLVERS

Features: Adjustable sights. Blue or stainless finish. Distributed by SGS Importers.
Price: I 22 LR, 6" bbl, 9-shot, blue **$236.95**
Price: I 22LR, 6" bbl, 9-shot, stainless **$258.95**
Price: II 38 Special, 3", 4" bbl, 6-shot, blue **$219.95**
Price: II 38 Special, 4" bbl, 6-shot, stainless **$236.95**
Price: III 357 Mag, 3", 4", 6" bbl, 6-shot, blue **$253.95**
Price: III 357 Mag, 3", 4", 6" bbl, 6-shot, stainless **$274.95**
Price: II 38 Special, 3" bbl, 6-shot, stainless steel **$236.95**

DAN WESSON 722M SMALL FRAME REVOLVER

Caliber: 22 WMR. **Barrel:** 2-1/2", 4", 6", 8" or 10"; interchangeable. **Weight:** 36 oz. (2-1/2"), 44 oz. (6"). **Length:** 9-1/4" overall (4" barrel). **Grips:** Hogue Gripper rubber (walnut, exotic woods optional). **Sights:** 1/8" serrated, interchangeable front, white outline rear adjustable for windage and elevation. **Features:** Built on the same frame as the Wesson 357; smooth, wide trigger with over-travel adjustment, wide spur hammer, with short double-action travel. Available in blue or stainless steel.
Price: Blued or stainless finish . . . . **$643.00 to $873.00**

DAN WESSON FIREARMS MODEL 15/715 and 32/732 REVOLVERS

Caliber: 32-20, 32 H&R Mag. (Model 32), 357 Mag. (Model 15). **Barrel:** 2-1/2", 4", 6", 8" (M32), 2-1/2", 4", 6", 8", 10" (M15); vent heavy. **Weight:** 36 oz. (2-1/2" barrel). **Length:** 9-1/4" overall (4" barrel). **Grips:** Checkered, interchangeable. **Sights:** 1/8" serrated front, fully adjustable rear. **Features:** New Generation Series. Interchangeable barrels; wide, smooth trigger, wide hammer spur; short double-action travel. Available in blue or stainless. Reintroduced 1997. Made in U.S.A. by Dan Wesson Firearms. Contact maker for full list of models.
Price: Model 15/715, 2-1/2" (blue or stainless) **$551.00**
Price: Model 15/715, 8" (blue or stainless) **$612.00**
Price: Model 15/715, compensated . . . . **$704.00 to $827.00**
Price: Model 32/732, 4" (blue or stainless) **$674.00**
Price: Model 32/732, 8" (blue or stainless) **$766.00**

DAN WESSON FIREARMS MODEL 41/741, 44/744 and 45/745 REVOLVERS

Caliber: 41 Mag., 44 Mag., 45 Colt, 6-shot. **Barrel:** 4", 6", 8", 10"; interchangeable; 4", 6", 8" Compensated. **Weight:** 48 oz. (4"). **Length:** 12" overall (6" bbl.) **Grips:** Smooth. **Sights:** 1/8" serrated front, white outline rear adjustable for windage and elevation. **Features:** Available in blue or stainless steel. Smooth, wide trigger with adjustable over-travel, wide hammer spur. Available in Pistol Pac set also. Reintroduced 1997. Contact Dan Wesson Firearms for complete price list.
Price: 41 Mag., 4", vent heavy (blue or stainless). **$643.00**
Price: 44 Mag., 6", vent heavy (blue or stainless). **$689.00**
Price: 45 Colt, 8", vent heavy (blue or stainless) **$766.00**
Price: Compensated models (all calibers) . . . . **$812.00 to $934.00**

DAN WESSON FIREARMS LARGE FRAME SERIES REVOLVERS

Caliber: 41, 741/41 Magnum; 44, 744/44 Magnum; 45, 745/45 Long Colt; 360, 7360/357; 460, 7460/45. **Barrel:** 2"-10". **Weight:** 49 oz.-69 oz. **Grips:** Standard, Hogue rubber Gripper Grips. **Sights:** Standard front, serrated ramp with color insert. Standard rear, adustable wide notch. Other sight options available. **Features:** Available in blue or stainless steel. Smooth, wide trigger with overtravel, wide hammer spur. Double and single action.
Price: . . . . **$769.00 to $889.00**

DAN WESSON FIREARMS MODEL 360/7360 REVOLVERS

Caliber: 357 Mag. **Barrel:** 4", 6", 8", 10"; vent heavy. **Weight:** 64 oz. (8" barrel). **Grips:** Hogue rubber finger groove. **Sights:** Interchangeable ramp or Patridge front, fully adjustable rear. **Features:** New Generation Large Frame Series. Interchangeable barrels and grips; smooth trigger, wide hammer spur. Blue (360) or stainless (7360). Introduced 1999. Made in U.S.A. by Dan Wesson Firearms.
Price: 4" bbl., blue or stainless **$735.00**
Price: 10" bbl., blue or stainless **$873.00**
Price: Compensated models . . . . **$858.00 to $980.00**

DAN WESSON FIREARMS MODEL 460/7460 REVOLVERS

Caliber: 45 ACP, 45 Auto Rim, 45 Super, 45 Winchester Magnum and 460 Rowland. **Barrel:** 4", 6", 8", 10"; vent heavy. **Weight:** 49 oz. (4" barrel). **Grips:** Hogue rubber finger groove; interchangeable. **Sights:** Interchangeable ramp or Patridge front, fully adjustable rear. **Features:** New Generation Large Frame Series. Shoots five cartridges (45 ACP, 45 Auto Rim, 45 Super, 45 Winchester Magnum and 460 Rowland; six half-moon clips for auto cartridges included). Interchangeable barrels and grips. Available with non-fluted cylinder and Slotted Lightweight barrel shroud. Introduced 1999. Made in U.S.A. by Dan Wesson Firearms.
Price: 4" bbl., blue or stainless **$735.00**
Price: 10" bbl., blue or stainless **$888.00**
Price: Compensated models . . . . **$919.00 to $1,042.00**

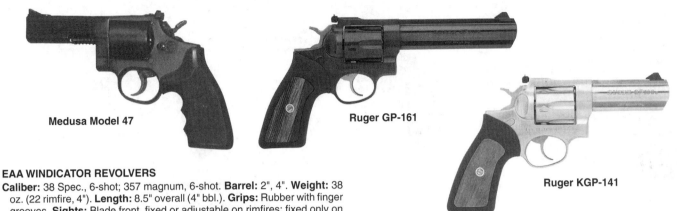

Medusa Model 47

Ruger GP-161

Ruger KGP-141

EAA WINDICATOR REVOLVERS
Caliber: 38 Spec., 6-shot; 357 magnum, 6-shot. **Barrel:** 2", 4". **Weight:** 38 oz. (22 rimfire, 4"). **Length:** 8.5" overall (4" bbl.). **Grips:** Rubber with finger grooves. **Sights:** Blade front, fixed or adjustable on rimfires; fixed only on 32, 38. **Features:** Swing-out cylinder; hammer block safety; blue finish. Introduced 1991. Imported from Germany by European American Armory.
Price: 38 Special 2" **$249.00**
Price: 38 Special, 4" **$259.00**
Price: 357 Magnum, 2" **$259.00**
Price: 357 Magnum, 4" **$279.00**

KORTH COMBAT REVOLVER
Caliber: .357 Mag., .32 S&W Long, 9mm Para., .22 WMR, .22 LR. **Barrel:** 3", 4", 5-1/4", 6", 8". **Sights:** Fully-adjustable, rear; Baughman ramp, front. **Grips:** Walnut (checkered or smooth). Also available as a Target model in .22 LR, .38 Spl., .32 S&W Long, .357 Mag. with undercut partridge front sight; fully-adjustable rear. Made in Germany. Imported by Korth USA.
Price: . . . . From **$5,442.00**

KORTH TROJA REVOLVER
Caliber: .357 Mag. **Barrel:** 6". **Finish:** Matte blue. **Grips:** Smooth, oversized finger contoured walnut. **Features:** Maintaining all of the precision German craftsmanship that has made this line famous, the final surface finish is not as finely polished as the firm's other products - thus the lower price. Introduced 2003. Imported from Germany by Korth USA.
Price: . . . . From **$3,995.00**

MEDUSA MODEL 47 REVOLVER
Caliber: Most 9mm, 38 and 357 caliber cartridges; 6-shot cylinder. **Barrel:** 2-1/2", 3", 4", 5", 6"; fluted. **Weight:** 39 oz. **Length:** 10" overall (4" barrel). **Grips:** Gripper-style rubber. **Sights:** Changeable front blades, fully adjustable rear. **Features:** Patented extractor allows gun to chamber, fire and extract over 25 different cartridges in the .355 to .357 range, without half-moon clips. Steel frame and cylinder; match quality barrel. Matte blue finish. Introduced 1996. Made in U.S.A. by Phillips & Rogers, Inc.
Price: **$899.00**

ROSSI MODEL 351/352 REVOLVERS
Caliber: 38 Special +P, 5-shot. **Barrel:** 2". **Weight:** 24 oz. **Length:** 6-1/2" overall. **Grips:** Rubber. **Sights:** Blade front, fixed rear. **Features:** Patented keylock Taurus Security System; forged steel frame handles +P ammunition. Introduced 2001. Imported by BrazTech/Taurus.
Price: Model 351 (blued finish) **$298.00**
Price: Model 352 (stainless finish) **$345.00**

ROSSI MODEL 461/462 REVOLVERS
Caliber: 357 Magnum +P, 6-shot. **Barrel:** 2". **Weight:** 26 oz. **Length:** 6-1/2" overall. **Grips:** Rubber. **Sights:** Fixed. **Features:** Single/double action. Patented keylock Taurus Security System; forged steel frame handles +P ammunition. Introduced 2001. Imported by BrazTech/Taurus.
Price: Model 461 (blued finish) **$298.00**
Price: Model 462 (stainless finish) **$345.00**

ROSSI MODEL 971/972 REVOLVERS
Caliber: 357 Magnum +P, 6-shot. **Barrel:** 4", 6". **Weight:** 40-44 oz. **Length:** 8-1/2" or 10-1/2" overall. **Grips:** Rubber. **Sights:** Fully adjustable. **Features:** Single/double action. Patented keylock Taurus Security System; forged steel frame handles +P ammunition. Introduced 2001. Imported by BrazTech/Taurus.
Price: Model 971 (blued finish, 4" barrel) **$345.00**
Price: Model 972 (stainless steel finish, 6" barrel) **$391.00**

Rossi Model 851
Similar to Model 971/972, chambered for 38 Special +P. Blued finish, 4" barrel. Introduced 2001. From BrazTech/Taurus.
Price: **$298.00**

RUGER GP-100 REVOLVERS
Caliber: 38 Spec., 357 Mag., 6-shot. **Barrel:** 3", 3" full shroud, 4", 4" full shroud, 6", 6" full shroud. **Weight:** 3" barrel-35 oz., 3" full shroud-36 oz., 4" barrel-37 oz., 4" full shroud-38 oz. **Sights:** Fixed; adjustable on 4" full shroud, all 6" barrels. **Grips:** Ruger Santoprene Cushioned Grip with Goncalo Alves inserts. **Features:** Uses action, frame incorporating improvements and features of both the Security-Six and Redhawk revolvers. Full length, short ejector shroud. Satin blue and stainless steel.
Price: GP-141 (357, 4" full shroud, adj. sights, blue) **$499.00**
Price: GP-160 (357, 6", adj. sights, blue) **$499.00**
Price: GP-161 (357, 6" full shroud, adj. sights, blue), 46 oz. **$499.00**
Price: GPF-331 (357, 3" full shroud) **$495.00**
Price: GPF-340 (357, 4") **$495.00**
Price: GPF-341 (357, 4" full shroud) **$495.00**
Price: KGP-141 (357, 4" full shroud, adj. sights, stainless) **$555.00**
Price: KGP-160 (357, 6", adj. sights, stainless), 43 oz. **$555.00**
Price: KGP-161 (357, 6" full shroud, adj. sights, stainless) 46 oz. **$555.00**
Price: KGPF-330 (357, 3", stainless) **$555.00**
Price: KGPF-331 (357, 3" full shroud, stainless) **$555.00**
Price: KGPF-340 (357, 4", stainless), KGPF-840 (38 Special) . . . **$555.00**
Price: KGPF-341 (357, 4" full shroud, stainless) **$555.00**
Price: KGPF-840 (38 Special, 4", stainless) **$555.00**

Ruger SP101 Double-Action-Only Revolver
Similar to standard SP101 except double-action-only with no single-action sear notch. Spurless hammer for snag-free handling, floating firing pin and Ruger's patented transfer bar safety system. Available with 2-1/4" barrel in 357 Magnum. Weighs 25 oz., overall length 7.06". Natural brushed satin, high-polish stainless steel. Introduced 1993.
Price: KSP321XL (357 Mag.) **$495.00**

RUGER SP101 REVOLVERS
Caliber: 22 LR, 32 H&R Mag., 6-shot; 38 Spec. +P, 357 Mag., 5-shot. **Barrel:** 2-1/4", 3-1/16", 4". **Weight:** (38 & 357 mag models) 2-1/4"-25 oz.; 3-1/16"-27 oz. **Sights:** Adjustable on 22, 32, fixed on others. **Grips:** Ruger Cushioned Grip with inserts. **Features:** Incorporates improvements and features found in the GP-100 revolvers into a compact, small frame, double-action revolver. Full-length ejector shroud. Stainless steel only. Introduced 1988.

Ruger KSP-331X

Smith & Wesson
Model 10

Smith & Wesson Model 36LS

Smith & Wesson Model 65LS

Price: KSP-821X (2-1/4", 38 Spec.) **$495.00**
Price: KSP-831X (3-1/16", 38 Spec.) **$495.00**
Price: KSP-241X (4" heavy bbl., 22 LR), 34 oz. **$495.00**
Price: KSP-3231X (3-1/16", 32 H&R), 30 oz. **$495.00**
Price: KSP-321X (2-1/4", 357 Mag.) **$495.00**
Price: KSP-331X (3-1/16", 357 Mag.) **$495.00**
Price: KSP-3241X (32 Mag., 4" bbl) **$495.00**

SMITH & WESSON MODEL 10 M&P HB REVOLVER
Caliber: 38 Spec., 6-shot. **Barrel:** 4". **Weight:** 33.5 oz. **Length:** 9-5/16" overall. **Grips:** Uncle Mike's Combat soft rubber; square butt. **Sights:** Fixed; ramp front, square notch rear.
Price: Blue **$496.00**

SMITH & WESSON COMMEMORATIVE MODEL 29
Features: Reflects original Model 29: 6-1/2" barrel, four-screw side plate, over-sized target grips, red vamp front and black blade rear sights, 150th Anniversary logo, engraved, gold-plated, blue, in wood presentation case. Limited.
Price: . . . . **NA**

SMITH & WESSON MODEL 629 REVOLVERS
Caliber: 44 Magnum, 44 S&W Special, 6-shot. **Barrel:** 5", 6", 8-3/8". **Weight:** 47 oz. (6" bbl.). **Length:** 11-3/8" overall (6" bbl.). **Grips:** Soft rubber; wood optional. **Sights:** 1/8" red ramp front, white outline rear, internal lock, adjustable for windage and elevation.
Price: Model 629, 4" **$717.00**
Price: Model 629, 6" **$739.00**
Price: Model 629, 8-3/8" barrel **$756.00**

Smith & Wesson Model 629 Classic Revolver
Similar to standard Model 629, full-lug 5", 6-1/2" or 8-3/8" barrel, chamfered front of cylinder, interchangeable red ramp front sight with adjustable white outline rear, Hogue grips with S&W monogram, frame is drilled and tapped for scope mounting. Factory accurizing and endurance packages. Overall length with 5" barrel is 10-1/2"; weighs 51 oz. Introduced 1990.
Price: Model 629 Classic (stainless), 5", 6-1/2" **$768.00**
Price: As above, 8-3/8" **$793.00**
Price: Model 629 with HiViz front sight **$814.00**

SMITH & WESSON MODEL 37 CHIEF'S SPECIAL & AIRWEIGHT
Caliber: 38 Spec. +P, 5-shot. **Barrel:** 1-7/8". **Weight:** 19-1/2 oz. (2" bbl.); 13-1/2 oz. (Airweight). **Length:** 6-1/2" (round butt). **Grips:** Round butt soft rubber. **Sights:** Fixed, serrated ramp front, square notch rear. Glass beaded finish.
Price: Model 37. . . . . **$523.00**

Smith & Wesson Model 637 Airweight Revolver
Similar to the Model 37 Airweight except has alloy frame, stainless steel barrel, cylinder and yoke; rated for 38 Spec. +P; Uncle Mike's Boot Grip. Weighs 15 oz. Introduced 1996. Made in U.S.A. by Smith & Wesson.
Price: **$548.00**

SMITH & WESSON MODEL 36LS, 60LS LADYSMITH
Caliber: .38 S&W Special +P, 5-shot. **Barrel:** 1-7/8". **Weight:** 20 oz. **Length:** 6-5/16 overall (1-7/8" barrel). **Grips:** Combat Dymondwood® grips with S&W monogram. **Sights:** Serrated ramp front, fixed notch rear. **Features:** Speedloader cutout. Comes in a fitted carry/storage case. Introduced 1989.
Price: Model 36LS **$518.00**
Price: Model 60LS, 2-1/8" barrel stainless, 357 Magnum **$566.00**

SMITH & WESSON MODEL 60 CHIEF'S SPECIAL
Caliber: 357 Magnum, 5-shot. **Barrel:** 2-1/8" or 3". **Weight:** 24 oz. **Length:** 7-1/2 overall (3" barrel). **Grips:** Rounded butt synthetic grips. **Sights:** Fixed, serrated ramp front, square notch rear. **Features:** Stainless steel construction. 3" full lug barrel, adjustable sights, internal lock. Made in U.S.A. by Smith & Wesson.
Price: 2-1/8" barrel **$541.00**
Price: 3" barrel **$574.00**

SMITH & WESSON MODEL 65
Caliber: 357 Mag. and 38 Spec., 6-shot. **Barrel:** 4". **Weight:** 34 oz. **Length:** 9-5/16" overall (4" bbl.). **Grips:** Uncle Mike's Combat. **Sights:** 1/8" serrated ramp front, fixed square notch rear. **Features:** Heavy barrel. Stainless steel construction. Internal lock.
Price: **$531.00**

SMITH & WESSON MODEL 317 AIRLITE, 317 LADYSMITH REVOLVERS
Caliber: 22 LR, 8-shot. **Barrel:** 1-7/8" 3". **Weight:** 9.9 oz. **Length:** 6-3/16" overall. **Grips:** Dymondwood Boot or Uncle Mike's Boot. **Sights:** Serrated ramp front, fixed notch rear. **Features:** Aluminum alloy, carbon and stainless steels, and titanium construction. Short spur hammer, smooth combat trigger. Clear Cote finish. Introduced 1997. Made in U.S.A. by Smith & Wesson.
Price: With Uncle Mike's Boot grip **$550.00**
Price: With DymondWood Boot grip, 3" barrel, HiViz front sight, internal lock **$600.00**
Price: Model 317 LadySmith (DymondWood only, comes with display case) **$596.00**

SMITH & WESSON MODEL 351PD
Caliber: 22 Mag. **Barrel:** 2". **Features:** Seven-shot, Scandium alloy.
Price: **$625.00**

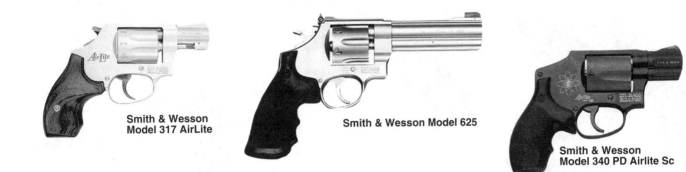

Smith & Wesson
Model 317 AirLite

Smith & Wesson Model 625

Smith & Wesson
Model 340 PD Airlite Sc

Smith & Wesson Model 360 PD
Airlite SC Chief's Special

SMITH & WESSON MODEL 64 STAINLESS M&P
Caliber: 38 Spec. +P, 6-shot. **Barrel:** 2", 3", 4". **Weight:** 34 oz. **Length:** 9-5/16" overall. **Grips:** Soft rubber. **Sights:** Fixed, 1/8" serrated ramp front, square notch rear. **Features:** Satin finished stainless steel, square butt.
Price: 2" **$522.00**
Price: 3", 4" **$532.00**

SMITH & WESSON MODEL 65LS LADYSMITH
Caliber: 357 Magnum, 38 Spec. +P, 6-shot. **Barrel:** 3". **Weight:** 31 oz. **Length:** 7.94" overall. **Grips:** Rosewood, round butt. **Sights:** Serrated ramp front, fixed notch rear. **Features:** Stainless steel with frosted finish. Smooth combat trigger, service hammer, shrouded ejector rod. Comes with case. Introduced 1992.
Price: **$584.00**

SMITH & WESSON MODEL 66 STAINLESS COMBAT MAGNUM
Caliber: 357 Mag. and 38 Spec. +P, 6-shot. **Barrel:** 2-1/2", 4", 6". **Weight:** 36 oz. (4" barrel). **Length:** 9-9/16" overall. **Grips:** Soft rubber. **Sights:** Red ramp front, micro-click rear adjustable for windage and elevation. **Features:** Satin finish stainless steel. Internal lock.
Price: 2-1/2" **$590.00**
Price: 4" **$579.00**
Price: 6" **$608.00**

SMITH & WESSON MODEL 67 COMBAT MASTERPIECE
Caliber: 38 Special, 6-shot. **Barrel:** 4". **Weight:** 32 oz. **Length:** 9-5/16" overall. **Grips:** Soft rubber. **Sights:** Red ramp front, micro-click rear adjustable for windage and elevation. **Features:** Stainless steel with satin finish. Smooth combat trigger, semi-target hammer. Introduced 1994.
Price: **$585.00**

Smith & Wesson Model 686 Magnum PLUS Revolver
Similar to the Model 686 except has 7-shot cylinder, 2-1/2", 4" or 6" barrel. Weighs 34-1/2 oz., overall length 7-1/2" (2-1/2" barrel). Hogue rubber grips. Internal lock. Introduced 1996. Made in U.S.A. by Smith & Wesson.
Price: 2-1/2" barrel **$631.00**
Price: 4" barrel **$653.00**
Price: 6" barrel **$663.00**

SMITH & WESSON MODEL 625 REVOLVER
Caliber: 45 ACP, 6-shot. **Barrel:** 5". **Weight:** 46 oz. **Length:** 11.375" overall. **Grips:** Soft rubber; wood optional. **Sights:** Patridge front on ramp, S&W micrometer click rear adjustable for windage and elevation. **Features:** Stainless steel construction with .400" semi-target hammer, .312" smooth combat trigger; full lug barrel. Glass beaded finish. Introduced 1989.
Price: 5" **$745.00**
Price: 4" with internal lock. **$745.00**

SMITH & WESSON MODEL 640 CENTENNIAL DA ONLY
Caliber: 357 Mag., 38 Spec. +P, 5-shot. **Barrel:** 2-1/8". **Weight:** 25 oz. **Length:** 6-3/4" overall. **Grips:** Uncle Mike's Boot Grip. **Sights:** Serrated ramp front, fixed notch rear. **Features:** Stainless steel. Fully concealed hammer, snag-proof smooth edges. Internal lock. Introduced 1995 in 357 Magnum.
Price: **$599.00**

SMITH & WESSON MODEL 617 K-22 MASTERPIECE
Caliber: 22 LR, 6- or 10-shot. **Barrel:** 4", 6", 8-3/8". **Weight:** 42 oz. (4" barrel). **Length:** NA. **Grips:** Soft rubber. **Sights:** Patridge front, adjustable rear. Drilled and tapped for scope mount. **Features:** Stainless steel with satin finish; 4" has .312" smooth trigger, .375" semi-target hammer; 6" has either .312" combat or .400" serrated trigger, .375" semi-target or .500" target hammer; 8-3/8" with .400" serrated trigger, .500" target hammer. Introduced 1990.
Price: 4" **$644.00**
Price: 6", target hammer, target trigger **$625.00**
Price: 6", 10-shot **$669.00**
Price: 8-3/8", 10 shot **$679.00**

SMITH & WESSON MODEL 610 CLASSIC HUNTER REVOLVER
Caliber: 10mm, 40 S&W, 6-shot cylinder. **Barrel:** 6-1/2" full lug. **Weight:** 52 oz. **Length:** 12" overall. **Grips:** Hogue rubber combat. **Sights:** Interchangeable blade front, micro-click rear adjustable for windage and elevation. **Features:** Stainless steel construction; target hammer, target trigger; unfluted cylinder; drilled and tapped for scope mounting. Introduced 1998.
Price: **$785.00**

SMITH & WESSON MODEL 340 PD AIRLITE Sc CENTENNIAL
Caliber: 357 Magnum, 38 Spec. +P, 5-shot. **Barrel:** 1-7/8". **Grips:** Rounded butt grip. **Sights:** HiViz front. **Features:** Synthetic grip, internal lock. Blue.
Price: **$799.00**

SMITH & WESSON MODEL 360 PD AIRLITE Sc CHIEF'S SPECIAL
Caliber: 357 Magnum, 38 Spec. +P, 5-shot. **Barrel:** 1-7/8". **Grips:** Rounded butt grip. **Sights:** Fixed. **Features:** Synthetic grip, internal lock. Stainless.
Price: Red ramp front **$767.00**
Price: HiViz front. **$781.00**

SMITH & WESSON MODEL 386 PD AIRLITE Sc
Caliber: 357 Magnum, 38 Spec. +P, 7-shot. **Barrel:** 2-1/2". **Grips:** Rounded butt grip. **Sights:** Adjustable, HiViz front. **Features:** Synthetic grip, internal lock.
Price: Blue **$815.00**

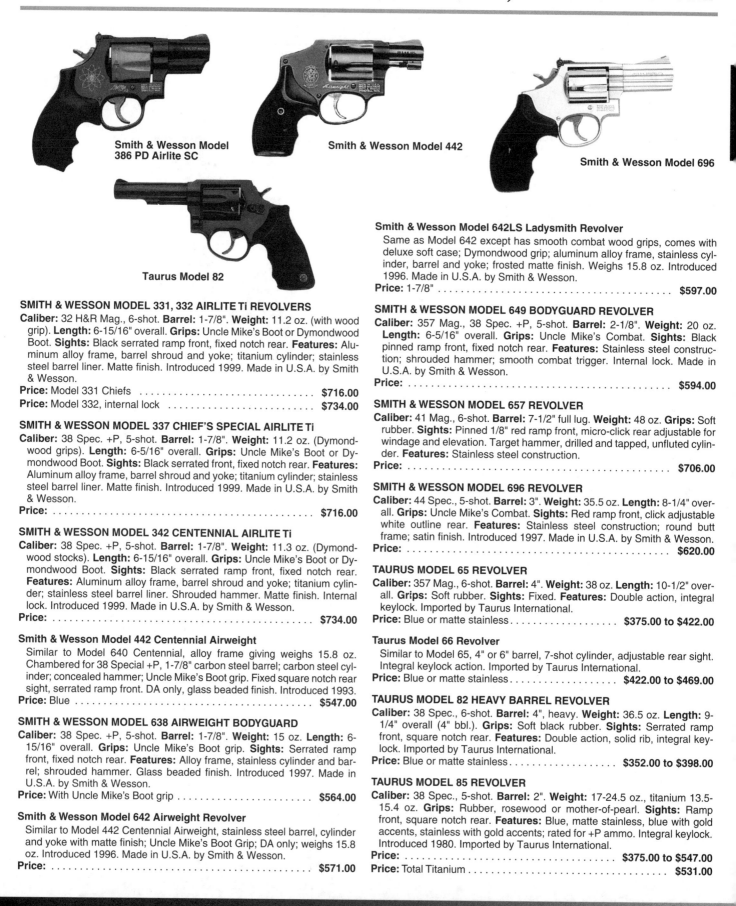

Smith & Wesson Model 386 PD Airlite SC

Smith & Wesson Model 442

Smith & Wesson Model 696

Taurus Model 82

SMITH & WESSON MODEL 331, 332 AIRLITE Ti REVOLVERS

Caliber: 32 H&R Mag., 6-shot. **Barrel:** 1-7/8". **Weight:** 11.2 oz. (with wood grip). **Length:** 6-15/16" overall. **Grips:** Uncle Mike's Boot or Dymondwood Boot. **Sights:** Black serrated ramp front, fixed notch rear. **Features:** Aluminum alloy frame, barrel shroud and yoke; titanium cylinder; stainless steel barrel liner. Matte finish. Introduced 1999. Made in U.S.A. by Smith & Wesson.
Price: Model 331 Chiefs **$716.00**
Price: Model 332, internal lock **$734.00**

SMITH & WESSON MODEL 337 CHIEF'S SPECIAL AIRLITE Ti

Caliber: 38 Spec. +P, 5-shot. **Barrel:** 1-7/8". **Weight:** 11.2 oz. (Dymondwood grips). **Length:** 6-5/16" overall. **Grips:** Uncle Mike's Boot or Dymondwood Boot. **Sights:** Black serrated front, fixed notch rear. **Features:** Aluminum alloy frame, barrel shroud and yoke; titanium cylinder; stainless steel barrel liner. Matte finish. Introduced 1999. Made in U.S.A. by Smith & Wesson.
Price: **$716.00**

SMITH & WESSON MODEL 342 CENTENNIAL AIRLITE Ti

Caliber: 38 Spec. +P, 5-shot. **Barrel:** 1-7/8". **Weight:** 11.3 oz. (Dymondwood stocks). **Length:** 6-15/16" overall. **Grips:** Uncle Mike's Boot or Dymondwood Boot. **Sights:** Black serrated ramp front, fixed notch rear. **Features:** Aluminum alloy frame, barrel shroud and yoke; titanium cylinder; stainless steel barrel liner. Shrouded hammer. Matte finish. Internal lock. Introduced 1999. Made in U.S.A. by Smith & Wesson.
Price: **$734.00**

Smith & Wesson Model 442 Centennial Airweight

Similar to Model 640 Centennial, alloy frame giving weighs 15.8 oz. Chambered for 38 Special +P, 1-7/8" carbon steel barrel; carbon steel cylinder; concealed hammer; Uncle Mike's Boot grip. Fixed square notch rear sight, serrated ramp front. DA only, glass beaded finish. Introduced 1993.
Price: Blue **$547.00**

SMITH & WESSON MODEL 638 AIRWEIGHT BODYGUARD

Caliber: 38 Spec. +P, 5-shot. **Barrel:** 1-7/8". **Weight:** 15 oz. **Length:** 6-15/16" overall. **Grips:** Uncle Mike's Boot grip. **Sights:** Serrated ramp front, fixed notch rear. **Features:** Alloy frame, stainless cylinder and barrel; shrouded hammer. Glass beaded finish. Introduced 1997. Made in U.S.A. by Smith & Wesson.
Price: With Uncle Mike's Boot grip **$564.00**

Smith & Wesson Model 642 Airweight Revolver

Similar to Model 442 Centennial Airweight, stainless steel barrel, cylinder and yoke with matte finish; Uncle Mike's Boot Grip; DA only; weighs 15.8 oz. Introduced 1996. Made in U.S.A. by Smith & Wesson.
Price: **$571.00**

Smith & Wesson Model 642LS Ladysmith Revolver

Same as Model 642 except has smooth combat wood grips, comes with deluxe soft case; Dymondwood grip; aluminum alloy frame, stainless cylinder, barrel and yoke; frosted matte finish. Weighs 15.8 oz. Introduced 1996. Made in U.S.A. by Smith & Wesson.
Price: 1-7/8" **$597.00**

SMITH & WESSON MODEL 649 BODYGUARD REVOLVER

Caliber: 357 Mag., 38 Spec. +P, 5-shot. **Barrel:** 2-1/8". **Weight:** 20 oz. **Length:** 6-5/16" overall. **Grips:** Uncle Mike's Combat. **Sights:** Black pinned ramp front, fixed notch rear. **Features:** Stainless steel construction; shrouded hammer; smooth combat trigger. Internal lock. Made in U.S.A. by Smith & Wesson.
Price: **$594.00**

SMITH & WESSON MODEL 657 REVOLVER

Caliber: 41 Mag., 6-shot. **Barrel:** 7-1/2" full lug. **Weight:** 48 oz. **Grips:** Soft rubber. **Sights:** Pinned 1/8" red ramp front, micro-click rear adjustable for windage and elevation. Target hammer, drilled and tapped, unfluted cylinder. **Features:** Stainless steel construction.
Price: **$706.00**

SMITH & WESSON MODEL 696 REVOLVER

Caliber: 44 Spec., 5-shot. **Barrel:** 3". **Weight:** 35.5 oz. **Length:** 8-1/4" overall. **Grips:** Uncle Mike's Combat. **Sights:** Red ramp front, click adjustable white outline rear. **Features:** Stainless steel construction; round butt frame; satin finish. Introduced 1997. Made in U.S.A. by Smith & Wesson.
Price: **$620.00**

TAURUS MODEL 65 REVOLVER

Caliber: 357 Mag., 6-shot. **Barrel:** 4". **Weight:** 38 oz. **Length:** 10-1/2" overall. **Grips:** Soft rubber. **Sights:** Fixed. **Features:** Double action, integral keylock. Imported by Taurus International.
Price: Blue or matte stainless.................... **$375.00 to $422.00**

Taurus Model 66 Revolver

Similar to Model 65, 4" or 6" barrel, 7-shot cylinder, adjustable rear sight. Integral keylock action. Imported by Taurus International.
Price: Blue or matte stainless.................... **$422.00 to $469.00**

TAURUS MODEL 82 HEAVY BARREL REVOLVER

Caliber: 38 Spec., 6-shot. **Barrel:** 4", heavy. **Weight:** 36.5 oz. **Length:** 9-1/4" overall (4" bbl.). **Grips:** Soft black rubber. **Sights:** Serrated ramp front, square notch rear. **Features:** Double action, solid rib, integral keylock. Imported by Taurus International.
Price: Blue or matte stainless.................... **$352.00 to $398.00**

TAURUS MODEL 85 REVOLVER

Caliber: 38 Spec., 5-shot. **Barrel:** 2". **Weight:** 17-24.5 oz., titanium 13.5-15.4 oz. **Grips:** Rubber, rosewood or mother-of-pearl. **Sights:** Ramp front, square notch rear. **Features:** Blue, matte stainless, blue with gold accents, stainless with gold accents; rated for +P ammo. Integral keylock. Introduced 1980. Imported by Taurus International.
Price: .... **$375.00 to $547.00**
Price: Total Titanium **$531.00**

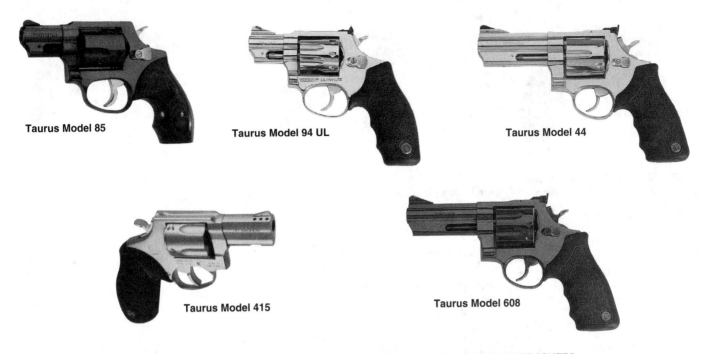

Taurus Model 85

Taurus Model 94 UL

Taurus Model 44

Taurus Model 415

Taurus Model 608

TAURUS MODEL 94 REVOLVER

Caliber: 22 LR, 9-shot cylinder. **Barrel:** 2", 4", 5". **Weight:** 18.5-27.5 oz. **Grips:** Soft black rubber. **Sights:** Serrated ramp front, click-adjustable rear. **Features:** Double action, integral keylock. Introduced 1989. Imported by Taurus International.
Price: Blue **$325.00**
Price: Matte stainless **$375.00**
Price: Model 94 UL, forged aluminum alloy, 18-18.5 oz. **$365.00**
Price: As above, stainless............................... **$410.00**

TAURUS MODEL 44 REVOLVER

Caliber: 44 Mag., 6-shot. **Barrel:** 4", 6-1/2", 8-3/8". **Weight:** 44-3/4 oz. **Grips:** Rubber. **Sights:** Adjustable. **Features:** Double action. Integral keylock. Introduced 1994. New Model 44S12 has 12" vent rib barrel. Imported from Brazil by Taurus International Manufacturing, Inc.
Price: Blue or stainless steel .... **$445.00 to $602.00**

TAURUS MODEL 415 REVOLVER

Caliber: 41 Mag., 5-shot. **Barrel:** 2-1/2". **Weight:** 30 oz. **Length:** 7-1/8" overall. **Grips:** Rubber. **Sights:** Fixed. **Features:** Stainless steel construction; matte finish; ported barrel. Double action. Integral keylock. Introduced 1999. Imported by Taurus International.
Price: **$508.00**
Price: Total Titanium **$602.00**

TAURUS MODEL 425/627 TRACKER REVOLVERS

Caliber: 357 Mag., 7-shot; 41 Mag., 5-shot. **Barrel:** 4" and 6". **Weight:** 28.8-40 oz. (titanium) 24.3-28. (6"). **Grips:** Rubber. **Sights:** Fixed front, adjustable rear. **Features:** Double action stainless steel, Shadow Gray or Total Titanium; vent rib (steel models only); integral keylock action. Imported by Taurus International.
Price: .... **$508.00 to $516.00**
Price: Total Titanium **$688.00**

TAURUS MODEL 445

Caliber: 44 Special, 5-shot. **Barrel:** 2". **Weight:** 20.3-28.25 oz. **Length:** 6-3/4" overall. **Grips:** Rubber. **Sights:** Ramp front, notch rear. **Features:** Blue or stainless steel. Standard or DAO concealed hammer, optional porting. Introduced 1997. Imported by Taurus International.
Price: .... **$345.00 to $500.00**
Price: Total Titanium 19.8 oz. **$600.00**

TAURUS MODEL 455 "STELLAR TRACKER"

Caliber: 45 ACP, 5-shot. **Barrel:** 2", 4", 6". **Weight:** 28/33/38.4 oz. **Grips:** Rubber. **Sights:** Adjustable. **Features:** Double action, matte stainless, includes five "Stellar" full-moon clips, integral keylock.
Price: **$523.00**

TAURUS MODEL 460 "TRACKER"

Caliber: 45 Colt, 5-shot. **Barrel:** 4" or 6". **Weight:** 33/38.4 oz. **Grips:** Rubber. **Sights:** Adjustable. **Features:** Double action, ventilated rib, matte stainless steel, comes with five "Stellar" full-moon clips.
Price: **$516.00**
Price: .... (Shadow gray, Total Titanium) **$688.00**

TAURUS MODEL 605 REVOLVER

Caliber: 357 Mag., 5-shot. **Barrel:** 2". **Weight:** 24 oz. **Grips:** Rubber. **Sights:** Fixed. **Features:** Double action, blue or stainless, concealed hammer models DAO, porting optional, integral keylock. Introduced 1995. Imported by Taurus International.
Price: .... **$375.00 to $438.00**

Taurus Model 731 Revolver

Similar to the Taurus Model 605, except in .32 Magnum.
Price: .... **$438.00 to $531.00**

TAURUS MODEL 608 REVOLVER

Caliber: 357 Mag. 38 Spec., 8-shot. **Barrel:** 4", 6-1/2", 8-3/8". **Weight:** 44-57 oz. **Length:** 9-3/8" overall. **Grips:** Soft black rubber. **Sights:** Adjustable. **Features:** Double action, integral keylock action. Available in blue or stainless. Introduced 1995. Imported by Taurus International.
Price: .... **$469.00 to $547.00**

Taurus Model 44 Series Revolver

Similar to Taurus Model 60 series, but in .44 Rem. Mag. With six-shot cylinder, blue and matte stainless finishes.
Price: .... **$500.00 to $578.00**

TAURUS MODEL 650CIA REVOLVER

Caliber: 357 Magnum, 5-shot. **Barrel:** 2". **Weight:** 24.5 oz. **Grips:** Rubber. **Sights:** Ramp front, square notch rear. **Features:** Double-action only, blue or matte stainless steel, integral keylock, internal hammer. Introduced 2001. From Taurus International.
Price: .... **$406.00 to $453.00**

Taurus Model 450

Taurus Model 817

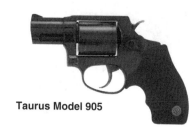

Taurus Model 905

TAURUS MODEL 651 CIA REVOLVER

Caliber: 357 Magnum, 5-shot. **Barrel:** 2". **Weight:** 17-24.5 oz. **Grips:** Rubber. **Sights:** Fixed. **Features:** Concealed single action/double action design. Shrouded cockable hammer, blue, matte stainless, Shadow Gray, Total Titanium, integral keylock. Made in Brazil. Imported by Taurus International Manufacturing, Inc.

Price: . . . . **$406.00 to $578.00**

TAURUS MODEL 450 REVOLVER

Caliber: 45 Colt, 5-shot. **Barrel:** 2". **Weight:** 21.2-22.3 oz. **Length:** 6-5/8" overall. **Grips:** Rubber. **Sights:** Ramp front, notch rear. **Features:** Double action, blue or stainless, ported, integral keylock. Introduced 1999. Imported from Brazil by Taurus International.

Price: **$492.00**
Price: Ultra-Lite (alloy frame) **$523.00**
Price: Total Titanium, 19.2 oz. **$600.00**

TAURUS MODEL 617 REVOLVER

Caliber: 357 Magnum, 7-shot. **Barrel:** 2". **Weight:** 28.3 oz. **Length:** 6-3/4" overall. **Grips:** Soft black rubber. **Sights:** Fixed. **Features:** Double action, blue, shadow gray, bright spectrum blue or matte stainless steel, integral keylock. Available with porting, concealed hammer. Introduced 1998. Imported by Taurus International.

Price: . . . . **$391.00 to $453.00**
Price: Total Titanium, 19.9 oz. **$602.00**

Taurus Model 445 Series Revolver

Similar to Taurus Model 617 series except in .44 Spl. with 5-shot cylinder.
Price: . . . . **$389.00 to $422.00**

Taurus Model 617ULT Revolver

Similar to Model 617 except aluminum alloy and titanium components, matte stainless finish, integral key-lock action. Weighs 18.5 oz. Available ported or non-ported. Introduced 2001. Imported by Taurus International.
Price: (5-shot cylinder) . . . . **$530.00 to $545.00**

TAURUS MODEL 817 ULTRA-LITE REVOLVER

Caliber: 38 Spec., 7-shot. **Barrel:** 2". **Weight:** 21 oz. **Length:** 6-1/2" overall. **Grips:** Soft rubber. **Sights:** Fixed. **Features:** Double action, integral keylock. Rated for +P ammo. Introduced 1999. Imported from Brazil by Taurus International.

Price: Blue **$375.00**
Price: Blue, ported **$395.00**
Price: Matte, stainless **$420.00**
Price: Matte, stainless, ported **$440.00**

TAURUS MODEL 850CIA REVOLVER

Caliber: 38 Special, 5-shot. **Barrel:** 2". **Weight:** 17-24.5 oz. **Grips:** Rubber. **Sights:** Ramp front, square notch rear. **Features:** Double action only, blue or matte stainless steel, rated for +P ammo, integral keylock, internal hammer. Introduced 2001. From Taurus International.

Price: . . . . **$406.00 to $453.00**
Price: Total Titanium **$578.00**

TAURUS MODEL 851CIA REVOLVER

Caliber: 38 Spec., 5-shot. **Barrel:** 2". **Weight:** 17-24.5 oz. **Grips:** Rubber. **Sights:** Fixed-UL/ULT adjustable. **Features:** Concealed single action/double action design. Shrouded cockable hammer, blue, matte stainless, Total Titanium, blue or stainless UL and ULT, integral keylock. Rated for +P ammo.

Price: . . . . **$406.00 to $578.00**

TAURUS MODEL 94, 941 REVOLVER

Caliber: 22 LR (Mod. 94), 22 WMR (Mod. 941), 8-shot. **Barrel:** 2", 4", 5". **Weight:** 27.5 oz. (4" barrel). **Grips:** Soft black rubber. **Sights:** Serrated ramp front, rear adjustable. **Features:** Double action, integral keylock. Introduced 1992. Imported by Taurus International.

Price: Blue . . . . **$328.00 to $344.00**
Price: Stainless (matte) . . . . **$375.00 to $391.00**
Price: Model 941 Ultra Lite,
forged aluminum alloy, 2" . . . . **$359.00 to $375.00**
Price: As above, stainless. . . . . **$406.00 to $422.00**

TAURUS MODEL 905, 405, 455 PISTOL CALIBER REVOLVERS

Caliber: 9mm, .40, .45 ACP, 5-shot. **Barrel:** 2", 4", 6-1/2". **Weight:** 21 oz. to 40.8 oz. **Grips:** Rubber. **Sights:** Fixed, adjustable on Model 455SS6 in .45 ACP. **Features:** Produced as a backup gun for law enforcement officers who desire to carry the same caliber ammunition in their backup revolver as they do in their service sidearm. Introduced 2003. Imported from Brazil by Taurus International Manufacturing, Inc.

Price: . . . . **$383.00 to $523.00**

Specially adapted single-shot and multi-barrel arms.

American Derringer Model 1

American Derringer Model 4

American Derringer Model 7

American Derringer Lady Derringer

American Derringer DA 38

AMERICAN DERRINGER MODEL 1

Caliber: 22 LR, 22 WMR, 30 Carbine, 30 Luger, 30-30 Win., 32 H&R Mag., 32-20, 380 ACP, 38 Super, 38 Spec., 38 Spec. shotshell, 38 Spec. +P, 9mm Para., 357 Mag., 357 Mag./45/410, 357 Maximum, 10mm, 40 S&W, 41 Mag., 38-40, 44-40 Win., 44 Spec., 44 Mag., 45 Colt, 45 Win. Mag., 45 ACP, 45 Colt/410, 45-70 single shot. **Barrel:** 3". **Weight:** 15-1/2 oz. (38 Spec.). **Length:** 4.82" overall. **Grips:** Rosewood, Zebra wood. **Sights:** Blade front. **Features:** Made of stainless steel with high-polish or satin finish. Two-shot capacity. Manual hammer block safety. Introduced 1980. Available in almost any pistol caliber. Contact the factory for complete list of available calibers and prices. From American Derringer Corp.

Price: 22 LR	POR
Price: 38 Spec.	POR
Price: 357 Maximum	POR
Price: 357 Mag.	POR
Price: 9mm, 380	POR
Price: 40 S&W	POR
Price: 44 Spec.	POR
Price: 44-40 Win.	POR
Price: 45 Colt	POR
Price: 30-30, 45 Win. Mag.	POR
Price: 41, 44 Mags.	POR
Price: 45-70, single shot	POR
Price: 45 Colt, 410, 2-1/2"	POR
Price: 45 ACP, 10mm Auto	POR

American Derringer Model 4

Similar to the Model 1 except has 4.1" barrel, overall length of 6", and weighs 16-1/2 oz.; chambered for 357 Mag., 357 Maximum, 45-70, 3" 410-bore shotshells or 45 Colt or 44 Mag. Made of stainless steel. Manual hammer block safety. Introduced 1980.

Price: 3" 410/45 Colt	$425.00
Price: 45-70	$560.00
Price: 44 Mag. with oversize grips	$515.00
Price: Alaskan Survival model (45-70 upper barrel, 410 or 45 Colt lower)	$475.00

American Derringer Model 7 Ultra Lightweight

Similar to Model 1 except made of high strength aircraft aluminum. Weighs 7-1/2 oz., 4.82" o.a.l., rosewood stocks. Available in 22 LR, 22 WMR, 32 H&R Mag., 380 ACP, 38 Spec., 44 Spec. Introduced 1980.

Price: 22 LR, WMR	$325.00
Price: 38 Spec.	$325.00
Price: 380 ACP	$325.00
Price: 32 H&R Mag/32 S&W Long	$325.00
Price: 44 Spec.	$565.00

American Derringer Model 10 Ultra Lightweight
Similar to the Model 1 except frame is of aluminum, giving weight of 10 oz. Stainless barrels. Available in 38 Spec., 45 Colt or 45 ACP only. Matte gray finish. Introduced 1980.

Price: 45 Colt	$385.00
Price: 45 ACP	$330.00
Price: 38 Spec.	$305.00

American Derringer Lady Derringer

Same as the Model 1 except has tuned action, is fitted with scrimshawed synthetic ivory grips; chambered for 32 H&R Mag. and 38 Spec.; 357 Mag., 45 Colt, 45/410. Deluxe Grade is highly polished; Deluxe Engraved is engraved in a pattern similar to that used on 1880s derringers. All come in a French-fitted jewelry box. Introduced 1989.

Price: 32 H&R Mag.	$375.00
Price: 357 Mag.	$405.00
Price: 38 Spec.	$360.00
Price: 45 Colt, 45/410	$435.00

American Derringer Texas Commemorative

A Model 1 Derringer with solid brass frame, stainless steel barrel and rosewood grips. Available in 38 Spec., 44-40 Win., or 45 Colt. Introduced 1980.

Price: 38 Spec.	$365.00
Price: 44-40	$420.00
Price: Brass frame, 45 Colt	$450.00

AMERICAN DERRINGER DA 38 MODEL

Caliber: 22 LR, 9mm Para., 38 Spec., 357 Mag., 40 S&W. **Barrel:** 3". **Weight:** 14.5 oz. **Length:** 4.8" overall. **Grips:** Rosewood, walnut or other hardwoods. **Sights:** Fixed. **Features:** Double-action only; two-shots. Manual safety. Made of satin-finished stainless steel and aluminum. Introduced 1989. From American Derringer Corp.

Price: 22 LR	$435.00
Price: 38 Spec.	$460.00
Price: 9mm Para.	$445.00
Price: 357 Mag.	$450.00
Price: 40 S&W	$475.00

ANSCHUTZ MODEL 64P SPORT/TARGET PISTOL

Caliber: 22 LR, 22 WMR, 5-shot magazine. **Barrel:** 10". **Weight:** 3 lbs., 8 oz. **Length:** 18-1/2" overall. **Stock:** Choate Rynite. **Sights:** None furnished; grooved for scope mounting. **Features:** Right-hand bolt; polished blue finish. Introduced 1998. Imported from Germany by AcuSport.

Price: 22 LR	$455.95
Price: 22 WMR	$479.95

Bond Arms Texas Defender

Bond Arms Century 2000 Defender

Cobra Big Bore

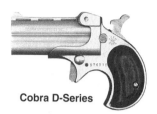

Cobra D-Series

Downsizer WSP Single Shot

Maximum Single Shot

BOND ARMS DEFENDER DERRINGER

Caliber: 410 Buckshot or slug, 45 Colt/45 Schofield (2.5" chamber), 45 Colt (only), 450 Bond Super/45 ACP/45 Super, 44 Mag./44 Special/44 Russian, 10mm, 40 S&W, 357 SIG, 357 Maximum/357 Mag./38 Special, 357 Mag/38 Special & 38 Long Colt, 38 Short Colt, 9mm Luger (9x19), 32 H&R Mag./38 S&W Long/32 Colt New Police, 22 Mag., 22 LR., 38-40, 44-40. **Barrel:** 3", 3-1/2". **Weight:** 20-21 oz. **Length:** 5"-5-1/2". **Grips:** Exotic woods or animal horn. **Sights:** Blade front, fixed rear. **Features:** Interchangeable barrels, retracting and rebounding firing pins, cross-bolt safety, automatic extractor for rimmed calibers. Stainless steel construction. Right- or left-hand.
Price: Texas (with TG) 3" bbl. **$379.00**
Price: Super (with TG) 3" bbl., 450 Bond Super and 45 ACP . . . **$379.00**
Price: Cowboy (no TG) **$379.00**
Price: Century 2000 (with TG), Cowboy Century 2000 (no TG), 3-1/2" bbls., 410/45 Colt **$394.00**
Price: Additional calibers - available separately

BROWN CLASSIC SINGLE SHOT PISTOL

Caliber: 17 Ackley Hornet through 375x444. **Barrel:** 15" air gauged match grade. **Weight:** About 3 lbs., 7 oz. **Grips:** Walnut; thumbrest target style. **Sights:** None furnished; drilled and tapped for scope mounting. **Features:** Falling block action gives rigid barrel-receiver mating; hand-fitted and headspaced. Introduced 1998. Made in U.S.A. by E.A. Brown Mfg.
Price: **$589.00**

COBRA BIG BORE DERRINGERS

Caliber: 22 WMR, 32 H&R Mag, 38 Spec., 9mm Para. **Barrel:** 2.75". **Weight:** 11.5 oz. **Length:** 4.65" overall. **Grips:** Textured black synthetic. **Sights:** Blade front, fixed notch rear. **Features:** Alloy frame, steel-lined barrels, steel breech block. Plunger-type safety with integral hammer block. Chrome or black Teflon finish. Introduced 2002. Made in U.S.A. by Cobra Enterprises.
Price: **$98.00**
Price: 9mm Para. **$136.00**

COBRA LONG-BORE DERRINGERS

Caliber: 22 WMR, 38 Spec., 9mm Para. **Barrel:** 3.5". **Weight:** 13 oz. **Length:** 5.65" overall. **Grips:** Textured black synthetic. **Sights:** Fixed.

Features: Chrome or black Teflon finish. Larger than Davis D-Series models. Introduced 2002. Made in U.S.A. by Cobra Enterprises.
Price: **$136.00**
Price: 9mm Para. **$136.00**
Price: Big-Bore models (same calibers, 3/4" shorter barrels). . . . **$136.00**

COBRA STARBIRD-SERIES DERRINGERS

Caliber: 22 LR, 22 WMR, 25 ACP, 32 ACP. **Barrel:** 2.4". **Weight:** 9.5 oz. **Length:** 4" overall. **Grips:** Laminated wood or pearl. **Sights:** Blade front, fixed notch rear. **Features:** Choice of black powder coat, satin nickel or chrome finish; spur trigger. Introduced 2002. Made in U.S.A. by Cobra Enterprises.
Price: **$112.00**

DOWNSIZER WSP SINGLE SHOT PISTOL

Caliber: 357 Magnum, 45 ACP, 38 Special. **Barrel:** 2.10." **Weight:** 11 oz. **Length:** 3.25" overall. **Grips:** Black polymer. **Sights:** None. **Features:** Single shot, tip-up barrel. Double action only. Stainless steel construction. Measures .900" thick. Introduced 1997. From Downsizer Corp.
Price: **$499.00**

MAXIMUM SINGLE SHOT PISTOL

Caliber: 22 LR, 22 Hornet, 22 BR, 22 PPC, 223 Rem., 22-250, 6mm BR, 6mm PPC, 243, 250 Savage, 6.5mm-35M, 270 MAX, 270 Win., 7mm TCU, 7mm BR, 7mm-35, 7mm INT-R, 7mm-08, 7mm Rocket, 7mm Super-Mag., 30 Herrett, 30 Carbine, 30-30, 308 Win., 30x39, 32-20, 350 Rem. Mag., 357 Mag., 357 Maximum, 358 Win., 375 H&H, 44 Mag., 454 Casull. **Barrel:** 8-3/4", 10-1/2", 14". **Weight:** 61 oz. (10-1/2" bbl.); 78 oz. (14" bbl.). **Length:** 15", 18-1/2" overall (with 10-1/2" and 14" bbl., respectively). **Grips:** Smooth walnut stocks and forend. Also available with 17" finger groove grip. **Sights:** Ramp front, fully adjustable open rear. **Features:** Falling block action; drilled and tapped for M.O.A. scope mounts; integral grip frame/receiver; adjustable trigger; Douglas barrel (interchangeable). Introduced 1983. Made in U.S.A. by M.O.A. Corp.
Price: Stainless receiver, blue barrel **$799.00**
Price: Stainless receiver, stainless barrel **$883.00**
Price: Extra blued barrel **$254.00**
Price: Extra stainless barrel **$317.00**
Price: Scope mount **$60.00**

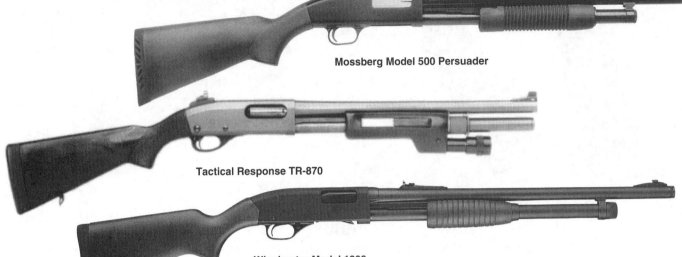

Mossberg Model 500 Persuader

Tactical Response TR-870

Winchester Model 1300 Camp Defender®

MOSSBERG MODEL 500 PERSUADER SECURITY SHOTGUNS

Gauge: 12, 20, .410, 3" chamber. **Barrel:** 18-1/2", 20" (Cyl.). **Weight:** 7 lbs. **Stock:** Walnut-finished hardwood or black synthetic. **Sights:** Metal bead front. **Features:** Available in 6- or 8-shot models. Top-mounted safety, double action slide bars, swivel studs, rubber recoil pad. Blue, Parkerized, Marinecote finishes. Mossberg Cablelock included. From Mossberg.

Price: 12 ga., 18-1/2", blue, wood or synthetic stock, 6-shot **$353.00**
Price: Cruiser, 12 ga., 18-1/2", blue, pistol grip, heat shield **$357.00**
Price: As above, 20 ga. or .410 bore.......................... **$345.00**

Mossberg Model 500, 590 Mariner Pump

Similar to the Model 500 or 590 Security except all metal parts finished with Marinecote metal finish to resist rust and corrosion. Synthetic field stock; pistol grip kit included. Mossberg Cablelock included.

Price: 6-shot, 18-1/2" barrel **$497.00**
Price: 9-shot, 20" barrel **$513.00**

Mossberg Model 500, 590 Ghost-Ring Shotguns

Similar to the Model 500 Security except has adjustable blade front, adjustable Ghost-Ring rear sight with protective "ears." Model 500 has 18.5" (Cyl.) barrel, 6-shot capacity; Model 590 has 20" (Cyl.) barrel, 9-shot capacity. Both have synthetic field stock. Mossberg Cablelock included. Introduced 1990. From Mossberg.

Price: 500 parkerized **$468.00**
Price: 590 parkerized **$543.00**
Price: 590 parkerized Speedfeed stock **$586.00**

Mossberg Model HS410 Shotgun

Similar to the Model 500 Security pump except chambered for 20 gauge or .410 with 3" chamber; has pistol grip forend, thick recoil pad, muzzle brake and has special spreader choke on the 18.5" barrel. Overall length is 37.5", weight is 6.25 lbs. Blue finish; synthetic field stock. Mossberg Cablelock and video included. Introduced 1990.

Price: HS 410 .... **$355.00**

MOSSBERG MODEL 590 SHOTGUN

Gauge: 12, 3" chamber. **Barrel:** 20" (Cyl.). **Weight:** 7-1/4 lbs. **Stock:** Synthetic field or Speedfeed. **Sights:** Metal bead front. **Features:** Top-mounted safety, double slide action bars. Comes with heat shield, bayonet lug, swivel studs, rubber recoil pad. Blue, Parkerized or Marinecote finish. Mossberg Cablelock included. From Mossberg.

Price: Blue, synthetic stock........................... **$417.00**
Price: Parkerized, synthetic stock...................... **$476.00**
Price: Parkerized, Speedfeed stock **$519.00**

TACTICAL RESPONSE TR-870 STANDARD MODEL SHOTGUN

Gauge: 12, 3" chamber, 7-shot magazine. **Barrel:** 18" (Cyl.). **Weight:** 9 lbs. **Length:** 38" overall. **Stock:** Fiberglass-filled polypropolene with non-snag recoil absorbing butt pad. Nylon tactical forend houses flashlight. **Sights:** Trak-Lock ghost ring sight system. Front sight has tritium insert. **Features:** Highly modified Remington 870P with Parkerized finish. Comes with nylon three-way adjustable sling, high visibility non-binding follower, high performance magazine spring, Jumbo Head safety, and Side Saddle extended 6-shot shell carrier on left side of receiver. Introduced 1991. From Scattergun Technologies, Inc.

Price: Standard model **$815.00**
Price: FBI model **$770.00**
Price: Patrol model **$595.00**
Price: Border Patrol model **$605.00**
Price: K-9 model (Rem. 11-87 action) **$995.00**
Price: Urban Sniper, Rem. 11-87 action **$1,290.00**
Price: Louis Awerbuck model **$705.00**
Price: Practical Turkey model **$725.00**
Price: Expert model **$1,350.00**
Price: Professional model **$815.00**
Price: Entry model **$840.00**
Price: Compact model **$635.00**
Price: SWAT model................................ **$1,195.00**

WINCHESTER MODEL 1300 DEFENDER PUMP GUN

Gauge: 12, 20, 3" chamber, 5- or 8-shot capacity. **Barrel:** 18" (Cyl.). **Weight:** 6-3/4 lbs. **Length:** 38-5/8" overall. **Stock:** Walnut-finished hardwood stock and ribbed forend. **Sights:** Metal bead front or TRUGLO® fiber-optic. **Features:** Cross-bolt safety, front-locking rotary bolt, twin action slide bars. Black rubber butt pad. From U.S. Repeating Arms Co.

Price: 8-Shot (black synthetic stock, TRUGLO® sight)........ **$343.00**
Price: 8-Shot Pistol Grip (pistol grip synthetic stock) **$343.00**

Winchester Model 1300 Coastal Pump Gun

Same as the Defender 8-Shot except has bright chrome finish, nickel-plated barrel, bead front sight. Phosphate coated receiver for corrosion resistance.

NEW!

Price: **$576.00**

Winchester Model 1300 Camp Defender®

Same as the Defender 8-Shot except has hardwood stock and forearm, fully adjustable open sights and 22" barrel with WinChoke® choke tube system (cylinder choke tube included). Weighs 6-7/8 lbs. Introduced 2001. From U.S. Repeating Arms Co.

Price: Camp Defender® **$392.00**

GRIPS

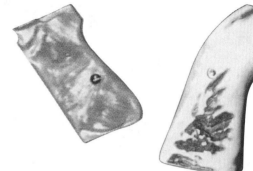

Ajax Grips

AJAX

Grip materials include genuine stag, buffalo horn, ivory polymer, white and black Pearlite, exotic woods, buffalo polymer, pewter, genuine ivory and Staglite (imitation stag horn). Available for most single- and double-action revolvers and semi-automatic pistols. Custom fittings are available.

Prices: Genuine stag . . . . **$199.95 to $249.95**
Prices: Genuine buffalo horn . . . . . . **$60.00 to $80.00**
Prices: Ivory polymer . . . . **$35.00 to $90.00**
Prices: Pearlite . . . . **$35.00 to $90.00**
Prices: Exotic woods (super walnut, cherrywood, black Silverwood) . . . . **$14.95 to $50.00**
Prices: Buffalo polymer. . . . . **$35.00 to $45.00**

Prices: Pewter . . . .**$50.00 to $60.00**
Prices: Genuine ivory . . . .**$325.00 to $350.00**
Prices: Staglite. . . . .**$49.95 to $59.95**
Textured decal grips in various textures also available from Ajax for many semi-automatic pistols.
Prices: **$9.95**

Alumna Grips

ALUMNA GRIPS

Aluminum handgun grips available in several configurations including checkered, UltraLight, ThinLine, olive gray finish, laser engraved and Custom Deluxe with up to 3 engraved initials. Anodized aluminum colors also available.
Prices: . . . .**$39.95 to $44.95**

BLU MAGNUM GRIPS

Makers of double- and single-action style grips in Skeeter Skelton, Sheriff Wilson and other styles, made of maple and exotic woods, ivory, stag, and Micarta.
Prices: . . . . **N/A**

BROWNELLS

Not a manufacturer, but an on-line and catalog retailer, supplying gunsmiths and retailers, as well as the shooting public. Many of the products shown in this section are also available from Brownells.

GRIPS

BUTLER CREEK (UNCLE MIKE'S)

Designed by handgun stock designer and craftsman Craig Spegel, revolver and pistol grips made of polymer are available for a wide range of handgun models. Revolver grips are made to be hand-filling, but not oversize. Finger grooves are provided on double-action revolver grips for good control. Revolver boot grips are designed not to "print" when used on concealed-carry revolvers, yet allow a controlled rapid draw. Pistol grips are specifically designed to maintain the original stock dimensions. Slip-on grips are offered in three sizes. Medium and large versions have finger grooves.

Prices: Revolver and handgun grips $20.95
Prices: Slip-on pistol grips $10.95

COAST IVORY

Offers handguns grips of elephant ivory, stag, California buckeye burl and other exotic woods, as well as polyester pearl.

Prices: Custom-fitted elephant ivory for 1911-style pistols **$450.00**
Prices: Custom-fitted ivory grips for Colt single-action revolvers . . . . **$500.00 and up**
Prices: Custom-fitted Derringer pistol ivory grips . . . . **$200.00 and up**
Prices: Custom-fitted genuine stag grips for Colt single-action revolvers **$190.00**
Prices: Polyester pearl grips . . . . . . **$60.00 to $85.00**

Crimson Trace Grips

CRIMSON TRACE

Makers of special grip replacements for many popular revolvers and pistols, including Lasergrip sighting systems. Lasergrips are intended for police agencies and military armed citizens.
Prices: . . . . **N/A**

GRIPS

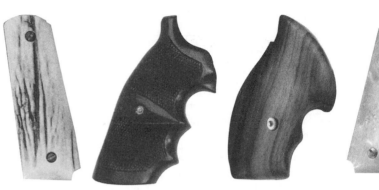

Eagle Grips

EAGLE GRIPS

Available grip materials include an extensive variety of rosewood, buffalo horn, ebony, mother-of-pearl, American elk, polymer and Ultra ivory (imitation of elephant ivory). Can produce grips for virtually any handgun. Custom-fittings available.

Prices: Rosewood or ebony handgun grips . . . . **$39.95 to $59.95**
Prices: Compact revolver Secret Service grips . . . . **$59.95 to $125.95**
Prices: Rosewood handgun thumb-rest grips (smooth finish) **$59.95**
Prices: Single-action revolver grips . . . . **$59.95 to $99.95**

FALCON INDUSTRIES, INC.

Producer of the Ergo Grip XT for 1911-type Government and Colt Commander-size frames. Made of textured nylon-based rigid polymer with pebble grain grip surface.

Price: **$22.00**

Falcon Industries Grip

HERRETT'S STOCKS, INC.

Standard and custom hand-fitted grips made of American walnut. Exotic woods such as cocobolo and bubinga are available on request. Grips are available in configurations including target, Camp Perry, combat, field, Jordan trooper, detective, and others. Offered in a variety of checkering patterns, or smooth finish.

Prices: . . . . **$19.95 to $329.95**

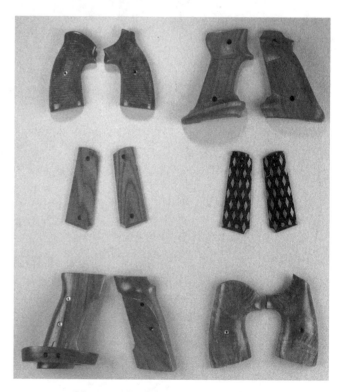

Herrett's Stocks, Inc. Grips

GRIPS

HOGUE, INC.

Producer of a wide range of grips including the Monogrip, a one-piece design that slides on revolver frames from the bottom. Hand-All grip sleeves fit over the original grips of over 50 handgun models. Grip materials include soft rubber, nylon, laminated hardwoods and fancy hardwoods such as cocobolo, goncalo alves, pau ferro, and kingwood. Single-action revolver grips are available in materials such as white and black Micarta, white and black pearlized polymer, ebony, fancy walnut, ivory polymer and exotic hardwoods.

Hogue, Inc. Grips

Prices: Revolver & pistol grips of rubber or nylon
. . . .**$14.95 to $22.95**
Prices: Revolver & pistol grips of goncalo alves or pau ferro . . . .**$24.95 to $59.95**
Prices: Revolver & pistol grips of laminated or fancy woods . . . .**$24.95 to $69.95**
Prices: Revolver & pistol grips of Kingwood, tulipwood or rosewood. . . . .**$24.95 to $79.95**
Prices: Single-action revolver grips wood, polymer or Micarta. . . . .**$39.95 to $79.95**

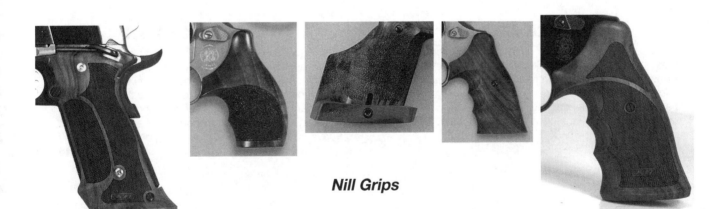

Nill Grips

NILL GRIPS

Double-action revolver grips are available with closed or open backstrap area in walnut with smooth, stippled, checkered or Rhomlas finishes, with or without finger grooves in a variety of styles. Anatomical match grips with or without adjustable palm rest are available for standard cartridge handguns and air pistols, as are match grips for Olympic rapid-fire and free pistols.

Prices: Closed back revolver combat-style grips . . . . $67.90 to $116.00
Prices: Open back revolver combat-style grips. . . . . $62.90 to $88.90
Prices: Combat-style grips for pistols . . . .$54.90 to $137.50
Prices: Palm rest grips for revolvers . . . .$109.90 to $164.50
Prices: Anatomical match grips with adjustable palm rest . . . .$137.50 to $155.00

GRIPS

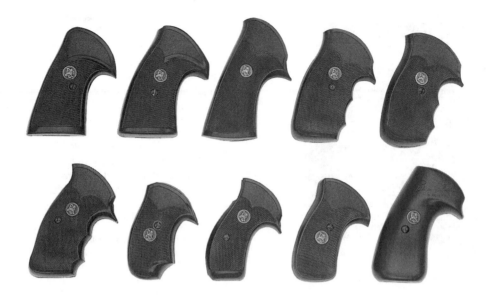

PACHMAYR

Models·available in rubber, combination wood and rubber (American Legend Series), and slip-on variations. Some have steel inserts to improve function and finger grooves and/or a palm swell is available on some models. Decelerator rubber grips are designed to dampen recoil on heavy-kicking handguns. Signature grips are available in full wrap-around or without coverage of the pistol backstrap for use on handguns such as the 1911-style pistols with grip safety mechanisms. Slip-on grips come in five sizes to fit virtually any handgun. Compact grips are for small, concealed carry handguns.

PEARCE GRIP

Producer of rubber grips for handgun models including those produced by Glock, Beretta, Colt, Makarov, Kahr Arms, Taurus and Para Ordnance. Highly contoured grips with palm swells, finger grooves and ultra-thin grip panels are available, depending on model.
Prices: . . . . **$9.95 to $24.95**

WILSON COMBAT

Grips for 1911-A1 style pistols in a variety of woods. Full-checkered models available in cocobolo and Diamondwood. Slim Line grips are laminated from cocobolo or Diamondwood and are 1/3 the thickness of standard 1911-style grips. Exotic wood 1911 grips are offered in cocobolo, Kingwood and Diamondwood and have a double-diamond checkering pattern.
Price: . . . . **$49.95 to $59**

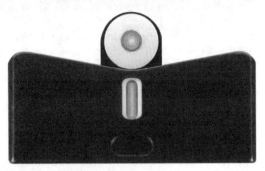

AO Express

Handgun Sights

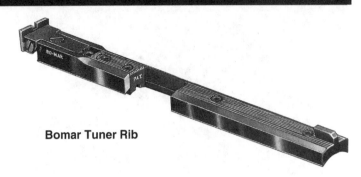

Bomar Tuner Rib

AO EXPRESS SIGHTS Low-profile, snag-free express-type sights. Shallow V rear with white vertical line, white dot front. All-steel, matte black finish. Rear is available in different heights. Made for most pistols, many with double set-screws. From AO Sight Systems, Inc.

Price: Standard Set, front and rear. **$60.00**
Price: Big Dot Set, front and rear. **$60.00**
Price: Tritium Set, Standard or Big Dot. **$90.00**
Price: 24/7 Pro Express, Std. or Big Dot Tritium **$120.00**

BO-MAR DELUXE BMCS Gives 3/8" windage and elevation adjustment at 50 yards on Colt Gov't 45; sight radius under 7". For GM and Commander models only. Uses existing dovetail slot. Has shield-type rear blade.

Bomar BMGS

Price: **$65.95**
Price: BMCS-2 (for GM and 9mm). **$68.95**
Price: Flat bottom. . . **$65.95**
Price: BMGC (for Colt Gold Cup), angled serrated blade, rear. **$68.95**
Price: BMGC front sight. **$12.95**
Price: BMCZ-75 (for CZ-75,TZ-75, P-9 and most clones). Works with factory front. **$68.95**

BO-MAR FRONT SIGHTS Dovetail style for S&W 4506, 4516, 1076; undercut style (.250", .280", 5/16" high); Fast Draw style (.210", .250", .230" high).
Price: **$12.95**

Bomar BMGC

BO-MAR BMU XP-100/T/C CONTENDER No gunsmithing required; has .080" notch.
Price: **$77.00**

BO-MAR BMML For muzzleloaders; has .062" notch, flat bottom.
Price: **$65.95**
Price: With 3/8" dovetail. **$65.95**

Bomar BMU XP-100

Bomar BMML

Bomar BMR

BO-MAR RUGER "P" ADJUSTABLE SIGHT Replaces factory front and rear sights.
Price: Rear sight. **$65.95**
Price: Front sight. **$12.00**

BO-MAR BMR Fully adjustable rear sight for Ruger MKI, MKII Bull barrel autos.
Price: Rear. **$65.95**
Price: Undercut front sight. **$12.00**

BO-MAR GLOCK Fully adjustable, all-steel replacement sights. Sight fits factory dovetail. Longer sight radius. Uses Novak Glock .275" high, .135" wide front, or similar.
Price: Rear sight. **$68.95**
Price: Front sight. **$20.95**

BO-MAR LOW PROFILE RIB & ACCURACY TUNER Streamlined rib with front and rear sights; 7 1/8" sight radius. Brings sight line closer to the bore than standard or extended sight and ramp. Weight 5 oz. Made for Colt Gov't 45, Super 38, and Gold Cup 45 and 38.
Price:. **$140.00**

Bomar Combat Rib

BO-MAR COMBAT RIB For S&W Model 19 revolver with 4" barrel. Sight radius 5 3/4", weight 5 1/2 oz.
Price:. **$127.00**

Bomar Winged Rib

BO-MAR WINGED RIB For S&W 4" and 6" length barrels-K-38, M10, HB 14 and 19. Weight for the 6" model is about 7 1/4 oz.
Price:. **$140.00**

Bomar Cover-Up Rib

BO-MAR COVER-UP RIB Adjustable rear sight, winged front guards. Fits right over revolver's original front sight. For S&W 4" M-10HB, M-13, M-58, M-64 & 65, Ruger 4" models SDA-34, SDA-84, SS-34, SS-84, GF-34, GF-84.
Price:. **$130.00**

Chip McCormick "Drop In"

CHIP MCCORMICK "DROP-IN" A low mount sight that fits any 1911-style slide with a standard military-type dovetail sight cut (60x.290"). Dovetail front sights also available. From Chip McCormick Corp.
Price: **$47.95**

CHIP MCCORMICK FIXED SIGHTS Same sight picture (.110" rear - .110" front) that's become the standard for pro combat shooters. Low mount design with rounded edges. For 1911-style pistols. May require slide machining for installation. From Chip McCormick Corp.
Price: **$24.95**

Chip McCormick Fixed Sight

C-MORE SIGHTS Replacement front sight blades offered in two types and five styles. Made of Du Pont Acetal, they come in a set of five high-contrast colors: blue, green, pink, red and yellow. Easy to install. Patridge style for Colt Python (all barrels), Ruger Super Blackhawk (7 1/2"), Ruger Blackhawk (4 5/8"); ramp style for Python (all barrels), Blackhawk (4 5/8"), Super Blackhawk (7 1/2" and 10 1/2"). From C-More Systems.
Price: Per set. $19.95

G.G. & G. GHOST RINGS Replaces the factory rear sight without gunsmithing. Black phosphate finish. Available for Colt M1911 and Commander, Beretta M92F, Glock, S&W, SIG Sauer.
Price: $65.00

Heinie Slant Pro

HEINIE SLANT PRO Made with a slight forward slant, the unique design of these rear sights is snag free for unimpeded draw from concealment. The combination of the slant and the rear serrations virtually eliminates glare. Made for most popular handguns. From Heinie Specialty Products.
Price: . . . . **$50.35 to $122.80**

HEINIE STRAIGHT EIGHT SIGHTS Consists of one tritium dot in the front sight and a slightly smaller Tritium dot in the rear sight. When aligned correctly, an elongated 'eight' is created. The Tritium dots are green in color. Designed with the belief that the human eye can correct vertical alignment faster than horizontal. Available for most popular handguns. From Heinie Specialty Products.
Price: . . . . **$104.95 to $122.80**

HEINIE CROSS DOVETAIL FRONT SIGHTS Made in a variety of heights, the standard dovetail is 60 degrees x .305" x .062" with a .002 taper. From Heinie Specialty Products.
Price: . . . . **$20.95 to $47.20**

JP GHOST RING Replacement bead front, ghost ring rear for Glock and M1911 pistols. From JP Enterprises.
Price: **$79.95**
Price: Bo-Mar replacement leaf with JP dovetail front bead. **$99.95**

LES BAER CUSTOM ADJUSTABLE LOW MOUNT REAR SIGHT Considered one of the top adjustable sights in the world for target shooting with 1911-style pistols. Available with Tritium inserts. From Les Baer Custom.
Price: . . . . **$49.00** (standard); **$99.00** (tritium)

LES BAER DELUXE FIXED COMBAT SIGHT A tactical-style sight with a very low profile. Incorporates a no-snag design and has serrations on sides. For 1911-style pistols. Available with Tritium inserts for night shooting. From Les Baer Custom.
Price: . . . . **$26.00** (standard); **$67.00** (with Tritium)

LES BAER DOVETAIL FRONT SIGHT Blank dovetail sight machined from bar stock. Can be contoured to many different configurations to meet user's needs. Available with Tritium insert. From Les Baer Custom.
Price: . . . . **$17.00** (standard); **$47.00** (with Tritium insert)

LES BAER FIBER OPTIC FRONT SIGHT Dovetail .330x65 degrees, .125" wide post, .185" high, .060" diameter. Red and green fiber optic. From Les Baer Custom.
Price: **$24.00**

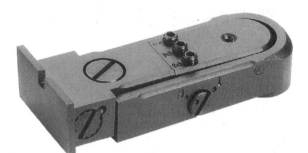

Les Baer PPC-Style Adjustable Rear Sight

LES BAER PPC-STYLE ADJUSTABLE REAR SIGHT Made for use with custom built 1911-style pistols, allows the user to preset three elevation adjustments for PPC-style shooting. Milling required for installation. Made from 4140 steel. From Les Baer Custom.
Price: $120.00

LES BAER DOVETAIL FRONT SIGHT WITH TRITIUM INSERT This fully contoured and finished front sight comes ready for gunsmith installation. From Les Baer Custom.
Price: $47.00

MMC TACTICAL ADJUSTABLE SIGHTS Low-profile, snag free design. Twenty-two click positions for elevation, drift adjustable for windage. Machined from 4140 steel and heat treated to 40 RC. Tritium and non-tritium. Ten different configurations and colors. Three different finishes. For 1911s, all Glock, HK USP, S&W, Browning Hi-Power.

Les Baer Dovetail

Price: Sight set, tritium. $144.92
Price: Sight set, white outline or white dot. $99.90
Price: Sight set, black. $93.90

MEPROLIGHT TRITIUM NIGHT SIGHTS Replacement sight assemblies for low-light conditions. Available for pistols (fixed and adj.),rifles, shotguns. 12-year warranty for useable illumination, while non-TRU-DOT have a 5-year warranty. Distributed in American by Kimber.

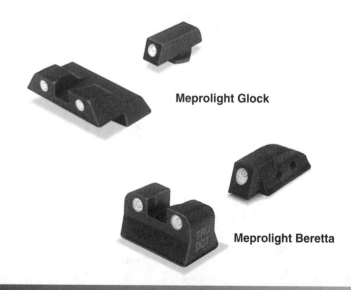

Meprolight Glock

Meprolight Beretta

METALLIC SIGHTS

Meprolight Colt

Meprolight Ruger

Meprolight Smith & Wesson

Meprolight H&K

Meprolight Taurus

Millett Colt

Millett Ruger

Price: Kahr K9, K40, fixed, TRU-DOT. **$100.00**
Price: Ruger P85, P89, P94, adjustable, TRU-DOT. **$156.00**
Price: Ruger Mini-14R sights. **$140.00**
Price: SIG Sauer P220, P225, P226, P228, adjustable, TRU-DOT. **$156.00**
Price: Smith&Wesson autos, fixed or adjustable, TRU-DOT. **$100.00**
Price: Taurus PT92, PT100, adjustable, TRU-DOT. **$156.00**
Price: Walther P-99, fixed, TRU-DOT. **$100.00**
Price: Shotgun bead. **$32.00**
Price: Beretta M92, Cougar, Brigadier, fixed, TRU-DOT. **$100.00**
Price: Browning Hi-Power, adjustable, TRU-DOT. **$156.00**
Price: Colt M1911 Govt., adjustable, TRU-DOT. **$156.00**

MILLETT SERIES 100 REAR SIGHTS All-steel highly visible, click adjustable. Blades in white outline, target black, silhouette, 3-dot. Fit most popular revolvers and autos.
Price:. . . . . **$51.77 to $84.00**

Millett Tritium Night Sight

MILLETT BAR-DOT-BAR TRITIUM NIGHT SIGHTS Replacement front and rear combos fit most automatics. Horizontal tritium bars on rear, dot front sight.
Price:. **$152.25**

MILLETT BAR/DOT Made with orange or white bar or dot for increased visibility. Available for Beretta 84, 85, 92S, 92SB, Browning, Colt Python & Trooper, Ruger GP 100, P85, Redhawk, Security Six.
Price:. . . . . **$14.99 to $24.99**

MILLETT 3-DOT SYSTEM SIGHTS The 3-Dot System sights use a single white dot on the front blade and two dots flanking the rear notch. Fronts available in Dual-Crimp and Wide Stake-On styles, as well as special applications. Adjustable rear sight available for most popular auto pistols and revolvers including Browning Hi-Power, Colt 1911 Government and Ruger P85.
Price: Front, from. **$16.80**
Price: Adjustable rear. **$55.60**

MILLETT REVOLVER FRONT SIGHTS All-steel replacement front sights with either white or orange bar. Easy to install. For Ruger GP-100, Redhawk, Security-Six, Police- Six, Speed-Six, Colt Trooper, Diamondback, King Cobra, Peacemaker, Python, Dan Wesson 22 and 15-2.
Price:. . . . . **$13.60 to $16.00**

MILLETT DUAL-CRIMP FRONT SIGHT Replacement front sight for automatic pistols. Dual-Crimp uses an all-steel two-point hollow rivet system. Available in eight heights and four styles. Has a skirted base that covers the front sight pad. Easily installed with the Millett Installation Tool Set. Available in Blaze Orange Bar, White Bar, Serrated Ramp, Plain Post. Available in heights of .185", .200", .225", .275", .312", .340" and .410".
Price:. **$16.80**

MILLETT STAKE-ON FRONT SIGHT Replacement front sight for automatic pistols. Stake-On sights have skirted base that covers the front sight pad. Easily installed with the Millet Installation Tool Set. Available in seven heights and four styles-Blaze Orange Bar, White Bar, Serrated Ramp, Plain Post. Available for Glock 17L and 24, others.
Price:. **$16.80**

METALLIC SIGHTS

MILLETT ADJUSTABLE TARGET Positive light-deflection serration and slant to eliminate glare and sharp edge sight notch. Audible "click" adjustments. For AMT Hardballer, Beretta 84, 85, 92S, 92SB, Browning Hi-Power, Colt 1911 Government and Gold Cup, Colt revolvers, Dan Wesson 15, 41, 44, Ruger revolvers, Glock 17, 17L, 19, 20, 21, 22, 23.
Price:. **$44.99**

MILLETT ADJUSTABLE WHITE OUTLINE Similar to the Target sight, except has a white outline on the blade to increase visibility. Available for the same handguns as the Target model, plus BRNO CZ-75/TZ-75/TA-90 without pin on front sight, and Ruger P85.
Price:. . . . . **$44.99 to $49.99**

OMEGA OUTLINE SIGHT BLADES Replacement rear sight blades for Colt and Ruger single action guns and the Interarms Virginian Dragoon. Standard Outline available in gold or white notch outline on blue metal. From Omega Sales, Inc.
Price:. **$10.00**

OMEGA MAVERICK SIGHT BLADES Replacement "peep-sight" blades for Colt, Ruger SAs, Virginian Dragoon. Three models available-No. 1, Plain; No. 2, Single Bar; No. 3, Double Bar Rangefinder. From Omega Sales, Inc.
Price: Each.. . . . . **$10.00**

ONE RAGGED HOLE Replacement rear sight ghost ring sight for Ruger handguns. Fits Blackhawks, Redhawks, Super Blackhawks, GP series and Mk. II target pistols with adjustable sights. From One Ragged Hole, Tallahassee, Florida.
Price:. . . . . **NA**

Pachmayr Accu-Set

PACHMAYR ACCU-SET Low-profile, fully adjustable rear sight to be used with existing front sight. Available with target, white outline or 3-dot blade. Blue finish. Uses factory dovetail and locking screw. For Browning, Colt, Glock, SIG Sauer, S&W and Ruger autos. From Pachmayr.
Price:. **$59.98**

P-T TRITIUM NIGHT SIGHTS Self-luminous tritium sights for most popular handguns, Colt AR-15, H&K rifles and shotguns. Replacement handgun sight sets available in 3- Dot style (green/green, green/yellow, green/orange) with bold outlines around inserts; Bar-Dot available in green/green with or without white outline rear sight. Functional life exceeds 15 years. From Innovative Weaponry, Inc.
Price: Handgun sight sets. **$99.95**
Price: Rifle sight sets. **$99.95**
Price: Rifle, front only. **$49.95**
Price: Shotgun, front only. **$49.95**

T/C Encore Fiber Optic Sight Set

T/C ENCORE FIBER OPTIC SIGHT SETS Click adjustable, steel rear sight and ramp-style front sight, both fitted with Tru-GloTM fiber optics. Specifically-designed for the T/C Encore pistol series. From Thompson/Center Arms.
Price:. **$49.35**

T/C ENCORE TARGET REAR SIGHT Precision, steel construction with click adjustments (via knurled knobs) for windage and elevation. Models available with low, medium and high blades. From Thompson/Center Arms.
Price:'. **$54.00**

T/C Encore Target Rear Sight

Trijicon Night Sight

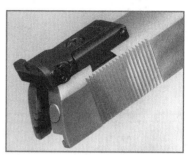

Wichita Series 70/80 Sight

TRIJICON NIGHT SIGHTS Three-dot night sight system uses tritium lamps in the front and rear sights. Tritium "lamps" are mounted in silicone rubber inside a metal cylinder. A polished crystal sapphire provides protection and clarity. Inlaid white outlines provide 3-dot aiming in daylight also. Available for most popular handguns including Glock 17, 19, 20, 21, 23, 24, 25, 26, 29, 30, H&K USP, Ruger P94, SIG P220, P225, 226, Colt 1911. Front and rear sets available. From Trijicon, Inc.
Price:. . . . . **$80.00 to $299.00**

TRIJICON 3-DOT Self-luminous front iron night sight for the Ruger SP101.
Price:. **$50.00**

WICHITA SERIES 70/80 SIGHT Provides click windage and elevation adjustments with precise repeatability of settings. Sight blade is grooved and angled back at the top to reduce glare. Available in Low Mount Combat or Low Mount Target styles for Colt 45s and their copies, S&W 645, Hi-Power, CZ 75 and others.
Price: Rear sight, target or combat. **$75.00**
Price: Front sight, Patridge or ramp. **$18.00**

WICHITA GRAND MASTER DELUXE RIBS Ventilated rib has wings machined into it for better sight acquisition and is relieved for Mag-Na-Porting. Milled to accept Weaver see-thru-style rings. Made of stainless; front and rear sights blued. Has Wichita Multi-Range rear sight system, adjustable front sight. Made for revolvers with 6" barrel.
Price: Model 301S, 301B (adj. sight K frames with custom bbl. of 1" to 1.032" dia. L and N frame with 1.062" to 1.100" dia. bbl.). **$225.00**
Price: Model 303S, 303B (adj. sight K, L, N frames with factory barrel). **$225.00**

WICHITA MULTI-RANGE QUICK CHANGE SIGHTING SYSTEM Multi-range rear sight can be pre-set to four positive repeatable range settings. Adjustable front sight allows compensation for changing lighting and weather conditions with just one front sight adjustment. Front sight comes with Lyman 17A Globe and set of apertures.
Price: Rear sight **$125.00**
Price: Front, sight **$95.00**

Williams Fire Sight Set

WILLIAMS FIRE SIGHT SETS Red fiber optic metallic sight replaces the original. Rear sight has two green fiber optic elements. Made of CNC-machined aluminum. Fits all Glocks, Ruger P-Series (except P-85), S&W 910, Colt Gov't. Model Series 80, Ruger GP 100 and Redhawk, and SIG Sauer (front only).
Price: Front and rear set **$39.95**
Price: SIG Sauer front. **$22.95**
Price: Browning BuckMark sight set **$44.95**
Price: Taurus PT111,PT140, PT145, PT1232, PT138 . . . . **$44.95**
Price: Ruger P Series, Glock, S&W 910, Colt Gov't. Series 80, Springfield XD. **$44.95**

WILSON ADJUSTABLE REAR SIGHTS Machined from steel, the click adjustment design requires simple cuts and no dovetails for installation. Available in several configurations: matte black standard blade with .128" notch; with .110" notch; with Tritium dots and .128" square or "U" shaped notch; and Combat Pyramid. From Wilson Combat.
Price:. . . . . **$24.95 to $69.95**

METALLIC SIGHTS

Wilson Nite-Eyes

WILSON NITE-EYES SIGHTS Low-profile, snag free design with green and yellow Tritium inserts. For 1911-style pistols. From Wilson Combat.

Price: **$119.95**

WILSON TACTICAL COMBAT SIGHTS Low-profile and snag-free in design, the sight employs the Combat Pyramid shape. For many 1911-style pistols and some Glock models. From Wilson Combat.

Price: **$139.95**

Sight Attachments

MERIT OPTICAL ATTACHMENT For iron sight shooting with handgun or rifle. Instantly attached by rubber suction cup to prescription or shooting glasses. Swings aside. Aperture adjustable from .020" to .156".

Price:. **$65.00**

Merit Optical Attachment

Alpec Mini Shot | Laseraim LA5X | Laseraim LAX

Maker and Model	Wave length (nm)	Beam Color	Lens	Operating Temp. (degrees F.)	Weight (ozs.)	Price	Other Data
ALPEC							[1]Range 1000 yards. [2]Range 300 yards. Mini Shot II range 500 yards, output 650mm, **$129.95**. [3]Range 300 yards; Laser Shot II 500 yards; Super Laser Shot 1000 yards. Black or stainless finish aluminum; removable pressure or push-button switch. Mounts for most handguns, many rifles and shotguns. From Alpec Team, Inc.
Power Shot[1]	635	Red	Glass	NA	2.5	$199.95	
Mini Shot[2]	670	Red	Glass	NA	2.5	99.95	
Laser Shot[3]	670	Red	Glass	NA	3.0	99.95	
BEAMSHOT							[1]Black or silver finish; adj. for windage and elevation; 300-yd. range; also M1000/S (500-yd. range), M1000/u (800-yd.). [2]Black finish; 300-, 500-, 800-yd. models. All come with removable touch pad switch, 5" cable. Mounts to fit virtually any firearm. From Quarton USA Co.
1000[1]	670	Red	Glass		3.8	NA	
3000[2]	635/670	Red	Glass		2	NA	
1001/u	635	Red	Glass		3.8	NA	
780	780	Red	Glass		3.8	NA	
BSA							[1]Comes with mounts for 22/air rifle and Weaver-style bases.
LS650[1]	N/A	Red	NA	NA	NA	49.95	
LASERAIM							[1]MOA dot at 100 yds: fits Weaver base. 3300-yd range; 2" dot at 100 yds.; rechargeable Nicad battery 41.5-mile range; 1" dot at 100 yds.; 20+ hrs. batt. life. [2]Laser projects 2" dot at 100 yds.: with rotary switch; with Hotdot **$237.00**; with Hotdot touch switch **$357.00**. [3]For Glock 17-27; G1 Hotdot **$299.00**; price installed. [10]Fits std. Weaver base, no rings required; 6-MOA dot; seven brightness settings. All have w&e adj.; black or satin silver finish. From Laseraim Technologies, Inc.
LA10 Hotdot[1]					NA	199.00	
Lasers							
MA-35RB Mini Aimer[2]					1.0	129.00	
G1 Laser[3]					2.0	229.00	
LASER DEVICES							[1]For S&W P99 semi-auto pistols; also BA-2, 5 oz., **$339.00**. [2]For revolvers. [3]For HK, Walther P99. [4]For semi-autos. [5]For rifles; also FA-4/ULS, 2.5 oz., $325.00. [6]For HK sub guns. [7]For military rifles. [8]For shotguns. [9]For SIG-Pro pistol. [10]Universal, semi-autos. All avail. with Magnum Power Point (650nM) or daytime-visible Super Power Point (632nM) diode. Infrared diodes avail. for law enforcement. From Laser Devices, Inc.
BA-1[1]	632	Red	Glass		2.4	372.00	
BA-3[2]	632	Red	Glass		3.3	332.50	
BA-5[3]	632	Red	Glass		3.2	372.00	
Duty-Grade[4]	632	Red	Glass		3.5	372.00	
FA-4[5]	632	Red	Glass		2.6	358.00	
LasTac[1]	632	Red	Glass		5.5	298.00 to 477.00	

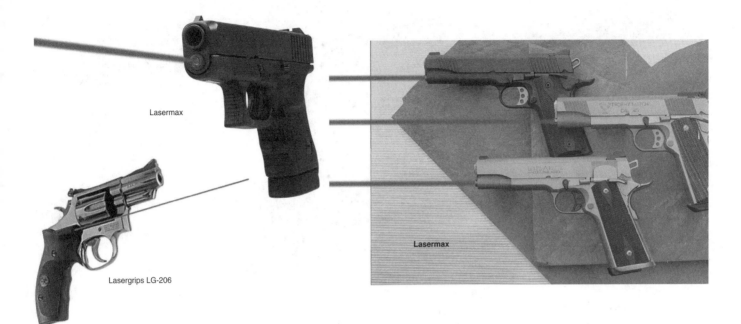

Lasermax

Lasergrips LG-206

Lasermax

Maker and Model	Wave length (nm)	Beam Color	Lens	Operating Temp. (degrees F.)	Weight (ozs.)	Price	Other Data
LASER DEVICES (cont.)							
MP-5[6]	632	Red	Glass		2.2	**495.00**	
MR-2[7]	632	Red	Glass		6.3	**485.00**	
SA-2[8]	632	Red	Glass		3.0	**360.00**	
SIG-Pro[9]	632	Red	Glass		2.6	**372.00**	
ULS-2001[10]	632	Red	Glass		4.5	**210.95**	
Universal AR-2A	632	Red	Glass		4.5	**445.00**	
LASERGRIPS							Replaces existing grips with built-in laser high in the right grip panel. Integrated pressure sensitive pad in grip activates the laser. Also has master on/off switch. [1]For Colt 1911/Commander. [2]For all Glock models. Option on/off switch. Requires factory installation. [3]For S&W K, L, N frames, round or square butt (LG-207); [4]For Taurus small-frame revolvers. [5]For Ruger SP-101. [6]For SIG Sauer P226. From Crimson Trace Corp. [7]For Beretta 92/96. [8]For Ruger MK II. [9]For S&W J-frame. [10]For Sig Sauer P228/229. [11]For Colt 1911 full size, wraparound. [12]For Beretta 92/96, wraparound. [13]For Colt 1911 compact, wraparound. [14]For S&W J-frame, rubber.
LG-201[1]	633	Red-Orange	Glass	NA		**299.00**	
LG-206[3]	633	Red-Orange	Glass	NA		**229.00**	
LG-085[4]	633	Red-Orange	Glass	NA		**229.00**	
LG-101[5]	633	Red-Orange	Glass	NA		**229.00**	
LG-226[6]	633	Red-Orange	Glass	NA		**229.00**	
GLS-630[2]	633	Red-Orange	Glass	NA		**595.00**	
LG202[7]	633	Red-Orange	Glass	NA		**299.00**	
LG203[8]	633	Red-Orange	Glass	NA		**299.00**	
LG205[9]	633	Red-Orange	Glass	NA		**299.00**	

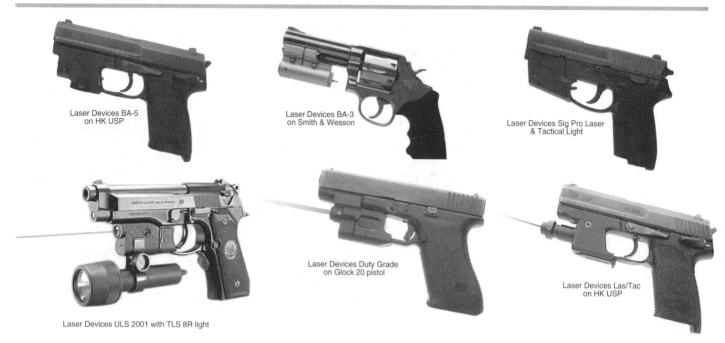

Laser Devices BA-5 on HK USP

Laser Devices BA-3 on Smith & Wesson

Laser Devices Sig Pro Laser & Tactical Light

Laser Devices ULS 2001 with TLS 8R light

Laser Devices Duty Grade on Glock 20 pistol

Laser Devices Las/Tac on HK USP

Maker and Model	Wave length (nm)	Beam Color	Lens	Operating Temp. (degrees F.)	Weight (ozs.)	Price	Other Data
LASERGRIPS *(cont.)*							
LG229[10]	633	Red-Orange	Glass	NA		**299.00**	
LG301[11]	633	Red-Orange	Glass	NA		**329.00**	
LG302[12]	633	Red-Orange	Glass	NA		**329.00**	
LG304[13]	633	Red-Orange	Glass	NA		**329.00**	
LG305[14]	633	Red-Orange	Glass	NA		**299.00**	
LASERLYTE							[1]Dot/circle or dot/crosshair projection; black or stainless. [2]Also 635/645mm model. From Tac Star Laserlyte. Laser's insta in grip activates the laser. Also has master on/off switch.
LLX-0006-140/090[1]	635/645	Red			1.4	**159.95**	
WPL-0004-140/090[2]	670	Red			1.2	**109.95**	
TPL-0004-140/090[2]	670	Red			1.2	**109.95**	
T7S-0004-140[2]	670	Red			0.8	**109.95**	
LASERMAX							Replaces the recoil spring guide rod; includes a customized takedown lever that serves as the laser's insta in grip activates the laser. Also has master on/off switch. For Glock, Smith & Wesson, Sigarms, Beretta, Colt, Kimber, Springfield Gov't. Model 1911, Heckler & Koch and select Taurus models. Installs in most pistols without gunsmithing. Battery life 1/2 hour to 2 hours in continuous use. From Laser Max.
LMS-1000 Internal Guide Rod	635	Red-Orange	Glass	40-120	.25	**389.00**	
NIGHT STALKER							Waterproof; LCD panel displays power remaining; programmable blink rate; con stant or memory on. From Wilcox Industri in grip activates the laser. Also has master on/off switch.
S0 Smart	635	Red	NA	NA	2.46	**515.00**	

COMPENDIUM OF STATE LAWS GOVERNING FIREARMS

The following chart lists the main provisions of state firearms laws as of the date of publication. In addition to the state provisions, the purchase, sale, and, in certain circumstances, the possession and interstate transportation of firearms are regulated by the Federal Gun Control Act of 1968 as amended by the Firearms Owners' Protection Act of 1986. Also, cities and localities may have their own gun ordinances in addition to federal and state restrictions. Details may be obtained by contacting local law enforcement authorities or by consulting your state's firearms law digest compiled by the NRA Institute for Legislative Action.

STATE	GUN BAN	EXEMPTIONS TO NICS[2]	STATE WAITING PERIOD - NUMBER OF DAYS		LICENSE OR PERMIT TO PURCHASE or other prerequesite		REGISTRATION		RECORD OF SALE REPORTED TO STATE OR LOCAL GOVT.
			HANDGUNS	LONG GUNS	HANDGUNS	LONG GUNS	HANDGUNS	LONG GUNS	
Alabama	—	—	—	—	—	—	—	—	—
Alaska	—	RTC	—	—	—	—	—	—	—
Arizona	—	RTC	—	—	—	—	—	—	—
Arkansas	—	RTC[3]	—	—	—	—	—	—	—
California	X_{20}	—	10_{14}	$10_{14,15}$	8, 23	—	X	24	X
Colorado	—	—	—	—	—	—	—	—	—
Connecticut	X_{20}	—	$14_{14,15}$	$14_{14,15}$	$X_{16, 23}$	—	—	24	X
Delaware	—	—	—	—	—	—	—	—	—
Florida	—	GRTC	$3_{14,15}$	—	—	—	—	—	—
Georgia	—	RTC	—	—	—	—	—	—	—
Hawaii	X_{20}	L, RTC	—	—	$X_{16, 23}$	X_{16}	X_{12}	X_{12}	X
Idaho	—	RTC	—	—	—	—	—	—	—
Illinois	20	—	3	2	X_{16}	X_{16}	4	4	X
Indiana	—	RTC, O_3	—	—	—	—	—	—	X
Iowa	—	L, RTC	—	—	X_{16}	—	—	—	—
Kansas	—	—	1	—	1	—	1	—	1
Kentucky	—	RTC[3]	—	—	—	—	—	—	—
Louisiana	—	GRTC	—	—	—	—	—	—	—
Maine	—	—	—	—	—	—	—	—	—
Maryland	X_{20}	O_3	7_{14}	$7_{9,14}$	8, 23	—	—	—	X
Massachusetts	X_{20}	GRTC	—	—	X_{16}	X_{16}	—	—	X
Michigan	—	O_3	—	—	$X_{16, 23}$	—	X	—	X
Minnesota	—	—	7_{16}	16	X_{16}	X_{16}	—	—	—
Mississippi	—	RTC[3]	—	—	—	—	—	—	—
Missouri	—	—	—	—	X_{16}	—	—	—	X
Montana	—	RTC	—	—	—	—	—	—	—
Nebraska	—	L	—	—	X	—	—	—	—
Nevada	—	RTC	1	—	—	—	1	—	—
New Hampshire	—	—	—	—	—	—	—	—	—
New Jersey	X_{20}	—	—	—	X_{16}	X_{16}	—	24	X
New Mexico	—	—	—	—	—	—	—	—	—
New York	X_{20}	L, RTC	—	—	$X_{16, 23}$	16	X	7	X
North Carolina	—	L, RTC	—	—	X_{16}	—	—	—	X
North Dakota	—	RTC	—	—	—	—	—	—	—
Ohio	20	—	1	—	16	—	1	—	1
Oklahoma	—	—	—	—	—	—	—	—	—
Oregon	—	GRTC	—	—	—	—	—	—	X
Pennsylvania	—	—	—	—	—	—	—	—	X
Rhode Island	—	—	7	7	23	—	—	—	X
South Carolina	—	RTC	8	—	8	—	—	—	X
South Dakota	—	GRTC	2	—	—	—	—	—	X
Tennessee	—	—	—	—	—	—	—	—	—
Texas	—	RTC[3]	—	—	—	—	—	—	—
Utah	—	RTC	—	—	—	—	—	—	—
Vermont	—	—	—	—	—	—	—	—	—
Virginia	X_{20}	—	1,8	—	1,8	—	—	—	1
Washington	—	O_3	5_{10}	—	—	—	—	—	X
West Virginia	—	—	—	—	—	—	—	—	—
Wisconsin	—	—	2	—	—	—	—	—	—
Wyoming	—	RTC	—	—	—	—	—	—	—
District of Columbia	X_{20}	L	—	—	X_{16}	X_{16}	X_{16}	X	X

COMPENDIUM OF STATE LAWS GOVERNING FIREARMS

Since state laws are subject to frequent change, this chart is
not to be considered legal advice or a restatement of the law.

All fifty states have sportsmen's protections laws to halt harrassment.

STATE	STATE PROVISION FOR RIGHT-TO-CARRY CONCEALED	CARRYING OPENLY PROHIBITED	OWNER ID CARDS OR LICENSING	FIREARM RIGHTS CONSTITU-TIONAL PROVISION	STATE FIREARMS PREEMPTION LAWS	RANGE PROTECTION LAW
Alabama	R	X_{11}	—	X	X	X
Alaska	R_{19}	—	—	X	—	X
Arizona	R	—	—	X	X	X
Arkansas	R	X_5	—	X	X	X
California	L	X_6	—	—	X	X
Colorado	R	25	—	X	X_{25}	X
Connecticut	R	X	—	X	X_{17}	X
Delaware	L	—	—	X	X	—
Florida	R	X	—	X	X	X
Georgia	R	X	—	X	X	X
Hawaii	L	X	X	X	—	X
Idaho	R	—	—	X	X	X
Illinois	D	X	X	X	—	X
Indiana	R	X	—	X	X_{18}	X
Iowa	L	X	—	—	X	X
Kansas	D	1	—	X	—	X
Kentucky	R	—	—	X	X	X
Louisiana	R	—	—	X	X	X
Maine	R	—	—	X	X	X
Maryland	L	X	—	—	X	X
Massachusetts	L	X	X	X	X_{17}	X
Michigan	R	X_{11}	—	X	X	X
Minnesota	R	X	—	—	X	X
Mississippi	R	—	—	X	X	X
Missouri	R	—	—	X	X	X
Montana	R	—	—	X	X	X
Nebraska	D	—	—	X	—	—
Nevada	R	—	—	X	X	X
New Hampshire	R	—	—	X	X	X
New Jersey	L	X	X	—	X_{17}	X
New Mexico	R	—	—	X	X	X
New York	L	X	X	—	X_{22}	X
North Carolina	R	—	—	X	X	X
North Dakota	R	X_6	—	X	X	X
Ohio	D	1	16	X	—	X
Oklahoma	R	X_6	—	X	X	X
Oregon	R	—	—	X	X	X
Pennsylvania	R	X_{11}	—	X	X	X
Rhode Island	L	X	—	X	X	X
South Carolina	R	X	—	X	X	X
South Dakota	R	—	—	X	X	X
Tennessee	R	X_5	—	X	X	X
Texas	R	X	—	X	X	X
Utah	R	X_6	—	X	X	X
Vermont	R_{19}	X_5	—	X	X	X
Virginia	R	—	—	X	X	X
Washington	R	X_{21}	—	X	X	—
West Virginia	R	—	—	X	X	X
Wisconsin	D	—	—	X	X	X
Wyoming	R	—	—	X	X	X
District of Columbia	D	X	X	NA	—	—

With over 20,000 "gun control" laws on the books in America, there are two challenges facing every gun owner. First, you owe it to yourself to become familiar with the federal laws on gun ownership. Only by knowing the laws can you avoid innocently breaking one.

Second, while federal legislation receives much more media attention, state legislatures and city councils make many more decisions regarding your right to own and carry firearms. NRA members and all gun owners must take extra care to be aware of anti-gun laws and ordinances at the state and local levels.

Notes:

1. In certain cities or counties.

2. **National Instant Check System (NICS) exemption codes:**
   RTC-Carry Permit Holders Exempt From NICS
   GRTC-Holders of RTC Permits issued before November 30, 1998 exempt from NICS. Holders of more recent permits are not exempt.
   L-Holders of state licenses to possess or purchase or firearms ID cards exempt from NICS.
   O-Other, See Note 3.

3. **NICS exemption notes: Arkansas:** RTC permits issued prior to 11/30/98 and those issued on and after 4/1/99 qualify. Those issued between 11/1/98 and 3/31/99 do not qualify. **Indiana:** Personal protection, hunting and target permits all qualify for exemptions. **Kentucky:** RTC permits issued after July 15, 1998 and prior to November 30, 1998 are exempt. **Maryland:** There are no exemptions for handgun purchases. For long gun purchases, those holding RTC permits issued before November 30, 1998 are exempt. **Michigan:** No exemptions for handguns, license for long guns. **Mississippi:** Permits issued to security guards do not qualify. **Texas:** Texas Peace Officer License, TCLEOSE Card, is valid only if issued prior to November 30, 1998. **Washington:** RTC permits issued after July 1, 1996 and prior to November 30, 1998 are exempt.

4. Chicago only. No handgun not already registered may be possessed.

5. **Arkansas** prohibits carrying a firearm "with a purpose to employ it as a weapon against a person." **Tennessee** prohibits carrying "with the intent to go armed." **Vermont** prohibits carrying a firearm "with the intent or purpose of injuring another."

6. Loaded.

7. New York City only.

8. A permit is required to acquire another handgun before 30 days have elapsed following the acquisition of a handgun.

9. **Maryland** subjects purchases of "assault weapons" to a 7-day waiting period.

10. May be extended by police to 30 days in some circumstances. An individual not holding a driver's license must wait 90 days.

11. Carrying a handgun openly in a motor vehicle requires a license.

12. Every person arriving in **Hawaii** is required to register any firearm(s) brought into the State within 3 days of arrival of the person or firearm(s), whichever occurs later. Handguns purchased from licensed dealers must be registered within 5 days.

13. Concealed carry laws vary significantly between the states. Ratings reflect the real effect a state's particular laws have on the ability of citizens to carry firearms for self-defense.

14. Purchases from dealers only. **Maryland:** 7 business days. Purchasers of regulated firearms must undergo background checks performed by the State Police, either through a dealer or directly through the State Police.

15. The waiting period does not apply to a person holding a valid permit or license to carry a firearm. In **Connecticut**, a hunting license also exempts the holder for long gun purchasers. **California:** transfers of a long gun to a person's parent, child or grandparent are exempt from the waiting period.

16. **Connecticut:** A certificate of eligibility or a carry permit is required to obtain a handgun and a carry permit is required to transport a handgun outside your home. **District of Columbia:** No handgun may be possessed unless it was registered prior to Sept. 23, 1976 and re-registered by Feb. 5, 1977. A permit to purchase is required for a rifle or shotgun. **Hawaii:** Purchase permits, required for all firearms, may not be issued until 14 days after application. A handgun purchase permit is valid for 10 days, for one handgun; a long gun permit is valid for one year, for multiple long guns. **Illinois:** A Firearm Owner's Identification Card (FOI) is required to possess or purchase a firearm, must be issued to qualified applicants within 30 days, and is valid for 5 years. **Iowa:** A purchase permit is required for handguns, and is valid for one year, beginning three days after issuance. **Massachusetts:** Firearms and feeding devices for firearms are divided into classes. Depending on the class, a firearm identification card (FID) or class A license or class B license is required to possess, purchase, or carry a firearm, ammunition thereof, or firearm feeding device, or "large capacity feeding device." **Michigan:** A handgun purchaser must obtain a license to purchase from local law enforcement, and within 10 days present the license and handgun to obtain a certificate of inspection. **Minnesota:** A handgun transfer or carrying permit, or a 7-day waiting period and handgun transfer report, is required to purchase handguns or "assault weapons" from a dealer. A permit or transfer report must be issued to qualified applicants within 7 days. A permit is valid for one year, a transfer report for

30 days. **Missouri:** A purchase permit is required for a handgun, must be issued to qualified applicants within 7 days, and is valid for 30 days. **New Jersey:** Firearm owners must possess a FID, which must be issued to qualified applicants within 30 days. To purchase a handgun, a purchase permit, which must be issued within 30 days to qualified applicants and is valid for 90 days, is required. An FID is required to purchase long guns. **New York:** Purchase, possession and/or carrying of a handgun require a single license, which includes any restrictions made upon the bearer. New York City also requires a license for long guns. **North Carolina:** To purchase a handgun, a license or permit is required, which must be issued to qualified applicants within 30 days. **Ohio:** Some cities require a permit-to-purchase or firearm owner ID card.

17. Preemption through judicial ruling. Local regulation may be instituted in **Massachusetts** if ratified by the legislature.

18. Except Gary and East Chicago and local laws enacted before January, 1994.

19. **Vermont and Alaska** law respect your right to carry without a permit. Alaska also has a permit to carry system to establish reciprocity with other states.

20. "Assault weapons" are prohibited in **California, Connecticut, New Jersey** and **New York**. Some local jurisdictions in **Ohio** also ban "assault weapons." **Hawaii** prohibits "assault pistols." **California** bans "unsafe handguns." **Illinois:** Chicago, Evanston, Oak Park, Morton Grove, Winnetka, Wilmette, and Highland Park prohibit handguns; some cities prohibit other kinds of firearms. **Maryland** prohibits "assault pistols" and the sale or manufacture of any handgun manufactured after Jan. 1, 1985, that appears on the Handgun Roster. **Massachusetts:** It is unlawful to sell, transfer or possess "any assault weapon or large capacity feeding device" [more than 10 rounds] that was not legally possessed on September 13, 1994. **Ohio:** some cities prohibit handguns of certain magazine capacities." **Virginia** prohibits "Street Sweeper" shotguns. The **District of Columbia** prohibits new acquisition of handguns and any semi-automatic firearm capable of using a detachable ammunition magazine of more than 12 rounds capacity. (With respect to some of these laws and ordinances, individuals may retain prohibited firearms owned previously, with certain restrictions.)

21. Local jurisdictions may opt out of prohibition.

22. Preemption only applies to handguns.

23. Requires proof of safety training for purchase. **California:** Must have Handgun Safety Certificate receipt which is valid for five years. **Connecticut:** To receive certificate of eligibility, must complete a handgun safety course approved by the Commissioner of Public Safety. **Hawaii:** Must have completed an approved handgun safety course. **Maryland:** Must complete an approved handgun safety course. **Michigan:** A person must correctly answer 70% of the questions on a basic safety review questionnaire in order to obtain a license to purchase. **New York:** Some counties require a handgun safety training course to receive a license. **Rhode Island:** Must receive a state-issued handgun safety card.

24. "Assault weapon" registration. **California** had two dates by which assault weapons had to be registered or possession after such date would be considered a felony: March 31, 1992 for the named make and model firearms banned in the 1989 legislation and December 31, 2000 for the firearms meeting the definition of the "assault weapons in the 1999 legislation. In **Connecticut**, those firearms banned by specific make and model in the 1993 law had to be registered by October 1, 1994 or possession would be considered a felony. A recent law requires registration of additional guns by October 1, 2003. In **New Jersey**, any "assault weapon" not registered, licensed, or rendered inoperable pursuant to a state police certificate by May 1, 1991, is considered contraband.

25. Local governments cannot enact ordinances that prohibit the sale, purchase, or possession of a firearm. Municipalities cannot restrict a person's ability to travel into, through, or within their jurisdiction for hunting or personal protection. Local governments, including law enforcement agencies, cannot maintain a database of guns or gun owners. Municipalities may prohibit open carry in government buildings if such prohibition is clearly posted.

Concealed carry codes:

R: Right-to-Carry "Shall issue" or less restrictive discretionary permit system (Ala., Conn.) (See also note #21.)

L: Right-to-Carry Limited by local authority's discretion over permit issuance.

D: Right-to-Carry Denied, no permit system exists; concealed carry is prohibited.

NL 00930

Rev. 9/2003 10m

Guide to Right-to-Carry Reciprocity and Recognition

- **The right to self-defense neither begins nor ends at a state border.**

- **A law-abiding citizen does not suffer a character change by crossing a state line.**

- **An "unalienable right" is not determined by geographical boundaries.**

- **A patchwork of state laws regarding the carrying of firearms can make criminals out of honest folks, especially those who frequently must travel the states to earn a living.**

- **Using data for all 3,054 U.S. counties from 1977 to 1994, University of Chicago Prof. John Lott finds that for each additional year a concealed handgun law is in effect the murder rate declines by 3%, robberies by over 2%, and the rape rate by 2%.**

In spite of the truth of these statements and the fact that nearly half of all Americans live in states that allow a law-abiding citizen to carry a firearm concealed for personal protection, it has not been commonplace that these same citizens could carry their firearm across states lines. NRA-ILA is working to pass right-to-carry reciprocity laws granting permit holders the ability to carry their firearms legally while visiting or traveling beyond their home state.

In order to assist NRA Members in determining which states recognize their permits, NRA-ILA has created this guide. This guide is not to be considered as legal advice or a restatement of the law. It is important to remember that state carry laws vary considerably. Be sure to check with state and local authorities outside your home state for a complete listing of restrictions on carrying concealed in that state. Many states restrict carrying in bars, restaurants (where alcohol is served), establishments where packaged alcohol is sold, schools, colleges, universities, churches, parks, sporting events, correctional facilities, courthouses, federal and state government offices/buildings, banks, airport terminals, police stations, polling places, any posted private property restricting the carrying of concealed firearms, etc. In addition to state restrictions, federal law prohibits carrying on military bases, in national parks and the sterile area of airports. National Forests usually follow laws of the state wherein the forest is located.

NOTE: Alaska and Vermont allow the concealed carry of firearms without a permit. Vermont residents traveling to other states must first obtain a non-resident permit from that state—if available—prior to carrying concealed. Alaska still issues permits to those who want them, allowing them to benefit by recognition and reciprocity laws.

NOTE TO READERS: Right To Carry reciprocity and recognition between the various states is subject to frequent change through legislative action and regulatory interpretation. This information is the best available at the time of publication. This summary is not intended as legal advice or restatement of law.

Rev. 3/2004

Alabama — Right-To-Carry Law Type: Reasonable May Issue

Issuing Authority:	County Sheriff
Contact agency for out of state permits:	Permits not granted.
These states recognize your permit:	Alaska, Colorado, Florida, Georgia, Idaho, Indiana, Kentucky, Michigan, Mississippi, Missouri, New Hampshire, North Carolina, North Dakota, Oklahoma, Utah, Tennessee, Vermont, Wyoming
This state recognizes permits from the following states:	Alaska, Colorado, Florida, Georgia, Idaho, Indiana, Kentucky, Michigan, Mississippi, New Hampshire, North Carolina, North Dakota, Oklahoma, Utah, Tennessee, Wyoming
Cost & Term of Permit:	$10 — 1 year

Key Government Offices:

Alabama Dept. of Public Safety
500 Dexter Ave.
Montgomery, Alabama 36130
Phone: (334)242-4392
Email: info@dps.state.al.us

Attorney General
Alabama State House
11 South Union Street, 3rd Floor
Montgomery, Alabama 36130
Phone: 334-242-7300

http://www.dps.state.al.us

Alaska — Right-To-Carry Law Type: Shall Issue

Issuing Authority:	State Trooper
Contact agency for out of state permits:	Permits not granted.
These states recognize your permit:	Alabama, Arizona, Colorado, Delaware, Florida, Idaho, Indiana, Kentucky, Michigan, Missouri, Montana, New Hampshire, North Carolina, North Dakota, Oklahoma, South Dakota, Utah, Vermont, Virginia, Wyoming
This state recognizes permits from the following states:	No permit required to carry concealed in Alaska.
Cost & Term of Permit:	$99 — 5 years

Key Government Offices:

Alaska Concealed Handgun Permit Program
5700 East Tudor Road
Anchorage, Alaska 99507
Phone: (907) 269-0392

http://www.dps.state.ak.us/ast/achp/

Arizona — Right-To-Carry Law Type: Shall Issue

Issuing Authority:	Arizona Department of Public Safety
Contact agency for out of state permits:	Arizona Department of Public Safety
These states recognize your permit:	Alaska, Arkansas, Colorado, Delaware, Florida, Idaho, Indiana, Kentucky, Michigan, Missouri, Montana, North Carolina, North Dakota, Oklahoma, Tennessee, Texas, Utah, Vermont, Virginia
This state recognizes permits from the following states:	Alaska, Arkansas, California, Colorado ,Connecticut, Deleware, Florida, Iowa, Kentucky, Louisiana, Maryland, Massachusetts, Michigan, Minnesota, Missouri, Montana, Nevada, New Mexico, North Carolina, North Dakota, Oklahoma, Oregon, South Carolina, Tennessee, Texas, Utah, West Virginia, Wyoming
Cost & Term of Permit:	$50 — 4 years

Key Government Offices:

Arizona Department of Public Safety
Attn: Concealed Weapons Permit Unit
P.O. Box 6488
Phoenix, Arizona 85005
Phone: (602) 256-6280 and (800) 256-6280
Fax: (602) 223-2928
Email: ccw@dps.state.az.us

Arizona Attorney General
1275 W. Washington Street
Phoenix, Arizona 85007
Phone: (602) 542-4266 and (888) 377-6108

http://www.dps.state.az.us/ccw/default.asp

Connecticut

Right-To-Carry Law Type: Reasonable May Issue

Issuing Authority:	Department of Public Safety, Special Licenses & Firearms Unit
Contact agency for out of state permits:	Department of Public Safety, Special Licenses & Firearms Unit
These states recognize your permit:	Alaska, Arizona, Idaho, Indiana, Kentucky, Michigan, Missouri, Montana, Oklahoma, Tennessee, Utah, Vermont
This state recognizes permits from the following states:	none
Cost & Term of Permit:	$35.00 plus $24.00 fingerprint processing fee — 5 years

Key Government Offices:

Department of Public Safety
1111 Country Club Road
Middletown, Connecticut 06450-9294
Phone: (860) 685-8000
Fax: (860) 685-8354
Email: DPS.Feedback@po.state.ct.us

Attorney General
55 Elm Street
Hartford, Connecticut 06106
Phone: 860-808-5318
Fax: 860 808-5387
Email: Attorney.General@po.state.ct.us

http://www.state.ct.us/dps/slfu/index.html

Delaware

Right-To-Carry Law Type: Restrictive May Issue

Issuing Authority:	Prothonotary of Superior Court
Contact agency for out of state permits:	Permits not granted.
These states recognize your permit:	Alaska, Arizona, Florida, Idaho, Indiana, Kentucky, Michigan, Missouri, Montana, North Carolina, Oklahoma, Tennessee, Utah, Vermont
This state recognizes permits from the following states:	Alaska, Arizona, Colorado, Florida, Michigan, North Carolina, North Dakota, Oklahoma, Tennessee, Utah
Cost & Term of Permit:	$34.50 plus other fees — Initially 2 years, renewal for 3 years.

Key Government Offices:

Delaware State Police
P.O. Box 430
Dover, Delaware 9903-0430
Phone: (302) 739-5900

Attorney General
Carvel State Office Building
820 N. French Street
Wilmington, Delaware 19801
Email: Attorney.General@State.DE.US

http://www.state.de.us/dsp/

Florida

Right-To-Carry Law Type: Shall Issue

Issuing Authority:	Department of Agriculture and Consumer Services, Division of Licensing
Contact agency for out of state permits:	Department of Agriculture and Consumer Services, Division of Licensing
These states recognize your permit:	Alabama, Alaska, Arizona, Arkansas, Colorado, Delaware, Georgia, Idaho, Indiana, Kentucky, Louisiana, Michigan, Mississippi, Missouri, Montana, New Hampshire, North Carolina, North Dakota, Oklahoma, Pennsylvania, South Dakota, Tennessee, Texas, Utah, Vermont, Wyoming
This state recognizes permits from the following states:	Alabama, Alaska, Arizona, Arkansas, Colorado, Delaware, Georgia, Idaho, Indiana, Kentucky, Louisiana, Michigan, Mississippi, Montana, New Hampshire, North Carolina, North Dakota*, Oklahoma, Pennsylvania, South Dakota*, Tennessee, Texas, Utah, Wyoming *must be 21
Cost & Term of Permit:	Residents: $75 plus fingerprinting fee, Renewal: $65 — 5 years

Key Government Offices:

Florida Dept. of Agriculture and Consumer Services,
Division of Licensing
P.O. Box 6687
Tallahassee, Florida 32314-6687
Phone: (850) 488-5381
email: springb@doacs.state.fl.us

Office of Attorney General
State of Florida The Capital
Tallahasse, Florida 32399-1050
Phone: 850-414-3300
Fax: 850-410-1630
email: ag@oag.state.fl.us

http://licgweb.doacs.state.fl.us/

Arkansas
Right-To-Carry Law Type: Shall Issue

Issuing Authority:	State Police
Contact agency for out of state permits:	Permits not granted.
These states recognize your permit:	Alaska, Arizona, Florida, Idaho, Indiana, Kentucky, Michigan, Missouri, Montana, North Carolina, Oklahoma, South Carolina, South Dakota, Tennessee, Texas, Utah, Vermont
This state recognizes permits from the following states:	Arizona, Florida, Kentucky, North Carolina, Oklahoma, South Carolina, Tennessee, Texas, Utah
Cost & Term of Permit:	$115 — 4 Years

Key Government Offices:

Regulatory Services Division
Attn: Arkansas State Police
#1 State Police Plaza Drive
Little Rock, Arkansas 72209-2971
Phone: 501-618-8627
Fax: 501-618-8647

Office of the Attorney General
200 Catlett-Prien Tower
323 Center Street
Little Rock, Arkansas 72201
Phone: 501-682-1323 (1-800-448-3014)
Email: oag@ag.state.ar.us

www.state.ar.us/chl/chl.html

California
Right-To-Carry Law Type: Restrictive May Issue

Issuing Authority:	County Sheriff
Contact agency for out of state permits:	Permits not granted.
These states recognize your permit:	Alaska, Arizona, Idaho, Indiana, Kentucky, Michigan, Missouri, Montana, Oklahoma, Tennessee, Utah, Vermont
This state recognizes permits from the following states:	none
Cost & Term of Permit:	varies — 2 years maximum

Key Government Offices:

California Attorney General
Attn: Department of Justice
P.O. Box 944255
Sacramento, California 94244-2550
Phone: (916) 445-9555

http://caag.state.ca.us/

Colorado
Right-To-Carry Law Type: Shall Issue

Issuing Authority:	County Sheriff
Contact agency for out of state permits:	Permits not granted.
These states recognize your permit:	Alabama, Alaska, Arizona, Florida, Georgia, Idaho, Indiana, Kentucky, Michigan, Missouri, Montana, New Hampshire, North Carolina, Oklahoma, South Dakota, Tennessee, Utah, Vermont, Wyoming
This state recognizes permits from the following states:	Alabama, Alaska, Arizona, Florida, Georgia, Idaho, Iowa, Indiana, Kentucky, Michigan, Montana, New Hampshire, North Carolina, Oklahoma, South Dakota, Tennessee, Utah, Wyoming
Cost & Term of Permit:	No more than $100 — 5 years

Key Government Offices:

Attorney General
1525 Sherman 5th Floor
Denver, Colorado 80203
Phone: (303) 866-4500
Fax: (303) 866-5691
Email: attorney.general@state.co.us

Colorado Bureau of Investigation
690 Kipling St. Suite 3000
Denver, Colorado 80215
Phone: (303) 239-5850
Email: james.spoden@cdps.state.co.us

http://cbi.state.co.us/ccw/reciprocity.asp

Georgia
Right-To-Carry Law Type: Shall Issue

Issuing Authority:	County Probate Judge
Contact agency for out of state permits:	Permits not granted.
These states recognize your permit:	Alabama, Alaska, Arizona, Colorado, Florida, Idaho, Indiana, Kentucky, Michigan, Missouri, Montana, New Hampshire, North Caolina, Oklahoma, Pennsylvania, South Dakota, Tennessee, Utah, Vermont, Wyoming
This state recognizes permits from the following states:	Alabama, Colorado, Florida, Idaho, Indiana, Kentucky, Michigan, Montana, New Hampshire, North Carolina, Pennsylvania, South Dakota, Tennessee, Wyoming
Cost & Term of Permit:	$24 to GBI and additional fee set by County. — 5 years
Key Government Offices:	Georgia Bureau of Investigation P.O. Box 370748 Decatur, Georgia 30037-0748 Phone: (404) 244-2501 Georgia Attorney General 40 Capitol Square, SW Atlanta, Georgia 30334-1300 Phone: 404-656-3300 http://www.ganet.org/ago/

Hawaii
Right-To-Carry Law Type: Restrictive May Issue

Issuing Authority:	Chief of Police
Contact agency for out of state permits:	Permits not granted.
These states recognize your permit:	Alaska, Idaho, Indiana, Kentucky, Michigan, Missouri, Montana, Oklahoma, Tennessee, Utah, Vermont
This state recognizes permits from the following states:	none
Cost & Term of Permit:	varies — varies
Key Government Offices:	Honolulu Police Department Attn: Firearms Division 801 S. Beretania Honolulu, Hawaii Phone: 808-529-3371, Fax: 808-529-3525 hpd@honolulupd.org http://www.honolulupd.org/service/gunlaw/htm Attorney General Department of the Attorney General 425 Queen Street Honolulu, Hawaii 96813 http://www.hawaii.gov/ag/index.html

Idaho
Right-To-Carry Law Type: Shall Issue

Issuing Authority:	County Sheriff
Contact agency for out of state permits:	Any Sheriffs' Department
These states recognize your permit:	Alabama, Alaska, Colorado, Florida, Georgia, Indiana, Kentucky, Michigan, Missouri, Montana, New Hampshire, North Carolina, North Dakota, Oklahoma, Tennessee, Utah, Vermont, Virginia, Wyoming
This state recognizes permits from the following states:	All state permits
Cost & Term of Permit:	$20 plus fingerprinting fee — 4 years
Key Government Offices:	Idaho Department of Law Enforcement 700 S. Stratford Dr P.O. Box 700 Meridian, Idaho 83680-0700 Phone: (208)884-7000 Idaho Attorney General 700 W. Jefferson Street P.O. Box 83720 Boise, Idaho 83720-0010 Phone: (208) 334-2400 Fax: (208) 334-2530 http://www.state.id.us/dle/dle.htm

Right-to-Carry Reciprocity and Recognition, cont.

Illinois — Right-To-Carry Law Type: Non-Issue

Issuing Authority:	Permits Not Available
Contact agency for out of state permits:	Permits not granted.
These states recognize your permit:	none
This state recognizes permits from the following states:	none
Cost & Term of Permit:	n/a | n/a

Key Government Offices:

Illinois State Police
P.O. Box 19461
Springfield, Illinois 62794-9461
Phone: 217-782-7263
Fax: 217-785-2821

Attorney General
500 South Second St.
Springfield, Illinois 62706
Phone: (217) 782-1090
Email: attorney_general@state.il.us

http://www.state.il.us/isp/isphpage.htm

Indiana — Right-To-Carry Law Type: Shall Issue

Issuing Authority:	State Police through Chief Law Enforcement Officer of Municipality
Contact agency for out of state permits:	Permits not granted.
These states recognize your permit:	Alabama, Alaska, Colorado, Florida, Georgia, Idaho, Kentucky, Michigan, Missouri, Montana, New Hampshire, North Carolina, North Dakota, Oklahoma, South Dakota, Tennessee, Utah, Vermont, Wyoming
This state recognizes permits from the following states:	All state permits recognized for non-Indiana residents.
Cost & Term of Permit:	$30 | 4 years

Key Government Offices:

State Police
100 North Senate Avenue
Indiana Government Center North, 3rd Floor
Indianapolis, Indiana 46204-2259
Phone: (317) 232-8200

Indiana Attorney General
State House, Room 219
Indianapolis, Indiana 46204
Phone: (317) 232 - 6201

http://www.state.in.us/isp/

Iowa — Right-To-Carry Law Type: Reasonable May Issue

Issuing Authority:	Sheriff for residents, Commissioner of Public Safety for non residents
Contact agency for out of state permits:	Commissioner of Public Safety
These states recognize your permit:	Alaska, Arizona, Idaho, Indiana, Kentucky, Michigan, Missouri, Montana, Oklahoma, Tennessee, Utah, Vermont
This state recognizes permits from the following states:	none
Cost & Term of Permit:	$10 for permit | 1 year

Key Government Offices:

Iowa Department of Public Safety
Wallace State Office Building
Des Moines, Iowa 50319
Phone: (515) 281-3211
Email: webteam@dps.state.ia.us

Attorney General
1305 E. Walnut Street
Des Moines, Iowa 50319
Phone: 515-281-5164
Fax: 515-281-4209
Email: webteam@ag.state.ia.us

http://www.state.ia.us/government/dps/index.html

Kansas — Right-To-Carry Law Type: Non-Issue

Issuing Authority:	Permits Not Available
Contact agency for out of state permits:	Permits Not Granted.
These states recognize your permit:	none
This state recognizes permits from the following states:	none
Cost & Term of Permit:	n/a · n/a

Key Government Offices:

Attorney General
301 S.W. 10th Avenue
Topeka, Kansas 66612-1597
Phone: (785) 296-2215
Fax: (785) 296-6296
Email: GENERAL@at01po.wpo.state.ks.us

Highway Patrol
General Headquarters
122 SW 7th Street
Topeka, Kansas 66603-3847
Phone: 785-296-6800
Fax: 785-296-3049

http://www.ink.org/public/ksag/

Kentucky — Right-To-Carry Law Type: Shall Issue

Issuing Authority:	State Police
Contact agency for out of state permits:	Permits not granted.
These states recognize your permit:	Alabama, Alaska, Arizona, Arkansas, Colorado, Florida, Georgia, Idaho, Indiana, Louisiana, Michigan, Mississippi, Missouri, Montana, New Hampshire, North Carolina, North Dakota, Oklahoma, South Dakota, Pennsylvania, Tennessee, Texas, Utah, West Virginia, Vermont, Wyoming
This state recognizes permits from the following states:	All state permits recognized.
Cost & Term of Permit:	$60 · 5 years

Key Government Offices:

Kentucky State Police
919 Versailles Road
Frankfort, Kentucky 40601
Phone: (502) 227-8725

Office of the Kentucky Attorney General
Frankfort, Kentucky 40601
Phone: (502) 696-5300

http://www.kentuckystatepolice.org/conceal.htm#recip

Louisiana — Right-To-Carry Law Type: Shall Issue

Issuing Authority:	Department of Public Safety & Corrections
Contact agency for out of state permits:	Permits not granted.
These states recognize your permit:	Alaska, Arizona, Florida, Idaho, Indiana, Kentucky, Michigan, Minnesota, Missouri, Montana, Oklahoma, Tennessee, Texas, Utah, Vermont, Virginia, Wyoming
This state recognizes permits from the following states:	Florida, Kentucky, Tennessee, Texas, Wyoming
Cost & Term of Permit:	$50 for 2 year permit, $100 for 4 year permit. · 2 years or 4 years

Key Government Offices:

Louisiana State Police/Department of Public Safety
P.O. Box 66614
Baton Rouge, Louisiana 70896-6614
Phone: 225-925-4239
Fax: 225-925-3717
Email: concealed-handguns@dps.state.la.us

Louisiana Attorney General
State Capitol, 22nd Floor
P.O. Bos 940005
Baton Rouge, Louisiana 70804-9005
Phone: (225) 342-7013 Fax: (225) 342-7335
http://www.ag.state.la.us

http://www.lsp.org/handguns

Right-to-Carry Reciprocity and Recognition, cont.

Maine

Right-To-Carry Law Type: Shall Issue

Issuing Authority:	Dept of Public Safety, Maine State Police, Licensing Division
Contact agency for out of state permits:	Chief of State Police
These states recognize your permit:	Alaska, Idaho, Indiana, Kentucky, Michigan, Missouri, Oklahoma, Tennessee, Utah, Vermont
This state recognizes permits from the following states:	none
Cost & Term of Permit:	Residents: new $35. renewal $20. Non residents: new & renewal $60. — 4 years

Key Government Offices:

Department of Public Safety Maine State Police, Licensing Division 164 State House Station Augusta, Maine 043333-0164 Phone: (207) 624-8775	Attorney General 6 State House Station Augusta, Maine 04333 Phone: (207) 626-8800 http://www.me.state.us.ag/homepage.htm

http://www.state.me.us.dps/msp

Maryland

Right-To-Carry Law Type: Restrictive May Issue

Issuing Authority:	Superintendent of State Police
Contact agency for out of state permits:	Superintendent of State Police
These states recognize your permit:	Alaska, Arizona, Idaho, Indiana, Kentucky, Michigan, Missouri, Montana, Oklahoma, Tennessee, Utah, Vermont
This state recognizes permits from the following states:	none
Cost & Term of Permit:	New $117 Renewal $74 — 2 years

Key Government Offices:

Maryland State Police Attn: Handgun Permit Section 7751 Washington Blvd Jessup, Maryland 20794 Phone: (410) 79-0191, (800) 525-5555	Attorney General 200 St. Paul Place Baltimore, Maryland 21202 Phone: (410) 576-6300 Fax: (410) 576-6447

http://www.mdsp.maryland.gov/mdsp/downloads/licensingapplications

Massachusetts

Right-To-Carry Law Type: Restrictive May Issue

Issuing Authority:	Department of State Police, Firearms Record Bureau
Contact agency for out of state permits:	Permits are technically available for non-residents, but are rarely granted.
These states recognize your permit:	Alaska, Arizona, Idaho, Indiana, Kentucky, Michigan, Missouri, Montana, Oklahoma, Tennessee, Utah, Vermont
This state recognizes permits from the following states:	none
Cost & Term of Permit:	Residents and Non-Residents: $100. — Residents: 4 years. Non res.: 1 year.

Key Government Offices:

Firearms Records Bureau Attn: Firearms License 200 Arlington Street Suite 2200 Chelsea, Massachusetts 02150 Phone: (617) 660-4780	Massachusetts State Police 470 Worcester Road Framingham, Massachusetts 01702 Phone: (508) 820-2300 Email: msp.webmaster@pol.state.ma.us

http://www.state.ma.us/msp/firearms/index.htm

Michigan

Right-To-Carry Law Type: Shall Issue

Issuing Authority:	County Gun Board/Sheriff
Contact agency for out of state permits:	Permits not granted.
These states recognize your permit:	Alabama, Alaska, Arizona, Colorado, Delaware, Florida, Georgia, Idaho, Indiana, Kentucky, Minnesota, Montana, Missouri, New Hampshire, North Carolina, North Dakota, Oklahoma, Pennsylvania, South Dakota, Tennessee, Utah, Vermont, Virginia, Wyoming
This state recognizes permits from the following states:	All state permits recognized, as long as permit holder is resident of issuing state.
Cost & Term of Permit:	$105 New and renewal. 5 years
Key Government Offices:	Michigan Department of State Police 714 S. Harrison Road East Lansing, Michigan 48823 Phone: (517) 332-2521 Michigan Attorney General P.O. Box 30212 Lansing, Michigan 48909 Phone: (517) 373-1110 Fax: (517) 241-1850 http://www.ag.state.mi.us
	http://www.michigan.gov/msp

Minnesota

Right-To-Carry Law Type: Shall Issue

Issuing Authority:	Chief of Police/County Sheriff
Contact agency for out of state permits:	Any Minnesota County Sheriff
These states recognize your permit:	Alaska, Arizona, Idaho, Indiana, Kentucky, Michigan, Missouri, Montana, Oklahoma, Tennessee, Utah, Vermont
This state recognizes permits from the following states:	Michigan, Louisiana, Wyoming
Cost & Term of Permit:	Not to exceed $100. 5 years
Key Government Offices:	Minnesota Department of Public Safety 444 Cedar Street Saint Paul, Minnesota 55101 Phone: (651) 282-6565 bca.permitstocarry@state.mn.us Minnesota Attorney General 102 State Capitol St. Paul, Minnesota 55155 Phone: (651) 296-6196 Fax: (651) 297-4193 http://www.ag.state.mn.us
	http://www.dps.state.mn.us/bca/CJIS/documents/carrypermits/states.html

Mississippi

Right-To-Carry Law Type: Shall Issue

Issuing Authority:	Department of Public Safety/Highway Patrol
Contact agency for out of state permits:	Permits not granted.
These states recognize your permit:	Alabama, Alaska, Florida, Idaho, Indiana, Kentucky, Michigan, Missouri, Montana, Oklahoma, Tennessee, Utah, Vermont, Wyoming
This state recognizes permits from the following states:	Alabama, Florida, Kentucky, Tennessee, Wyoming
Cost & Term of Permit:	New: $100. Renewal: $50. 4 years
Key Government Offices:	Mississippi State Police P. O. Box 958 Jackson, Mississippi 39205-0958 Phone: (601) 987-1586 Email: jtucker@dps.state.ms.us Attorney General P.O. Box 220 Jackson, Mississippi 39205-0220 Phone: (601) 359-3680 http://www.ago.state.ms.us
	http://www.dps.state.ms.us/dps/dps.nsf

Missouri — Right-To-Carry Law Type: Shall Issue

Issuing Authority:	County Sheriff
Contact agency for out of state permits:	Permits not granted.
These states recognize your permit:	Alaska, Arizona, Idaho, Indiana, Kentucky, Michigan, New Hampshire, Oklahoma, Tennessee, Utah, Vermont
This state recognizes permits from the following states:	All state permits are recognized.
Cost & Term of Permit:	$100 — 3 years

Key Government Offices:

Deparment of Public Safety
P.O. Box 749
Jefferson City, Missouri 65102-0749
Phone: (573) 751-4905   Fax: (573) 751-5399

Attorney General
Supreme Court Building 207 W. High St.
P.O. Box 899
Jefferson City, Missouri 65102
Phone: (573) 751-3321
Fax: (573) 751-0774

http://www.dps.state.mo.us

Montana — Right-To-Carry Law Type: Shall Issue

Issuing Authority:	County Sheriff
Contact agency for out of state permits:	Permits not granted.
These states recognize your permit:	Alaska, Arizona, Colorado, Florida, Idaho, Indiana, Kentucky, Michigan, Missouri, North Carolina, North Dakota, Oklahoma, South Carolina, Tennessee, Utah, Vermont, Wyoming
This state recognizes permits from the following states:	Alaska, Arizona, Arkansas, California, Colorado, Connecticut, Florida, Georgia, Idaho, Indiana, Iowa, Kentucky, Louisiana, Maryland, Massachusetts, Michigan, Minnesota, Mississippi, Nevada, New Jersey, New Mexico, New York, North Carolina, North Dakota, Oklahoma, Oregon, Pennsylvania, South Carolina, South Dakota, Tennessee, Texas, Utah, Virginia, Washington, West Virginia, Wyoming
Cost & Term of Permit:	New: $50. Renewal: $25. — 4 years

Key Government Offices:

Montana Highway Patrol
2550 Prospect Ave.
P.O. Box 201419
Helena, Montana 59620-1419
Phone: (406) 444-3780
Fax: (406) 444-4169

Montana Attorney General
P.O. Box 201401
Helena, Montana 59620-1401
Phone: 406-444-2026
Fax: 406-444-3549
contact:doj@state.mt.us

http://www.doj.state.mt.us/enforcement/concealedweapons.asp

Nebraska — Right-To-Carry Law Type: Non-Issue

Issuing Authority:	Permits not available
Contact agency for out of state permits:	Permits not granted.
These states recognize your permit:	none
This state recognizes permits from the following states:	none
Cost & Term of Permit:	n.a — n.a

Key Government Offices:

Nebraska State Patrol
P.O. Box 94907
Lincoln, Nebraska 68509
Phone: 402-471-4545

Attorney General
2115 State Capitol
P.O. Box 98920
Lincoln, Nebraska 68509-8920
Phone: 402-471-2682
Fax: 402-471-3297

http://www.nsp.state.ne.us

Nevada

Right-To-Carry Law Type: Shall Issue

Issuing Authority:	County Sheriff
Contact agency for out of state permits:	In person with any County Sheriff
These states recognize your permit:	Alaska, Arizona, Idaho, Indiana, Kentucky, Michigan, Missouri, Montana, Oklahoma, Tennessee, Utah, Vermont
This state recognizes permits from the following states:	none
Cost & Term of Permit:	New $60. Renewal $25 — 5 years; 3 years non-resident
Key Government Offices:	Office of the Attorney General 100 N. Carson Street Carson City, Nevada 89701-4717 Phone: (775)684-1100 Fax: (775) 684-1108 Email: aginfo@ag.state.nv.us

http://www.ag.state.nv.us

New Hampshire

Right-To-Carry Law Type: Shall Issue

Issuing Authority:	Selectman/Mayor or Chief of Police
Contact agency for out of state permits:	Director of State Police
These states recognize your permit:	Alabama, Alaska, Colorado, Florida, Georgia, Idaho, Indiana, Kentucky, Michigan, Missouri, North Carolina, North Dakota, Oklahoma, Tennessee, Utah, Vermont, Wyoming
This state recognizes permits from the following states:	Alabama, Alaska, Colorado, Florida, Georgia, Idaho, Indiana, Kentucky, Michigan, North Carolina, North Dakota, Oklahoma, Tennesse, Wyoming
Cost & Term of Permit:	Residents: $10. Non Residents: $20. — 4 years
Key Government Offices:	Director of State Police Permits and Licensing Unit 10 Hazen Drive Concord, New Hampshire 03301 Phone: (603) 271-3575 Fax: (603) 271-1153

http://www.state.nh.us/safety/nhsp/plupr.html

New Jersey

Right-To-Carry Law Type: Restrictive May Issue

Issuing Authority:	Chief of Police/Superintendent of State Police
Contact agency for out of state permits:	Superintendent of State Police--Permits are technically available for non-residents, but are rarely granted.
These states recognize your permit:	Alaska, Idaho, Indiana, Kentucky, Michigan, Missouri, Montana, Oklahoma, Tennessee, Utah, Vermont
This state recognizes permits from the following states:	none
Cost & Term of Permit:	$20 — 2 years
Key Government Offices:	New Jersey State Police Firearms Investigation Unit PO Box 7068 West Trenton, NJ 08628-0068 609-882-2000 ext. 2664	Office of the Attorney General Dept. of Law & Public Safety P.O. Box 080 Trenton, New Jersey 08625-0080 Phone: (609) 292-4925, Fax: (609) 292-3508 http://www.njpublicsafety.com

http://www.njsp.org/faq.html#firearms

New Mexico

Right-To-Carry Law Type: Shall Issue

Issuing Authority:	Department of Public Safety
Contact agency for out of state permits:	Permits not granted.
These states recognize your permit:	Alaska, Arizona, Colorado, Idaho, Indiana, Kentucky, Michigan, Missouri, Oklahoma, Tennessee, Utah, Vermont
This state recognizes permits from the following states:	A list of reciprocal states is not available at this time, since New Mexico's new law was implemented 1/1/2004.

Cost & Term of Permit:	$100 for initial permit plus fingerprint fee. $50 for renewal.	2 years

Key Government Offices:	Department of Public Safety P.O. Box 1628 Santa Fe, New Mexico 87504 Phone: (505) 827-3370 or (505) 827-9000	Attorney General 407 Galisteo Street Bataan Memorial Building, Rm 260 Santa Fe, New Mexico 87501 Phone: (505) 827-6000, Fax: (505) 827-5826 http://www.ago.state.nm.us
	http://www.dps.nm.org/	

New York

Right-To-Carry Law Type: Restrictive May Issue

Issuing Authority:	Varies by county
Contact agency for out of state permits:	Permits not granted.
These states recognize your permit:	Alaska, Idaho, Indiana, Kentucky, Michigan, Missouri, Montana, Oklahoma, Tennessee, Utah, Vermont
This state recognizes permits from the following states:	none

Cost & Term of Permit:	Varies by county	Varies, 2 years to lifetime

Key Government Offices:	State Police Counsel's Office Bldg. 22, 1220 Washington Ave. Albany, New York 12226 Phone: (518) 457-6811	Attorney General 120 Broadway New York, New York 10271-0332 Phone: (212)416-8050 http://www.oag.state.ny.us
	http://www.troopers.state.ny.us/firearms/firearmsindex.html	

North Carolina

Right-To-Carry Law Type: Shall Issue

Issuing Authority:	County Sheriff
Contact agency for out of state permits:	Permits not granted.
These states recognize your permit:	Alabama, Alaska, Arizona, Colorado, Delaware, Florida, Georgia, Idaho, Indiana, Kentucky, Michigan, Missouri, Montana, New Hampshire, Oklahoma, Pennsylvania, South Carolina, South Dakota, Tennessee, Utah, Vermont, Virginia
This state recognizes permits from the following states:	Alabama, Alaska, Arkansas, Arizona, Colorado, Delaware, Florida, Georgia, Idaho, Indiana, Kentucky, Michigan, Montana, New Hampshire, Oklahoma, Pennsylvania, South Carolina, South Dakota, Tennessee, Utah, Virginia, Wyoming

Cost & Term of Permit:	$80 permit fee	5 years

Key Government Offices:	North Carolina Highway Partol 512 N. Salisbury Street 4702 Mail Service Center Raleigh, North Carolina 27699-4702 Phone: (919) 733-7952 Email: Webmaster@ncshp.org	Attorney General North Carolina Department of Justice P.O. Box 629 Raleigh, North Carolina 27602-0629 Phone: 919-716-6400 Fax: 919-716-6750 Email: agjus@mail.jus.state.nc.us
	http://www.jus.state.nc.us/	

North Dakota

Right-To-Carry Law Type: Shall Issue

Issuing Authority:	Chief of the Bureau of Criminal Investigation
Contact agency for out of state permits:	Chief of the Bureau of Criminal Investigation
These states recognize your permit:	Alabama, Alaska*, Arizona, Delaware, Florida*, Idaho, Indiana, Kentucky, Michigan, Missouri, Montana, New Hampshire, Oklahoma, South Dakota, Tennessee, Utah, Vermont, Wyoming *Must be 21 years old
This state recognizes permits from the following states:	Alabama, Alaska*, Arizona, Florida*, Indiana, Kentucky, Michigan, Montana, New Hampshire, Oklahoma, South Dakota, Tennessee**, Utah, Wyoming *Must be 21 years old **Handguns only
Cost & Term of Permit:	$25 — 3 years

Key Government Offices:	North Dakota Office of Attorney General Bureau of Criminal Investigation Bismarck, North Dakota 58502-1054 Phone: (701) 328-5500 Fax: (701) 328-5510 Email: bciinfo@state.nd.us	Office of Attorney General State Capitol 600 E Boulevard Ave. Dept 125 Bismarck, North Dakota 58505-0040 Phone: (701) 328-2210 Fax: (701) 328-2226 Email: ndag@state.nd.us
	http://www.ag.state.nd.us/BCI/reciprocity.htm	

Ohio

Right-To-Carry Law Type: Shall Issue

Issuing Authority:	County Sheriff
Contact agency for out of state permits:	Permits not granted.
These states recognize your permit:	Many states will recognize Ohio permits, once Ohio begins issuing them and the Attorney General has reciprocal agreements in place.
This state recognizes permits from the following states:	HB 12, which gave Ohio citizens the right to carry a firearm concealed, become law in January, 2004. The Attorney General must now negotiate reciprocal agreements with other states.
Cost & Term of Permit:	$45 new and renewal — 4 years

Key Government Offices:	Ohio Highway Patrol P O Box 182074 Columbus, Ohio 43232 http://www.state.oh.us/ohiostatepatrol	Attorney General 30 E. Broad Street 17th Floor Columbus, Ohio 43215-3420 Phone: (614) 466-4320 Fax: (614) 466-5057
	http://www.ag.state.oh.us/	

Oklahoma

Right-To-Carry Law Type: Shall Issue

Issuing Authority:	State Bureau of Investigation
Contact agency for out of state permits:	Permits not granted.
These states recognize your permit:	Alabama, Alaska, Arkansas, Arizona, Colorado, Delaware, Florida. Idaho, Indiana, Kentucky, Michigan, Missouri, Montana, New Hampshire, North Carolina, North Dakota, Tennessee, Texas, Utah, Virginia, Vermont, Wyoming
This state recognizes permits from the following states:	All state permits recognized.
Cost & Term of Permit:	New $100, Renewal $85. — 5 years

Key Government Offices:	Oklahoma State Bureau of Investigation 6600 N. Harvey Suite 300 Oklahoma City, Oklahoma 73116 Phone: (405) 848-6724 or (800)207-6724 outside OK City sda@osbi.state.ok.us	Attorney General 112 State Capitol 2300 N. Lincoln Blvd. Oklahoma City, Oklahoma 73105 Phone: (405) 521-3921, Fax: (405) 521-6246 http://www.oag.state.of.us
	http://www.osbi.state.ok.us/sda.htm	

Oregon

Right-To-Carry Law Type: Shall Issue

Issuing Authority:	County Sheriff
Contact agency for out of state permits:	Discretionary to residents of contiguous states only
These states recognize your permit:	Alaska, Arizona, Idaho, Indiana, Kentucky, Michigan, Missouri, Montana, Oklahoma, Tennessee, Utah, Vermont
This state recognizes permits from the following states:	none
Cost & Term of Permit:	New: $65. Renewal $50. — 4 years

Key Government Offices:

State Police
400 Public Service Bldg.
255 Capitol St. N.E.
Salem, Oregon 97310
Phone: (503) 378-3720 Fax: (503) 378-8282
http://www.osp.state.or.us

Attorney General
Justice Department
1162 Court St. NE
Salem Oregon, 97310
Phone: (503) 378-4400, Fax: (503) 378-5938
http://www.doj.state.or.us

http://www.osp.state.or.us

Pennsylvania

Right-To-Carry Law Type: Shall Issue

Issuing Authority:	County Sheriff or Chief of Police
Contact agency for out of state permits:	Any Sheriff's Department
These states recognize your permit:	Alaska, Florida, Georgia, Idaho, Indiana, Kentucky, Michigan, Missouri, Montana, North Carolina, Oklahoma, Tennessee, Utah, Vermont, Wyoming
This state recognizes permits from the following states:	Florida, Georgia, Kentucky, Michigan, North Carolina, Wyoming
Cost & Term of Permit:	$19 — 5 years

Key Government Offices:

State Police
1800 Elmerton Avenue
Harrisburg, Pennsylvania 17110-9758
Phone: (717) 783-5599
Fax: (717) 787-2948

Attorney General
16th Floor, Strawberry Square
Harrisburg, Pennsylvania 17120
Phone: 717-787-3391
Fax: (717) 787-8242
http://www.attorneygeneral.gov

http://www.psp.state.pa.us

Rhode Island

Right-To-Carry Law Type: Restrictive May Issue

Issuing Authority:	Attorney General
Contact agency for out of state permits:	Attorney General by mail only. Permits are technically available for non-residents, but are rarely granted.
These states recognize your permit:	Alaska, Idaho, Indiana, Kentucky, Michigan, Missouri, Oklahoma, Tennessee, Utah, Vermont
This state recognizes permits from the following states:	none
Cost & Term of Permit:	$40 — 4 years

Key Government Offices:

State Police
311 Danielson Pike
North Scituate, Rhode Island 02857
Phone: (401) 444-1000
Fax: (401) 444-1105
http://www.risp.state.ri.us

Attorney General
150 South Main Street
Providence, Rhode Island 02903
Phone: (401) 274-4400
Fax: (401) 222-1331
http://www.riag.state.ri.us

http://www.riag.state.ri.us/

South Carolina

Right-To-Carry Law Type: Shall Issue

Issuing Authority:	S.C. Law Enforcement Division
Contact agency for out of state permits:	Permits not granted.
These states recognize your permit:	Alaska, Arizona, Arkansas, Idaho, Indiana, Kentucky, Michigan, Missouri, Montana, North Carolina, Oklahoma, Tennessee, Utah, Vermont, Virginia, Wyoming
This state recognizes permits from the following states:	Arkansas, North Carolina, Tennessee, Wyoming
Cost & Term of Permit:	$50 — 4 years

Key Government Offices:	South Carolina Law Enforcement Division Attn: Regulatory Services Unit P.O. Box 21398 Columbia, South Carolina 29221 Phone: 803-896-7014	Attorney General Box 11549 Columbia, South Carolina 29211 Phone: (803) 734-3970 Fax: (803) 253-6283 http://www.scattorneygeneral.org
	http://www.sled.state.sc.us	

South Dakota

Right-To-Carry Law Type: Shall Issue

Issuing Authority:	Chief of Police/County Sheriff
Contact agency for out of state permits:	Permits not granted.
These states recognize your permit:	Alaska, Colorado, Florida*, Georgia, Idaho, Indiana, Kentucky, Michigan, Missouri, Montana, North Carolina, North Dakota, Oklahoma, Tennessee, Utah, Vermont, Wyoming *must be 21
This state recognizes permits from the following states:	Alaska, Colorado*, Florida, Georgia, Indiana, Kentucky, Michigan, Montana, North Carolina, North Dakota, Tennessee, Utah, Wyoming *must be 21
Cost & Term of Permit:	$10 — 4 years

Key Government Offices:	Highway Patrol 118 West Capitol Pierre, South Dakota 57501 Phone: (605) 773-3105 Fax: (605) 773-6046 http://hp.state.sd.us/information.htm	Attorney General 500 East Capitol Ave. Pierre, South Dakota 57501-5070 Phone: (605)-773-3215 Fax: 605)773-4106 http://www.state.sd.attorney/office/news/concealed.asp
	http://sdsos.gov/firearms	

Tennessee

Right-To-Carry Law Type: Shall Issue

Issuing Authority:	Department of Public Safety
Contact agency for out of state permits:	Permits not granted.
These states recognize your permit:	Alaska, Arizona, Arkansas, Colorado, Delaware, Florida, Georgia, Idaho, Indiana, Kentucky, Louisiana, Michigan, Mississippi, Missouri, Montana, New Hampshire, North Carolina, North Dakota, Oklahoma, South Carolina, South Dakota, Texas, Utah, Virginia, Vermont, Wyoming
This state recognizes permits from the following states:	All state permits recognized.
Cost & Term of Permit:	New: $115; Renewal: $50 — 4 years

Key Government Offices:	Tennessee Department of Safety Attn: Handgun Carry Permit Office 1150 Foster Ave Nashville, Tennessee 37249-1000 Phone: (615) 251-8590	Attorney General P.O. Box 20207 Nashville, Tennessee 37202 Phone: (615) 741-3491 Fax: (615) 741-2009 http://www.attorneygeneral.state.tn.us
	http://www.state.tn.us/safety/	

Texas

Right-To-Carry Law Type: Shall Issue

Issuing Authority:	Department of Public Safety
Contact agency for out of state permits:	Department of Public Safety
These states recognize your permit:	Alaska, Arizona, Arkansas, Florida, Idaho, Indiana, Kentucky, Louisiana, Michigan, Missouri, Montana, Oklahoma, Tennessee, Utah, Virginia, Vermont, Wyoming
This state recognizes permits from the following states:	Arizona, Arkansas, Florida, Kentucky, Louisiana, Oklahoma, Tennessee. Wyoming
Cost & Term of Permit:	$140 ($70 for seniors)　　　　　4 years
Key Government Offices:	Texas Department of Public Safety Concealed Handgun Licensing Section P O Box 4143 Austin, Texas 78791-4143 Phone: (512) 424-7293 or (800) 224-5744 http://www.txdps.state.tx.us　　　Attorney General P. O. Box 12548 Austin, Texas 78711-2548 Phone: (512) 463-2100 Fax: (512) 463-2063 http://www.oag.state.tx.us
	http://www.txdps.state.tx.us/administration/crime_records/chl/reciprocity.htm

Utah

Right-To-Carry Law Type: Shall Issue

Issuing Authority:	Department of Public Safety
Contact agency for out of state permits:	Department of Public Safety
These states recognize your permit:	Alabama, Alaska, Arizona, Arkansas, Delaware, Florida, Idaho, Indiana, Kentucky, Michigan, Missouri, Montana, North Carolina, North Dakota, Oklahoma, South Dakota, Vermont, Wyoming
This state recognizes permits from the following states:	All state permits recognized.
Cost & Term of Permit:	New $35, $10 Renewal　　　　　5 years
Key Government Offices:	Utah Department of Public Safety Bureau of Criminal Identification 3888 W. 5400 S. P.O. Box 148280 Salt Lake City, Utah 84114-8280 Phone: (801) 965-4445　　　Utah Attorney General 236 State Capitol Salt Lake City, Utah 84114 Phone: (801) 366-0260 Fax: (801) 538-1121 http://www.attorneygeneral.utah.gov
	http://bci.utah.gov/cfp/cfphome.html

Vermont

Right-To-Carry Law Type: Permits Not Required

Issuing Authority:	Permits Not Required
Contact agency for out of state permits:	Permits Not Required
These states recognize your permit:	none
This state recognizes permits from the following states:	Permits Not Required
Cost & Term of Permit:	n/a　　　　　n/a
Key Government Offices:	Attorney General 109 State Street Montpelier, Vermont 05609-1001 Phone: (802) 828 3171 Fax: (802) 828 2154
	http://www.state.vt.us/atg/

Virginia

Right-To-Carry Law Type: Shall Issue

Issuing Authority:	State Circuit Court of residence
Contact agency for out of state permits:	Permits not granted.
These states recognize your permit:	Alaska, Idaho, Indiana, Kentucky, Michigan, Missouri, Montana, North Carolina, Oklahoma, Tennessee, Utah, West Virginia, Vermont
This state recognizes permits from the following states:	Alaska, Arizona, Arkansas, Idaho, Louisiana, Michigan, North Carolina, Oklahoma, South Carolina, Tennessee, Texas, Utah, Washington, West Virginia
Cost & Term of Permit:	no more than $50 — 5 years
Key Government Offices:	Virginia State Police P.O. Box 27472 Richmond, Virginia 23261 Phone: (804) 674-2000	Attorney General 900 East Main Street Richmond, Virginia 23219 Phone: (804) 786-2071 Fax: (804) 786-1991 http://www.oag.state.va.us
	http://www.vsp.state.va.us/vsp.html

Washington

Right-To-Carry Law Type: Shall Issue

Issuing Authority:	Chief of Police/Sheriff
Contact agency for out of state permits:	Permits not granted.
These states recognize your permit:	Alaska, Idaho, Indiana, Kentucky, Michigan, Missouri, Montana, Oklahoma, Tennessee, Utah, Vermont, Virginia
This state recognizes permits from the following states:	none
Cost & Term of Permit:	New: $36; Renewal: $32 — 5 years
Key Government Offices:	Washington State Patrol General Administration Building PO Box 42600 Olympia, Washington 98504-2600 Phone: (360) 753-6540 Fax: (360) 753-2492	Attorney General 1125 Washington St. SE Olympia, Washington 98504-0100 Phone: (360) 753-6200 Fax: (360) 664-0988 http://www.atg.wa.gov
	http://www.wsp.wa.gov/newsfaqs/answers.htm#weapons

West Virginia

Right-To-Carry Law Type: Shall Issue

Issuing Authority:	County Sheriff
Contact agency for out of state permits:	Permits not granted.
These states recognize your permit:	Alaska, Arizona, Idaho, Indiana, Kentucky, Michigan, Missouri, Montana, Oklahoma, Tennessee, Utah, Vermont, Virginia
This state recognizes permits from the following states:	Kentucky, Virginia
Cost & Term of Permit:	$60 — 5 years
Key Government Offices:	West Virginia State Police 725 Jefferson Road South Charleston, West Virginia 25309 Phone: (304) 746-2100 Fax: (304) 746-2246	Attorney General State Capitol, Room 26-E 1900 Kanawha Blvd. East Charleston, West Virginia 25305-0220 Phone: (304) 558-2021 Fax: (304) 558-0140
	http://www.wvstatepolice.com/legal/legal.shtml

Right-to-Carry Reciprocity and Recognition, cont.

Wisconsin
Right-To-Carry Law Type: Non-Issue

Issuing Authority:	Permits not available
Contact agency for out of state permits:	Permits not granted.
These states recognize your permit:	none
This state recognizes permits from the following states:	none
Cost & Term of Permit:	n/a n/a
Key Government Offices:	Attorney General 123 West Washington Ave. PO Box 7857 Madison, Wisconsin 53707-7857 Phone: 608-266-1221 Fax: 608-267-2779

http://www.doj.state.wi.us/

Wyoming
Right-To-Carry Law Type: Shall Issue

Issuing Authority:	Attorney General
Contact agency for out of state permits:	Permits not granted.
These states recognize your permit:	Alabama, Alaska, Arizona, Colorado, Florida, Georgia, Idaho, Indiana, Kentucky, Louisiana, Michigan, Minnesota, Mississippi, Missouri, Montana, New Hampshire, North Carolina, North Dakota, Oklahoma, Pennsylvania, South Carolina, South Dakota, Tennessee, Texas, Utah, Vermont
This state recognizes permits from the following states:	Alabama, Alaska, Colorado, Florida, Georgia, Idaho, Indiana, Kentucky, Louisiana, Michigan, Mississippi, Montana, New Hampshire, North Carolina, North Dakota, Oklahoma, Pennsylvania, South Carolina, South Dakota, Tennessee, Texas, Utah
Cost & Term of Permit:	$74 5 years
Key Government Offices:	Wyoming Attorney General's Office 123 Capitol Building 200 W. 24th Street Cheyenne, Wyoming 82002 Phone: (307) 777-7841 Fax: (307) 777-6869

http://attorneygeneral.state.dci.cwp.html

PRODUCT & SERVICE DIRECTORY

AMMUNITION COMPONENTS, SHOTSHELL

A.W. Peterson Gun Shop, Inc.
Ballistic Product, Inc.
Blount, Inc., Sporting Equipment Div.
CCI Ammunition ATK
Cheddite, France S.A.
Claybuster Wads & Harvester Bullets
Garcia National Gun Traders, Inc.
Peterson Gun Shop, Inc., A.W.
Precision Reloading, Inc.
Ravell Ltd.
Tar-Hunt Custom Rifles, Inc.
Vitt/Boos

AMMUNITION COMPONENTS-- BULLETS, POWDER, PRIMERS, CASES

A.W. Peterson Gun Shop, Inc.
Acadian Ballistic Specialties
Accuracy Unlimited
Accurate Arms Co., Inc.
Action Bullets & Alloy Inc.
ADCO Sales, Inc.
Alaska Bullet Works, Inc.
Alliant Techsystems Smokeless Powder Group
Allred Bullet Co.
Alpha LaFranck Enterprises
American Products, Inc.
Arizona Ammunition, Inc.
Armfield Custom Bullets
A-Square Co.
Atlantic Rose, Inc.
Baer's Hollows
Ballard Rifle & Cartridge Co., LLC
Barnes
Barnes Bullets, Inc.
Beartooth Bullets
Bell Reloading, Inc.
Berger Bullets Ltd.
Berry's Mfg., Inc.
Big Bore Bullets of Alaska
Big Bore Express
Bitterroot Bullet Co.
Black Belt Bullets (See Big Bore Express)
Black Hills Shooters Supply
Black Powder Products
Blount, Inc., Sporting Equipment Div.
Blue Mountain Bullets
Brenneke GmbH
Briese Bullet Co., Inc.
Brown Co., E. Arthur
Brown Dog Ent.
BRP, Inc. High Performance Cast Bullets
Buck Stix-SOS Products Co.
Buckeye Custom Bullets
Buckskin Bullet Co.
Buffalo Arms Co.
Buffalo Bullet Co., Inc.
Buffalo Rock Shooters Supply
Bullseye Bullets
Bull-X, Inc.
Butler Enterprises
Cambos Outdoorsman
Canyon Cartridge Corp.
Cascade Bullet Co., Inc.
Cast Performance Bullet Company
Casull Arms Corp.
CCI Ammunition ATK
Champion's Choice, Inc.
Cheddite, France S.A.
CheVron Bullets
Chuck's Gun Shop

Clean Shot Technologies
Competitor Corp., Inc.
Cook Engineering Service
Corbin Mfg. & Supply, Inc.
Cummings Bullets
Curtis Cast Bullets
Curtis Gun Shop (See Curtis Cast Bullets)
Custom Bullets by Hoffman
Dakota Arms, Inc.
Davide Pedersoli and Co.
DKT, Inc.
Dohring Bullets
Eichelberger Bullets, Wm.
Federal Cartridge Co.
Fiocchi of America, Inc.
Forkin, Ben (See Belt MTN Arms)
Forkin Arms
Fowler Bullets
Fowler, Bob (See Black Powder Products)
Foy Custom Bullets
Freedom Arms, Inc.
Garcia National Gun Traders, Inc.
Gehmann, Walter (See Huntington Die Specialties)
GOEX, Inc.
Golden Bear Bullets
Gotz Bullets
Grayback Wildcats
Green Mountain Rifle Barrel Co., Inc.
Grier's Hard Cast Bullets
GTB
Gun City
Harris Enterprises
Harrison Bullets
Hart & Son, Inc.
Hawk Laboratories, Inc. (See Hawk, Inc.)
Hawk, Inc.
Haydon Shooters Supply, Russ
Heidenstrom Bullets
Hercules, Inc. (See Alliant Techsystems, Smokeless)
Hi-Performance Ammunition Company
Hirtenberger AG
Hobson Precision Mfg. Co.
Hodgdon Powder Co.
Hornady Mfg. Co.
HT Bullets
Hunters Supply, Inc.
Huntington Die Specialties
Impact Case & Container, Inc.
Imperial Magnum Corp.
IMR Powder Co.
Intercontinental Distributors, Ltd.
J&D Components
J&L Superior Bullets (See Huntington Die Special)
J.R. Williams Bullet Co.
James Calhoon Mfg.
James Calhoon Varmint Bullets
Jamison International
Jensen Bullets
Jensen's Firearms Academy
Jericho Tool & Die Co., Inc.
Jester Bullets
JLK Bullets
JRP Custom Bullets
Ka Pu Kapili
Kaswer Custom, Inc.
Keith's Bullets
Keng's Firearms Specialty, Inc./US Tactical Systems
Ken's Kustom Kartridges
Kent Cartridge Mfg. Co. Ltd.
KLA Enterprises
Knight Rifles
Knight Rifles (See Modern Muzzle Loading, Inc.)
Lapua Ltd.

Lawrence Brand Shot (See Precision Reloading)
Legend Products Corp.
Liberty Shooting Supplies
Lightning Performance Innovations, Inc.
Lindsley Arms Cartridge Co.
Littleton, J. F.
Lomont Precision Bullets
Lyman Products Corp.
Magnus Bullets
Maine Custom Bullets
Maionchi-L.M.I.
Marchmon Bullets
Markesbery Muzzle Loaders, Inc.
MarMik, Inc.
Marshall Fish Mfg. Gunsmith Sptg. Co.
MAST Technology, Inc.
McMurdo, Lynn (See Specialty Gunsmithing)
Meister Bullets (See Gander Mountain)
Men-Metallwerk Elisenhuette GmbH
Merkuria Ltd.
Michael's Antiques
Midway Arms, Inc.
Mitchell Bullets, R.F.
MI-TE Bullets
Montana Precision Swaging
Mountain State Muzzleloading Supplies, Inc.
Mulhern, Rick
Murmur Corp.
Nagel's Custom Bullets
National Bullet Co.
Naval Ordnance Works
North American Shooting Systems
North Devon Firearms Services
Northern Precision Custom Swaged Bullets
Nosler, Inc.
OK Weber, Inc.
Oklahoma Ammunition Co.
Old Wagon Bullets
Oregon Trail Bullet Company
Pacific Cartridge, Inc.
Pacific Rifle Co.
Page Custom Bullets
Pease Accuracy
Penn Bullets
Peterson Gun Shop, Inc., A.W.
Petro-Explo Inc.
Phillippi Custom Bullets, Justin
Pinetree Bullets
PMC/Eldorado Cartridge Corp.
Polywad, Inc.
Pony Express Reloaders
Power Plus Enterprises, Inc.
Precision Delta Corp.
Prescott Projectile Co.
Price Bullets, Patrick W.
PRL Bullets, c/o Blackburn Enterprises
Professional Hunter Supplies (See Star Custom Bullets)
Proofmark Corp.
R.I.S. Co., Inc.
Rainier Ballistics Corp.
Ramon B. Gonzalez Guns
Ravell Ltd.
Redwood Bullet Works
Reloading Specialties, Inc.
Remington Arms Co., Inc.
Rhino
Robinson H.V. Bullets
Rubright Bullets
Russ Haydon's Shooters' Supply
SAECO (See Redding Reloading Equipment)
Scharch Mfg., Inc.-Top Brass
Schneider Bullets
Schroeder Bullets

Schumakers Gun Shop
Scot Powder
Seebeck Assoc., R.E.
Shappy Bullets
Sharps Arms Co., Inc., C.
Shilen, Inc.
Sierra Bullets
SOS Products Co. (See Buck Stix-SOS Products Co.)
Southern Ammunition Co., Inc.
Specialty Gunsmithing
Speer Bullets
Spencer's Rifle Barrels, Inc.
SSK Industries
Stanley Bullets
Star Ammunition, Inc.
Star Custom Bullets
Starke Bullet Company
Starline, Inc.
Stewart's Gunsmithing
Swift Bullet Co.
T.F.C. S.p.A.
Taracorp Industries, Inc.
Tar-Hunt Custom Rifles, Inc.
TCCI
TCSR
The A.W. Peterson Gun Shop, Inc.
The Gun Works
The Ordnance Works
Thompson Bullet Lube Co.
Thompson Precision
TMI Products (See Haselbauer Products, Jerry)
Traditions Performance Firearms
Trico Plastics
True Flight Bullet Co.
Tucson Mold, Inc.
Unmussig Bullets, D. L.
USAC
Vann Custom Bullets
Vihtavuori Oy/Kaltron-Pettibone
Vincent's Shop
Viper Bullet and Brass Works
Walters Wads
Warren Muzzleloading Co., Inc.
Watson Trophy Match Bullets
Weatherby, Inc.
Western Nevada West Coast Bullets
Widener's Reloading & Shooting Supply, Inc.
Winchester Div. Olin Corp.
Winkle Bullets
Woodleigh (See Huntington Die Specialties)
Worthy Products, Inc.
Wyant Bullets
Wyoming Custom Bullets
Zero Ammunition Co., Inc.

AMMUNITION, COMMERCIAL

3-Ten Corp.
A.W. Peterson Gun Shop, Inc.
Ace Custom 45's, Inc.
Ad Hominem
Air Arms
American Ammunition
Arizona Ammunition, Inc.
Arms Corporation of the Philippines
Arundel Arms & Ammunition, Inc., A.
A-Square Co.
Atlantic Rose, Inc.
Badger Shooters Supply, Inc.
Ballistic Product, Inc.
Ben William's Gun Shop
Benjamin/Sheridan Co., Crosman
Big Bear Arms & Sporting Goods, Inc.
Black Hills Ammunition, Inc.

Blammo Ammo
Blount, Inc., Sporting Equipment Div.
Brenneke GmbH
Buffalo Bullet Co., Inc.
Bull-X, Inc.
Cabela's
Cambos Outdoorsman
Casull Arms Corp.
CBC
Champion's Choice, Inc.
Cor-Bon Inc./Glaser LLC
Crosman Airguns
Cubic Shot Shell Co., Inc.
Daisy Outdoor Products
Dead Eye's Sport Center
Delta Arms Ltd.
Delta Frangible Ammunition LLC
Dynamit Nobel-RWS, Inc.
Effebi SNC-Dr. Franco Beretta
Eley Ltd.
Elite Ammunition
Estate Cartridge, Inc.
Federal Cartridge Co.
Fiocchi of America, Inc.
Garcia National Gun Traders, Inc.
Garrett Cartridges, Inc.
Garthwaite Pistolsmith, Inc., Jim
Gibbs Rifle Co., Inc.
Gil Hebard Guns Inc.
Glaser LLC
Glaser Safety Slug, Inc.
GOEX, Inc.
Goodwin's Gun Shop
Gun City
Hansen & Co.
Hart & Son, Inc.
Hi-Performance Ammunition Company
Hirtenberger AG
Hornady Mfg. Co.
Hunters Supply, Inc.
Intercontinental Distributors, Ltd.
Ion Industries, Inc.
Keng's Firearms Specialty, Inc./US Tactical Systems
Kent Cartridge America, Inc.
Kent Cartridge Mfg. Co. Ltd.
Knight Rifles
Lapua Ltd.
Lethal Force Institute (See Police Bookshelf)
Lock's Philadelphia Gun Exchange
Magnum Research, Inc.
MagSafe Ammo Co.
Magtech Ammunition Co. Inc.
Maionchi-L.M.I.
Mandall Shooting Supplies Inc.
Markell,Inc.
Marshall Fish Mfg. Gunsmith Sptg. Co.
McBros Rifle Co.
Men-Metallwerk Elisenhuette GmbH
Mullins Ammunition
New England Ammunition Co.
Oklahoma Ammunition Co.
Omark Industries, Div. of Blount, Inc.
Outdoor Sports Headquarters, Inc.
P.S.M.G. Gun Co.
Pacific Cartridge, Inc.
Paragon Sales & Services, Inc.
Parker & Sons Shooting Supply
Parker Gun Finishes
Peterson Gun Shop, Inc., A.W.
PMC/Eldorado Cartridge Corp.
Police Bookshelf
Polywad, Inc.
Pony Express Reloaders
Precision Delta Corp.
Pro Load Ammunition, Inc.
R.E.I.
Ravell Ltd.

Remington Arms Co., Inc.
Rucker Dist. Inc.
RWS (See US Importer-Dynamit Nobel-RWS, Inc.)
Sellier & Bellot, USA Inc.
Southern Ammunition Co., Inc.
Speer Bullets
TCCI
The A.W. Peterson Gun Shop, Inc.
The BulletMakers Workshop
The Gun Room Press
The Gun Works
Thompson Bullet Lube Co.
USAC
VAM Distribution Co. LLC
Victory USA
Vihtavuori Oy/Kaltron-Pettibone
Visible Impact Targets
Voere-KGH GmbH
Weatherby, Inc.
Westley Richards & Co.
Whitestone Lumber Corp.
Widener's Reloading & Shooting Supply, Inc.
William E. Phillips Firearms
Winchester Div. Olin Corp.
Zero Ammunition Co., Inc.

AMMUNITION, CUSTOM

3-Ten Corp.
A.W. Peterson Gun Shop, Inc.
Accuracy Unlimited
AFSCO Ammunition
Allred Bullet Co.
American Derringer Corp.
American Products, Inc.
Arizona Ammunition, Inc.
Arms Corporation of the Philippines
Atlantic Rose, Inc.
Ballard Rifle & Cartridge Co., LLC
Bear Arms
Belding's Custom Gun Shop
Berger Bullets Ltd.
Big Bore Bullets of Alaska
Black Hills Ammunition, Inc.
Blue Mountain Bullets
Brynin, Milton
Buckskin Bullet Co.
CBC
CFVentures
Champlin Firearms, Inc.
Cubic Shot Shell Co., Inc.
Custom Tackle and Ammo
Dakota Arms, Inc.
Dead Eye's Sport Center
Delta Frangible Ammunition LLC
DKT, Inc.
Elite Ammunition
Estate Cartridge, Inc.
GDL Enterprises
GOEX, Inc.
Grayback Wildcats
Hirtenberger AG
Hobson Precision Mfg. Co.
Horizons Unlimited
Hornady Mfg. Co.
Hunters Supply, Inc.
James Calhoon Mfg.
James Calhoon Varmint Bullets
Jensen Bullets
Jensen's Custom Ammunition
Jensen's Firearms Academy
Kaswer Custom, Inc.
Kent Cartridge Mfg. Co. Ltd.
L. E. Jurras & Assoc.
L.A.R. Mfg., Inc.
Lethal Force Institute (See Police Bookshelf)
Lindsley Arms Cartridge Co.
Linebaugh Custom Sixguns
Loch Leven Industries/Convert-A-Pell

MagSafe Ammo Co.
MAST Technology, Inc.
McBros Rifle Co.
McMurdo, Lynn (See Specialty Gunsmithing)
Men-Metallwerk Elisenhuette GmbH
Milstor Corp.
Mullins Ammunition
Oklahoma Ammunition Co.
P.S.M.G. Gun Co.
Peterson Gun Shop, Inc., A.W.
Phillippi Custom Bullets, Justin
Police Bookshelf
Power Plus Enterprises, Inc.
Precision Delta Corp.
Professional Hunter Supplies (See Star Custom Bullets)
R.E.I.
Ramon B. Gonzalez Guns
Sandia Die & Cartridge Co.
SOS Products Co. (See Buck Stix-SOS Products Co.)
Specialty Gunsmithing
Spencer's Rifle Barrels, Inc.
SSK Industries
Star Custom Bullets
Stewart's Gunsmithing
The A.W. Peterson Gun Shop, Inc.
The BulletMakers Workshop
The Country Armourer
Unmussig Bullets, D. L.
Vitt/Boos
Vulpes Ventures, Inc. Fox Cartridge Division
Warren Muzzleloading Co., Inc.
Watson Trophy Match Bullets
Worthy Products, Inc.
Zero Ammunition Co., Inc.

AMMUNITION, FOREIGN

A.W. Peterson Gun Shop, Inc.
Ad Hominem
AFSCO Ammunition
Armscorp USA, Inc.
Atlantic Rose, Inc.
B&P America
Beeman Precision Airguns
Cape Outfitters
CBC
Cheddite, France S.A.
Cubic Shot Shell Co., Inc.
Dead Eye's Sport Center
DKT, Inc.
Dynamit Nobel-RWS, Inc.
E. Arthur Brown Co.
Fiocchi of America, Inc.
First Inc., Jack
Gamebore Division, Polywad Inc.
Gibbs Rifle Co., Inc.
GOEX, Inc.
Goodwin's Gun Shop
Gunsmithing, Inc.
Hansen & Co.
Heidenstrom Bullets
Hirtenberger AG
Hornady Mfg. Co.
I.S.S.
Intrac Arms International
K.B.I. Inc.
MagSafe Ammo Co.
Maionchi-L.M.I.
Mandall Shooting Supplies Inc.
Marksman Products
MAST Technology, Inc.
Merkuria Ltd.
Mullins Ammunition
Navy Arms Company
Oklahoma Ammunition Co.
P.S.M.G. Gun Co.
Paragon Sales & Services, Inc.
Peterson Gun Shop, Inc., A.W.
Petro-Explo Inc.

Precision Delta Corp.
R.E.T. Enterprises
Ramon B. Gonzalez Guns
RWS (See US Importer-Dynamit Nobel-RWS, Inc.)
Samco Global Arms, Inc.
Sentinel Arms
Southern Ammunition Co., Inc.
Speer Bullets
Stratco, Inc.
T.F.C. S.p.A.
The A.W. Peterson Gun Shop, Inc.
The BulletMakers Workshop
The Paul Co.
Victory Ammunition
Vihtavuori Oy/Kaltron-Pettibone
Vulpes Ventures, Inc. Fox Cartridge Division
Wolf Performance Ammunition

BOOKS & MANUALS (PUBLISHERS & DEALERS)

"Su-Press-On", Inc.
Alpha 1 Drop Zone
American Handgunner Magazine
Armory Publications
Arms & Armour Press
Ballistic Product, Inc.
Ballistic Product, Inc.
Barnes Bullets, Inc.
Bauska Barrels
Beartooth Bullets
Beeman Precision Airguns
Blacksmith Corp.
Blacktail Mountain Books
Blue Book Publications, Inc.
Blue Ridge Machinery & Tools, Inc.
Boone's Custom Ivory Grips, Inc.
Brown Co., E. Arthur
Brownells, Inc.
Bullet N Press
C. Sharps Arms Co. Inc./Montana Armory
Cape Outfitters
Cheyenne Pioneer Products
Colonial Repair
Corbin Mfg. & Supply, Inc.
DBI Books Division of Krause Publications
deHaas Barrels
Dixon Muzzleloading Shop, Inc.
Excalibur Publications
Executive Protection Institute
Galati International
Gerald Pettinger Books (See Pettinger Books)
Golden Age Arms Co.
Gun City
Gun List (See Krause Publications)
Guncraft Books (See Guncraft Sports Inc.)
Guncraft Sports Inc.
Gunnerman Books
GUNS Magazine
Gunsmithing, Inc.
H&P Publishing
Handgun Press
Harris Publications
Hawk Laboratories, Inc. (See Hawk, Inc.)
Hawk, Inc.
Heritage/VSP Gun Books
Hodgdon Powder Co.
Home Shop Machinist, The Village Press Publications
Hornady Mfg. Co.
Huntington Die Specialties
I.D.S.A. Books
Info-Arm
Ironside International Publishers, Inc.

Jantz Supply
Kelley's
King & Co.
Koval Knives
Krause Publications, Inc.
L.B.T.
Lapua Ltd.
Lebeau-Courally
Lethal Force Institute (See Police Bookshelf)
Lyman Products Corp.
Madis Books
Magma Engineering Co.
Mandall Shooting Supplies Inc.
MarMik, Inc.
Montana Armory, Inc .(See C. Sharps Arms Co. Inc.)
Mountain South
Mountain State Muzzleloading Supplies, Inc.
Mulberry House Publishing
Navy Arms Company
Numrich Gun Parts Corporation
OK Weber, Inc.
Outdoor Sports Headquarters, Inc.
Paintball Games International Magazine Aceville
Pejsa Ballistics
Petersen Publishing Co.
Pettinger Books, Gerald
PFRB Co.
Police Bookshelf
Precision Shooting, Inc.
Professional Hunter Supplies (See Star Custom Bullets)
Ravell Ltd.
Ray Riling Arms Books Co.
Remington Double Shotguns
Russ Haydon's Shooters' Supply
Rutgers Book Center
S&S Firearms
Safari Press, Inc.
Saunders Gun & Machine Shop
Scharch Mfg., Inc.-Top Brass
Scharch Mfg., Inc.-Top Brass
Semmer, Charles (See Remington Double Shotguns)
Sharps Arms Co., Inc., C.
Shotgun Sports Magazine, dba Shootin' Accessories Ltd.
Sierra Bullets
Speer Bullets
SPG LLC
Stackpole Books
Star Custom Bullets
Stewart Game Calls, Inc., Johnny
Stoeger Industries
Stoeger Publishing Co. (See Stoeger Industries)
Swift Bullet Co.
The A.W. Peterson Gun Shop, Inc.
The Gun Room Press
The Gun Works
The NgraveR Co.
Thomas, Charles C.
Track of the Wolf, Inc.
Trafalgar Square
Trotman, Ken
Tru-Balance Knife Co.
Vega Tool Co.
Vintage Industries, Inc.
VSP Publishers (See Heritage/VSP Gun Books)
W.E. Brownell Checkering Tools
WAMCO-New Mexico
Wells Creek Knife & Gun Works
Wilderness Sound Products Ltd.
Williams Gun Sight Co.
Wolfe Publishing Co.
Wolf's Western Traders

CASES, CABINETS, RACKS & SAFES - GUN

All Rite Products, Inc.
Allen Co., Bob
Allen Co., Inc.
Allen Sportswear, Bob (See Allen Co., Bob)
Alumna Sport by Dee Zee
American Display Co.
American Security Products Co.
Americase
Art Jewel Enterprises Ltd.
Ashby Turkey Calls
Bagmaster Mfg., Inc.
Barramundi Corp.
Berry's Mfg., Inc.
Big Spring Enterprises "Bore Stores"
Bill's Custom Cases
Bison Studios
Black Sheep Brand
Brauer Bros.
Brown, H. R. (See Silhouette Leathers)
Browning Arms Co.
Bushmaster Hunting & Fishing
Cannon Safe, Inc.
Chipmunk (See Oregon Arms, Inc.)
Cobalt Mfg., Inc.
CONKKO
Connecticut Shotgun Mfg. Co.
D&L Industries (See D.J. Marketing)
D.J. Marketing
Dara-Nes, Inc. (See Nesci Enterprises, Inc.)
Deepeeka Exports Pvt. Ltd.
Doskocil Mfg. Co., Inc.
DTM International, Inc.
EMF Co., Inc.
English, Inc., A.G.
Enhanced Presentations, Inc.
Eversull Co., Inc.
Fort Knox Security Products
Freedom Arms, Inc.
Frontier Safe Co.
Galati International
GALCO International Ltd.
Gun-Ho Sports Cases
Hall Plastics, Inc., John
Hastings
Homak
Hoppe's Div. Penguin Industries, Inc.
Hunter Co., Inc.
Hydrosorbent Products
Impact Case & Container, Inc.
Johanssons Vapentillbehor, Bert
Johnston Bros. (See C&T Corp. TA Johnson Brothers)
Kalispel Case Line
Kane Products, Inc.
KK Air International (See Impact Case & Container Co.)
Knock on Wood Antiques
Kolpin Mfg., Inc.
Lakewood Products LLC
Liberty Safe
Mandall Shooting Supplies Inc.
Marsh, Mike
McWelco Products
Morton Booth Co.
MPC
MTM Molded Products Co., Inc.
Nalpak
Necessary Concepts, Inc.
Nesci Enterprises, Inc.
Oregon Arms, Inc. (See Rogue Rifle Co., Inc.)
Outa-Site Gun Carriers
Pflumm Mfg. Co.
Poburka, Philip (See Bison Studios)

PRODUCT & SERVICE DIRECTORY

Powell & Son (Gunmakers) Ltd., William
Protektor Model
Prototech Industries, Inc.
Rogue Rifle Co., Inc.
Schulz Industries
Southern Security
Sportsman's Communicators
Sun Welding Safe Co.
Sweet Home, Inc.
Talmage, William G.
The Outdoor Connection, Inc.
The Surecase Co.
Tinks & Ben Lee Hunting Products (See Wellington)
Trulock Tool
Universal Sports
W. Waller & Son, Inc.
Whitestone Lumber Corp.
Wilson Case, Inc.
Woodstream
Zanotti Armor, Inc.
Ziegel Engineering

CLEANING & REFINISHING SUPPLIES

AC Dyna-tite Corp.
Alpha 1 Drop Zone
American Gas & Chemical Co., Ltd
Answer Products Co.
Armite Laboratories
Atlantic Mills, Inc.
Atsko/Sno-Seal, Inc.
Barnes Bullets, Inc.
Battenfeld Technologies
Beeman Precision Airguns
Belltown Ltd.
Bill's Gun Repair
Birchwood Casey
Blount, Inc., Sporting Equipment Div.
Blount/Outers ATK
Blue and Gray Products Inc. (See Ox-Yoke Originals)
Break-Free, Inc.
Bridgers Best
Brown Co., E. Arthur
Brownells, Inc.
C.S. Van Gorden & Son, Inc.
Cambos Outdoorsman
Cambos Outdoorsman
Camp-Cap Products
CONKKO
Connecticut Shotgun Mfg. Co.
Creedmoor Sports, Inc.
CRR, Inc./Marble's Inc.
Custom Products (See Jones Custom Products)
Cylinder & Slide, Inc., William R. Laughridge
Dara-Nes, Inc. (See Nesci Enterprises, Inc.)
Deepeeka Exports Pvt. Ltd.
Desert Mountain Mfg.
Du-Lite Corp.
Dykstra, Doug
E&L Mfg., Inc.
Eezox, Inc.
Ekol Leather Care
Faith Associates
Flitz International Ltd.
Fluoramics, Inc.
Frontier Products Co.
G96 Products Co., Inc.
Golden Age Arms Co.
Guardsman Products
Gunsmithing, Inc.
Hafner World Wide, Inc.
Half Moon Rifle Shop
Heatbath Corp.
Hoppe's Div. Penguin Industries, Inc.

Hornady Mfg. Co.
Hydrosorbent Products
Iosso Products
J. Dewey Mfg. Co., Inc.
Jantz Supply
Jantz Supply
Johnston Bros. (See C&T Corp. TA Johnson Brothers)
Jonad Corp.
K&M Industries, Inc.
Kellogg's Professional Products
Kent Cartridge Mfg. Co. Ltd.
Kesselring Gun Shop
Kleen-Bore,Inc.
Knight Rifles
Laurel Mountain Forge
Lee Supplies, Mark
LEM Gun Specialties, Inc. The Lewis Lead Remover
List Precision Engineering
LPS Laboratories, Inc.
Lyman Products Corp.
Mac-1 Airgun Distributors
Mandall Shooting Supplies Inc.
Marble Arms (See CRR, Inc./Marble's Inc.)
Mark Lee Supplies
Micro Sight Co.
Minute Man High Tech Industries
Mountain State Muzzleloading Supplies, Inc.
MTM Molded Products Co., Inc.
Muscle Products Corp.
Nesci Enterprises Inc.
Northern Precision Custom Swaged Bullets
Now Products, Inc.
October Country Muzzleloading
Old World Oil Products
Omark Industries, Div. of Blount, Inc.
Original Mink Oil, Inc.
Otis Technology, Inc.
Outers Laboratories Div. of ATK
Ox-Yoke Originals, Inc.
Parker & Sons Shooting Supply
Parker Gun Finishes
Pendleton Royal, c/o Swingler Buckland Ltd.
Perazone-Gunsmith, Brian
Pete Rickard, Inc.
Peter Dyson & Son Ltd.
Precision Airgun Sales, Inc.
PrOlixr Lubricants
Pro-Shot Products, Inc.
R&S Industries Corp.
Radiator Specialty Co.
Rooster Laboratories
Russ Haydon's Shooters' Supply
Rusteprufe Laboratories
Rusty Duck Premium Gun Care Products
Saunders Gun & Machine Shop
Schumakers Gun Shop
Sheffield Knifemakers Supply, Inc.
Shooter's Choice Gun Care
Shotgun Sports Magazine, dba Shootin' Accessories Ltd.
Silencio/Safety Direct
Sinclair International, Inc.
Sno-Seal, Inc. (See Atsko/Sno-Seal, Inc.)
Southern Bloomer Mfg. Co.
Splitfire Sporting Goods, L.L.C.
Starr Trading Co., Jedediah
Stoney Point Products, Inc.
Svon Corp.
T.F.C. S.p.A.
TDP Industries, Inc.
Tetra Gun Care
Texas Platers Supply Co.
The A.W. Peterson Gun Shop, Inc.
The Dutchman's Firearms, Inc.

The Lewis Lead Remover (See LEM Gun Specialties)
The Paul Co.
Track of the Wolf, Inc.
United States Products Co.
Van Gorden & Son Inc., C. S.
Venco Industries, Inc. (See Shooter's Choice Gun Care)
VibraShine, Inc.
Volquartsen Custom Ltd.
Warren Muzzleloading Co., Inc.
Watson Trophy Match Bullets
WD-40 Co.
Wick, David E.
Willow Bend
Wolf's Western Traders
Young Country Arms

CUSTOM GUNSMITH

A&W Repair
A.A. Arms, Inc.
Acadian Ballistic Specialties
Accuracy Unlimited
Ace Custom 45's, Inc.
Acra-Bond Laminates
Adair Custom Shop, Bill
Ahlman Guns
Al Lind Custom Guns
Aldis Gunsmithing & Shooting Supply
Alpha Precision, Inc.
Alpine Indoor Shooting Range
Amrine's Gun Shop
Answer Products Co.
Antique Arms Co.
Armament Gunsmithing Co., Inc.
Arms Craft Gunsmithing
Arms Ingenuity Co.
Armscorp USA, Inc.
Artistry in Wood
Art's Gun & Sport Shop, Inc.
Arundel Arms & Ammunition, Inc., A.
Autauga Arms, Inc.
Badger Creek Studio
Baelder, Harry
Baer Custom Inc., Les
Bain & Davis, Inc.
Bansner's Ultimate Rifles, LLC
Barnes Bullets, Inc.
Baron Technology
Barta's Gunsmithing
Bear Arms
Bear Mountain Gun & Tool
Beaver Lodge (See Fellowes, Ted)
Behlert Precision, Inc.
Beitzinger, George
Belding's Custom Gun Shop
Ben William's Gun Shop
Bengtson Arms Co., L.
Bill Adair Custom Shop
Billings Gunsmiths
BlackStar AccuMax Barrels
BlackStar Barrel Accurizing (See BlackStar AccuMax)
Bob Rogers Gunsmithing
Bond Custom Firearms
Borden Ridges Rimrock Stocks
Borovnik KG, Ludwig
Bowen Classic Arms Corp.
Brace, Larry D.
Briese Bullet Co., Inc.
Briganti, A.J.
Briley Mfg. Inc.
Broad Creek Rifle Works, Ltd.
Brockman's Custom Gunsmithing
Broken Gun Ranch
Brown Precision, Inc.
Brown Products, Inc., Ed
Buchsenmachermeister
Buckhorn Gun Works
Budin, Dave
Bull Mountain Rifle Co.

Bullberry Barrel Works, Ltd.
Burkhart Gunsmithing, Don
Cache La Poudre Rifleworks
Cambos Outdoorsman
Cambos Outdoorsman
Campbell, Dick
Carolina Precision Rifles
Carter's Gun Shop
Caywood, Shane J.
CBC-BRAZIL
Chambers Flintlocks Ltd., Jim
Champlin Firearms, Inc.
Chicasaw Gun Works
Chuck's Gun Shop
Chuilli, Stephen
Clark Custom Guns, Inc.
Clark Firearms Engraving
Classic Arms Company
Classic Arms Corp.
Clearview Products
Cleland's Outdoor World, Inc
Coffin, Charles H.
Cogar's Gunsmithing
Cole's Gun Works
Colonial Arms, Inc.
Colonial Repair
Colorado Gunsmithing Academy
Colorado School of Trades
Colt's Mfg. Co., Inc.
Conrad, C. A.
Corkys Gun Clinic
Cox, Ed. C.
Cullity Restoration
Custom Gun Stocks
Custom Single Shot Rifles
D&D Gunsmiths, Ltd.
Dangler, Homer L.
D'Arcy Echols & Co.
Darlington Gun Works, Inc.
Dave's Gun Shop
David Miller Co.
David R. Chicoine
David W. Schwartz Custom Guns
Davis, Don
Delorge, Ed
Del-Sports, Inc.
DGR Custom Rifles
DGS, Inc., Dale A. Storey
Dietz Gun Shop & Range, Inc.
Dilliott Gunsmithing, Inc.
Donnelly, C. P.
Duane A. Hobbie Gunsmithing
Duane's Gun Repair (See DGR Custom Rifles)
Duffy, Charles E (See Guns Antique & Modern DBA)
Duncan's Gun Works, Inc.
E. Arthur Brown Co.
Eckelman Gunsmithing
Ed Brown Products, Inc.
Eggleston, Jere D.
Entre`prise Arms, Inc.
Erhardt, Dennis
Eversull Co., Inc.
Evolution Gun Works Inc.
F.I., Inc. - High Standard Mfg. Co.
FERLIB
Ferris Firearms
Fisher, Jerry A.
Fisher Custom Firearms
Fleming Firearms
Flynn's Custom Guns
Forkin, Ben (See Belt MTN Arms)
Forkin Arms
Forster, Kathy (See Custom Checkering)
Forster, Larry L.
Forthofer's Gunsmithing & Knifemaking
Francesca, Inc.
Francotte & Cie S.A. Auguste
Fred F. Wells/Wells Sport Store
Frontier Arms Co.,Inc.
Fullmer, Geo. M.

G.G. & G.
Galaxy Imports Ltd., Inc.
Garthwaite Pistolsmith, Inc., Jim
Gary Reeder Custom Guns
Gator Guns & Repair
Genecco Gun Works
Gene's Custom Guns
Gentry Custom Gunmaker, David
George E. Mathews & Son, Inc.
George Hoenig, Inc.
Gillmann, Edwin
Gilman-Mayfield, Inc.
Gilmore Sports Concepts
Giron, Robert E.
Goens, Dale W.
Gonic Arms/North American Arm
Goodling's Gunsmithing
Goodwin's Gun Shop
Grace, Charles E.
Grayback Wildcats
Graybill's Gun Shop
Green, Roger M.
Greg Gunsmithing Repair
Gre-Tan Rifles
Griffin & Howe, Inc.
Griffin & Howe, Inc.
Griffin & Howe, Inc.
Gruning Precision Inc.
Guncraft Books (See Guncraft Sports Inc.)
Guncraft Sports Inc.
Guncraft Sports, Inc.
Guns Antique & Modern DBA / Charles E. Duffy
Gunsite Custom Shop
Gunsite Gunsmithy (See Gunsite Custom Shop)
Gunsite Training Center Gunsmithing Ltd.
Hamilton, Alex B (See Ten-Ring Precision, Inc)
Hammans, Charles E.
Hammerli Service-Precision Mac
Hammond Custom Guns Ltd.
Hank's Gun Shop
Hanson's Gun Center, Dick
Harris Gunworks
Harry Lawson Co.
Hart & Son, Inc.
Hart Rifle Barrels,Inc.
Hartmann & Weiss GmbH
Harwood, Jack O.
Hawken Shop, The (See Dayton Traister)
Hecht, Hubert J, Waffen-Hecht
Heilmann, Stephen
Heinie Specialty Products
Hensley, Gunmaker, Darwin
High Bridge Arms, Inc
High Performance International
High Precision
Highline Machine Co.
Hill, Loring F.
Hiptmayer, Armurier
Hiptmayer, Klaus
Hoag, James W.
Hodgson, Richard
Hoehn Sales, Inc.
Hofer Jagdwaffen, P.
Holland's Gunsmithing
Huebner, Corey O.
Hunkeler, A (See Buckskin Machine Works
Imperial Magnum Corp.
Irwin, Campbell H.
Island Pond Gun Shop
Israel Arms International, Inc.
Ivanoff, Thomas G. (See Tom's Gun Repair)
J&S Heat Treat
J.J. Roberts / Engraver
Jack Dever Co.
Jackalope Gun Shop
James Calhoon Mfg.

James Calhoon Varmint Bullets
Jamison's Forge Works
Jarrett Rifles, Inc.
Jarvis, Inc.
Jay McCament Custom Gunmaker
Jeffredo Gunsight
Jensen's Custom Ammunition
Jim Norman Custom Gunstocks
Jim's Gun Shop (See Spradlin's)
Jim's Precision, Jim Ketchum
John Norrell Arms
John Rigby & Co.
Jones Custom Products, Neil A.
Juenke, Vern
K. Eversull Co., Inc.
KDF, Inc.
Keith's Custom Gunstocks
Ken Eyster Heritage Gunsmiths, Inc.
Ken Starnes Gunmaker
Ketchum, Jim (See Jim's Precision)
Kilham & Co.
King's Gun Works
KLA Enterprises
Klein Custom Guns, Don
Kleinendorst, K. W.
KOGOT
Korzinek Riflesmith, J.
L. E. Jurras & Assoc.
LaFrance Specialties
Lampert, Ron
LaRocca Gun Works
Larry Lyons Gunworks
Lathrop's, Inc.
Laughridge, William R (See Cylinder & Slide Inc)
Lawson Co., Harry
Lazzeroni Arms Co.
LeFever Arms Co., Inc.
Linebaugh Custom Sixguns
List Precision Engineering
Lock's Philadelphia Gun Exchange
Lone Star Rifle Company
Long, George F.
Mag-Na-Port International, Inc.
Mahony, Philip Bruce
Mahony, Philip Bruce
Mahovsky's Metalife
Makinson, Nicholas
Mandall Shooting Supplies Inc.
Marshall Fish Mfg. Gunsmith Sptg. Co.
Martin's Gun Shop
Martz, John V.
Mathews & Son, Inc., George E.
Mazur Restoration, Pete
McCann's Muzzle-Gun Works
McCluskey Precision Rifles
McGowen Rifle Barrels
McMillan Rifle Barrels
MCS, Inc.
Mercer Custom Guns
Michael's Antiques
Mid-America Recreation, Inc.
Middlebrooks Custom Shop
Miller Arms, Inc.
Miller Custom
Mills Jr., Hugh B.
Moeller, Steve
Monell Custom Guns
Montgomery Community College
Morrison Custom Rifles, J. W.
Morrow, Bud
Mo's Competitor Supplies (See MCS, Inc.)
Mowrey's Guns & Gunsmithing
Mullis Guncraft
Muzzleloaders Etcetera, Inc.
NCP Products, Inc.
Neil A. Jones Custom Products
Nelson's Custom Guns, Inc.
Nettestad Gun Works
New England Arms Co.

New England Custom Gun Service
Newman Gunshop
Nicholson Custom
Nickels, Paul R.
Nicklas, Ted
Nitex Gun Shop
North American Shooting Systems
Nu-Line Guns,Inc.
Old World Gunsmithing
Olson, Vic
Ottmar, Maurice
Ox-Yoke Originals, Inc.
Ozark Gun Works
P&M Sales & Services, LLC
P.S.M.G. Gun Co.
PAC-NOR Barreling
Pagel Gun Works, Inc.
Parker & Sons Shooting Supply
Parker Gun Finishes
Pasadena Gun Center
Paterson Gunsmithing
Paulsen Gunstocks
Peacemaker Specialists
PEM's Mfg. Co.
Pence Precision Barrels
Pennsylvania Gunsmith School
Penrod Precision
Pentheny de Pentheny
Performance Specialists
Pete Mazur Restoration
Peter Dyson & Son Ltd.
Peterson Gun Shop, Inc., A.W.
Piquette's Custom Engraving
Plum City Ballistic Range
Powell & Son (Gunmakers) Ltd., William
Power Custom, Inc.
Professional Hunter Supplies (See Star Custom Bullets)
Quality Custom Firearms
R&J Gun Shop
R.A. Wells Custom Gunsmith
Ramon B. Gonzalez Guns
Ray's Gunsmith Shop
Renfrew Guns & Supplies
Ridgetop Sporting Goods
Ries, Chuck
RMS Custom Gunsmithing
Robert Valade Engraving
Robinson, Don
Rocky Mountain Arms, Inc.
Romain's Custom Guns, Inc.
Ron Frank Custom Classic Arms
Ruger's Custom Guns
Rupert's Gun Shop
Savage Arms, Inc.
Schiffman, Mike
Schumakers Gun Shop
Score High Gunsmithing
Sharp Shooter Supply
Shaw, Inc., E. R. (See Small Arms Mfg. Co.)
Shay's Gunsmithing
Shockley, Harold H.
Shooters Supply
Shootin' Shack
Shooting Specialties (See Titus, Daniel)
Shotguns Unlimited
Silver Ridge Gun Shop (See Goodwin, Fred)
Simmons Gun Repair, Inc.
Singletary, Kent
Siskiyou Gun Works (See Donnelly, C. P.)
Skeoch, Brian R.
Sklany's Machine Shop
Slezak, Jerome F.
Small Arms Mfg. Co.
Small Arms Specialists
Smith, Art
Snapp's Gunshop
Sound Technology
Speiser, Fred D.

Spencer Reblue Service
Spencer's Rifle Barrels, Inc.
Splitfire Sporting Goods, L.L.C.
Sportsmen's Exchange & Western Gun Traders, Inc.
Springfield Armory
Springfield, Inc.
SSK Industries
Star Custom Bullets
Steelman's Gun Shop
Steffens, Ron
Steven Dodd Hughes
Stiles Custom Guns
Stott's Creek Armory, Inc.
Sturgeon Valley Sporters
Sullivan, David S .(See Westwind Rifles Inc.)
Swann, D. J.
Swenson's 45 Shop, A. D.
Swift River Gunworks
Szweda, Robert (See RMS Custom Gunsmithing)
Taconic Firearms Ltd., Perry Lane
Talmage, William G.
Tank's Rifle Shop
Tar-Hunt Custom Rifles, Inc.
Tarnhelm Supply Co., Inc.
Taylor & Robbins
Ten-Ring Precision, Inc.
Terry K. Kopp Professional Gunsmithing
The A.W. Peterson Gun Shop, Inc.
The Competitive Pistol Shop
The Custom Shop
The Gun Shop
The Gun Works
The Orvis Co.
The Robar Co.'s, Inc.
The Swampfire Shop (See Peterson Gun Shop, Inc.)
Theis, Terry
Thompson, Randall (See Highline Machine Co.)
Thurston Sports, Inc.
Time Precision
Tom's Gun Repair, Thomas G. Ivanoff
Tom's Gunshop
Trevallion Gunstocks
Trulock Tool
Tucker, James C.
Turnbull Restoration, Doug
Unmussig Bullets, D. L.
Upper Missouri Trading Co.
Van Horn, Gil
Van Patten, J. W.
Van's Gunsmith Service
Vest, John
Vic's Gun Refinishing
Vintage Arms, Inc.
Virgin Valley Custom Guns
Volquartsen Custom Ltd.
Walker Arms Co., Inc.
Wallace, Terry
Wasmundt, Jim
Wayne E. Schwartz Custom Guns
Weatherby, Inc.
Weber & Markin Custom Gunsmiths
Weems, Cecil
Werth, T. W.
Wessinger Custom Guns & Engraving
Western Design (See Alpha Gunsmith Division)
Westley Richards & Co.
Westwind Rifles, Inc., David S. Sullivan
White Barn Wor
White Rifles, Inc.
Wichita Arms, Inc.
Wiebe, Duane
Wild West Guns
William E. Phillips Firearms

Williams Gun Sight Co.
Williams Shootin' Iron Service, The Lynx-Line
Williamson Precision Gunsmithing
Wilsom Combat
Winter, Robert M.
Wise Guns, Dale
Wiseman and Co., Bill
Wood, Frank (See Classic Guns, Inc.)
Working Guns
Wright's Gunstock Blanks
Yankee Gunsmith "Just Glocks"
Zeeryp, Russ

GUN PARTS, U.S. & FOREIGN

"Su-Press-On", Inc.
A.A. Arms, Inc.
Ahlman Guns
Amherst Arms
Antique Arms Co.
Armscorp USA, Inc.
Auto-Ordnance Corp.
B.A.C.
Badger Shooters Supply, Inc.
Ballard Rifle & Cartridge Co., LLC
Bar-Sto Precision Machine
Bear Mountain Gun & Tool
Billings Gunsmiths
Bill's Gun Repair
Bob's Gun Shop
Briese Bullet Co., Inc.
Brown Products, Inc., Ed
Brownells, Inc.
Bryan & Assoc.
Buffer Technologies
Cambos Outdoorsman
Cambos Outdoorsman
Cape Outfitters
Caspian Arms, Ltd.
CBC-BRAZIL
Chicasaw Gun Works
Ciener Inc., Jonathan Arthur
Cole's Gun Works
Colonial Arms, Inc.
Colonial Repair
Colt's Mfg. Co., Inc.
Custom Riflestocks, Inc., Michael M. Kokolus
Cylinder & Slide, Inc., William R. Laughridge
David R. Chicoine
Delta Arms Ltd.
DGR Custom Rifles
Dibble, Derek A.
Dixie Gun Works
Duane's Gun Repair (See DGR Custom Rifles)
Duffy, Charles E (See Guns Antique & Modern DBA)
E.A.A. Corp.
Elliott Inc., G. W.
EMF Co., Inc.
Enguix Import-Export
Entre`prise Arms, Inc.
European American Armory Corp (See E.A.A. Corp)
Evolution Gun Works Inc.
F.I., Inc. - High Standard Mfg. Co.
Faloon Industries, Inc.
Federal Arms Corp. of America
Fleming Firearms
Forrest Inc., Tom
Gentry Custom Gunmaker, David
Glimm's Custom Gun Engraving
Goodwin's Gun Shop
Granite Mountain Arms, Inc.
Greider Precision
Gre-Tan Rifles
Groenewold, John

Gun Hunter Books (See Gun Hunter Trading Co.)
Gun Hunter Trading Co.
Guns Antique & Modern DBA / Charles E. Duffy Gunsmithing, Inc.
Hastings
Hawken Shop, The (See Dayton Traister)
High Performance International I.S.S.
Irwin, Campbell H.
Jack First, Inc.
Jamison's Forge Works
Jonathan Arthur Ciener, Inc.
Kimber of America, Inc.
Knight's Mfg. Co.
Krico Deutschland GmbH
LaFrance Specialties
Lampert, Ron
LaPrade
Laughridge, William R (See Cylinder & Slide Inc)
Leapers, Inc.
List Precision Engineering
Lodewick, Walter H.
Logdewood Mfg.
Long, George F.
Mandall Shooting Supplies Inc.
Markell,Inc.
Martin's Gun Shop
McCormick Corp., Chip
MCS, Inc.
Merkuria Ltd.
Mid-America Recreation, Inc.
Morrow, Bud
Mo's Competitor Supplies (See MCS, Inc.)
North Star West
Northwest Arms
Nu-Line Guns,Inc.
Numrich Gun Parts Corporation
Nygord Precision Products, Inc.
Olathe Gun Shop
Olympic Arms Inc.
P.S.M.G. Gun Co.
Pacific Armament Corp
Pennsylvania Gun Parts Inc
Performance Specialists
Peter Dyson & Son Ltd.
Peterson Gun Shop, Inc., A.W.
Ranch Products
Randco UK
Ravell Ltd.
Retting, Inc., Martin B
Romain's Custom Guns, Inc.
Ruger (See Sturm, Ruger & Co., Inc.)
Rutgers Book Center
S&S Firearms
Sabatti SPA
Samco Global Arms, Inc.
Sarco, Inc.
Shockley, Harold H.
Shootin' Shack
Silver Ridge Gun Shop (See Goodwin, Fred)
Simmons Gun Repair, Inc.
Smires, C. L.
Smith & Wesson
Southern Ammunition Co., Inc.
Sportsmen's Exchange & Western Gun Traders, Inc.
Springfield Sporters, Inc.
Springfield, Inc.
Steyr Mannlicher GmbH P Co KG
STI International
Strayer-Voigt, Inc.
Sturm Ruger & Co. Inc.
Sunny Hill Enterprises, Inc.
T&S Industries, Inc.
Tank's Rifle Shop
Tarnhelm Supply Co., Inc.

Terry K. Kopp Professional Gunsmithing
The A.W. Peterson Gun Shop, Inc.
The Gun Room Press
The Gun Shop
The Gun Works
The Southern Armory
The Swampfire Shop (See Peterson Gun Shop, Inc.)
VAM Distribution Co. LLC
Vektor USA
Vintage Arms, Inc.
W. Waller & Son, Inc.
W.C. Wolff Co.
Walker Arms Co., Inc.
Wescombe, Bill (See North Star West)
Whitestone Lumber Corp.
Wild West Guns
Williams Mfg. of Oregon
Winchester Sutler, Inc., The
Wise Guns, Dale
Wisners Inc/Twin Pine Armory

GUNS, FOREIGN MANUFACTURER U.S. IMPORTER

Accuracy Internationl Precision Rifles (See U.S.)
Accuracy Int'l. North America, Inc.
Ad Hominem
Air Arms
Armas Garbi, S.A.
Armas Kemen S. A. (See U.S. Importers)
Armi Perazzi S.p.A.
Armi San Marco (See U.S. Importers-Taylor's & Co I
Armi Sport (See U.S. Importers-Cape Outfitters)
Arms Corporation of the Philippines
Armscorp USA, Inc.
Arrieta S.L.
Astra Sport, S.A.
Atamec-Bretton
AYA (See U.S. Importer-New England Custom Gun Serv
B.A.C.
B.C. Outdoors
BEC, Inc.
Benelli Armi S.p.A.
Benelli USA Corp
Beretta S.p.A., Pietro
Beretta U.S.A. Corp.
Bernardelli S.p.A., Vincenzo
Bersa S.A.
Bertuzzi (See U.S. Importer-New England Arms Co)
Bill Hanus Birdguns
Blaser Jagdwaffen GmbH
Borovnik KG, Ludwig
Bosis (See U.S. Importer-New England Arms Co.)
Brenneke GmbH
Browning Arms Co.
Bryan & Assoc.
BSA Guns Ltd.
Cabanas (See U.S. Importer-Mandall Shooting Supply)
Cabela's
Cape Outfitters
CBC
Chapuis Armes
Churchill (See U.S. Importer-Ellett Bros.)
Conetrol Scope Mounts
Cosmi Americo & Figlio s.n.c.
Crucelegui, Hermanos (See U.S. Importer-Mandall)
Cubic Shot Shell Co., Inc.
Daewoo Precision Industries Ltd.

Dakota (See U.S. Importer-EMF Co., Inc.)
Dakota Arms, Inc.
Daly, Charles (See U.S. Importer)
Davide Pedersoli and Co.
Domino
Dumoulin, Ernest
Eagle Imports, Inc.
EAW (See U.S. Importer-New England Custom Gun Serv
Ed's Gun House
Effebi SNC-Dr. Franco Beretta
EMF Co., Inc.
Eversull Co., Inc.
F.A.I.R.
Fabarm S.p.A.
FEG
Feinwerkbau Westinger & Altenburger
Felk Pistols Inc.
FERLIB
Fiocchi Munizioni S.p.A. (See U.S. Importer-Fiocch
Firearms Co Ltd. / Alpine (See U.S. Importer-Mandall
Firearms International
Flintlocks, Etc.
Franchi S.p.A.
Galaxy Imports Ltd., Inc.
Gamba S.p.A. Societa Armi Bresciane Srl
Gamo (See U.S. Importers-Arms United Corp, Daisy M
Gaucher Armes, S.A.
Gibbs Rifle Co., Inc.
Glock GmbH
Goergen's Gun Shop, Inc.
Griffin & Howe, Inc.
Griffin & Howe, Inc.
Griffin & Howe, Inc.
Grulla Armes
Hammerli Ltd.
Hammerli USA
Hartford (See U.S. Importer-EMF Co. Inc.)
Hartmann & Weiss GmbH
Heckler & Koch, Inc.
Hege Jagd-u. Sporthandels GmbH
Helwan (See U.S. Importer-Interarms)
Holland & Holland Ltd.
Howa Machinery, Ltd.
I.A.B. (See U.S. Importer-Taylor's & Co Inc.)
IAR Inc.
IGA (See U.S. Importer-Stoeger Industries)
Ignacio Ugartechea S.A.
Imperial Magnum Corp.
Imperial Miniature Armory
Import Sports Inc.
Inter Ordnance of America LP
Intrac Arms International
J.G. Anschutz GmbH & Co. KG
JSL Ltd (See U.S. Importer-Specialty Shooters)
K. Eversull Co., Inc.
Kimar (See U.S. Importer-IAR,Inc)
Korth Germany GmbH
Krico Deutschland GmbH
Krieghoff Gun Co., H.
Lakefield Arms Ltd. (See Savage Arms, Inc.)
Lapua Ltd.
Laurona Armas Eibar, S.A.L.
Lebeau-Courally
Lever Arms Service Ltd.
Llama Gabilondo Y Cia
London Guns Ltd.
M. Thys (See U.S. Importer-Champlin Firearms Inc)
Magtech Ammunition Co. Inc.
Mandall Shooting Supplies Inc.
Marocchi F.lli S.p.A

Mauser Werke Oberndorf Waffensysteme GmbH
McCann Industries
MEC-Gar S.R.L.
Merkel
Miltex, Inc
Morini (See U.S. Importers-Mandall Shooting Supply)
New England Custom Gun Service
New SKB Arms Co.
Norica, Avnda Otaola
Norinco
Norma Precision AB (See U.S. Importers-Dynamit)
Northwest Arms
Nygord Precision Products, Inc.
OK Weber, Inc.
Para-Ordnance Mfg., Inc.
Pardini Armi Srl
Perugini Visini & Co. S.r.l.
Peters Stahl GmbH
Pietta (See U.S. Importers-Navy Arms Co, Taylor's
Piotti (See U.S. Importer-Moore & Co, Wm. Larkin)
PMC/Eldorado Cartridge Corp.
Powell & Son (Gunmakers) Ltd., William
Prairie Gun Works
Ramon B. Gonzalez Guns
Rizzini F.lli (See U.S. Importers-Moore & C England)
Rizzini SNC
Robinson Armament Co.
Rossi Firearms
Rottweil Compe
Rutten (See U.S. Importer-Labanu Inc)
RWS (See US Importer-Dynamit Nobel-RWS, Inc.)
S.A.R.L. G. Granger
S.I.A.C.E. (See U.S. Importer-IAR Inc)
Sabatti SPA
Sako Ltd (See U.S. Importer-Stoeger Industries)
San Marco (See U.S. Importers-Cape Outfitters-EMF
Sarsilmaz Shotguns - Turkey (see B.C. Outdoors)
Sauer (See U.S. Importers-Paul Co., The, Sigarms I
Savage Arms (Canada), Inc.
SIG
Sigarms, Inc.
SIG-Sauer (See U.S. Importer-Sigarms Inc.)
SKB Shotguns
Small Arms Specialists
Societa Armi Bresciane Srl (See U.S. Importer-Cape
Sphinx Systems Ltd.
Springfield Armory
Springfield, Inc.
Starr Trading Co., Jedediah
Steyr Mannlicher GmbH P Co KG
T.F.C. S.p.A.
Tanfoglio Fratelli S.r.l.
Tanner (See U.S. Importer-Mandall Shooting Supply)
Tar-Hunt Custom Rifles, Inc.
Taurus International Firearms (See U.S. Importer)
Taurus S.A. Forjas
Taylor's & Co., Inc.
Techno Arms (See U.S. Importer-Auto-Ordnance Corp
The A.W. Peterson Gun Shop, Inc.
Tikka (See U.S. Importer-Stoeger Industries)
TOZ (See U.S. Importer-Nygord Precision Products)
Ugartechea S. A., Ignacio

Ultralux (See U.S. Importer-Keng's Firearms)
Unique/M.A.P.F.
Valtro USA, Inc
Verney-Carron
Voere-KGH GmbH
Walther GmbH, Carl
Weatherby, Inc.
Webley and Scott Ltd.
Weihrauch KG, Hermann
Westley Richards & Co.
Whiscombe (See U.S. Importer-Pelaire Products)
Wolf (See J.R. Distributing)
Yankee Gunsmith "Just Glocks"
Zabala Hermanos S.A.

GUNS, FOREIGN-IMPORTER

Accuracy International
AcuSport Corporation
Air Rifle Specialists
American Frontier Firearms Mfg., Inc
Auto-Ordnance Corp.
B.A.C.
B.C. Outdoors
Bell's Legendary Country Wear
Benelli USA Corp
Big Bear Arms & Sporting Goods, Inc.
Bill Hanus Birdguns
Bridgeman Products
British Sporting Arms
Browning Arms Co.
Cape Outfitters
Century International Arms, Inc.
Champion Shooters' Supply
Champion's Choice, Inc.
Chapuis USA
Cimarron F.A. Co.
CVA
CZ USA
Dixie Gun Works
Dynamit Nobel-RWS, Inc.
E&L Mfg., Inc.
E.A.A. Corp.
Eagle Imports, Inc.
Ellett Bros.
EMF Co., Inc.
Euroarms of America, Inc.
Eversull Co., Inc.
Fiocchi of America, Inc.
Flintlocks, Etc.
Franzen International,Inc (See U.S. Importer for)
G.U. Inc (See U.S. Importer for New SKB Arms Co.)
Galaxy Imports Ltd., Inc.
Gamba, USA
Gamo USA, Inc.
Giacomo Sporting USA
Glock, Inc.
Gremmel Enterprises
GSI, Inc.
Guncraft Books (See Guncraft Sports Inc.)
Guncraft Sports Inc.
Gunsite Custom Shop
Gunsite Training Center
Hammerli USA
I.S.S.
IAR Inc.
Imperial Magnum Corp.
Imperial Miniature Armory
Import Sports Inc.
Intrac Arms International
K. Eversull Co., Inc.
K.B.I. Inc.
Kemen America
Keng's Firearms Specialty, Inc./US Tactical Systems

Krieghoff International,Inc.
Labanu, Inc.
Legacy Sports International
Lion Country Supply
London Guns Ltd.
Magnum Research, Inc.
Marx, Harry (See U.S. Importer for FERLIB)
MCS, Inc.
MEC-Gar U.S.A., Inc.
Navy Arms Company
New England Arms Co.
Nygord Precision Products, Inc.
OK Weber, Inc.
P.S.M.G. Gun Co.
Para-Ordnance, Inc.
Parker Reproductions
Pelaire Products
Perazzi U.S.A. Inc.
Powell Agency, William
Precision Sales International, Inc.
Rocky Mountain Armoury
S.D. Meacham
Safari Arms/Schuetzen Pistol Works
Samco Global Arms, Inc.
Savage Arms, Inc.
Scott Fine Guns Inc., Thad
Sigarms, Inc.
SKB Shotguns
Small Arms Specialists
Southern Ammunition Co., Inc.
Specialty Shooters Supply, Inc.
Springfield, Inc.
Stoeger Industries
Stone Enterprises Ltd.
Swarovski Optik North America Ltd.
Tar-Hunt Custom Rifles, Inc.
Taurus Firearms, Inc.
Taylor's & Co., Inc.
The A.W. Peterson Gun Shop, Inc.
The Gun Shop
The Orvis Co.
The Paul Co.
Track of the Wolf, Inc.
Traditions Performance Firearms
Tristar Sporting Arms, Ltd.
Trooper Walsh
U.S. Importer-Wm. Larkin Moore
VAM Distribution Co. LLC
Vektor USA
Vintage Arms, Inc.
VTI Gun Parts
Westley Richards Agency USA (See U.S. Importer for Wingshooting Adventures

GUNS, SURPLUS, PARTS & AMMUNITION

Ahlman Guns
Alpha 1 Drop Zone
Armscorp USA, Inc.
Arundel Arms & Ammunition, Inc., A.
B.A.C.
Bondini Paolo
Cambos Outdoorsman
Century International Arms, Inc.
Cole's Gun Works
Conetrol Scope Mounts
Delta Arms Ltd.
Ed's Gun House
First Inc., Jack
Fleming Firearms
Forrest Inc., Tom
Garcia National Gun Traders, Inc.
Goodwin's Gun Shop
Gun City
Gun Hunter Books (See Gun Hunter Trading Co.)
Gun Hunter Trading Co.

Hank's Gun Shop
Hege Jagd-u. Sporthandels GmbH
Jackalope Gun Shop
Ken Starnes Gunmaker
LaRocca Gun Works
Lever Arms Service Ltd.
Log Cabin Sport Shop
Martin's Gun Shop
Navy Arms Company
Nevada Pistol Academy, Inc.
Northwest Arms
Numrich Gun Parts Corporation
Oil Rod and Gun Shop
Olathe Gun Shop
Paragon Sales & Services, Inc.
Pasadena Gun Center
Power Plus Enterprises, Inc.
Ravell Ltd.
Retting, Inc., Martin B
Rutgers Book Center
Samco Global Arms, Inc.
Sarco, Inc.
Shootin' Shack
Silver Ridge Gun Shop (See
    Goodwin, Fred)
Simmons Gun Repair, Inc.
Sportsmen's Exchange & Western
    Gun Traders, Inc.
Springfield Sporters, Inc.
T.F.C. S.p.A.
Tarnhelm Supply Co., Inc.
The A.W. Peterson Gun Shop, Inc.
The Gun Room Press
Thurston Sports, Inc.
Williams Shootin' Iron Service, The
    Lynx-Line

GUNS, U.S. MADE

3-Ten Corp.
A.A. Arms, Inc.
Accu-Tek
Ace Custom 45's, Inc.
Acra-Bond Laminates
Ad Hominem
Airrow
Allred Bullet Co.
American Derringer Corp.
American Frontier Firearms Mfg.,
    Inc
AR-7 Industries, LLC
ArmaLite, Inc.
Armscorp USA, Inc.
A-Square Co.
Austin & Halleck, Inc.
Autauga Arms, Inc.
Auto-Ordnance Corp.
Baer Custom Inc., Les
Ballard Rifle & Cartridge Co., LLC
Barrett Firearms Manufacturer, Inc.
Bar-Sto Precision Machine
Benjamin/Sheridan Co., Crosman
Beretta S.p.A., Pietro
Beretta U.S.A. Corp.
Big Bear Arms & Sporting Goods,
    Inc.
Bill Russ Trading Post
Bond Arms, Inc.
Borden Ridges Rimrock Stocks
Borden Rifles Inc.
Brockman's Custom Gunsmithing
Brown Co., E. Arthur
Brown Products, Inc., Ed
Browning Arms Co.
Bryan & Assoc.
Bushmaster Firearms
C. Sharps Arms Co. Inc./Montana
    Armory
Cabela's
Calico Light Weapon Systems
Cambos Outdoorsman
Cape Outfitters
Casull Arms Corp.
CCL Security Products

Century Gun Dist. Inc.
Champlin Firearms, Inc.
Charter 2000
Cobra Enterprises, Inc.
Colt's Mfg. Co., Inc.
Competitor Corp., Inc.
Conetrol Scope Mounts
Connecticut Shotgun Mfg. Co.
Connecticut Valley Classics (See
    CVC, BPI)
Cooper Arms
Crosman Airguns
Cumberland Arms
Cumberland Mountain Arms
CVA
Daisy Outdoor Products
Dakota Arms, Inc.
Dan Wesson Firearms
Dayton Traister
Dixie Gun Works
Downsizer Corp.
DS Arms, Inc.
DunLyon R&D Inc.
E&L Mfg., Inc.
E. Arthur Brown Co.
Eagle Arms, Inc. (See ArmaLite,
    Inc.)
Ed Brown Products, Inc.
Emerging Technologies, Inc. (See
    Laseraim Technologies, Inc.)
Entre'prise Arms, Inc.
Essex Arms
Excel Industries Inc.
F.I., Inc. - High Standard Mfg. Co.
Fletcher-Bidwell, LLC.
FN Manufacturing
Fort Worth Firearms
Freedom Arms, Inc.
Fulton Armory
Galena Industries AMT
Garcia National Gun Traders, Inc.
Gary Reeder Custom Guns
Genecco Gun Works
Gentry Custom Gunmaker, David
George Hoenig, Inc.
George Madis Winchester
    Consultants
Gibbs Rifle Co., Inc.
Gil Hebard Guns Inc.
Gilbert Equipment Co., Inc.
Goergen's Gun Shop, Inc.
Goodwin's Gun Shop
Granite Mountain Arms, Inc.
Grayback Wildcats
Gunsite Custom Shop
Gunsite Gunsmithy (See Gunsite
    Custom Shop)
H&R 1871.LLC
Hammans, Charles E.
Hammerli USA
Harrington & Richardson (See
    H&R 1871, Inc.)
Harris Gunworks
Hart & Son, Inc.
Hatfield Gun
Hawken Shop, The (See Dayton
    Traister)
Heritage Firearms (See Heritage
    Mfg., Inc.)
Heritage Manufacturing, Inc.
Hesco-Meprolight
High Precision
Hi-Point Firearms/MKS Supply
HJS Arms, Inc.
H-S Precision, Inc.
Hutton Rifle Ranch
IAR Inc.
Imperial Miniature Armory
Israel Arms International, Inc.
Ithaca Classic Doubles
Ithaca Gun Company LLC
J.P. Enterprises Inc.
Jim Norman Custom Gunstocks
John Rigby & Co.

John's Custom Leather
K.B.I. Inc.
Kahr Arms
Kehr, Roger
Kelbly, Inc.
Kel-Tec CNC Industries, Inc.
Kimber of America, Inc.
Knight Rifles
Knight's Mfg. Co.
Kolar
L.A.R. Mfg., Inc.
L.W. Seecamp Co., Inc.
LaFrance Specialties
Lakefield Arms Ltd. (See Savage
    Arms, Inc.)
Laseraim Technologies, Inc.
Lever Arms Service Ltd.
Ljutic Industries, Inc.
Lock's Philadelphia Gun Exchange
Lomont Precision Bullets
Lone Star Rifle Company
Mag-Na-Port International, Inc.
Magnum Research, Inc.
Mandall Shooting Supplies Inc.
Marlin Firearms Co.
Maverick Arms, Inc.
McBros Rifle Co.
McCann Industries
Mid-America Recreation, Inc.
Miller Arms, Inc.
MKS Supply, Inc. (See Hi-Point
    Firearms)
MOA Corporation
Montana Armory, Inc .(See C.
    Sharps Arms Co. Inc.)
MPI Stocks
Navy Arms Company
NCP Products, Inc.
New Ultra Light Arms, LLC
Noreen, Peter H.
North American Arms, Inc.
North Star West
Northwest Arms
Nowlin Mfg. Co.
Olympic Arms Inc.
Oregon Arms, Inc. (See Rogue
    Rifle Co., Inc.)
P&M Sales & Services, LLC
Parker & Sons Shooting Supply
Parker Gun Finishes
Phillips & Rogers, Inc.
Phoenix Arms
Precision Small Arms Inc.
ProWare, Inc.
Ramon B. Gonzalez Guns
Rapine Bullet Mould Mfg. Co.
Remington Arms Co., Inc.
Robinson Armament Co.
Rock River Arms
Rocky Mountain Arms, Inc.
Rogue Rifle Co., Inc.
Rogue River Rifleworks
Rohrbaugh
Romain's Custom Guns, Inc.
RPM
Ruger (See Sturm, Ruger & Co.,
    Inc.)
Safari Arms/Schuetzen Pistol
    Works
Savage Arms (Canada), Inc.
Searcy Enterprises
Sharps Arms Co., Inc., C.
Shiloh Rifle Mfg.
Sklany's Machine Shop
Small Arms Specialists
Smith & Wesson
Sound Technology
Spencer's Rifle Barrels, Inc.
Springfield Armory
Springfield, Inc.
SSK Industries
STI International
Stoeger Industries
Strayer-Voigt, Inc.

Sturm Ruger & Co. Inc.
Sunny Hill Enterprises, Inc.
T&S Industries, Inc.
Taconic Firearms Ltd., Perry Lane
Tank's Rifle Shop
Tar-Hunt Custom Rifles, Inc.
Taurus Firearms, Inc.
Texas Armory (See Bond Arms,
    Inc.)
The A.W. Peterson Gun Shop, Inc.
The Gun Room Press
The Gun Works
Thompson/Center Arms
Tristar Sporting Arms, Ltd.
U.S. Fire Arms Mfg. Co., Inc.
U.S. Repeating Arms Co., Inc.
Visible Impact Targets
Volquartsen Custom Ltd.
Wallace, Terry
Weatherby, Inc.
Wescombe, Bill (See North Star
    West)
Wessinger Custom Guns &
    Engraving
Whildin & Sons Ltd, E.H.
Whitestone Lumber Corp.
Wichita Arms, Inc.
Wichita Arms, Inc.
Wildey, Inc.
Wilsom Combat
Z-M Weapons

GUNSMITH SCHOOL

American Gunsmithing Institute
Bull Mountain Rifle Co.
Colorado Gunsmithing Academy
Colorado School of Trades
Cylinder & Slide, Inc., William R.
    Laughridge
Lassen Community College,
    Gunsmithing Dept.
Laughridge, William R (See
    Cylinder & Slide Inc)
Log Cabin Sport Shop
Modern Gun Repair School
Montgomery Community College
Murray State College
North American Correspondence
    Schools The Gun Pro
Nowlin Mfg. Co.
NRI Gunsmith School
Pennsylvania Gunsmith School
Piedmont Community College
Pine Technical College
Professional Gunsmiths of America
Smith & Wesson
Southeastern Community College
Spencer's Rifle Barrels, Inc.
Trinidad St. Jr. Col. Gunsmith Dept.
Wright's Gunstock Blanks
Yavapai College

GUNSMITH SUPPLIES, TOOLS & SERVICES

Ace Custom 45's, Inc.
Actions by "T" Teddy Jacobson
Alaskan Silversmith, The
Aldis Gunsmithing & Shooting
    Supply
Alley Supply Co.
Allred Bullet Co.
Alpec Team, Inc.
American Frontier Firearms Mfg.,
    Inc
American Gunsmithing Institute
Baer Custom Inc., Les
Ballard Rifle & Cartridge Co., LLC
Bar-Sto Precision Machine
Bauska Barrels
Bear Mountain Gun & Tool
Bengtson Arms Co., L.

Bill's Gun Repair
Blue Ridge Machinery & Tools, Inc.
Boyds' Gunstock Industries, Inc.
Break-Free, Inc.
Briley Mfg. Inc.
Brockman's Custom Gunsmithing
Brown Products, Inc., Ed
Brownells, Inc.
Bryan & Assoc.
B-Square Company, Inc.
Buffer Technologies
Bull Mountain Rifle Co.
Bushmaster Firearms
C.S. Van Gorden & Son, Inc.
Carbide Checkering Tools (See
    J&R Engineering)
Carter's Gun Shop
Caywood, Shane J.
CBC-BRAZIL
Chapman Manufacturing Co.
Chicasaw Gun Works
Choate Machine & Tool Co., Inc.
Ciener Inc., Jonathan Arthur
Colonial Arms, Inc.
Colorado School of Trades
Colt's Mfg. Co., Inc.
Conetrol Scope Mounts
Corbin Mfg. & Supply, Inc.
CRR, Inc./Marble's Inc.
Cumberland Arms
Cumberland Mountain Arms
Custom Checkering Service, Kathy
    Forster
D'Arcy Echols & Co.
Dem-Bart Checkering Tools, Inc.
Dixie Gun Works
Dixie Gun Works
Dremel Mfg. Co.
Du-Lite Corp.
Efficient Machinery Co.
Entre'prise Arms, Inc.
Erhardt, Dennis
Evolution Gun Works Inc.
Faith Associates
Faloon Industries, Inc.
FERLIB
Fisher, Jerry A.
Forgreens Tool & Mfg., Inc.
Forkin, Ben (See Belt MTN Arms)
Forster, Kathy (See Custom
    Checkering)
Gentry Custom Gunmaker, David
Goodwin's Gun Shop
Grace Metal Products
Gre-Tan Rifles
Gruning Precision Inc.
Gunline Tools
Half Moon Rifle Shop
Hammond Custom Guns Ltd.
Hastings
Henriksen Tool Co., Inc.
High Performance International
High Precision
Holland's Gunsmithing
Ironsighter Co.
Israel Arms International, Inc.
Ivanoff, Thomas G. (See Tom's
    Gun Repair)
J&R Engineering
J&S Heat Treat
J. Dewey Mfg. Co., Inc.
Jantz Supply
Jenkins Recoil Pads, Inc.
JGS Precision Tool Mfg., LLC
Jonathan Arthur Ciener, Inc.
Jones Custom Products, Neil A.
Kailua Custom Guns Inc.
Kasenit Co., Inc.
Kleinendorst, K. W.
Korzinek Riflesmith, J.
LaBounty Precision Reboring, Inc
LaFrance Specialties
Laurel Mountain Forge
Lea Mfg. Co.

Lee Supplies, Mark
List Precision Engineering
Lock's Philadelphia Gun Exchange
London Guns Ltd.
Mahovsky's Metalife
Marble Arms (See CRR, Inc./Marble's Inc.)
Mark Lee Supplies
Marsh, Mike
Martin's Gun Shop
McFarland, Stan
Menck, Gunsmith Inc., T.W.
Metalife Industries (See Mahovsky's Metalife)
Michael's Antiques
Micro Sight Co.
Midway Arms, Inc.
MMC
Mo's Competitor Supplies (See MCS, Inc.)
Mowrey's Guns & Gunsmithing
Neil A. Jones Custom Products
New England Custom Gun Service
Ole Frontier Gunsmith Shop
Olympic Arms Inc.
Parker & Sons Shooting Supply
Parker Gun Finishes
Paulsen Gunstocks
PEM's Mfg. Co.
Perazone-Gunsmith, Brian
Peter Dyson & Son Ltd.
Power Custom, Inc.
Practical Tools, Inc.
Precision Specialties
R.A. Wells Custom Gunsmith
Ranch Products
Ransom International Corp.
Reardon Products
Rice, Keith (See White Rock Tool & Die)
Robert Valade Engraving
Rocky Mountain Arms, Inc.
Romain's Custom Guns, Inc.
Royal Arms Gunstocks
Rusteprufe Laboratories
Sharp Shooter Supply
Shooter's Choice Gun Care
Simmons Gun Repair, Inc.
Smith Abrasives, Inc.
Southern Bloomer Mfg. Co.
Spencer Reblue Service
Spencer's Rifle Barrels, Inc.
Spradlin's
Starr Trading Co., Jedediah
Starrett Co., L. S.
Stiles Custom Guns
Stoney Point Products, Inc.
Sullivan, David S .(See Westwind Rifles Inc.)
Sunny Hill Enterprises, Inc.
T&S Industries, Inc.
T.W. Menck Gunsmith Inc.
Tank's Rifle Shop
Texas Platers Supply Co.
The A.W. Peterson Gun Shop, Inc.
The Dutchman's Firearms, Inc.
The Gun Works
The NgraveR Co.
The Robar Co.'s, Inc.
Theis, Terry
Tom's Gun Repair, Thomas G. Ivanoff
Track of the Wolf, Inc.
Trinidad St. Jr. Col. Gunsmith Dept.
Trulock Tool
Turnbull Restoration, Doug
United States Products Co.
Van Gorden & Son Inc., C. S.
Venco Industries, Inc. (See Shooter's Choice Gun Care)
W.C. Wolff Co.
Warne Manufacturing Co.
Washita Mountain Whetstone Co.
Weigand Combat Handguns, Inc.

Wessinger Custom Guns & Engraving
White Rock Tool & Die
Wilcox All-Pro Tools & Supply
Wild West Guns
Will-Burt Co.
Williams Gun Sight Co.
Williams Shootin' Iron Service, The Lynx-Line
Willow Bend
Windish, Jim
Winter, Robert M.
Wise Guns, Dale
Wright's Gunstock Blanks
Yavapai College
Ziegel Engineering

HANDGUN ACCESSORIES

"Su-Press-On", Inc.
A.A. Arms, Inc.
Ace Custom 45's, Inc.
Action Direct, Inc.
ADCO Sales, Inc.
Aimtech Mount Systems
Ajax Custom Grips, Inc.
Alpha 1 Drop Zone
American Derringer Corp.
American Frontier Firearms Mfg., Inc
Arms Corporation of the Philippines
Astra Sport, S.A.
Autauga Arms, Inc.
Badger Creek Studio
Baer Custom Inc., Les
Bagmaster Mfg., Inc.
Bar-Sto Precision Machine
Behlert Precision, Inc.
Berry's Mfg., Inc.
Bill's Custom Cases
Blue and Gray Products Inc. (See Ox-Yoke Originals)
Bond Custom Firearms
Bowen Classic Arms Corp.
Bridgeman Products
Broken Gun Ranch
Brooks Tactical Systems-Agrip
Brown Products, Inc., Ed
Bushmaster Hunting & Fishing
Butler Creek Corp.
Cannon Safe, Inc.
Centaur Systems, Inc.
Central Specialties Ltd (See Trigger Lock Division)
Charter 2000
Cheyenne Pioneer Products
Chicasaw Gun Works
Ciener Inc., Jonathan Arthur
Clark Custom Guns, Inc.
Classic Arms Company
Conetrol Scope Mounts
Crimson Trace Lasers
CRR, Inc./Marble's Inc.
Cylinder & Slide, Inc., William R. Laughridge
D&L Industries (See D.J. Marketing)
D.J. Marketing
Dade Screw Machine Products
Delhi Gun House
DeSantis Holster & Leather Goods, Inc.
Dixie Gun Works
Doskocil Mfg. Co., Inc.
E&L Mfg., Inc.
E. Arthur Brown Co.
E.A.A. Corp.
Ed Brown Products, Inc.
Essex Arms
European American Armory Corp (See E.A.A. Corp)

Evolution Gun Works Inc.
F.I., Inc. - High Standard Mfg. Co.
Faloon Industries, Inc.
Federal Arms Corp. of America
Feinwerkbau Westinger & Altenburger
Fisher Custom Firearms
Fleming Firearms
Freedom Arms, Inc.
G.G. & G.
Galati International
GALCO International Ltd.
Garcia National Gun Traders, Inc.
Garthwaite Pistolsmith, Inc., Jim
Gil Hebard Guns Inc.
Gilmore Sports Concepts
Glock, Inc.
Goodwin's Gun Shop
Gould & Goodrich
Gremmel Enterprises
Gun-Alert
Gun-Ho Sports Cases
H.K.S. Products
Hafner World Wide, Inc.
Hammerli USA
Heinie Specialty Products
Henigson & Associates, Steve
Hill Speed Leather, Ernie
Hi-Point Firearms/MKS Supply
Hobson Precision Mfg. Co.
Hoppe's Div. Penguin Industries, Inc.
H-S Precision, Inc.
Hunter Co., Inc.
Impact Case & Container, Inc.
J.P. Enterprises Inc.
Jarvis, Inc.
JB Custom
Jeffredo Gunsight
Jim Noble Co.
John's Custom Leather
Jonathan Arthur Ciener, Inc.
Kalispel Case Line
KeeCo Impressions, Inc.
King's Gun Works
KK Air International (See Impact Case & Container Co.)
L&S Technologies Inc. (See Aimtech Mount Systems)
Lakewood Products LLC
LaserMax, Inc.
Loch Leven Industries/Convert-A-Pell
Lock's Philadelphia Gun Exchange
Lohman Mfg. Co., Inc.
Mag-Na-Port International, Inc.
Magnolia Sports,Inc.
Mag-Pack Corp.
Mahony, Philip Bruce
Mandall Shooting Supplies Inc.
Marble Arms (See CRR, Inc./Marble's Inc.)
Markell,Inc.
McCormick Corp., Chip
MEC-Gar S.R.L.
Menck, Gunsmith Inc., T.W.
Merkuria Ltd.
Middlebrooks Custom Shop
Millett Sights
Mogul Co./Life Jacket
MTM Molded Products Co., Inc.
No-Sho Mfg. Co.
Numrich Gun Parts Corporation
Omega Sales
Outdoor Sports Headquarters, Inc.
Ox-Yoke Originals, Inc.
Pachmayr Div. Lyman Products
Pager Pal
Palmer Security Products
Parker & Sons Shooting Supply
Pearce Grip, Inc.
Perazone-Gunsmith, Brian
Phoenix Arms
Practical Tools, Inc.

Precision Small Arms Inc.
Protektor Model
Ram-Line ATK
Ranch Products
Ransom International Corp.
Ringler Custom Leather Co.
RPM
Seecamp Co. Inc., L. W.
Simmons Gun Repair, Inc.
Sound Technology
Southern Bloomer Mfg. Co.
Springfield Armory
Springfield, Inc.
SSK Industries
Sturm Ruger & Co. Inc.
T.F.C. S.p.A.
Tactical Defense Institute
Tanfoglio Fratelli S.r.l.
The A.W. Peterson Gun Shop, Inc.
The Concealment Shop, Inc.
The Gun Works
The Keller Co.
The Protector Mfg. Co., Inc.
Thompson/Center Arms
Trigger Lock Division / Central Specialties Ltd.
Trijicon, Inc.
Triple-K Mfg. Co., Inc.
Truglo, Inc.
Tyler Manufacturing & Distributing
United States Products Co.
Universal Sports
Volquartsen Custom Ltd.
W. Waller & Son, Inc.
W.C. Wolff Co.
Warne Manufacturing Co.
Weigand Combat Handguns, Inc.
Wessinger Custom Guns & Engraving
Western Design (See Alpha Gunsmith Division)
Whitestone Lumber Corp.
Wild West Guns
Williams Gun Sight Co.
Wilsom Combat
Yankee Gunsmith "Just Glocks"
Ziegel Engineering

HANDGUN GRIPS

A.A. Arms, Inc.
African Import Co.
Ahrends, Kim (See Custom Firearms, Inc)
Ajax Custom Grips, Inc.
Altamont Co.
American Derringer Corp.
American Frontier Firearms Mfg., Inc
American Gripcraft
Arms Corporation of the Philippines
Art Jewel Enterprises Ltd.
Baelder, Harry
Baer Custom Inc., Les
Big Bear Arms & Sporting Goods, Inc.
Bob's Gun Shop
Boone Trading Co., Inc.
Boone's Custom Ivory Grips, Inc.
Boyds' Gunstock Industries, Inc.
Brooks Tactical Systems-Agrip
Brown Products, Inc., Ed
Clark Custom Guns, Inc.
Cole-Grip
Colonial Repair
Crimson Trace Lasers
Custom Firearms (See Ahrends, Kim)
Cylinder & Slide, Inc., William R. Laughridge
Dixie Gun Works
E.A.A. Corp.
EMF Co., Inc.

Essex Arms
European American Armory Corp (See E.A.A. Corp)
F.I., Inc. - High Standard Mfg. Co.
Faloon Industries, Inc.
Feinwerkbau Westinger & Altenburger
Fibron Products, Inc.
Fisher Custom Firearms
Forrest Inc., Tom
Garthwaite Pistolsmith, Inc., Jim
Goodwin's Gun Shop
Herrett's Stocks, Inc.
HIP-GRIP Barami Corp.
Hogue Grips
H-S Precision, Inc.
Huebner, Corey O.
I.S.S.
Israel Arms International, Inc.
John Masen Co. Inc.
KeeCo Impressions, Inc.
Kim Ahrends Custom Firearms, Inc.
Korth Germany GmbH
Lett Custom Grips
Linebaugh Custom Sixguns
Lyman Products Corp.
Mandall Shooting Supplies Inc.
Michaels Of Oregon, Co.
Millett Sights
N.C. Ordnance Co.
Newell, Robert H.
Northern Precision Custom Swaged Bullets
Pachmayr Div. Lyman Products
Pardini Armi Srl
Parker & Sons Shooting Supply
Perazone-Gunsmith, Brian
Pilgrim Pewter,Inc. (See Bell Originals Inc. Sid)
Precision Small Arms Inc.
Radical Concepts
Rosenberg & Son, Jack A
Roy's Custom Grips
Spegel, Craig
Stoeger Industries
Sturm Ruger & Co. Inc.
Sunny Hill Enterprises, Inc.
Tactical Defense Institute
Taurus Firearms, Inc.
The A.W. Peterson Gun Shop, Inc.
Tirelli
Triple-K Mfg. Co., Inc.
Tyler Manufacturing & Distributing
U.S. Fire Arms Mfg. Co., Inc.
Uncle Mike's (See Michaels of Oregon Co.)
Vintage Industries, Inc.
Volquartsen Custom Ltd.
Western Mfg. Co.
Whitestone Lumber Corp.
Wright's Gunstock Blanks

HOLSTERS & LEATHER GOODS

A&B Industries,Inc (See Top-Line USA Inc)
A.A. Arms, Inc.
Action Direct, Inc.
Action Products, Inc.
Aker International, Inc.
AKJ Concealco
Alessi Holsters, Inc.
Arratoonian, Andy (See Horseshoe Leather Products)
Autauga Arms, Inc.
Bagmaster Mfg., Inc.
Baker's Leather Goods, Roy
Bandcor Industries, Div. of Man-Sew Corp.
Bang-Bang Boutique (See Holster Shop, The)

PRODUCT & SERVICE DIRECTORY

Beretta S.p.A., Pietro
Bianchi International, Inc.
Bond Arms, Inc.
Brocock Ltd.
Brooks Tactical Systems-Agrip
Brown, H. R. (See Silhouette Leathers)
Browning Arms Co.
Bull-X, Inc.
Cape Outfitters
Cathey Enterprises, Inc.
Chace Leather Products
Churchill Glove Co., James
Cimarron F.A. Co.
Classic Old West Styles
Clements' Custom Leathercraft, Chas
Cobra Sport S.r.l.
Colonial Repair
Counter Assault
Delhi Gun House
DeSantis Holster & Leather Goods, Inc.
Dillon Precision Products, Inc.
Dixie Gun Works
Ekol Leather Care
El Paso Saddlery Co.
EMF Co., Inc.
Faust Inc., T. G.
Freedom Arms, Inc.
Gage Manufacturing
GALCO International Ltd.
Garcia National Gun Traders, Inc.
Gil Hebard Guns Inc.
Gilmore Sports Concepts
GML Products, Inc.
Goodwin's Gun Shop
Gould & Goodrich
Gun Leather Limited
Gunfitters
Hafner World Wide, Inc.
HandCrafts Unltd (See Clements' Custom Leather)
Hank's Gun Shop
Heinie Specialty Products
Henigson & Associates, Steve
Hill Speed Leather, Ernie
HIP-GRIP Barami Corp.
Hobson Precision Mfg. Co.
Hogue Grips
Horseshoe Leather Products
Hume, Don
Hunter Co., Inc.
Jim Noble Co.
John's Custom Leather
K.L. Null Holsters Ltd.
Kane Products, Inc.
Kirkpatrick Leather Co.
Kolpin Mfg., Inc.
Korth Germany GmbH
Kramer Handgun Leather
L.A.R. Mfg., Inc.
Lawrence Leather Co.
Lock's Philadelphia Gun Exchange
Lone Star Gunleather
Magnolia Sports,Inc.
Mandall Shooting Supplies Inc.
Markell,Inc.
Marksman Products
Michaels Of Oregon, Co.
Minute Man High Tech Industries
Navy Arms Company
No-Sho Mfg. Co.
Null Holsters Ltd. K.L.
October Country Muzzleloading
Ojala Holsters, Arvo
Oklahoma Leather Products,Inc.
Old West Reproductions,Inc. R.M. Bachman
Pager Pal
Parker & Sons Shooting Supply
Pathfinder Sports Leather
Protektor Model
PWL Gunleather

Ramon B. Gonzalez Guns
Renegade
Ringler Custom Leather Co.
Rogue Rifle Co., Inc.
Safariland Ltd., Inc.
Safety Speed Holster, Inc.
Scharch Mfg., Inc.-Top Brass
Schulz Industries
Second Chance Body Armor
Silhouette Leathers
Smith Saddlery, Jesse W.
Sparks, Milt
Stalker, Inc.
Starr Trading Co., Jedediah
Strong Holster Co.
Stuart, V. Pat
Tabler Marketing
Tactical Defense Institute
Ted Blocker Holsters, Inc.
Tex Shoemaker & Sons, Inc.
Thad Rybka Custom Leather Equipment
The A.W. Peterson Gun Shop, Inc.
The Concealment Shop, Inc.
The Gun Works
The Keller Co.
The Outdoor Connection, Inc.
Torel, Inc.
Triple-K Mfg. Co., Inc.
Tristar Sporting Arms, Ltd.
Tyler Manufacturing & Distributing
Uncle Mike's (See Michaels of Oregon Co.)
Venus Industries
Walt's Custom Leather, Walt Whinnery
Watson Trophy Match Bullets
Westley Richards & Co.
Whinnery, Walt (See Walt's Custom Leather)
Wild Bill's Originals
Wilsom Combat

PISTOLSMITH

A.W. Peterson Gun Shop, Inc.
Acadian Ballistic Specialties
Accuracy Unlimited
Ace Custom 45's, Inc.
Actions by "T" Teddy Jacobson
Adair Custom Shop, Bill
Ahlman Guns
Ahrends, Kim (See Custom Firearms, Inc)
Aldis Gunsmithing & Shooting Supply
Alpha Precision, Inc.
Alpine Indoor Shooting Range
Armament Gunsmithing Co., Inc.
Arundel Arms & Ammunition, Inc., A.
Badger Creek Studio
Baer Custom Inc., Les
Bain & Davis, Inc.
Banks, Ed
Bar-Sto Precision Machine
Behlert Precision, Inc.
Ben William's Gun Shop
Bengtson Arms Co., L.
Bill Adair Custom Shop
Billings Gunsmiths
Bowen Classic Arms Corp.
Broken Gun Ranch
Caraville Manufacturing
Chicasaw Gun Works
Clark Custom Guns, Inc.
Cleland's Outdoor World, Inc
Colonial Repair
Colorado School of Trades
Colt's Mfg. Co., Inc.
Corkys Gun Clinic
Custom Firearms (See Ahrends, Kim)

Cylinder & Slide, Inc., William R. Laughridge
D&D Gunsmiths, Ltd.
D&L Sports
David R. Chicoine
Dayton Traister
Dilliott Gunsmithing, Inc.
Ellicott Arms, Inc. / Woods Pistolsmithing
Evolution Gun Works Inc.
F.I., Inc. - High Standard Mfg. Co.
Ferris Firearms
Fisher Custom Firearms
Forkin, Ben (See Belt MTN Arms)
Forkin Arms
Francesca, Inc.
G.G. & G.
Garthwaite Pistolsmith, Inc., Jim
Gary Reeder Custom Guns
Genecco Gun Works
Gentry Custom Gunmaker, David
George E. Mathews & Son, Inc.
Greider Precision
Guncraft Sports Inc.
Guncraft Sports, Inc.
Gunsite Custom Shop
Gunsite Gunsmithy (See Gunsite Custom Shop)
Gunsite Training Center
Hamilton, Alex B (See Ten-Ring Precision, Inc)
Hammerli Service-Precision Mac
Hammond Custom Guns Ltd.
Hank's Gun Shop
Hanson's Gun Center, Dick
Harris Gunworks
Harwood, Jack O.
Hawken Shop, The (See Dayton Traister)
Heinie Specialty Products
High Bridge Arms, Inc
Highline Machine Co.
Hoag, James W.
Irwin, Campbell H.
Island Pond Gun Shop
Ivanoff, Thomas G. (See Tom's Gun Repair)
J&S Heat Treat
Jarvis, Inc.
Jeffredo Gunsight
Jensen's Custom Ammunition
Jungkind, Reeves C.
Kaswer Custom, Inc.
Ken Starnes Gunmaker
Kilham & Co.
Kim Ahrends Custom Firearms, Inc.
King's Gun Works
La Clinique du .45
LaFrance Specialties
LaRocca Gun Works
Lathrop's, Inc.
Lawson, John G (See Sight Shop, The)
Leckie Professional Gunsmithing
Linebaugh Custom Sixguns
List Precision Engineering
Long, George F.
Mag-Na-Port International, Inc.
Mahony, Philip Bruce
Mahovsky's Metalife
Mandall Shooting Supplies Inc.
Marvel, Alan
Mathews & Son, Inc., George E.
McCann's Machine & Gun Shop
MCS, Inc.
Middlebrooks Custom Shop
Miller Custom
Mitchell's Accuracy Shop
MJK Gunsmithing, Inc.
Modern Gun Repair School
Montgomery Community College
Mo's Competitor Supplies (See MCS, Inc.)

Mowrey's Guns & Gunsmithing
Mullis Guncraft
NCP Products, Inc.
Novak's, Inc.
Nowlin Mfg. Co.
Olathe Gun Shop
Paris, Frank J.
Pasadena Gun Center
Peacemaker Specialists
PEM's Mfg. Co.
Performance Specialists
Peterson Gun Shop, Inc., A.W.
Pierce Pistols
Piquette's Custom Engraving
Power Custom, Inc.
Precision Specialties
Ramon B. Gonzalez Guns
Randco UK
Ries, Chuck
Rim Pac Sports, Inc.
Rocky Mountain Arms, Inc.
RPM
Ruger's Custom Guns
Score High Gunsmithing
Shooters Supply
Shootin' Shack
Singletary, Kent
Springfield, Inc.
SSK Industries
Swenson's 45 Shop, A. D.
Swift River Gunworks
Ten-Ring Precision, Inc.
Terry K. Kopp Professional Gunsmithing
The A.W. Peterson Gun Shop, Inc.
The Gun Works
The Robar Co.'s, Inc.
The Sight Shop
Thompson, Randall (See Highline Machine Co.)
Thurston Sports, Inc.
Tom's Gun Repair, Thomas G. Ivanoff
Turnbull Restoration, Doug
Vic's Gun Refinishing
Volquartsen Custom Ltd.
Walker Arms Co., Inc.
Walters Industries
Wardell Precision Handguns Ltd.
Wessinger Custom Guns & Engraving
White Barn Wor
Wichita Arms, Inc.
Wild West Guns
Williams Gun Sight Co.
Williamson Precision Gunsmithing
Wilsom Combat
Wright's Gunstock Blanks

RELOADING TOOLS AND ACCESSORIES

4-D Custom Die Co.
Advance Car Mover Co., Rowell Div.
American Products, Inc.
Ammo Load, Inc.
Armfield Custom Bullets
Armite Laboratories
Arms Corporation of the Philippines
Atlantic Rose, Inc.
Atsko/Sno-Seal, Inc.
Bald Eagle Precision Machine Co.
Ballistic Product, Inc.
Belltown Ltd.
Ben William's Gun Shop
Ben's Machines
Berger Bullets Ltd.
Berry's Mfg., Inc.
Blount, Inc., Sporting Equipment Div.
Blue Mountain Bullets

Blue Ridge Machinery & Tools, Inc.
Bonanza (See Forster Products)
Break-Free, Inc.
Brown Co., E. Arthur
BRP, Inc. High Performance Cast Bullets
Brynin, Milton
B-Square Company, Inc.
Buck Stix-SOS Products Co.
Buffalo Arms Co.
Bull Mountain Rifle Co.
Bullseye Bullets
C&D Special Products (See Claybuster Wads & Harvester Bullets)
Camdex, Inc.
Camp-Cap Products
Canyon Cartridge Corp.
Case Sorting System
CH Tool & Die Co. (See 4-D Custom Die Co.)
CheVron Bullets
Claybuster Wads & Harvester Bullets
CONKKO
Cook Engineering Service
Crouse's Country Cover
Cumberland Arms
Curtis Cast Bullets
Custom Products (See Jones Custom Products)
CVA
D.C.C. Enterprises
Davide Pedersoli and Co.
Davis, Don
Davis Products, Mike
Denver Instrument Co.
Dillon Precision Products, Inc.
Dropkick
E&L Mfg., Inc.
Eagan, Donald V.
Eezox, Inc.
Eichelberger Bullets, Wm.
Enguix Import-Export
Euroarms of America, Inc.
E-Z-Way Systems
Federated-Fry (See Fry Metals)
Feken, Dennis
Ferguson, Bill
First Inc., Jack
Fisher Custom Firearms
Flambeau Products Corp.
Flitz International Ltd.
Forster Products
Fremont Tool Works
Fry Metals
Gehmann, Walter (See Huntington Die Specialties)
Graf & Sons
Graphics Direct
Graves Co.
Green, Arthur S.
Greenwood Precision
GTB
Gun City
Hanned Precision (See The Hanned Line)
Harrell's Precision
Harris Enterprises
Harrison Bullets
Haydon Shooters Supply, Russ
Heidenstrom Bullets
High Precision
Hirtenberger AG
Hodgdon Powder Co.
Hoehn Sales, Inc.
Holland's Gunsmithing
Hondo Ind.
Hornady Mfg. Co.
Howell Machine
Hunters Supply, Inc.
Hutton Rifle Ranch
Image Ind. Inc.
Imperial Magnum Corp.

PRODUCT & SERVICE DIRECTORY

INTEC International, Inc.
Iosso Products
J&L Superior Bullets (See
　Huntington Die Special)
Javelina Lube Products
JGS Precision Tool Mfg., LLC
JLK Bullets
Jonad Corp.
Jones Custom Products, Neil A.
Jones Moulds, Paul
K&M Services
Kapro Mfg. Co. Inc. (See R.E.I.)
Knoell, Doug
Korzinek Riflesmith, J.
L.A.R. Mfg., Inc.
L.E. Wilson, Inc.
Lapua Ltd.
Le Clear Industries (See E-Z-Way
　Systems)
Lee Precision, Inc.
Legend Products Corp.
Liberty Metals
Liberty Shooting Supplies
Lightning Performance
　Innovations, Inc.
Lithi Bee Bullet Lube
Littleton, J. F.
Lock's Philadelphia Gun Exchange
Lortone Inc.
Lyman Instant Targets, Inc. (See
　Lyman Products)
Lyman Products Corp.
MA Systems
Magma Engineering Co.
MarMik, Inc.
Marquart Precision Co.
Match Prep-Doyle Gracey
Mayville Engineering Co. (See
　MEC, Inc.)
MCS, Inc.
MEC, Inc.
Midway Arms, Inc.
MI-TE Bullets
Montana Armory, Inc .(See C.
　Sharps Arms Co. Inc.)
Mo's Competitor Supplies (See
　MCS, Inc.)
Mountain South
Mountain State Muzzleloading
　Supplies, Inc.
MTM Molded Products Co., Inc.
Multi-Scale Charge Ltd.
MWG Co.
Navy Arms Company
Newman Gunshop
North Devon Firearms Services
Old West Bullet Moulds
Omark Industries, Div. of Blount,
　Inc.
Original Box, Inc.
Outdoor Sports Headquarters, Inc.
Paco's (See Small Custom Mould
　& Bullet Co.)
Paragon Sales & Services, Inc.
Pease Accuracy
Pinetree Bullets
Ponsness/Warren
Prairie River Arms
Prime Reloading

Professional Hunter Supplies (See
　Star Custom Bullets)
Pro-Shot Products, Inc.
R.A. Wells Custom Gunsmith
R.E.I.
R.I.S. Co., Inc.
Rapine Bullet Mould Mfg. Co.
Reloading Specialties, Inc.
Rice, Keith (See White Rock Tool &
　Die)
Rochester Lead Works
Rooster Laboratories
Rorschach Precision Products
SAECO (See Redding Reloading
　Equipment)
Sandia Die & Cartridge Co.
Saunders Gun & Machine Shop
Saville Iron Co. (See Greenwood
　Precision)
Seebeck Assoc., R.E.
Sharp Shooter Supply
Sharps Arms Co., Inc., C.
Shiloh Rifle Mfg.
Sierra Specialty Prod. Co.
Silver Eagle Machining
Skip's Machine
Small Custom Mould & Bullet Co.
Sno-Seal, Inc. (See Atsko/Sno-
　Seal, Inc.)
SOS Products Co. (See Buck Stix-
　SOS Products Co.)
Spencer's Rifle Barrels, Inc.
SPG LLC
SSK Industries
Stalwart Corporation
Star Custom Bullets
Starr Trading Co., Jedediah
Stillwell, Robert
Stoney Point Products, Inc.
Stratco, Inc.
Tamarack Products, Inc.
Taracorp Industries, Inc.
TCCI
TCSR
TDP Industries, Inc.
Tetra Gun Care
The Hanned Line
The Protector Mfg. Co., Inc.
Thompson/Center Arms
TMI Products (See Haselbauer
　Products, Jerry)
Vega Tool Co.
Venco Industries, Inc. (See
　Shooter's Choice Gun Care)
VibraShine, Inc.
Vibra-Tek Co.
Vihtavuori Oy/Kaltron-Pettibone
Vitt/Boos
W.B. Niemi Engineering
W.J. Riebe Co.
WD-40 Co.
Webster Scale Mfg. Co.
White Rock Tool & Die
Widener's Reloading & Shooting
　Supply, Inc.
Wise Custom Guns
Woodleigh (See Huntington Die
　Specialties)

Yesteryear Armory & Supply
Young Country Arms

SHOOTING/TRAINING SCHOOL

Alpine Indoor Shooting Range
American Gunsmithing Institute
American Small Arms Academy
Auto Arms
Beretta U.S.A. Corp.
Bob's Tactical Indoor Shooting
　Range & Gun Shop
Bridgeman Products
Chapman Academy of Practical
　Shooting
Chelsea Gun Club of New York City
　Inc.
Cherry Creek State Park Shooting
　Center
CQB Training
Defense Training International, Inc.
Executive Protection Institute
Ferris Firearms
Front Sight Firearms Training
　Institute
G.H. Enterprises Ltd.
Gene's Custom Guns
Griffin & Howe, Inc.
Griffin & Howe, Inc.
Griffin & Howe, Inc.
Guncraft Books (See Guncraft
　Sports Inc.)
Guncraft Sports Inc.
Guncraft Sports, Inc.
Gunsite Training Center
Henigson & Associates, Steve
Jensen's Custom Ammunition
Jensen's Firearms Academy
Kemen America
L.L. Bean, Inc.
Lethal Force Institute (See Police
　Bookshelf)
Loch Leven Industries/Convert-A-
　Pell
Long, George F.
McMurdo, Lynn (See Specialty
　Gunsmithing)
Mendez, John A.
NCP Products, Inc.
Nevada Pistol Academy, Inc.
North American Shooting Systems
North Mountain Pine Training
　Center (See Executive
Nowlin Mfg. Co.
Paxton Quigley's Personal
　Protection Strategies
Pentheny de Pentheny
Performance Specialists
Police Bookshelf
SAFE
Shoot Where You Look
Shooter's World
Shooters, Inc.
Sigarms, Inc.
Smith & Wesson
Specialty Gunsmithing
Starlight Training Center, Inc.

Tactical Defense Institute
The Firearm Training Center
The Midwest Shooting School
The Shooting Gallery
Thunden Ranch
Western Missouri Shooters
　Alliance
Yankee Gunsmith "Just Glocks"
Yavapai Firearms Academy Ltd.

SIGHTS, METALLIC

100 Straight Products, Inc.
Accura-Site (See All's, The Jim
　Tembelis Co., Inc.)
Ad Hominem
Alley Supply Co.
All's, The Jim J. Tembelis Co., Inc.
Alpec Team, Inc.
Andela Tool & Machine, Inc.
AO Sight Systems
ArmaLite, Inc.
Ashley Outdoors, Inc.
Aspen Outfitting Co.
Axtell Rifle Co.
B.A.C.
Baer Custom Inc., Les
Ballard Rifle & Cartridge Co., LLC
BEC, Inc.
Bob's Gun Shop
Bo-Mar Tool & Mfg. Co.
Bond Custom Firearms
Bowen Classic Arms Corp.
Brockman's Custom Gunsmithing
Brooks Tactical Systems-Agrip
Brown Co., E. Arthur
Brown Dog Ent.
Brownells, Inc.
Buffalo Arms Co.
Bushmaster Firearms
C. Sharps Arms Co. Inc./Montana
　Armory
California Sights (See Fautheree,
　Andy)
Campbell, Dick
Cape Outfitters
Cape Outfitters
Cash Mfg. Co., Inc.
Center Lock Scope Rings
Champion's Choice, Inc.
C-More Systems
Colonial Repair
CRR, Inc./Marble's Inc.
Davide Pedersoli and Co.
DHB Products
Dixie Gun Works
DPMS (Defense Procurement
　Manufacturing Services, Inc.)
E. Arthur Brown Co.
Evolution Gun Works Inc.
Faloon Industries, Inc.
Farr Studio, Inc.
G.G. & G.
Garthwaite Pistolsmith, Inc., Jim
Goergen's Gun Shop, Inc.
Goodwin's Gun Shop
Guns Div. of D.C. Engineering, Inc.
Gunsmithing, Inc.

Hank's Gun Shop
Heidenstrom Bullets
Heinie Specialty Products
Hesco-Meprolight
Hiptmayer, Armurier
Hiptmayer, Klaus
I.S.S.
Innovative Weaponry Inc.
J.G. Anschutz GmbH & Co. KG
J.P. Enterprises Inc.
Keng's Firearms Specialty, Inc./US
　Tactical Systems
Knight Rifles
Knight's Mfg. Co.
L.P.A. Inc.
Leapers, Inc.
List Precision Engineering
London Guns Ltd.
Lyman Instant Targets, Inc. (See
　Lyman Products)
Mandall Shooting Supplies Inc.
Marble Arms (See CRR,
　Inc./Marble's Inc.)
MCS, Inc.
MEC-Gar S.R.L.
Meprolight (See Hesco-
　Meprolight)
Merit Corp.
Mid-America Recreation, Inc.
Middlebrooks Custom Shop
Millett Sights
MMC
Modern Muzzleloading, Inc.
Montana Armory, Inc .(See C.
　Sharps Arms Co. Inc.)
Montana Vintage Arms
Mo's Competitor Supplies (See
　MCS, Inc.)
Navy Arms Company
New England Custom Gun Service
Newman Gunshop
Novak's, Inc.
OK Weber, Inc.
One Ragged Hole
Parker & Sons Shooting Supply
PEM's Mfg. Co.
Perazone-Gunsmith, Brian
RPM
Sharps Arms Co., Inc., C.
Slug Site
STI International
T.F.C. S.p.A.
Talley, Dave
Tank's Rifle Shop
The A.W. Peterson Gun Shop, Inc.
The Gun Doctor
Trijicon, Inc.
Truglo, Inc.
United States Optics Technologies,
　Inc.
Warne Manufacturing Co.
Weigand Combat Handguns, Inc.
Wichita Arms, Inc.
Wild West Guns
Williams Gun Sight Co.
Wilsom Combat
Wilsom Combat